SMP Further Mathematics Series

Extensions of Calculus

COLIN GOLDSMITH and DAVID NELSON

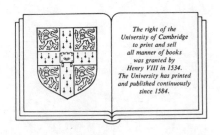

The right of the
University of Cambridge
to print and sell
all manner of books
was granted by
Henry VIII in 1534.
The University has printed
and published continuously
since 1584.

CAMBRIDGE UNIVERSITY PRESS

Cambridge

New York   Port Chester   Melbourne   Sydney

Published by the Press Syndicate of the University of Cambridge
The Pitt Building, Trumpington Street, Cambridge CB2 1RP
40 West 20th Street, New York, NY 10011, USA
10 Stamford Road, Oakleigh, Melbourne 3166, Australia

© Cambridge University Press 1990

First published 1990

Printed in Great Britain
at the University Press, Cambridge

British Library cataloguing in publication data
Goldsmith, Colin
Extensions of calculus.
1. Calculus
I. Title II. Nelson, David III. Series
515
ISBN 0 521 37702 1

Contents

Preface   *page* vii

1 Hyperbolic functions   1
   1 Introduction   1
   2 Basic properties   2
   3 The inverse hyperbolic functions   7

2 De Moivre's theorem   12
   1 Introduction   12
   2 Polynomial equations   13
   3 De Moivre's theorem   16

3 Limits   20
   1 Introduction   20
   2 Functions $n \mapsto f(n)$ with domain $\mathbb{N}$ 21
   3 Functions $x \mapsto f(x)$ with domain $\mathbb{R}$ 26
   4 Some standard results   28
   5 Continuity and differentiability   31

4 Infinite series   37
   1 An example   37
   2 Sums of finite series   39
   3 Infinite series   40
   4 Taylor series   44
   5 Derivation of power series by integration   47
   6 Applications to the evaluation of functions   48

5 Euler's relation   55
   1 Limits of complex sequences   55
   2 Series of complex terms   56
   3 The exponential function   57
   4 Euler's relation   59
   5 The link between the circular and hyperbolic functions 61

6 Reduction formulae   65
   1 The basic idea   65
   2 Reduction formulae with two parameters   67

7 Second-order differential equations ... 71
    1 Foundations ... 71
    2 Second-order equations with constant coefficients ... 77
    3 Simple harmonic motion ... 79
    4 Control mechanisms ... 83
    5 Forced oscillations ... 84
    6 Formulation of differential equations ... 86

8 Differential geometry ... 91
    1 Arc length ... 91
    2 Polar coordinates ... 94
    3 Areas of polar curves ... 96
    4 Radius of curvature ... 100
    5 Signs ... 104

9 Improper integrals and limits of sequences ... 108
    1 Improper integrals ... 108
    2 Convergence of sequences ... 112
    3 Proof ... 116
    4 Second-order convergence ... 117

10 Differential equations and substitution ... 124
    1 Introduction ... 124
    2 Critical damping ... 126
    3 Resonance ... 127
    4 Examples summarised ... 129
    5 Differential equations associated with electrical circuits ... 130

11 Complex-number geometry ... 136
    1 Lines and circles ... 136
    2 Further loci ... 139
    3 The transformation $z \mapsto 1/z$ ... 143
    4 Geometry using complex numbers ... 146

12 Partial differentiation ... 151
    1 Tangent planes ... 152
    2 Tangents and tangent planes; increment notation ... 154
    3 Function notation and Taylor approximations ... 156

13 Double integrals ... 165
    1 Volumes ... 165
    2 Polar coordinates ... 170
    3 Applications to probability ... 172

14 Conformal transformations of the complex plane   177
    1 Transformation diagrams   177
    2 Orthogonal families   180
    3 The Newton–Raphson process   186

15 Jacobians   192
    1 Local distortions   192
    2 The Jacobian matrix   194
    3 Functions mapping $\mathbb{R}^m$ to $\mathbb{R}^n$ 197

16 Triple integrals and substitution   202
    1 Applications to mechanics   202
    2 Substitution in double integrals   207
    3 Polar coordinates in three dimensions   212
    4 Two important applications   215

Answers, hints and comments on the exercises   222

Index   344

Preface

In the preparation of this book, I have made extensive use of a partial draft written by David Nelson. The original SMP book with the same title has also had an important influence. Thanks are also due to many others, pupils as well as teachers, who have provided valuable criticism and constructive ideas. Special mention must be made of Terry Hawkes, who has worked through all the exercise material, and of Sam Boardman, Michael Hall and Donald Miller for their contribution to the development of the book in the early stages.

The book interweaves a number of mathematical threads which are more usually developed separately. As the title suggests, a basic knowledge of calculus, such as is included in any British sixth-form mathematics course, is assumed (though this course could be started well before the single-subject calculus is completed). Several of the chapters in the first half of the book develop this work on functions of a single real variable, introducing hyperbolic functions and reduction formulae and then extending techniques for solving differential equations. The second major strand involves complex numbers, with Euler's relation providing useful connections with the two-dimensional calculus. Then the geometry of the complex plane prepares the ground for the third ingredient, the higher-dimension calculus. The treatment of partial differentiation and of double and triple integrals is kept simple, but it is hoped that the concentration on geometrical illustrations will make difficult ideas come alive. The differentiation of functions of a complex variable provides an important link and is interpreted in terms of special transformations of two-dimensional space.

The fourth main theme is the one that students find the most difficult: the encouragement of greater rigour and the habit of proof. Two early chapters, on limits and infinite series, set the scene, and opportunities to develop one's expertise occur thereafter. It is believed that, even more than other aspects of mathematics, the philosophy and practice of proof only grows through experience. Largely for this reason, the text has been kept fairly brief, while the answers to the exercises are given in considerable detail.

There are many occasions when a programmable calculator or computer will be found valuable, not all of them indicated as such explicitly. There are also plenty of opportunities for the curious reader to investigate topics which are only touched on in the text.

The book is designed to cover the appropriate section of the SMP Further Mathematics syllabus, and a number of questions from past SMP A-level papers are included. The Oxford and Cambridge Schools Examination Board is thanked for permission to reproduce these. Much of the material here is more often found in higher education than in school courses, and the book should be found useful also in colleges and universities.

Colin Goldsmith

1

Hyperbolic functions

1. INTRODUCTION

We recollect that inverse circular functions are very useful in integration. Thus

$$\int \frac{1}{\sqrt{(1 - x^2)}} dx = \sin^{-1} x + k$$

$$\int \frac{1}{1 + x^2} dx \quad = \tan^{-1} x + k.$$

We cannot at the moment integrate the similar functions $1/\sqrt{(1 + x^2)}$ and $1/\sqrt{(x^2 - 1)}$, and in order to do this we introduce new functions called *hyperbolic functions*, which behave in many ways like the circular functions. (The reason for their name is that they are connected with the rectangular hyperbola $x^2 - y^2 = 1$ in much the same way as the circular functions are connected with the circle $x^2 + y^2 = 1$.) The hyperbolic functions were first studied by the Swiss mathematician Johann Lambert (1728–1777).

We first define the functions then, in Exercise 1A, provide the opportunity to develop their simple properties.

Definition 1
For all real values of x,

$$\sinh x = \tfrac{1}{2}(e^x - e^{-x}), \qquad \cosh x = \tfrac{1}{2}(e^x + e^{-x}).$$

Example 1
Simplify $\sinh a \cosh b + \cosh a \sinh b$.

Solution
In exponentials we have

$$\tfrac{1}{2}(e^a - e^{-a}) \times \tfrac{1}{2}(e^b + e^{-b}) + \tfrac{1}{2}(e^a + e^{-a}) \times \tfrac{1}{2}(e^b - e^{-b})$$
$$= \tfrac{1}{4}(e^{a+b} + e^{a-b} - e^{-a+b} - e^{-a-b} + e^{a+b} - e^{a-b} + e^{-a+b} - e^{-a-b})$$
$$= \tfrac{1}{4}(2e^{a+b} - 2e^{-a-b})$$
$$= \sinh(a + b).$$

This is reminiscent of the addition formula for $\sin(a + b)$. □

Exercise 1A

1   Express each of the following in terms of exponential functions and simplify:

1

(a) $2 \sinh x \cosh x$ (b) $\cosh^2 x + \sinh^2 x$
(c) $\cosh^2 x - \sinh^2 x$ (d) $\cosh a \cosh b + \sinh a \sinh b$
(e) $2 \cosh^2 x - 1$ (f) $1 + 2 \sinh^2 x$
Comment on your results.

2   From the graphs of e^x and e^{-x} (Figure 1), sketch the graphs of $y = \sinh x$ and $y = \cosh x$. For each of the hyperbolic functions, state (a) whether it is odd or even, (b) whether it is periodic, and (c) the range of the function. Carefully define the inverse functions $\sinh^{-1} x$ and $\cosh^{-1} x$ and state their domains.

3   Find the derivatives of $\sinh x$ and $\cosh x$. Are your answers consistent with the graphs from question 2? What is the gradient of $y = \sinh x$ at the origin?

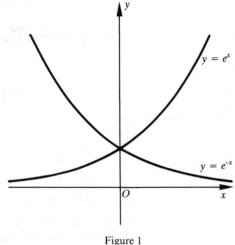

Figure 1

2. BASIC PROPERTIES

When developing the long list of formulae for sines and cosines, we started with the four 'addition formulae' and deduced all the others from these. The same can be done for the hyperbolic functions. First, as in Example 1 and Exercise 1A, question 1(d), we can prove that

$$\sinh(a + b) = \sinh a \cosh b + \cosh a \sinh b$$
$$\sinh(a - b) = \sinh a \cosh b - \cosh a \sinh b$$
$$\cosh(a + b) = \cosh a \cosh b + \sinh a \sinh b$$
$$\cosh(a - b) = \cosh a \cosh b - \sinh a \sinh b.$$

Replacing both a and b by x, we then obtain

$$\sinh 2x = 2 \sinh x \cosh x$$
$$\cosh 2x = \cosh^2 x + \sinh^2 x$$
$$1 = \cosh^2 x - \sinh^2 x.$$

We combined the formulae

$$\cos 2\theta = \cos^2 \theta - \sin^2 \theta \quad \text{and} \quad 1 = \cos^2 \theta + \sin^2 \theta$$

to give two further formulae for $\cos 2\theta$, one involving $\cos \theta$ only, the other involving $\sin \theta$ only. Similarly, we find that

$$\cosh 2x = 2 \cosh^2 x - 1$$
$$= 1 + 2 \sinh^2 x.$$

Derivatives
From the definitions, we obtain

$$f(x) = \sinh x \quad \Rightarrow \quad f'(x) = \cosh x$$

and
$$g(x) = \cosh x \quad \Rightarrow \quad g'(x) = \sinh x.$$

Graphs

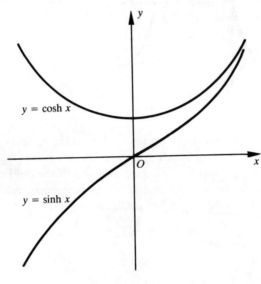

Figure 2

The graph of $y = \sinh x$ has rotational symmetry about the origin because $\sinh x$ is an odd function. The graph of $y = \cosh x$ (an even function) has reflectional symmetry in the y-axis. Note that for large positive x, both $\sinh x$ and $\cosh x$ are approximately equal to $\frac{1}{2} e^x$.

It can be proved that a thin, flexible cable supported at either end and hanging freely under gravity takes up a shape similar to the graph of $y = \cosh x$. We call such a curve a *catenary* (from the Latin *catena*, a chain).

2.1 Inverse functions

Before introducing the important inverse functions for sinh and cosh, it would be sensible to review ideas about the inverse circular functions, which may not be familiar.

A calculator will give $\quad \sin 0.850 = 0.751$

and $\quad \sin^{-1} 0.751 = 0.850 \quad$ (to 3 SF in both cases).

It also gives $\quad \sin 3.910 = -0.695,$

but $\quad \sin^{-1}(-0.695) = -0.768.$

Many different numbers have the same sine, but the inverse sine button on a

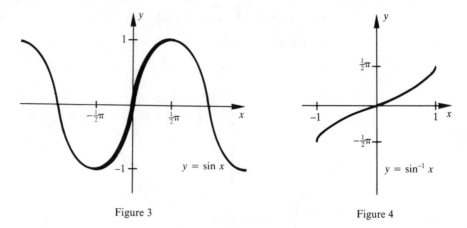

Figure 3   Figure 4

calculator gives only one number for each specific number in the domain. Graphs provide the best explanation of this.

The graph of Figure 4 is the reflection in $y = x$ of the bold part of Figure 3. This indicates how the inverse sine function is defined, and calculator and computer software is designed accordingly.

When the integral $\int \dfrac{1}{\sqrt{(1 - x^2)}}\,dx$ was first encountered, it was found that the substitution $u = \sin^{-1} x$ was effective:

$$\int \frac{1}{\sqrt{(1 - x^2)}}\,dx = \int \frac{\cos u}{\sqrt{(1 - \sin^2 u)}}\,du$$

$$= \int \frac{\cos u}{\cos u}\,du$$

$$= u + k$$

$$= \sin^{-1} x + k.$$

$$\begin{aligned} u &= \sin^{-1} x \\ &\Rightarrow \quad x = \sin u \\ &\Rightarrow \quad \frac{dx}{du} = \cos u \end{aligned}$$

The Pythagoras relation $1 - \sin^2 u = \cos^2 u$ is crucial here, of course. It should be noted, moreover, that u is restricted by the definition of $\sin^{-1} x$ to the interval from $-\tfrac{1}{2}\pi$ to $\tfrac{1}{2}\pi$, and so $\sqrt{(\cos^2 u)} = +\cos u$, since $\cos u$ cannot be negative.

There is no difficulty in defining the inverse function for $\sinh x$, but for $\cosh^{-1} x$ we have to restrict ourselves to one half of the graph of $\cosh x$; Figures 5 and 6 illustrate this.

Exercise 1B

1 Write down the indefinite integrals of $\sinh x$ and $\cosh x$.

2 From the graphs, estimate the values of $\displaystyle\int_0^2 \sinh x\,dx$ and $\displaystyle\int_0^2 \cosh x\,dx$. Then obtain values to 3 SF by integration.

3 (a) Simplify $\cosh a + \sinh a$.
   (b) Show that $(\cosh a + \sinh a)(\cosh b + \sinh b) = \cosh(a + b) + \sinh(a + b)$.
   (c) Show that $(\cosh a + \sinh a)^n = \cosh na + \sinh na$.

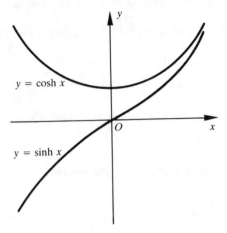

Figure 5

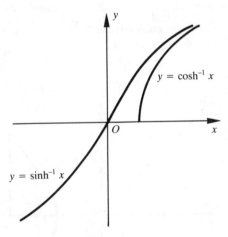

Figure 6

(d) What are the results analogous to those in (b) and (c) involving the circular functions?

4 (a) Show that $29^2 - 21^2 = 20^2$.
   (b) If $\sin \theta = \frac{21}{29}$, what are the possible values of $\cos \theta$?
   (c) If $\sinh u = \frac{21}{20}$, what is the value of $\cosh u$?
   (d) If $\cosh u = \frac{13}{5}$, what are the possible values of $\sinh u$?

5 Use your calculator to complete this table. Then sketch the graph of $y = \cos^{-1} x$.

x	-1	-0.5	0	0.5	1
$\cos^{-1} x$					

Sketch the graph of $y = \cos x$ from $x = -2\pi$ to $x = 2\pi$ and indicate the portion for which the $\cos^{-1} x$ graph is a reflection in $y = x$.

6 State the range of the function $\tan^{-1} x$ and sketch its graph.

7   (a) If sinh $u = 2$, find the values of cosh u and e^u, and hence write u as a natural logarithm.

    (b) If $v = \cosh^{-1} 3$, write down the values of cosh v, sinh v and e^v. Hence obtain v as a natural logarithm.

    (c) Use the method of (a) and (b) to show that

$$\cosh^{-1} x = \ln(x + \sqrt{(x^2 - 1)}) \quad \text{and} \quad \sinh^{-1} x = \ln(x + \sqrt{(1 + x^2)}).$$

8   Find $\int \dfrac{1}{\sqrt{(1 + x^2)}} dx$, (a) using the substitution $x = \sinh y$, and (b) using the substitution $x = \tan \theta$.

9   Find $\int \dfrac{1}{\sqrt{(x^2 - a^2)}} dx$, (a) using a suitable hyperbolic substitution, and (b) using a different substitution.

10   Use the chain rule to differentiate $\ln(x + \sqrt{(1 + x^2)})$; simplify the result.

11   Using the Newton–Raphson method, solve the equation $\cosh x = 2x$, giving answers correct to 3 SF.

12   Find the indefinite integrals $\int \sinh^2 x \, dx$ and $\int \cosh^2 x \, dx$.

13   (a) Show that for all u, the point P (cosh u, sinh u) lies on the right-hand branch of the rectangular hyperbola $x^2 - y^2 = 1$.

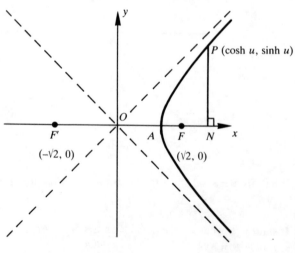

Figure 7

    (b) Show that $FP = \sqrt{2} \cosh u - 1$, where F is $(\sqrt{2}, 0)$, and find $F'P$. Deduce that $F'P - FP = 2$.

    (c) Show that the region bounded by the lines PN and AN and by the arc AP has area $\int_0^u \sinh^2 t \, dt$, and deduce that the area bounded by the lines OA and OP and the arc AP equals $\tfrac{1}{2} u$.

3. THE INVERSE HYPERBOLIC FUNCTIONS

Since $\cosh^2 u - \sinh^2 u = 1$, $\sqrt{(1 + \sinh^2 u)} = \cosh u$, and this suggests that to integrate $1/\sqrt{(a^2 + x^2)}$ we should try $x = a \sinh u$.

Then
$$\int \frac{1}{\sqrt{(a^2 + x^2)}}dx = \int \frac{1}{a \cosh u} \times a \cosh u \, du$$

$$= \int 1 \, du$$
$$= u + k$$
$$= \sinh^{-1}(x/a) + k.$$

Note that $\cosh u > 0$ for all u, so we have indeed taken the positive square root.

Example 2

Find $I = \displaystyle\int_1^3 \frac{1}{\sqrt{(1 + x^2)}}dx$ to 3 SF.

Solution
The integral is represented by the shaded area in Figure 8, and this gives an approximate value of 1.

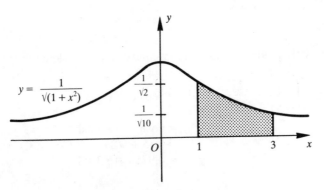

Figure 8

Now $I = \left[\sinh^{-1}x\right]_1^3 = \sinh^{-1}3 - \sinh^{-1}1 = 0.937$ (to 3 SF). ☐

However, you may have a calculator which does not provide hyperbolic functions. Luckily, the inverse functions have alternative forms involving logarithms. The key to obtaining these is the relation $\sinh u + \cosh u = e^u$, which follows immediately from the definitions of the hyperbolic functions, for

$$\sinh^{-1}\frac{x}{a} = u \;\Rightarrow\; x = a \sinh u$$
$$\Rightarrow\; \sqrt{(a^2 + x^2)} = a \cosh u, \quad \text{as we have seen.}$$

It follows that $x + \sqrt{(a^2 + x^2)} = a(\sinh u + \cosh u) = a e^u,$

and hence $u = \sinh^{-1}\dfrac{x}{a} = \ln\left(\dfrac{x}{a} + \sqrt{\left(1 + \left(\dfrac{x}{a}\right)^2\right)}\right).$

Example 2 (contd)

$$I = \sinh^{-1} 3 - \sinh^{-1} 1$$
$$= \ln(3 + \sqrt{10}) - \ln(1 + \sqrt{2})$$
$$= 0.937 \quad \text{(to 3 SF)}.$$
☐

3.1 The second standard integral and its logarithmic form

In a similar way, we can show that if $x > a > 0$, then

$$\int \frac{1}{\sqrt{(x^2 - a^2)}}\,dx = \cosh^{-1}\frac{x}{a} + k$$

$$= \ln\left(\frac{x}{a} + \sqrt{\left(\left(\frac{x}{a}\right)^2 - 1\right)}\right) + k.$$

Example 3

Evaluate $\displaystyle\int_5^8 \frac{1}{\sqrt{(x^2 - 6x + 8)}}\,dx.$

Solution
As so often with quadratic functions, we must first complete the square:

$$\int_5^8 \frac{1}{\sqrt{((x-3)^2 - 1)}}\,dx = \Big[\cosh^{-1}(x - 3)\Big]_5^8$$

$$= \cosh^{-1} 5 - \cosh^{-1} 2$$
$$= \ln(5 + \sqrt{24}) - \ln(2 + \sqrt{3})$$
$$= 0.975 \quad \text{(to 3 SF)}.$$
☐

Exercise 1C

1 If $u = \cosh^{-1}(x/a)$, show that $\sqrt{(x^2 - a^2)} = a \sinh u$, and that
$$\cosh^{-1}\frac{x}{a} = \ln\left(\frac{x}{a} + \sqrt{\left(\left(\frac{x}{a}\right)^2 - 1\right)}\right).$$

2 Express the following as natural logarithms:
   (a) $\sinh^{-1} 4$ (b) $\cosh^{-1} 2$ (c) $\sinh^{-1}(-2)$ (d) $\cosh^{-1} 1.5$

3 Show that $\ln(-x + \sqrt{(1 + x^2)}) = -\ln(x + \sqrt{(1 + x^2)})$. What is the significance of this relation?

4 Differentiate:
   (a) $\sinh 2x$ (b) $\cosh(\tfrac{1}{2}x + 3)$ (c) $x \sinh x$ (d) $\sinh^{-1} 3x$
   (e) $\cosh^{-1}(x + 5)$ (f) $\cosh^{-1}\tfrac{1}{2}x$ (g) $\sinh^{-1}(1/x)$

5 Find:

(a) $\displaystyle\int_5^7 \frac{1}{\sqrt{(x^2 - 9)}}\,dx$ (b) $\displaystyle\int_1^4 \frac{1}{\sqrt{(x^2 + 9)}}\,dx$

(c) $\displaystyle\int_{-2}^2 \frac{1}{\sqrt{(4x^2 + 1)}}\,dx$ (d) $\displaystyle\int_2^5 \frac{1}{\sqrt{(4x^2 - 9)}}\,dx$

Use rough sketch graphs to check your answers.

6 $\cosh^{-1} x$ is defined only for $x > 1$. If $a, b > 0$, show by putting $u = -x$ (or from graphical considerations) that

$$\int_{-a}^{-b} \frac{1}{\sqrt{(x^2 - 1)}}\,dx = \cosh^{-1} a - \cosh^{-1} b = \left[-\cosh^{-1}(-x) \right]_{-a}^{-b}$$

and hence that

$$\int \frac{1}{\sqrt{(x^2 - 1)}}\,dx = -\cosh^{-1}(-x) + k \quad \text{if } x < -1.$$

7 Find:

(a) $\displaystyle\int_0^1 \frac{1}{\sqrt{((x + 2)^2 + 9)}}\,dx$ (b) $\displaystyle\int_2^3 \frac{1}{\sqrt{(x^2 + 4x + 5)}}\,dx$

(c) $\displaystyle\int_2^3 \frac{1}{\sqrt{(x^2 + 4x - 5)}}\,dx$

8 Evaluate the following integrals:

(a) $\displaystyle\int_0^1 \cosh^2 x\,dx$ (b) $\displaystyle\int_0^1 \sqrt{(1 + x^2)}\,dx$ (c) $\displaystyle\int_0^1 \sqrt{(x^2 + 4x + 5)}\,dx$

9 Evaluate the following integrals:

(a) $\displaystyle\int_0^1 \frac{1}{\sqrt{(5 + 4x - x^2)}}\,dx$ (b) $\displaystyle\int_0^1 \frac{1}{x^2 + 4x + 5}\,dx$

(c) $\displaystyle\int_0^1 \frac{12}{x^2 + 6x + 8}\,dx.$

10 Use integration by parts to find:

(a) $\displaystyle\int x \sinh x\,dx$ (b) $\displaystyle\int 1 \times \sinh^{-1} x\,dx$

Miscellaneous exercise 1

1 Differentiate $\sinh 2x$ by the chain rule and $2 \sinh x \cosh x$ by the product rule. What do you find? Find the second derivatives in each case.

2 We define the hyperbolic tangent, $\tanh x$, as $\sinh x / \cosh x$. Investigate its properties (e.g. addition formula, derivative, integral, graph).

3 Prove that $\tanh y = 1 - 2/(e^{2y} + 1)$, and hence obtain a logarithmic form for $\tanh^{-1} x$.

4 Given that $y = \sinh^{-1} x$, show that $u = e^y$ satisfies the equation $u^2 - 2xu - 1 = 0$, and hence obtain the logarithmic form for $\sinh^{-1} x$.

5 Show that $y = A \sinh nx + B \cosh nx \Rightarrow \dfrac{d^2y}{dx^2} = n^2y.$

What is the corresponding result for the circular functions?

6 Obtain Taylor approximations for $\sinh x$ and $\cosh x$ for small x.

7 Obtain the first three non-zero terms of a Taylor approximation for $\sinh^{-1} x$ for small x.

8 Test and explain the following recipe for calculating $\cosh x$:
'Divide $|x|$ by 2 repeatedly until the result is less than 0.005 (call the number of divisions n). Square the result, divide by 2 and add 1. Finally, perform the operation 'square, multiply by 2 and subtract 1'; do this n times.'

(*Hint:* $\cosh x \approx 1 + \dfrac{x^2}{2!} + \dfrac{x^4}{4!} + \ldots;\quad \cosh 2u = 2\cosh^2 u - 1.$)

9 Turn the recipe of question 8 into a computer program.

10 Investigate the shape of the graph of $y = \cosh x + p \sinh x$ for different values of p.

11 (*a*) We can solve the equation $3 \cosh x + 4 \sinh x = 10$ by first writing the left-hand side as $R \sinh(x + \alpha)$. Show that $R = \sqrt{7}$ and $\alpha = \sinh^{-1}(3/\sqrt{7})$; complete the solution.

(*b*) Solve the equation in (*a*) by writing $\sinh x$ and $\cosh x$ in exponential form and hence obtaining a quadratic equation in e^x.

12 Solve the following equations:
(*a*) $10 \cosh x + 8 \sinh x = 13$ (*b*) $10 \cosh x - 8 \sinh x = 7$

13 Evaluate $\displaystyle\int_0^1 \dfrac{1}{\sqrt{(x^2 + 4x)}}\,dx.$

14 Use the substitution $x = a/u$ to show that for $x > 0$, $a > 0$,

$$\int \frac{1}{x\sqrt{(x^2 + a^2)}}\,dx = -\frac{1}{a}\sinh^{-1}\left(\frac{a}{x}\right) + k.$$

Verify the result by differentiating $\sinh^{-1}(a/x)$.   [SMP]

15 Draw a sketch of the curve with equation $y = 1/\cosh x$, and find in the form $\pm \ln k$ (where the value of k is to be found) the x-coordinates of its points of inflexion.
     [SMP]

16 Sketch the graph whose equation is $x^2 - y^2 = a^2$ $(a > 0)$. Prove that the point P $(a \cosh t, a \sinh t)$ lies on this graph for all real values of t, but that there are points of the graph which cannot be expressed in this form.

If U is the point of the graph for which $t = u$, find the area of the region $\mathcal{R}$ bounded by the curve, the line OU and the x-axis. (You may assume that $u > 0$.)

Prove that the transformation with matrix

$$\begin{bmatrix} \cosh \alpha & \sinh \alpha \\ \sinh \alpha & \cosh\alpha \end{bmatrix}$$

transforms the point P into another point of the curve. Into what region is $\mathcal{R}$ transformed by this? What is the area of the transformed region? Give reasons for your answers.
     [SMP]

17 Question 8 gives an algorithm for calculating cosh x without using exponential or logarithmic functions. By reversing the process, obtain an algorithm for calculating $\cosh^{-1} x$.

SUMMARY

(1) $$\sinh x = \tfrac{1}{2}(e^x - e^{-x}), \qquad \cosh x = \tfrac{1}{2}(e^x + e^{-x})$$

(2) $$\sinh(a + b) = \sinh a \cosh b + \cosh a \sinh b$$
$$\cosh(a + b) = \cosh a \cosh b + \sinh a \sinh b, \text{ etc.}$$

$$\sinh 2x = 2 \sinh x \cosh x$$
$$\cosh 2x = \cosh^2 x + \sinh^2 x$$
$$= 2 \cosh^2 x - 1$$
$$= 1 + 2 \sinh^2 x$$

$$1 = \cosh^2 x - \sinh^2 x$$

A further list of formulae can be found on page 63.

(3) $$\int \frac{1}{\sqrt{(a^2 + x^2)}}\,dx = \sinh^{-1}\left(\frac{x}{a}\right) + k = \ln\left(\frac{x}{a} + \sqrt{\left(1 + \left(\frac{x}{a}\right)^2\right)}\right) + k$$

$$\int \frac{1}{\sqrt{(x^2 - a^2)}}\,dx = \cosh^{-1}\left(\frac{x}{a}\right) + k = \ln\left(\frac{x}{a} + \sqrt{\left(\left(\frac{x}{a}\right)^2 - 1\right)}\right) + k$$

(4) $x = a \cosh t$, $y = a \sinh t$ is a parametric representation of the right-hand branch of the hyperbola $x^2 - y^2 = a^2$.

2

De Moivre's theorem

1. INTRODUCTION

We assume here familiarity with the addition, subtraction, multiplication and division of complex numbers, representation of $a + bj$ by the point (a, b) in an Argand diagram, and the terms modulus and argument for the polar coordinates of the point in the Argand diagram.

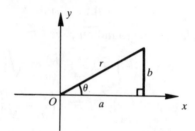

Figure 1

We recollect that the polar form is of particular value in any situation involving multiplication or division of complex numbers, because if

$$z_1 = a + bj = r \cos \theta + r \sin \theta \times j \quad \text{(see Figure 1)}$$
$$= r(\cos \theta + j \sin \theta)$$

and $\qquad z_2 = s(\cos \phi + j \sin \phi),$

then $\qquad z_1 z_2 = rs (\cos \theta + j \sin \theta)(\cos \phi + j \sin \phi)$
$$= rs\{(\cos \theta \cos \phi - \sin \theta \sin \phi) + j (\sin \theta \cos \phi + \cos \theta \sin \phi)\}$$
$$= rs(\cos(\theta + \phi) + j \sin(\theta + \phi)).$$

In short, $\qquad\qquad [r, \theta] \times [s, \phi] = [rs, \theta + \phi].$ \hfill (1)

It follows that if $z_1 = [r, \theta],$
then $z_1{}^2 = [r^2, 2\theta], z_1{}^3 = [r^3, 3\theta],$ etc.

Example 1
Find a square root of $-4 - 9j$ in the form $a + bj$, giving a and b to 3 SF.

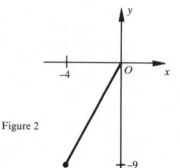

Figure 2

12

Solution
$-4 - 9j$ may be written as $(-4, -9)$ in Cartesian coordinates or as $[\sqrt{97}, \pi + \tan^{-1}\frac{9}{4}] = [9.849, 4.294]$ in polar coordinates.

From equation (1) above, a square root of $-4 - 9j$ is given in polar form as $[\sqrt{9.849}, \frac{1}{2} \times 4.294] = [3.138, 2.147]$. In Cartesian form, this is the number

$$3.138(\cos 2.147 + j \sin 2.147) = -1.71 + 2.63j \quad \text{(to 3 SF)}.$$

Your calculator probably effects the conversion from Cartesian to polar coordinates (and vice versa) easily. Check that

$$(-1.71 + 2.63j)^2 = -3.99 - 8.99j \quad \text{to 3 SF}.$$

$+1.71 - 2.63j$ is also a square root, and this would have been obtained directly if $-4 - 9j$ had been expressed initially as $[\sqrt{97}, -\pi + \tan^{-1}\frac{9}{4}]$. □

Exercise 2A

1   If $z_1 = 2 + 3j$ and $z_2 = 4 - j$, find in the form $a + bj$ each of the following:
    (a) $z_1 z_2$ (b) z_2^2 (c) z_1^3
    (d) z_1/z_2 (remember to multiply top and bottom by $4 + j$)   (e) z_2/z_1
    Find the modulus and argument of each of your five answers and also of z_1 and z_2.
    Check that your answers are consistent, based on $[r, \theta] \times [s, \phi] = [rs, \theta + \phi]$.

2   Find (in Cartesian form) the two square roots of:
    (a) $3 + 4j$ (b) $-2 + 6j$ (c) $2 - 6j$

3   (a) -8 can be written as $[8, \pi]$ or $[8, 3\pi]$ or $[8, 5\pi]$. Use these representations to find, in Cartesian form, three different solutions of $z^3 = -8$.
    (b) Factorise $z^3 + 8$ over the real numbers, and hence obtain the answers to (a) by an independent method.
    (c) Find the three cube roots of $7 + 5j$ in Cartesian form, rounding to 3 SF.
    (d) Show that $(a + bj)^3 = (a^3 - 3ab^2) + (3a^2b - b^3)j$, and hence check *one* answer to (c).

4   Explain why $\cos 3\theta + j \sin 3\theta = (\cos \theta + j \sin \theta)^3$ and why it follows that $\cos 3\theta = \cos^3 \theta - 3 \cos \theta \sin^2 \theta$. Hence obtain the formula for $\cos 3\theta$ in terms of $\cos \theta$ alone.

5   Solve the equation $z^2 + (7 + 2j)z + (-3 + 5j) = 0$, and check one answer.

2. POLYNOMIAL EQUATIONS

One consequence of extending the number system to include complex numbers is that equations of the form $ax^2 + bx + c = 0$ (where a, b and c are real) have two roots. We need only exclude the special case when $a = 0$ and interpret equations where $b^2 - 4ac = 0$ as having two coincident roots. Now that we realise that two square roots can be obtained for any complex number by the method of Example 1, the result is seen to hold for any quadratic equation with complex coefficients; the roots may be found from the usual formula.

Exercise 2A, question 3 shows how the cube roots can be obtained from any complex number, and it will transpire that every cubic equation with complex coefficients has three roots in the complex field. The general result for equations of degree n is of great importance.

Example 2

Show the three cube roots of $3 + 8j$ on an Argand diagram.

Solution

$$3 + 8j = [r, \theta] \quad \text{or} \quad [r, \theta + 2\pi] \quad \text{or} \quad [r, \theta + 4\pi]$$

where
$$r = \sqrt{73} \quad \text{and} \quad \theta = \tan^{-1}\tfrac{8}{3},$$

so the cube roots are given by $[\sqrt[3]{r}, \tfrac{1}{3}\theta]$, $[\sqrt[3]{r}, \tfrac{1}{3}\theta + \tfrac{2}{3}\pi]$ and $[\sqrt[3]{r}, \tfrac{1}{3}\theta + \tfrac{4}{3}\pi]$.

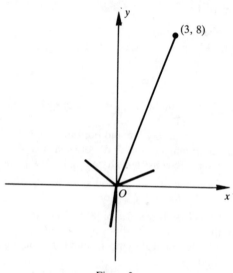

Figure 3

The line segments from the origin to the three points form a propeller-like configuration. This will always be the case in questions of this kind. ☐

Example 3

Solve $(z + 1)^4 = 16z^4$, and show the answers on an Argand diagram.

Solution

Clearly one solution comes from $z + 1 = 2z$, but there are three others since 16 has four fourth roots: $2, 2j, -2$ and $-2j$ (see Figure 4).

So
$$z + 1 = 2z \quad \text{or} \quad 2jz \quad \text{or} \quad -2z \quad \text{or} \quad -2jz.$$

The solutions are $\quad 1, \quad \dfrac{1}{2j-1}, \quad -\tfrac{1}{3} \quad \text{and} \quad \dfrac{1}{-2j-1},$

that is, $\quad 1, \quad -\tfrac{1}{5} - \tfrac{2}{5}j, \quad -\tfrac{1}{3} \quad \text{and} \quad -\tfrac{1}{5} + \tfrac{2}{5}j.$

The fourth roots of 16 form a pattern with rotational symmetry of order 4. Figure 5, on the other hand, does not have this symmetry. ☐

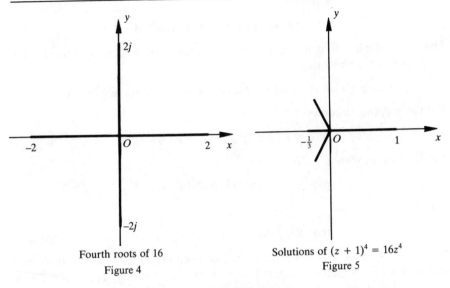

Fourth roots of 16   Solutions of $(z + 1)^4 = 16z^4$

Figure 4   Figure 5

Exercise 2B

1   Solve the following equations:
   (a) $z^3 = 1$ (b) $z^3 = j$ (c) $z^3 = 1 + j$
   (d) $z^3 = -1$ (e) $z^3 + 8j = 0$ (f) $z^6 = -1$
   and give sketches of the geometrical representations of the roots.

2   Solve the following equations:
   (a) $4z^4 - 11z^2 - 3 = 0$ (b) $z^5 - z^3 + z^2 - 1 = 0$ (c) $z^4 + z^2 + 1 = 0$

3   The equation of Example 3 can be solved by other, more elementary methods. Follow through one of these.

4   Form cubic equations whose roots are:
   (a) $\frac{1}{2}, -\frac{1}{2}, 2j$ (b) $-1, j, 2 - j$

5   Solve $z^7 = 1$. The sum of the roots is zero; from this fact show that
   $$\cos \tfrac{2}{7}\pi + \cos \tfrac{4}{7}\pi + \cos \tfrac{6}{7}\pi = -\tfrac{1}{2}.$$

6   One vertex of a square inscribed in the unit circle is $(1, \tfrac{3}{16}\pi)$. Of which complex number do these vertices represent the fourth roots? Illustrate with a diagram.

7   If $z^6 = j$, what are the possible values of z^5?   [SMP]

8   By considering the solutions, other than 1, of the equation $z^4 = 1$, or otherwise, solve the equation $(z + 1)^4 = z^4$.   [SMP]

9   Solve $(1 + j)z^2 - (1 + 4j)z - 1 + 2j = 0$.

10   Find approximately the three solutions of $z^3 = 12 - 7j$.

11   Investigate $\cos \tfrac{2}{5}\pi + \cos \tfrac{4}{5}\pi$ in a similar way to question 5, and deduce that $\sin 18° = \tfrac{1}{4}(\sqrt{5} - 1)$.

12   If $z = \cos \theta + j \sin \theta$, find the values of
   $$z + \frac{1}{z}, \quad z^2 + \frac{1}{z^2}, \quad z^n + \frac{1}{z^n} \quad \text{and} \quad z^n - \frac{1}{z^n}$$
   in terms of θ.

3. DE MOIVRE'S THEOREM

The basis of all our work so far in this chapter, $[r, \theta] \times [s, \phi] = [rs, \theta + \phi]$, depends upon the identity

$$(\cos \theta + j \sin \theta)(\cos \phi + j \sin \phi) = \cos(\theta + \phi) + j \sin(\theta + \phi).$$

With $\phi = \theta$, this becomes

$$(\cos \theta + j \sin \theta)^2 = \cos 2\theta + j \sin 2\theta,$$

and then again with $\phi = 2\theta$,

$$(\cos \theta + j \sin \theta)^3 = \cos 3\theta + j \sin 3\theta.$$

Induction leads to

$$(\cos \theta + j \sin \theta)^n = \cos n\theta + j \sin n\theta$$

for any positive integral n (i.e. $n \in \mathbb{Z}^+$). This is known as de Moivre's theorem* and it holds for negative integers (see Exercise 2C, question 2) and also, with suitable interpretation, for rational numbers. It can be used to deduce a number of trigonometric formulae more simply than by repeated use of the elementary formulae.

Example 4
Express $\tan 5\theta$ in terms of $\tan \theta$.

Solution
We have $(\cos \theta + j \sin \theta)^5 = \cos 5\theta + j \sin 5\theta$, and writing $c = \cos \theta$ and $s = \sin \theta$, the binomial theorem gives

$$(\cos \theta + j \sin \theta)^5 = c^5 + 5c^4 sj + 10c^3 s^2 j^2 + 10c^2 s^3 j^3 + 5cs^4 j^4 + s^5 j^5$$
$$= c^5 - 10c^3 s^2 + 5cs^4 + j(5c^4 s - 10c^2 s^3 + s^5).$$

We now have two versions of the *same* complex number; the real parts must be equal and so must the imaginary parts. Hence,

$$\cos 5\theta = \cos^5 \theta - 10 \cos^3 \theta \sin^2 \theta + 5 \cos \theta \sin^4 \theta$$

and
$$\sin 5\theta = 5 \cos^4 \theta \sin \theta - 10 \cos^2 \theta \sin^3 \theta + \sin^5 \theta.$$

Dividing corresponding sides of these equations gives

$$\tan 5\theta = \frac{5 \cos^4 \theta \sin \theta - 10 \cos^2 \theta \sin^3 \theta + \sin^5 \theta}{\cos^5 \theta - 10 \cos^3 \theta \sin^2 \theta + 5 \cos \theta \sin^4 \theta}$$

$$= \frac{5 \tan \theta - 10 \tan^3 \theta + \tan^5 \theta}{1 - 10 \tan^2 \theta + 5 \tan^4 \theta}, \quad \text{dividing each term by } \cos^5 \theta. \quad \square$$

---

* Abraham de Moivre (1667–1754) was a French Huguenot who moved to London in 1685. A friend of Newton, he made important contributions to the theory of probability and to trigonometry. He is credited with the first study of the normal distribution, and 'Stirling's formula' is in fact due to de Moivre.

Example 5

Express $\cos^4 \theta$ as a sum of cosines, and hence obtain $\int \cos^4 \theta \, d\theta$.

Solution

Writing $z = \cos \theta + j \sin \theta$, we have $z^{-1} = \cos \theta - j \sin \theta$, so

$$z + z^{-1} = 2 \cos \theta.$$

Also, $z^n = \cos n\theta + j \sin n\theta$ and $z^{-n} = \cos n\theta - j \sin n\theta$ give

$$z^n + z^{-n} = 2 \cos n\theta.$$

Now
$$\begin{aligned}
2^4 \cos^4 \theta &= (z + z^{-1})^4 \\
&= z^4 + 4z^3 z^{-1} + 6z^2 z^{-2} + 4zz^{-3} + z^{-4} \\
&= z^4 + z^{-4} + 4(z^2 + z^{-2}) + 6 \\
&= 2 \cos 4\theta + 8 \cos 2\theta + 6.
\end{aligned}$$

Hence,
$$\cos^4 \theta = \tfrac{1}{8} \cos 4\theta + \tfrac{1}{2} \cos 2\theta + \tfrac{3}{8}$$

and
$$\int \cos^4 \theta \, d\theta = \tfrac{1}{32} \sin 4\theta + \tfrac{1}{4} \sin 2\theta + \tfrac{3}{8}\theta + k.$$

This technique will enable us to express $\cos^n \theta$, $\sin^n \theta$ or $\cos^m \theta \sin^n \theta$ as a sum of cosines and sines. □

Exercise 2C

1   Use de Moivre's theorem to express $\cos 3\theta$, $\sin 3\theta$ and $\tan 3\theta$ in terms of $\cos \theta$, $\sin \theta$ and $\tan \theta$, respectively.

2   Simplify $(\cos n\theta + j \sin n\theta)(\cos n\theta - j \sin n\theta)$, and hence show that
$$(\cos \theta + j \sin \theta)^{-m} = \cos(-m\theta) + j \sin(-m\theta), \quad m \in \mathbb{Z}^+.$$

3   Show that $\cos(\theta/n) + j \sin(\theta/n)$ is an nth root of $\cos \theta + j \sin \theta$ if $n \in \mathbb{Z}^+$.

4   Simplify:

(a) $(\cos \tfrac{1}{3}\pi + j \sin \tfrac{1}{3}\pi)^6$

(b) $(\cos \theta - j \sin \theta)^5$

(c) $\{\cos(\tfrac{1}{4}\pi - \theta) + j \sin(\tfrac{1}{4}\pi - \theta)\}^4$

(d) $\dfrac{1}{(\cos \tfrac{1}{2}\theta - j \sin \tfrac{1}{2}\theta)^6}$

5   Express in the form $a + bj$:

(a) $(\cos 2\theta - j \sin 2\theta)^2 (\cos 2\phi + j \sin 2\phi)^2$

(b) $\dfrac{(\cos \theta + j \sin \theta)^5}{(\cos \theta - j \sin \theta)^4}$

(c) $(\sin \theta + j \cos \theta)^4$

(d) $(\sin \theta - j \cos \theta)^6$

(e) $\dfrac{1}{(1 + \cos 2\theta + j \sin 2\theta)^2}$

6   Prove that
$$(1 + j)^n = 2^{n/2}(\cos \tfrac{1}{4}n\pi + j \sin \tfrac{1}{4}n\pi)$$
and
$$(1 + j\sqrt{3})^n + (1 - j\sqrt{3})^n = 2^{n+1} \cos \tfrac{1}{3}n\pi.$$

Verify these results by multiplying out the brackets directly when $n = 2$ and $n = 3$.

7   Find one value of each of the following:

(a) $(\cos \tfrac{2}{3}\pi + j \sin \tfrac{2}{3}\pi)^{1/4}$ (b) $(\cos \tfrac{3}{2}\pi + j \sin \tfrac{3}{2}\pi)^{1/6}$

(c) $\sqrt{(\cos 2\theta + j \sin 2\theta)}$ (d) $\sqrt{(\cos 2\theta - j \sin 2\theta)^5}$.

8 Use de Moivre's theorem to express $\cos 4\theta$ and $\tan 4\theta$ in terms of $\cos \theta$ and $\tan \theta$, respectively.

9 Determine constants a, b, c, d such that

$$\cos^6 \theta = a + b \cos 2\theta + c \cos 4\theta + d \cos 6\theta.$$

Evaluate $\int_0^{\pi/3} \cos^6 \theta \, d\theta$.

10 (a) Starting from $(2j \sin \theta)^4 = (z - z^{-1})^4$, where $z = \cos \theta + j \sin \theta$, express $\sin^4 \theta$ as a sum of cosines and hence obtain $\int \sin^4 \theta \, d\theta$.

(b) Find $\int \cos^5 \theta \, d\theta$.

11 Repeat question 10(a) starting from $\sin^4\theta = (\sin^2 \theta)^2 = \left(\dfrac{1 - \cos 2\theta}{2}\right)^2$.

Also repeat question 10(b) starting from

$$\cos^5 \theta = \cos^2 \theta \cos^3 \theta = \left(\frac{1 + \cos 2\theta}{2}\right)\left(\frac{\cos 3\theta + 3 \cos \theta}{4}\right).$$

Miscellaneous exercise 2

1 Show that the patterns of points on five faces of a die are given by the geometrical representations of the roots of the following equations:

$$z = 0, \quad z^2 + j = 0, \quad z^3 - jz = 0, \quad z^4 + 1 = 0, \quad z^5 + z = 0.$$

Form an equation which would give the pattern on the sixth face.

2 Draw a diagram showing the 14 points round the circle $|z| = 1$ which represent all the possible powers of $\cos \frac{3}{7}\pi + j \sin \frac{3}{7}\pi$.

3 $z^2 + 4 = 0 \Rightarrow z = \pm 2j$. Hence $z^2 + 4$ can be factorised as $(z - 2j)(z + 2j)$. Factorise the following into linear factors over the complex numbers:
(a) $z^2 - 4j$ (b) $z^2 - 2z + 17$ (c) $4z^2 + 4z + 10$
(d) $z^2 + 4j - 4$ (e) $z^2 + 4jz - 4$

4 Given that $-j$ is a zero of each of the following polynomials, factorise them into linear factors:
(a) $z^3 - j$ (b) $z^3 + jz^2 - 3z - 3j$ (c) $z^4 + 5z^2 + 4$
(d) $z^4 + (1 + j)z^3 + (1 + j)z^2 + (-3 + j)z - 3j$

5 Factorise $z^5 + 1$ into one linear and two quadratic factors with real coefficients, using $\sin 18° = \frac{1}{4}(\sqrt{5} - 1)$ (see Exercise 2B, question 11).

6 Solve $(z + j)^3 = (z - j)^3$; check your answers by taking the modulus and argument of both sides of the equation. In a similar way, solve and check the roots of the equation $(z + j)^4 = (z - j)^4$.

7 Determine k, l and m such that

$$P(z) = z^4 + 3z^2 + 6z + 10 = (z^2 - kz + l)(z^2 + kz + m).$$

Hence solve the equation $P(z) = 0$. (This is known as Descartes' method for solving quartic equations.)

8 Show that the product of the distinct nth roots of unity is $(-1)^{n-1}$.

9   Given that $\omega = \cos \frac{2}{3}\pi + j \sin \frac{2}{3}\pi$, show that $\omega^3 = 1$ and $\omega^2 + \omega + 1 = 0$.
Simplify:

(a) $\dfrac{1}{1+\omega} + \dfrac{1}{1+\omega^2}$ (b) $\dfrac{1}{z-\omega} + \dfrac{1}{z-\omega^2}$ (c) $\dfrac{\omega^2}{z-\omega} + \dfrac{\omega}{z-\omega^2}$

10   With ω defined as in question 9, multiply out

$$(z - a - b)(z - a\omega - b\omega^2)(z - a\omega^2 - b\omega).$$

Show that these are factors of $z^3 + 3z - 2$ if $ab = -1$ and $a^3 + b^3 = 2$. Find a and b, and hence the three roots of $z^3 + 3z - 2 = 0$, rounding to 2 DP.

11   Use the method of question 10 to solve:
    (a) $z^3 + 9z + 26 = 0$ (b) $z^3 - 6z - 4 = 0$.

12   Show that if a and b are complex conjugates, then $a + b$, $a\omega + b\omega^2$ and $a\omega^2 + b\omega$ are all real.

13   Use the Newton–Raphson method to find the real root α of $z^3 + 3z - 2 = 0$ to 2 DP. Divide $z^3 + 3z - 2$ by $z - \alpha$ and proceed to find the two complex roots. Check that your answers agree with those of question 10.

SUMMARY

Multiplying and dividing complex numbers is especially simple in polar form (modulus and argument), since

$$[r, \ \theta] \times [s, \ \phi] = [rs, \ \theta + \phi].$$

Polar form is also useful when finding square roots, cube roots, etc., of complex numbers.

De Moivre's theorem states that

$$(\cos \theta + j \sin \theta)^n = \cos n\theta + j \sin n\theta;$$

it is true for all rational values of n.

If $z = \cos \theta + j \sin \theta$,   then $\dfrac{1}{z} = \cos \theta - j \sin \theta.$

Also $z^n + \dfrac{1}{z^n} = 2 \cos n\theta$ and $z^n - \dfrac{1}{z^n} = 2j \sin n\theta.$

3
Limits

1. INTRODUCTION

Many issues in the development of the calculus have been glossed over so far, especially concerning the limits of sequences and functions. Consider the following questions:

(i) How does the graph of $y = \dfrac{x^3}{x^2 - 3x + 1}$ behave for large positive x?

(ii) How does the graph of $y = x^5 e^{-x}$ behave for large positive x?

(iii) What is the limit of $\dfrac{\sqrt{x} - \sqrt{3}}{x - 3}$ as x tends to 3 (the derivative of $\sqrt{x}$ at $x = 3$)?

(iv) Does $(1 + 3/x)^x$ tend to a limit as x tends to infinity?

(v) Does the sequence $x_1 = 1$, $x_{i+1} = 2/x_i^2$ tend to a limit? If so, what is it?

(vi) Does the sequence $x_1 = 1$, $x_{i+1} = \sqrt{(2/x_i)}$ tend to a limit?

(vii) How quickly does the sequence $x_1 = 1$, $x_{i+1} = x_i - \left(\dfrac{x_i^3 - 2}{3x_i^2} \right)$ tend to its limit (the Newton–Raphson process)?

You probably feel confident about the answers to many of these questions, but could you justify these answers convincingly? We shall look at a number of ways of tackling such problems theoretically. First, though, it is a good idea to make numerical investigations.

Question (iv) above cannot be answered at a glance. We note that $(1 + \frac{3}{100})^x$ tends to infinity as x tends to infinity, whereas $(1 + 3/x)^{100}$ tends to 1 as x tends to infinity. The behaviour of $(1 + 3/x)^x$ is hard to predict.

However, a calculator soon gives us the information

x	10	20	100	500	1000
$(1 + 3/x)^x$	13.79	16.37	19.22	19.91	20.00

It would seem that there is a limit of 20, or some number close to 20.

Exercise 3A

1 Investigate by numerical methods the behaviour of the following as $n \to \infty$:
    (a) $n^{0.2}$ (b) 0.2^n (c) $0.2^{1/n}$ (d) $n^{1/n}$

2 Investigate the behaviour of the following as $n \to \infty$:
    (a) $(1 - 1/n)^n$ (b) $(1 + 1/\sqrt{n})^n$ (c) $(1 + 1/n)^{\sqrt{n}}$ (d) $(1 + 1/n)^n$

3 If the sequence $u_1 = 1$, $u_{i+1} = 2/u_i^2$ tends to a limit l, then l must be a solution of $l = 2/l^2$, that is, $l = \sqrt[3]{2}$.

Similarly, if $v_1 = 1$, $v_{i+1} = \sqrt{(2/v_i)}$ tends to a limit, this must also be $\sqrt[3]{2}$.

Show numerically that one sequence converges and one diverges. Compare the first four terms of the convergent sequence with the first four terms of the Newton–Raphson sequence (§1, question (vii)).

4 Investigate the following sequences:

(a) $u_1 = 1$, $u_{i+1} = \sqrt{(u_i + 1)}$ (b) $v_1 = 1$, $v_{i+1} = 1 + 1/v_i$

5 Answer §1, questions (i), (ii) and (iii), using numerical methods where necessary.

Sometimes we are concerned with functions whose domain is $\mathbb{N}$, the natural numbers $1, 2, 3, \ldots$, and sometimes with functions whose domain is $\mathbb{R}$, the real numbers; question 5 is of the latter kind.

We shall introduce a formal treatment of limits in terms of functions of natural numbers and pick up functions of real numbers in §3.

2. FUNCTIONS $n \mapsto f(n)$ WITH DOMAIN $\mathbb{N}$

The behaviour as $n \to \infty$ can take four different forms. We give an example of each.

(i) $f(n) \to \infty$ or $f(n) \to -\infty$, for example, $f(n) = n^2$.

(ii) $f(n)$ tends to a limit, for example, $f(n) = (2n + 1)/(n - 3)$; the limit is 2.

(iii) $f(n)$ oscillates finitely, for example, $f(n) = 3 + (-1)^n$.

(iv) $f(n)$ oscillates infinitely, for example, $f(n) = 3 + n(-1)^n$.

It is helpful to express the ideas behind (i) and (ii) in a formal manner. For (i), we say '$f(n) \to +\infty$ if, for every k (however large), we can find an integer n_0 such that $f(n) > k$ for all $n > n_0$.'

This can be thought of as a game of challenge and response. For the squaring function, suppose you suggest the number 1000 for k; I can then give 31 (or any larger number) for n_0, since $n^2 > 1000$ for all $n > 31$. If, instead, you choose $k = 1\,000\,000$, I can select 1000 for n_0, since it is true that $n^2 > 1\,000\,000$ for all $n > 1000$.

A similar idea works for (ii). We say '$f(n) \to l$ if, for every positive number k (however small), we can find an integer n_0 such that $|f(n) - l| < k$ for all $n > n_0$.'

For
$$f(n) = \frac{2n + 1}{n - 3}, \qquad f(n) - 2 = \frac{7}{n - 3}.$$

If you take $k = 0.01$, I can select n_0 as 703, since $|f(n) - 2| < 0.01$ for all $n > 703$. It is also possible to formalise (iii) and (iv), but this is less useful.

2.1 Standard results and use of inequalities

There is no difficulty in establishing the following well-known facts.

Theorem 1
(a) For $\alpha > 0$, $\quad n^\alpha \to \infty \quad$ as $\quad n \to \infty$.
(b) For $\alpha < 0$, $\quad n^\alpha \to 0 \quad$ as $\quad n \to \infty$.

Inequalities often help us to use these results in the formal treatment of more complicated functions.

Example 1

Prove that the limit of $f(n) = \dfrac{3n^2 + 7n - 2}{n^2 - n + 4}$ is 3 as $n \to \infty$.

Solution

$$\frac{3n^2 + 7n - 2}{n^2 - n + 4} - 3 = \frac{10n - 14}{n^2 - n + 4} < \frac{10n - 10}{n^2 - n} = \frac{10(n-1)}{n(n-1)} = \frac{10}{n}.$$

The inequality holds if $n > 1$ (so that both numerator and denominator are positive), and is certainly correct for large positive n. Also $f(n) - 3 > 0$ if $n > 1$.
    Consequently,

$$\left| \frac{3n^2 + 7n - 2}{n^2 - n + 4} - 3 \right| < k \quad \text{for all } n > 10/k.$$

Notice that we are *not* saying that

$$|f(n) - 3| < k \quad \Rightarrow \quad n > 10/k;$$

this is untrue. All we require is

$$n > 10/k \quad \Rightarrow \quad |f(n) - 3| < k. \qquad \square$$

In practice, we more often invoke the following results, which are not too difficult to prove.

Theorem 2
Given that $f(n)$ and $g(n)$ tend to l and m respectively as $n \to \infty$, then $\lambda f(n)$, $f(n) + g(n)$, $f(n)\, g(n)$ and $f(n)/g(n)$ tend to λl, $l + m$, lm and l/m $(m \neq 0)$, respectively.

Theorem 3
If $g(n) \to 0$ as $n \to \infty$ and if $0 < |f(n)| < |g(n)|$ for all n, then $f(n) \to 0$ as $n \to \infty$.

Example 1: alternative solution

$$\frac{3n^2 + 7n - 2}{n^2 - n + 4} = \frac{\left(3 + \dfrac{7}{n} - \dfrac{2}{n^2} \right)}{\left(1 - \dfrac{1}{n} + \dfrac{4}{n^2} \right)}$$

and
$$3 + \frac{7}{n} - \frac{2}{n^2} \rightarrow 3 + 0 + 0 \quad \text{(by theorems 1 and 2).}$$

Similarly,
$$1 - \frac{1}{n} + \frac{4}{n^2} \rightarrow 1 - 0 + 0,$$

so
$$\frac{3n^2 + 7n - 2}{n^2 - n + 4} \rightarrow \frac{3}{1} = 3 \quad \text{(by theorem 2).}$$

Theorem 4
Given that $h(n) < f(n) < g(n)$ for all $n > n_1$, and that both $h(n)$ and $g(n)$ tend to a common limit l as $n \rightarrow \infty$, then $f(n)$ also tends to l as $n \rightarrow \infty$.

This result is closely related to theorem 3. For obvious reasons, it is sometimes called the method of 'squeezing'.

Exercise 3B

1 Classify the behaviour of the following functions as $n \rightarrow \infty$, as in §2:

(a) $1 + 0.8^n$ (b) $(-n)^n$ (c) $\dfrac{n^2}{n+1}$ (d) $\dfrac{\sin n}{n}$

(e) $\dfrac{2n+1}{n^2 + 3n + 5}$ (f) $2^{1/n}$ (g) $n^{1/2}$

For the functions in category (i), suggest values of n_0 for $k = 100$ and $k = 1000$; for the functions in category (ii), suggest values of n_0 for $k = 0.01$ and $k = 0.001$.

2 Use theorem 2 to find the limits of the following as $n \rightarrow \infty$:

(a) $\dfrac{n+1}{2n-5}$ (b) $\dfrac{(n+1)^2}{2n(3n-1)}$ (c) $\dfrac{\sqrt{n+1}}{n}$ (d) $\dfrac{\sqrt{(2n^2 + n)} - n}{n-1}$

3 Find the limit of $\dfrac{\cos n}{\sqrt{n}}$ as $n \rightarrow \infty$.

4 If $f(n) = \dfrac{n^2 + 1}{n^2 + n + 1}$, prove that $0 < 1 - f(n) < \dfrac{1}{n}$ for $n > 0$. Find the limit of $f(n)$ as $n \rightarrow \infty$. [SMP]

5 (a) Consider $u_n = nx^n$ when $x = 0.9$. Show that $u_{n+1}/u_n < 0.95$ when $n > 18$, and hence that $u_n < 0.95^{n-19} \times u_{19}$ for $n > 19$. Deduce that $u_n \rightarrow 0$ as $n \rightarrow \infty$.
 (b) Show that $v_n = nx^n \rightarrow 0$ as $n \rightarrow \infty$ when $x = 0.96$.
 (c) Show that $w_n = n^2 x^n \rightarrow 0$ as $n \rightarrow \infty$ when $x = 0.9$.

6 Show that $x^n/n!$ tends to 0 as n tends to infinity, whatever the value of x.

7 If $f(n) \rightarrow l$ and $g(n) \rightarrow m$ as $n \rightarrow \infty$, and $|f(n) - l| < \frac{1}{2}k$ for all $n > n_1$, while $|g(n) - m| < \frac{1}{2}k$ for all $n > n_2$, explain why

$$|f(n) + g(n) - l - m| < k \quad \text{for all } n > n_1 + n_2.$$

Does this prove that $f(n) + g(n) \rightarrow l + m$ as $n \rightarrow \infty$?

8 Prove that $(\sqrt{(n^2 + 1)} - n)(\sqrt{(n^2 + 1)} + n) = 1$.

Deduce the limit of $\sqrt{(n^2 + 1)} - n$ as $n \rightarrow \infty$. [SMP]

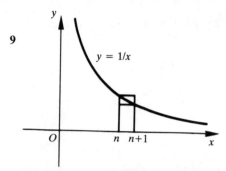

Figure 1

9 Use areas from Figure 1 to show that

$$\frac{1}{n+1} < \ln(n+1) - \ln n < \frac{1}{n} \quad \text{for } n>0,$$

and hence that

$$\frac{n}{n+1} < n \ln\left(1 + \frac{1}{n}\right) < 1.$$

Deduce the limit of $(1 + 1/n)^n$ as $n \to \infty$.

10 Use the method of question 9 to prove that the limit of $(1 + 3/n)^n$ as $n \to \infty$ is e^3. What is its value to 4 SF? Is this consistent with the findings of §1?

11 Use the binomial theorem to show that

$$\left(1 + \frac{1}{n}\right)^n < n < \left(1 + \frac{2}{\sqrt{n}}\right)^n \quad \text{for all } n \geqslant 3.$$

Deduce the limit of $n^{1/n}$ as $n \to \infty$.

2.2 The limit of $(1 + a/n)^n$ as $n \to \infty$

This limit is connected with the Poisson distribution in probability theory and has several other applications.

In Figure 2, the shaded area is $a/(n + a)$, the area under the curve over the same domain is $\ln(n + a) - \ln n$, and the area of the largest rectangle is a/n.

Hence
$$\frac{a}{n+a} < \ln(n+a) - \ln n < \frac{a}{n} \quad \text{if } a>0.$$

This leads to
$$a\left(\frac{n}{n+a}\right) < n \ln\left(\frac{n+a}{n}\right) < a,$$

therefore
$$a\left(\frac{n}{n+a}\right) < \ln\left(1 + \frac{a}{n}\right)^n < a.$$

Now let $n \to \infty$. By theorem 4, we have $\ln(1 + a/n)^n \to a$. Since the exponential function is continuous, this means that

$$\left(1 + \frac{a}{n}\right)^n \to e^a.$$

(In effect we are saying that as $y \to b$, $e^y \to e^b$.)

From Figure 3, if $b>0$, we obtain in the same way

$$\left(1 - \frac{b}{n}\right)^n \to e^{-b} \quad \text{as } n \to \infty.$$

Arguing from areas, as we have done above, is equivalent to saying

$$f(x)<g(x) \text{ for } a<x<b \quad \Rightarrow \quad \int_a^b f(x)\,dx < \int_a^b g(x)\,dx.$$

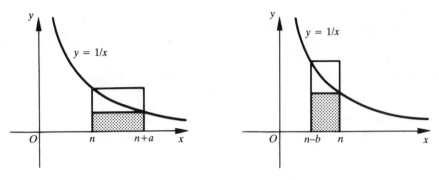

Figure 2   Figure 3

This is often fruitful, and a number of examples using this idea are included in Miscellaneous exercise 3.

Example 2

Find an approximate value of $\int_0^{\pi/4} \frac{1}{\sqrt{(25 - 4 \sin^2 x)}} dx$.

Solution

Instead of using Simpson's rule, we can argue as follows.

In the interval $0 < x < \pi/4$,

$$23 < \quad 25 - 4 \sin^2 x \quad < 25$$

and hence

$$\frac{1}{5} < \frac{1}{\sqrt{(25 - 4 \sin^2 x)}} < \frac{1}{\sqrt{23}}.$$

$$\int_0^{\pi/4} \frac{1}{5} dx < \int_0^{\pi/4} \frac{1}{\sqrt{(25 - 4 \sin^2 x)}} dx < \int_0^{\pi/4} \frac{1}{\sqrt{23}} dx,$$

i.e.

$$\frac{\pi}{20} < \int_0^{\pi/4} \frac{1}{\sqrt{(25 - 4 \sin^2 x)}} dx < \frac{\pi}{4\sqrt{23}},$$

which shows that the integral has a value between 0.157 and 0.164.   □

Exercise 3C

1 Write down the limits of the following as $n \to \infty$:

    (a) $(1 + 1/n)^n$ (b) $(1 - 1/n)^n$ (c) $(1 + 2/n)^n$ (d) $(1 + 1/n)^{2n}$

2 Instead of charging interest annually at 18%, a credit card company charges interest monthly at $1\frac{1}{2}\%$. Show that the effective annual rate of interest on a fixed sum is 19.56%. What is the effect of charging interest half-monthly at $\frac{3}{4}\%$? Consumed with greed, the Devil's Credit Card Company decides to charge interest at $18/n\%$, n times a year, where n is large. What is the maximum effective annual rate that can be achieved in this way?

3 Replacing x by $\ln u$ in the approximation $(1 + x/n)^n \approx e^x$, derive the approximation

$$\ln u \approx n(u^{1/n} - 1), \quad \text{for } u > 0.$$

An algorithm for finding ln u on a calculator with only a square root key and the elementary arithmetic functions is: 'Enter u, press the square root key m times, subtract 1, then multiply by two m times'. Verify that with $m = 18$, ln 6.5 is obtained correct to 5 SF by this method.

4   By considering the area under $y = 1/x$ from $x = 1$ to $x = u$ (where $u > 1$), show that $\dfrac{n(n^{1/n} - 1)}{\ln u}$ lies between $u^{1/n}$ and 1.

(a) Deduce that $n(u^{1/n} - 1) \to \ln u$ as $n \to \infty$.

(b) Show also that the percentage error in the approximation $n(u^{1/n} - 1) \approx \ln u$ is less than $100(u^{1/n} - 1)$.

(c) Use the approximation to evaluate ln 2 to within 1%.

5   Explain   why $\sin x < \sqrt{\sin x} < \sqrt{x}$ for $0 < x < \tfrac{1}{2}\pi$.   Deduce   that $\displaystyle\int_0^{\pi/2} \sqrt{(\sin x)}\,dx$ lies between 1 and 1.3125.

3. FUNCTIONS $x \mapsto f(x)$ with domain $\mathbb{R}$

The formal definitions of §2 require only minor modifications:

(i) $f(x) \to l$ as $x \to \infty$ if for every positive real number k, we can find x_0 so that $|f(x) - l| < k$ for all $x > x_0$;

(ii) $f(x) \to l$ as $x \to a$ if for every positive real number k, we can find a positive number δ so that $|f(x) - l| < k$ for all x such that $0 < |x - a| < \delta$.

One subtle consequence of the definition in (ii) should be noted: if $f(x) \to l$ as $x \to a$, the value of l need not be equal to $f(a)$, and indeed $f(a)$ may not exist. Consider, for example, the function $[x]$, the integer part of x, at $x = 1$ (see Figure 4). If we try to find the limit of $f(x)$ as $x \to 1$, we cannot produce a δ if $k = \tfrac{1}{2}$, say. Nevertheless, if x approaches 1 *from below*, the definition is satisfied with $l = 0$ (even though $f(1) = 1$), and we write $\lim\limits_{x \to 1^-} [x] = 0$.

Similarly, if x approaches 1 *from above*, the limit definition is satisfied and we write $\lim\limits_{x \to 1^+} [x] = 1$.

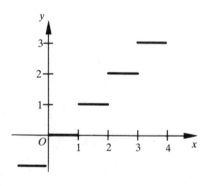

Figure 4

Theorems 1 to 4 in §2 have exact counterparts when we are concerned with real numbers (see the chapter summary), and enable us to tackle questions like (i) in §1 more satisfactorily than before.

Example 3

Investigate the graphs of

(a) $y = \dfrac{3x + 2}{x^2 - 9}$ (b) $y = \dfrac{3x^2 + 2x}{x^2 - 9}$ (c) $y = \dfrac{3x^2 + 2x}{x - 9}$ for large x.

Solution
One approach is to retain only the dominant terms in the numerator and denominator, saying that for large x, in (a) $y \approx 3x/x^2 = 3/x$, in (b) $y \approx 3x^2/x^2 = 3$, and in (c) $y \approx 3x^2/x = 3x$. This is only partially successful, as we shall see.

Another simple method is to choose a specific large value for x, 1000 say, and obtain from a calculator in (a) $y \approx 0.003\,002$, in (b) $y \approx 3.002$, and in (c) $y \approx 3029$. What does this tell us?

In (c), we can carry out a long division, and then write

$$y = \frac{3x^2 + 2x}{x - 9} = 3x + 29 + \frac{261}{x - 9} = 3x + 29 + \frac{261/x}{1 - 9/x}$$

$$
\begin{array}{r}
3x + 29 \\
x - 9 \overline{)\,3x^2 + 2x} \\
\underline{3x^2 - 27x} \\
29x \\
\underline{29x - 261} \\
261
\end{array}
$$

As $x \to \infty$, $\qquad \dfrac{261}{x} \to 0 \quad \text{and} \quad 1 - \dfrac{9}{x} \to 1.$

It follows that $y = 3x + 29$ is an asymptote, approached from above for positive x and from below for negative x. The complete graph is the hyperbola of Figure 5.

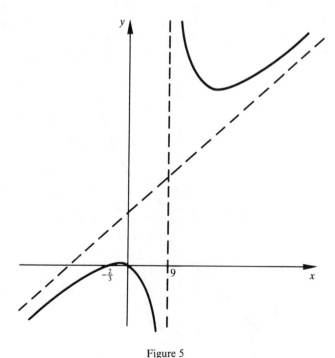

Figure 5

Exercise 3D

1 Discuss the behaviour as x tends to infinity of

(a) $\dfrac{3x + 2}{x^2 - 9}$, and (b) $\dfrac{3x^2 + 2x}{x^2 - 9}$

(see Example 3) by dividing top and bottom by x^2 in each case.

2 By long division, as in Example 3, find the asymptotes of:

(a) $y = \dfrac{x^2 + 5x + 2}{x + 3}$ (b) $y = \dfrac{x^3 + 5x^2 + 2}{x^2 + x + 3}$ (c) $y = \dfrac{4x^3 + x - 7}{x^2 - 2x + 3}$

In each case, confirm your answer by finding y when $x = 100$.

3 Use numerical methods to investigate the behaviour of the following as x tends to infinity:

(a) $\dfrac{\ln x}{x}$ (b) $\dfrac{\ln x}{\sqrt{x}}$ (c) $x\,e^{-x}$ (d) $x^3\,e^{-x}$ (e) $\dfrac{e^x}{x^2 + 10}$

4 Investigate the behaviour of the following as x tends to 0:

(a) $\dfrac{\sin 2x}{x}$ (b) $x \ln x$ (c) $x^2 \ln x$ (d) $x^3\,e^{-x}$ (e) $\dfrac{e^x + 10}{x^2}$

4. SOME STANDARD RESULTS

A number of limits involving the logarithmic and exponential functions are important; some have arisen informally already, for example in the study of continuous probability distributions.

If we draw graphs of e^x, x and $\ln x$ on one diagram (Figure 6), it seems plausible that x/e^x and $(\ln x)/x$ both tend to zero as $x \to \infty$. We establish the second result by returning to the definition of $\ln x$ as an integral. Results about the exponential function are then deduced by means of substitutions.

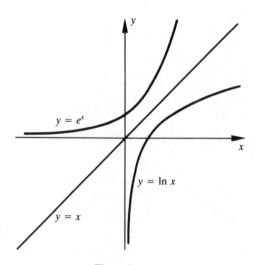

Figure 6

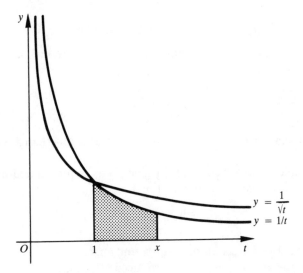

Figure 7

Figure 7 shows the graphs of $y = 1/t$ and $y = 1/\sqrt{t}$.

If $x > 1$, $\qquad 0 < \displaystyle\int_1^x 1/t \, dt < \int_1^x 1/\sqrt{t} \, dt$

$\Rightarrow \quad 0 < \quad \ln x \quad < 2\sqrt{x} - 2$

$\Rightarrow \quad 0 < \quad \dfrac{\ln x}{x} \quad < \dfrac{2\sqrt{x} - 2}{x} = \dfrac{2}{\sqrt{x}} - \dfrac{2}{x}.$

Since the right-hand side of this inequality tends to 0 as $x \to \infty$,

$$\frac{\ln x}{x} \to 0 \quad \text{as } x \to \infty. \tag{1}$$

A more powerful result is given by replacing x by u^α, where α may be any positive number.

Then $\qquad\qquad \dfrac{\ln u^\alpha}{u^\alpha} \to 0 \quad \text{as } u \to \infty,$

that is, $\qquad\qquad \dfrac{\alpha \ln u}{u^\alpha} \to 0 \quad \text{as } u \to \infty,$

or $\qquad\qquad \dfrac{\ln u}{u^\alpha} \to 0 \quad \text{as } u \to \infty.$

This result, like the others that follow, may be re-stated with x as the variable:

$$\frac{\ln x}{x^\alpha} \to 0 \quad \text{as } x \to \infty. \tag{2}$$

Putting $x = 1/y$ and then $x = e^t$ in (2), we get

$$y^\alpha \ln y \to 0 \quad \text{as } y \to 0, \tag{3}$$

and

$$t\, e^{-\alpha t} \to 0 \quad \text{as } t \to \infty. \tag{4}$$

The special cases where $\alpha = 1$ have been met in Exercise 3D.

Finally, if $m > 0$, then $\qquad U^m \to 0 \quad \text{as } U \to 0$.

Hence $\lim_{t \to \infty} (t\, e^{-\alpha t}) = 0 \quad \Rightarrow \quad \lim_{t \to \infty} (t^m\, e^{-m\alpha t}) = 0$

$$\Rightarrow \quad \lim_{t \to \infty} (t^m\, e^{-t}) = 0, \quad \text{choosing } \alpha = 1/m.$$

In colloquial terms, 'e^t tends to infinity more rapidly than any positive power of t'.

For completeness, we conclude by giving a more formal treatment of the limit crucial to all our work on circular functions,

$$\frac{\sin x}{x} \to 1 \quad \text{as } x \to 0. \tag{5}$$

In Figure 8, OAB is a sector of radius r, and angle AOB measures x radians. The tangent to the arc at A meets OB produced at T. Since

$$\text{area } \triangle OAB < \text{area sector } OAB < \text{area } \triangle OAT \quad \text{and } 0 < x < \tfrac{1}{2}\pi,$$

we have

$$\tfrac{1}{2}r^2 \sin x < \tfrac{1}{2}r^2 x < \tfrac{1}{2}r^2 \tan x;$$

thus $\quad \sin x < \quad x \quad < \tan x.$

Hence $\qquad 1 < \dfrac{x}{\sin x} < \dfrac{1}{\cos x}$

or $\qquad \cos x < \dfrac{\sin x}{x} < 1.$

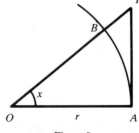

Figure 8

Now let $x \to 0$: $\qquad 1 \le \lim \left(\dfrac{\sin x}{x} \right) \le 1.$

Hence $\dfrac{\sin x}{x} \to 1$ as $x \to 0$ through positive values.

To complete the proof, we have to discuss negative values of x. So let $x = -y$ where $y > 0$:

$$\frac{\sin x}{x} = \frac{\sin(-y)}{-y} = \frac{\sin y}{y}.$$

$$\lim_{x \to 0^-} \left(\frac{\sin x}{x} \right) = \lim_{y \to 0^+} \left(\frac{\sin y}{y} \right) = 1,$$

and the proof is complete.

Exercise 3E

1 Sketch the graphs of:
   (a) $y = (\ln x)/x$ (b) $y = x^2 e^{-x}$ (c) $y = x \ln x$

2 Prove that $x^{1/x} \to 1$ as $x \to \infty$. Does $x^{1/x}$ tend to a limit as $x \to 0$? Find the maximum value of $x^{1/x}$ for $x > 0$. Sketch the graph of $y = x^{1/x}$ for positive x.

3 Use the fact that, if $\alpha > 0$, $x e^{-\alpha x} \to 0$ as $x \to \infty$, to show that $nx^n \to 0$ as $n \to \infty$ if $0 < x < 1$. (Compare Exercise 3B, question 5.)

4 Find the limits as $x \to 0$:

   (a) $\dfrac{\sin x}{3x^2 + 2x}$ (b) $\dfrac{\sin x - x}{4x - 6}$ (c) $\dfrac{\sin x - 3x}{5 \sin x - x}$

5 Sketch the graphs of:

   (a) $y = \dfrac{\sin x}{x}$ (b) $y = \sin \dfrac{1}{x}$

6 By writing $x = 1/u$, find the limit of $x \sin(1/x)$ as $x \to \infty$. Sketch the graph of $y = x \sin(1/x)$ for positive x.

5. CONTINUITY AND DIFFERENTIABILITY

The idea that a graph is 'continuous' when it is joined up and has a 'discontinuity' when there is a break or sudden jump is familiar. Thus the graph of $y = x^3/(x^2 + 1)$ is continuous everywhere, since $x^2 + 1 > 0$ for all real x; $y = x^3/(x^2 - 1)$ has discontinuities at $x = +1$ and $x = -1$; $y = x - [x]$ (where $[x]$ denotes the integer part of x) has discontinuities at all integer values of x.

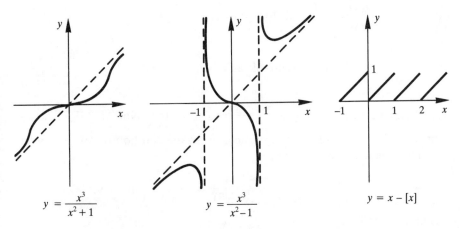

$$y = \frac{x^3}{x^2 + 1}$$

$$y = \frac{x^3}{x^2 - 1}$$

$$y = x - [x]$$

Figure 9

Continuity is really concerned with limits. We recall the definition '$f(x) \to l$ as $x \to a$ if for every positive real number k, we can find a positive number δ so that $|f(x) - l| < k$ for all x such that $0 < |x - a| < \delta$'.
Consider the function $x - [x]$ at $x = 2$. If we try to find the limit of $f(x)$ as $x \to 2$, we cannot produce a δ if $k = \frac{1}{2}$, say. Nevertheless, if x approaches 2

from below, the definition is satisfied with $l = 1$ (even though $f(2) = 0$), and we write $\lim\limits_{x \to 2^-} x - [x] = 1$.

Similarly, if x approaches 2 *from above*, the limit definition is satisfied and we write $\lim\limits_{x \to 2^+} x - [x] = 0$.

We can now define formally the assertion '$f(x)$ is continuous at $x = c$'. We require that (i) $f(c)$ exists, (ii) $f(x) \to f(c)$ as $x \to c^+$, and (iii) $f(x) \to f(c)$ as $x \to c^-$. Thus the function $x - [x]$ is continuous at $x = \frac{1}{2}$ but discontinuous at $x = 2$ since it fails the third of our conditions there.

5.1 Differentiability

All our early experience of differentiating was concerned with limits. For example, with $f(x) = \sqrt{x}$, the process is illuminated by the following table:

a	b	$\dfrac{f(b) - f(a)}{b - a}$
8.9	9	0.167 13
8.99	9	0.166 71
9	9.01	0.166 62
9	9.1	0.166 21

In general, the assertion '$f(x)$ is differentiable at $x = c$' requires that (i) $f(c)$ exists, and (ii) $\dfrac{f(x) - f(c)}{x - c}$ tends to a limit as $x \to c$.

Example 4
Show that $f(x) = \sqrt{x}$ is differentiable at $x = 9$.

Solution
$f(9) = 3$, so we want the limit of $\dfrac{\sqrt{x} - 3}{x - 9}$ as x tends to 9. Note that this fraction is undefined when $x = 9$. It was sensible to make definition (ii) of §3 in what may have seemed a perverse way.

Now $\dfrac{\sqrt{x} - 3}{x - 9} = \dfrac{\sqrt{x} - 3}{(\sqrt{x} - 3)(\sqrt{x} + 3)} = \dfrac{1}{\sqrt{x} + 3}$ if $x \neq 9$.

The limit as $x \to 9$ is $\frac{1}{6}$. $\square$

Example 5
Is the function $f(x) = |x|$ differentiable at $x = 0$?

Solution
Since the graph has a sharp bend at the origin, we expect the formal definition to fail there.

Now

$$\frac{f(x) - f(0)}{x - 0} \to 1 \quad \text{as } x \to 0^+$$

and

$$\frac{f(x) - f(0)}{x - 0} \to -1 \quad \text{as } x \to 0^-,$$

so the function is not differentiable at $x = 0$.

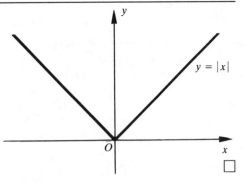

Figure 10

Exercise 3F

1 Explain why $f: x \mapsto [x]$ is not differentiable at $x = 1$.

2 Devise a function which is continuous everywhere and differentiable everywhere except at $x = \pm 1$.

3 The function $f(x) = \begin{cases} ax(x - 1) + b, & x < 1 \\ x - 1, & 1 \leqslant x \leqslant 3 \\ px^2 + qx + 2, & x > 3. \end{cases}$

Find values for the constants a, b, p and q so that simultaneously
  (i) $f(x)$ is continuous for all x,
  (ii) $f'(x)$ does not exist at $x = 1$, and
  (iii) $f'(x)$ is continuous at $x = 3$.
Does $f''(3)$ exist in your example?   [SMP]

4 Discuss the existence of the derivative at $x = 0$ of the function $f: x \mapsto x|x|$, showing that you have considered both positive and negative values as x tends to 0.
  State with reasons which of the following are true and which are false:
  (i) f is an even function.
  (ii) f is continuous at $x = 0$.
  (iii) f is differentiable at $x = 0$.
Sketch a graph of the function f and find the derived function f'. Is f' differentiable at $x = 0$?   [SMP]

Miscellaneous exercise 3

1 (a) Given that $f(n) = \dfrac{1}{2} \times \dfrac{3}{4} \times \dfrac{5}{6} \times \ldots \times \dfrac{2n - 1}{2n}$,

express $f(n + 1)$ in terms of $f(n)$ and use your calculator (or a computer) to make a conjecture about the value of $f(n)$ as $n \to \infty$.
  (b) Repeat (a) for

$$f(n) = \frac{3}{4} \times \frac{15}{16} \times \frac{35}{36} \times \ldots \times \frac{(2n)^2 - 1}{(2n)^2}.$$

2 Suppose an equilateral triangle is inscribed in a circle of radius 20 cm, then S_3, the inscribed circle of the triangle, has radius r_3 equal to $20 \cos \frac{1}{3}\pi = 10$ cm.
  Next inscribe a square in the circle S_3 and let S_4, the incircle of the square, have radius r_4. Show that

$$r_4 = 20 \cos \tfrac{1}{3}\pi \cos \tfrac{1}{4}\pi = 7.071 \text{ cm.}$$

Continue the process by inscribing a regular pentagon inside S_4, then a regular hexagon inside S_5, and so on.

Complete the following table:

n	3	4	5	6
r_n	10	7.071		

What happens to r_n as $n \to \infty$? Compute values, graph results and make a conjecture.

3   Let
$$f(n) = \left(\frac{2}{1} \times \frac{2}{3}\right)\left(\frac{4}{3} \times \frac{4}{5}\right) \cdots \left(\frac{2n}{2n-1} \times \frac{2n}{2n+1}\right).$$

Evaluate $f(1)$, $f(2)$ and $f(3)$.
   (a) Prove that $f(n)$ is a monotonic increasing function.
   (b) Prove that $f(n) < 2$ for all n, and deduce that $f(n)$ tends to a limit as $n \to \infty$.

4   If $t > 0$, prove that $(1 + t)^n > 1 + nt$ for all integers $n > 1$. Deduce that if $x > 1$, $x^n \to \infty$ as $n \to \infty$.   [SMP]

5   With the help of a graph of $\sin x$ for $0 \leqslant x \leqslant \tfrac{1}{6}\pi$, give the values of the constants a and b, as close to each other as possible, such that $ax \leqslant \sin x \leqslant bx$ for $0 \leqslant x \leqslant \tfrac{1}{6}\pi$.

Deduce two numbers between which the value of $\displaystyle\int_0^{\pi/6} \sqrt{(\sin x)}\,dx$ lies, and which differ by not more than 0.007. (Give three decimal places in your answers.)

6   By integrating a suitable inequality, prove that $u < \tan u$ for $0 < u < \tfrac{1}{2}\pi$.

7   Use the inequality of question 6 to prove that $e^{-x^2/2} \geqslant \cos x$ for $0 \leqslant x \leqslant \tfrac{1}{2}\pi$.

8   (a) Use your calculator to evaluate $\sqrt{(x^2 + 3x)} - \sqrt{(x^2 - 5)}$ for several large values of x.
   (b) Simplify $[\sqrt{(x^2 + 3x)} - \sqrt{(x^2 - 5)}][\sqrt{(x^2 + 3x)} + \sqrt{(x^2 - 5)}]$, and hence establish the limit of $\sqrt{(x^2 + 3x)} - \sqrt{(x^2 - 5)}$ as $x \to \infty$.

9   Prove that the function $u(x) = x - \sin x$ increases steadily with x. Deduce that $\displaystyle\int_1^2 \frac{\sin x\,dx}{x^3} < \tfrac{1}{2}$. Obtain for the right-hand side a value k, less than $\tfrac{1}{2}$, such that the integral is less than k.   [SMP]

10   By considering the integrals $\displaystyle\int_1^{\sqrt{3}} \frac{2}{1 + x^2}\,dx$ and $\displaystyle\int_1^{\sqrt{3}} \frac{dx}{x}$, prove that $\ln 3 > \tfrac{1}{3}\pi$.

11   Sketch on the same diagram the graphs of $1/x$ and $1/\sqrt{x}$ for $x \geqslant 1$, labelling the graphs clearly.

By comparing the areas under the two graphs over the interval $1 \leqslant x \leqslant t$, show that for $t \geqslant 1$,
$$\frac{\ln t}{t} \leqslant \frac{2}{\sqrt{t}} - \frac{2}{t}.$$

What can you deduce about the behaviour of the function $t \to (\ln t)/t$ for large values of t? Sketch the graph of this function for $t > 0$, paying particular attention to the asymptotes and turning values.   [SMP]

12   Prove that, if $x > 0$ and $x \neq 1$, then
$$\frac{1}{1 + \sqrt{x}} = \frac{(1 - \sqrt{x})(1 + x)}{1 - x^2}.$$

If $0 < x < \frac{1}{4}$, between what bounds does $1 - x^2$ lie? Deduce that

$$0.198 > \int_0^{1/4} \frac{1}{1 + \sqrt{x}} dx > 0.185. \qquad \text{[SMP]}$$

13 Let $S(n) = \cos(\pi/4) \cos(\pi/8) \ldots \cos(\pi/2^n)$, where n is a positive integer.
  (a) Prove that $S(n) \sin(\pi/2^n) = 1/2^{n-1}$.
  (b) Deduce that $S(n) \to 2/\pi$ as $n \to \infty$.
This result was first obtained by Francois Viète (1540–1603).

14 By repeated use of the identity $\cos 2\phi = 2 \cos^2 \phi - 1$, express Viète's limit in the form

$$\frac{2}{\pi} = \frac{\sqrt{2}}{2} \times \frac{\sqrt{(2 + \sqrt{2})}}{2} \times \frac{\sqrt{(2 + \sqrt{(2 + \sqrt{2})})}}{2} \ldots$$

SUMMARY

Definitions
(1) $f(x) \to \infty$ as $x \to \infty$ if for every positive number k (however large), we can find a number x_0 such that $f(x) > k$ for all $x > x_0$.

(2) $f(x) \to l$ as $x \to \infty$ if for every positive number k (however small), we can find x_0 so that $|f(x) - l| < k$ for all $x > x_0$.

(3) $f(x) \to l$ as $x \to a$ if for every positive number k, we can find a positive number δ such that $|f(x) - l| < k$ for all x such that $0 < |x - a| < \delta$.

Theorems
(1) For $\alpha > 0$, $x^\alpha \to \infty$ as $x \to \infty$. For $\alpha < 0$, $x^\alpha \to 0$ as $x \to \infty$.

(2) If $f(x) \to l$ and $g(x) \to m$ as $x \to \infty$,

then $\qquad\qquad\qquad \lambda f(x) \to \lambda l, \qquad f(x) + g(x) \to l + m,$

$$f(x) g(x) \to lm \quad \text{and} \quad f(x)/g(x) \to l/m \quad \text{(provided } m \neq 0).$$

(3) If $g(x) \to 0$ as $x \to \infty$ and if $0 < |f(x)| < |g(x)|$ for all $x > x_0$, then $f(x) \to 0$ as $x \to \infty$.

(4) If $h(x) < f(x) < g(x)$ for all $x > x_0$, and both $h(x)$ and $g(x)$ tend to the same limit l as $x \to \infty$, then $f(x)$ also tends to l as $x \to \infty$.

Important results
(1) As $n \to \infty$, $\qquad (1 + x/n)^n \to e^x$
$$x^n/n! \to 0$$
$$n^\alpha x^n \to 0 \quad \text{for all } \alpha, |x| < 1$$

(2) As $x \to \infty$, $\qquad\qquad \dfrac{\ln x}{x^\alpha} \to 0 \quad \text{for all } \alpha > 0$

$$x\, e^{-\alpha x} \to 0 \quad \text{for all } \alpha > 0$$
$$x^{\alpha}\, e^{-x} \to 0 \quad \text{for all } \alpha > 0$$

(3)   As $x \to 0$, $x^{\alpha} \ln x \to 0 \quad \text{for all } \alpha > 0$

$$\frac{\sin x}{x} \to 1$$

4

Infinite series

1. AN EXAMPLE

Here is a game for two players. They take turns to draw a ball from a bag and replace it. The bag contains just two red and three blue balls. The first player, A, has to draw a red ball to win; the second player, B, must draw a blue to win. Which player has the better chance of winning?

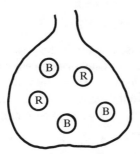

Figure 1

The probability that A wins in the first round is $\frac{2}{5}$; the probability that B wins is $\frac{3}{5} \times \frac{3}{5} = \frac{9}{25}$ (remember that A must fail to draw red if B is to get a draw at all). So A has a slightly better chance in the first round. But the game may not be concluded in the first round; it may go on and on. To find A's chance of winning, we have to add together his chance of winning in rounds 1, 2, 3, ... Noting that the probability of an inconclusive round is $\frac{3}{5} \times \frac{2}{5} = \frac{6}{25}$, we have

$$P \text{ (A wins)} = \frac{2}{5} + \frac{6}{25} \times \frac{2}{5} + \frac{6}{25} \times \frac{6}{25} \times \frac{2}{5} + \ldots$$
$$P \text{ (B wins)} = \frac{9}{25} + \frac{6}{25} \times \frac{9}{25} + \frac{6}{25} \times \frac{6}{25} \times \frac{9}{25} + \ldots$$

Since $\frac{2}{5} > \frac{9}{25}$, we conclude, without further calculation, that A has the better chance since each term of his series is larger than the corresponding term of B's. Nevertheless, A's chance can be found as follows:

$$P \text{ (A wins)} = \frac{2}{5}(1 + \frac{6}{25} + (\frac{6}{25})^2 + \ldots)$$

Now we know that the sum of the first n terms of the geometric series in the bracket is

$$\frac{1 - (\frac{6}{25})^n}{1 - \frac{6}{25}}.$$

As $n \to \infty$, $(\frac{6}{25})^n \to 0$, so the sum tends to $1/(1 - \frac{6}{25})$ in value.

37

We conclude that $\quad P\,(A\text{ wins}) = \dfrac{2}{5}\left(\dfrac{1}{1 - \frac{6}{25}}\right) = \dfrac{10}{19}\,,$

and $\qquad\qquad\quad P\,(B\text{ wins}) = \dfrac{9}{25}\left(\dfrac{1}{1 - \frac{6}{25}}\right) = \dfrac{9}{19}\,.$

This problem contains two important ideas, the summation of an infinite series and the comparison between two infinite series. These form the substance of this chapter.

In general, we shall denote the terms of a series $u_1, u_2, u_3, \ldots$, and use S_n to denote the sum of the first n terms.

Thus
$$S_1 = u_1,$$
$$S_2 = u_1 + u_2,$$
$$S_{n-1} = u_1 + u_2 + \ldots + u_{n-1},$$
$$S_n = u_1 + u_2 + \ldots + u_{n-1} + u_n,$$

so that $\qquad\qquad S_n = S_{n-1} + u_n.$

Since S_n is a function whose domain is the positive integers, its behaviour as $n \to \infty$ falls into one of the four categories given in §2 of Chapter 3.

If S_n tends to a limit l as $n \to \infty$, we say that the series is *convergent* and has 'sum to infinity' or 'sum' l. In the game for two players we found that the sum to infinity of $1 + \frac{6}{25} + (\frac{6}{25})^2 + \ldots$ was $\frac{25}{19}$. Conventionally, we write this in the form

$$1 + \tfrac{6}{25} + (\tfrac{6}{25})^2 + \ldots = \tfrac{25}{19}.$$

Exercise 4A

1 Find S_6, S_7, S_8 and an expression for S_n for each of the following series:
   (a) $1 + 2 + 3 + \ldots$
   (b) $1 - 1 + 1 - 1 + \ldots$
   (c) $1 - 2 + 3 - 4 + \ldots$
   and confirm that these series respectively diverge, oscillate finitely and oscillate infinitely.

2 For the geometric series $a + ar + ar^2 + \ldots + ar^{n-1}$,

$$S_n = a\left(\frac{1 - r^n}{1 - r}\right).$$

   Discuss the behaviour as $n \to \infty$ in each of the following cases:
   (a) $a = 1, r = \frac{1}{2}$ (b) $a = 1, r = -\frac{1}{2}$
   (c) $a = 1, r = 2$ (d) $a = 1, r = -2$

3 Players A and B take turns to roll a die. A goes first and needs a six to win. B needs 1 or 2 to win. Which player has the better chance of winning?

4 Find the fraction whose decimal expansion is $0.373\,737 \ldots$ recurring.

5 A ball is dropped from a height h metres onto a horizontal plane, and at each bounce its speed is halved. Show that the bouncing ceases $3\sqrt{(2h/g)}$ seconds after the ball is dropped.

6 Players A and B take turns to roll two dice. A goes first and needs a total of 7 or 10 to win, while B needs a total of 8, 9 or 10 to win. Find the probability of A winning.

7 For what values of x does $1 + \dfrac{x}{1-x} + \left(\dfrac{x}{1-x}\right)^2 + \ldots$ converge? What is then the sum to infinity?

8 Using partial fractions or otherwise, find the sum of the first n terms of the series

$$\frac{1}{1 \times 2} + \frac{1}{2 \times 3} + \frac{1}{3 \times 4} + \ldots + \frac{1}{r(r+1)} + \ldots.$$

Deduce the sum to infinity.

9 Prove that the sum of the first k terms of the series

$$\frac{2}{1 \times 3} + \frac{2}{3 \times 5} + \ldots + \frac{2}{(2n-1)(2n+1)} + \ldots$$

is $1 - 1/(2k+1)$. How many terms of this series must be taken to bring the sum to within 10^{-6} of its limiting value? [SMP]

10 For the series $\quad \dfrac{1}{2!} + \dfrac{2}{3!} + \dfrac{3}{4!} + \ldots + \dfrac{r}{(r+1)!} + \ldots,$

find S_2, S_3 and S_4 as simple fractions. Suggest a formula for S_n and prove it, by induction or otherwise. Hence show that the series is convergent.

11 By multiplying S_n by $1 - x$, find the sum to n terms of the series

$$1 + 2x + 3x^2 + \ldots + rx^{r-1} + \ldots.$$

Find the sum to infinity if $|x| < 1$. You may assume that $nx^n \to 0$, which was proved in Chapter 3.

12 Obtain S_n for the series in question 11 by differentiating a suitable expression.

13 Use a calculator to find S_{10}, S_{15} and S_{20} for:

(a) $\displaystyle\sum_1^n \frac{1}{r}$ (b) $\displaystyle\sum_1^n \frac{1}{r^2}$ (c) $\displaystyle\sum_1^n \frac{1}{\sqrt{r}}$

14 Use a computer to find S_{100}, S_{150} and S_{200} for each of the series in question 13. Can you guess how many of these series converge?

2. SUMS OF FINITE SERIES

Whenever we can find a concise form for the finite sum S_n, it is easy to discuss the behaviour as n tends to infinity.

For the geometric series $\quad S_n = a\left(\dfrac{1 - r^n}{1 - r}\right),$

the infinite series converges if $|r| < 1$, and the sum to infinity is $a/(1 - r)$.

One common method of summing a finite series is by the method of differences. Sometimes we can find a function $f(n)$ such that $u_n = f(n) - f(n-1)$ for all $n \geq 1$.

Then $\quad S_n = f(1) - f(0) + f(2) - f(1) + \ldots + f(n) - f(n-1)$
$\qquad\quad = f(n) - f(0).$

Such a method is applicable in Exercise 4A, question 10, where we can write

$$\frac{r}{(r+1)!} \quad \text{as} \quad \frac{r+1}{(r+1)!} - \frac{1}{(r+1)!} \quad \text{or} \quad \frac{1}{r!} - \frac{1}{(r+1)!},$$

and also in questions 8 and 9.

There are many occasions when we cannot obtain an explicit form for S_n. It may nevertheless be possible (i) to decide whether or not the series converges and (ii) to find the sum to infinity of a convergent series. For example, the familiar series

$$x - \frac{x^2}{2} + \frac{x^3}{3} - \frac{x^4}{4} + \dots$$

will be shown to converge if $-1 < x \le 1$, and the sum to infinity is then $\ln(1 + x)$.

We shall start by considering the convergence/divergence decision.

3. INFINITE SERIES

3.1 The method of comparison

In this method, we compare term by term a series whose behaviour is unknown with a familiar one. For example, we can show that

$$x + \frac{x^2}{2} + \frac{x^3}{3} + \dots + \frac{x^r}{r} + \dots$$

is convergent if $0 < x < 1$.

Since $\qquad\qquad S_n < x + x^2 + x^3 + \dots + x^{n-1},$

and we know that this geometric series converges if $0 < x < 1$, then the original series must converge.

3.2 The harmonic series and its relatives

For comparison purposes, a particularly important series is

$$1 + \frac{1}{2} + \frac{1}{3} + \dots + \frac{1}{r} + \dots.$$

Because of the link between its terms and the length of string or pipe required to produce musical harmonics,* the series is known as the harmonic series.

Is the harmonic series convergent or divergent? If you experimented in Exercise 4A with a calculator or computer, you will have found that S_n grows very slowly.

Thus $\qquad\qquad S_{10} \approx 2.929, \quad S_{20} \approx 3.656, \quad S_{40} \approx 4.337.$

However, a grouping of the terms of the series shows that we can increase S_n indefinitely, for

* If length 1 gives middle C, the other terms give C', G', C", E", G", B ", C''', D''', E''', F#'''', etc.

$$1 + \tfrac{1}{2} + (\tfrac{1}{3} + \tfrac{1}{4}) + (\tfrac{1}{5} + \tfrac{1}{6} + \tfrac{1}{7} + \tfrac{1}{8}) + \ldots$$
$$> 1 + \tfrac{1}{2} + (\tfrac{1}{4} + \tfrac{1}{4}) + (\tfrac{1}{8} + \tfrac{1}{8} + \tfrac{1}{8} + \tfrac{1}{8}) + \ldots$$
$$= 1 + \tfrac{1}{2} + \quad \tfrac{1}{2} \quad + \quad\quad \tfrac{1}{2} \quad\quad + \ldots$$

Thus

$$S_8 > 1 + \tfrac{1}{2} + \tfrac{1}{2} + \tfrac{1}{2} = 2\tfrac{1}{2}, \quad S_{16} > 1 + \tfrac{1}{2} + \tfrac{1}{2} + \tfrac{1}{2} + \tfrac{1}{2} = 3, \quad S_{32} > 3\tfrac{1}{2}, \quad \text{etc.}$$

Clearly, the harmonic series is divergent. But divergence is slow. The above argument only shows that S_n exceeds 10 when $n > 2^{18}$ (over a quarter of a million!); more precise information about the behaviour of S_n is provided by Miscellaneous exercise 4, question 12.

The series $S = 1 + \dfrac{1}{2^s} + \dfrac{1}{3^s} + \dfrac{1}{4^s} + \ldots$

The harmonic series is one of this family, corresponding to the case $s = 1$. It divides the family into two groups:

(i) if $s < 1$, the series $\sum \dfrac{1}{r^s}$ is divergent, and

(ii) if $s > 1$, the series is convergent.

Proof of (i)

If $s < 1$, $\qquad 1 + \dfrac{1}{2^s} + \dfrac{1}{3^s} + \ldots > 1 + \dfrac{1}{2} + \dfrac{1}{3} + \ldots,$

which was proved above to be divergent.

Proof of (ii)
We need to show that the series is less than one known to be convergent. A method similar to that used for the harmonic series is found to be effective:

$$S_n = 1 + \left(\frac{1}{2^s} + \frac{1}{3^s}\right) + \left(\frac{1}{4^s} + \frac{1}{5^s} + \frac{1}{6^s} + \frac{1}{7^s}\right) + \ldots \quad \text{to } n \text{ terms}$$

$$< 1 + \left(\frac{1}{2^s} + \frac{1}{2^s}\right) + \left(\frac{1}{4^s} + \frac{1}{4^s} + \frac{1}{4^s} + \frac{1}{4^s}\right) + \ldots \quad \text{to infinity}$$

$$= 1 + \frac{1}{2^{s-1}} + \frac{1}{4^{s-1}} + \ldots$$

$$= \frac{1}{1 - 2^{s-1}}$$

since it is a geometric series with ratio $1/2^{s-1} < 1$.

Now S_n is a steadily increasing function of n and we have shown it to be bounded above. So S_n tends to a limit, and $\sum 1/r^s$ is convergent.

There is no formula for the sum of n terms of this series, nor a general formula for the sum to infinity, but there are simple (and surprising) results when s is a positive even integer.

For example, $1 + \dfrac{1}{2^2} + \dfrac{1}{3^2} + \ldots = \dfrac{\pi^2}{6}$

(see Miscellaneous exercise 4, questions 4 and 14)

and $1 + \dfrac{1}{2^4} + \dfrac{1}{3^4} + \ldots = \dfrac{\pi^4}{90}.$

3.3 Alternating series

Some series consist of terms which are alternatively positive and negative. We shall find that an alternating series may converge even though the corresponding series of positive terms diverges.

For example, $1 - \dfrac{1}{\sqrt{2}} + \dfrac{1}{\sqrt{3}} - \dfrac{1}{\sqrt{4}} + \ldots$ converges,

while $1 + \dfrac{1}{\sqrt{2}} + \dfrac{1}{\sqrt{3}} + \dfrac{1}{\sqrt{4}} + \ldots$ diverges.

Exercise 4B

Questions 5 and 10 provide important results which are required in subsequent questions and included in the chapter summary.

1 Show that $x + \frac{1}{2}x^2 + \frac{1}{3}x^3 + \ldots$ is divergent if $x > 1$.

2 Show that $1 + \frac{1}{3} + \frac{1}{5} + \ldots$ is divergent.

3 Use the inequality $\ln u < u - 1$ (see Chapter 3) to show that $\displaystyle\sum_{2}^{\infty} \dfrac{1}{\ln r}$ is divergent.

4 (a) By writing $\displaystyle\sum_{0}^{\infty} \dfrac{x^r}{r!}$ in the form

$$1 + x + \frac{x^2}{2!} + \frac{x^3}{3!} + \frac{x^4}{4!}\left(1 + \frac{x}{5} + \frac{x^2}{5 \times 6} + \ldots\right),$$

show that the series is convergent if $0 < x < 4$.
  (b) Show that the series is convergent for any positive value of x.

5 (a) Show that if $u_r > 0$ and there exists a fixed value $k < 1$ for which $u_{r+1} < ku_r$ for all r, then Σu_r is convergent.
  (b) Show that the series is still convergent if we only have the weaker condition $u_{r+1} < ku_r$ for all $r > m$, where m is a fixed positive integer.

6 Use question 5 to show that (a) $\Sigma x^r/r$, and (b) $\Sigma r^2 x^r$ are convergent if $0 < x < 1$.

7 If m and x are both negative, show that all the terms of the binomial series

$$1 + mx + \frac{m(m-1)}{2!}x^2 + \frac{m(m-1)(m-2)}{3!}x^3 + \ldots$$

are positive, and that the series converges if $-1 < x < 0$.

8 Copy Figure 2 and continue it for $n = 4, 5, 6, 7, 8$, given that

$$S_n = 1 - \tfrac{1}{2} + \tfrac{1}{4} - \tfrac{1}{8} + \ldots + (-\tfrac{1}{2})^r + \ldots.$$

What is the limit of S_n as $n \to \infty$?

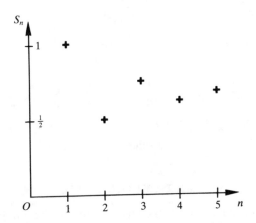

Figure 2

9   Draw graphs like Figure 2 for:
     (a) $S_n = 1 + \frac{1}{2} + \frac{1}{3} + \dots$ (b) $S_n = 1 - \frac{1}{2} + \frac{1}{3} - \frac{1}{4} + \dots$
     (c) $S_n = 1 - \frac{1}{3} + \frac{1}{5} - \frac{1}{7} + \dots$

10 Explain why an alternating series is convergent if (a) $u_n \to 0$ as $n \to \infty$, and
     (b) $|u_n| > |u_{n+1}|$ for all n.

11 Use question 10 to show that:

     (a) $\dfrac{1}{\ln 2} - \dfrac{1}{\ln 3} + \dfrac{1}{\ln 4} - \dots$ is convergent;

     (b) $x - \frac{1}{2}x^2 + \frac{1}{3}x^3 - \frac{1}{4}x^4 + \dots$ is convergent if $0 < x \leqslant 1$.

12 Show that (a) the exponential series

$$1 + x + \frac{x^2}{2!} + \frac{x^3}{3!} + \dots$$

     converges for all negative x, and (b) the binomial series

$$1 + mx + \frac{m(m-1)}{2!}x^2 + \frac{m(m-1)(m-2)}{3!}x^3 + \dots$$

     converges for all x such that $0 < x < 1$.

13 Show that the series for $\sin x$ and $\cos x$ are convergent for all values of x. (You may
     assume that the exponential series is convergent for all values of x.)

14 Which of the following statements are correct?

     (a) $\displaystyle\sum_1^\infty u_r$ is convergent $\Rightarrow u_n \to 0$ as $n \to \infty$.

     (b) $u_n \to 0$ as $n \to \infty \Rightarrow \Sigma u_r$ is convergent.

     (c) $-1 < \dfrac{u_{r+1}}{u_r} < 0$ for all $r \Rightarrow \Sigma u_r$ is convergent.

     (d) $\dfrac{u_{r+1}}{u_r} \geqslant 1$ for all $r \Rightarrow \Sigma u_r$ is divergent.

     (e) If $u_r > 0$ for all r, then Σu_r converges $\Rightarrow u_1 - u_2 + u_3 - u_4 + \dots$ converges.
     (f) If $u_r > 0$ for all r, then Σu_r converges $\Leftarrow u_1 - u_2 + u_3 - u_4 + \dots$ converges.
     Illustrate each false statement with an example.

15   Show that

$$\frac{1}{r} - \frac{1}{r-1} = \frac{1}{r(r+1)} < \frac{1}{r^2} < \frac{1}{r^2-1} = \frac{1}{2}\left(\frac{1}{r-1} - \frac{1}{r+1}\right).$$

Hence show that

$$\frac{20}{220} < \sum_{11}^{\infty} \frac{1}{r^2} < \frac{21}{220} \quad \text{and} \quad \frac{40}{840} < \sum_{21}^{\infty} \frac{1}{r^2} < \frac{41}{840}$$

Use your value of $\sum_{1}^{20} 1/r^2$ from Exercise 4A, question 13 to obtain a good estimate for $\sum_{1}^{\infty} 1/r^2$. Compare it with the value of $\frac{1}{6}\pi^2$ given by your calculator.

4. TAYLOR SERIES

The Taylor approximations, which we assume to be familiar, can now be extended to give the following infinite Taylor series:

$$e^x = 1 + x + \frac{x^2}{2!} + \frac{x^3}{3!} + \dots \qquad \text{for all } x \qquad (1)$$

$$\sin x = x - \frac{x^3}{3!} + \frac{x^5}{5!} - \dots \qquad \text{for all } x \qquad (2)$$

$$\cos x = 1 - \frac{x^2}{2!} + \frac{x^4}{4!} - \dots \qquad \text{for all } x \qquad (3)$$

$$\ln(1+x) = x - \frac{x^2}{2} + \frac{x^3}{3} - \dots \qquad \text{if } -1 < x \leq 1 \qquad (4)$$

and $$(1+x)^m = 1 + mx + \frac{m(m-1)}{2!}x^2 + \dots \quad \text{if } -1 < x < 1, \text{ for any } m \quad (5)$$

It is important to be clear that a statement such as (4) says, 'If $-1 < x \leq 1$, the series on the right-hand side is a convergent series, and its sum equals $\ln(1+x)$.'

Earlier in this chapter we established the convergence of all these series. We have yet to show that the sums of these series are in fact e^x, $\sin x$, etc. For this we shall use Taylor's theorem,* the proof of which can be found in any advanced text.

4.1 Taylor's theorem

Provided that the function $x \mapsto f(x)$ is continuous and all derivatives exist throughout the range from $x = a$ to $x = a + h$,

$$f(a+h) = f(a) + h f'(a) + \frac{h^2}{2!} f''(a) + \dots + \frac{h^n}{n!} f^{(n)}(a + \theta h),$$

where $0 < \theta < 1$.

---

* Brooke Taylor (1685–1731) published his theorem in 1715.

The term
$$\frac{h^n}{n!} f^{(n)}(a + \theta h)$$

is called the 'remainder after n terms' and constitutes the error in taking the first n terms of the series as an approximation to the given function.

In the simple case, $n = 1$, we have $f(a + h) = f(a) + h f'(a + \theta h)$. This is equivalent to

$$\frac{f(a + h) - f(a)}{h} = f'(a + \theta h)$$

and can be interpreted geometrically as saying that in Figure 3, the chord PQ is parallel to the tangent to the curve somewhere between P and Q.

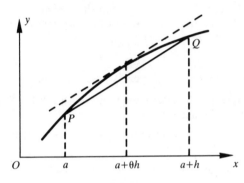

Figure 3

We shall be taking $a = 0$ from now on, that is, applying Taylor's theorem in the form

$$f(h) = f(0) + h f'(0) + \frac{h^2}{2!} f''(0) + \ldots + \frac{h^n}{n!} f^{(n)}(\theta h),$$

where θ is some number between 0 and 1.

Example 1
Find the remainder after n terms and the Taylor series for the function $x \mapsto e^x$.

Solution
Writing $f(x) = e^x$, we have $f'(x) = e^x$ and $f^{(n)}(x) = e^x$ for all n. Thus $f(0) = f'(0) = f''(0) = \ldots = 1$, and we have

$$e^h = 1 + h + \frac{h^2}{2!} + \ldots + \frac{h^{n-1}}{(n-1)!} + \frac{h^n}{n!} e^{\theta h}.$$

The remainder is $R_n = \dfrac{h^n}{n!} e^{\theta h}$, where $0 < \theta < 1$. Although we cannot tell what value θ has (indeed it will vary with n), we can say that $e^{\theta h}$ lies between 1 and e^h, and since we know, from Chapter 3, that $h^n/n! \to 0$ as $n \to \infty$, it follows that $R_n \to 0$.

Hence for all values of h, the series

$$1 + h + \frac{h^2}{2!} + \ldots \quad \text{has sum to infinity } e^h.$$

This is the Taylor series, which is often written with x for h throughout:

$$e^x = 1 + x + \frac{x^2}{2!} + \frac{x^3}{3!} + \ldots. \qquad \square$$

The remainder after n terms is valuable when we approximate by calculating the first few terms of a Taylor series. For example, as well as saying $e^{0.2} \approx 1 + 0.2 + 0.2^2/2! = 1.22$, we know that the error is $(0.2)^3 \, e^{0.2\theta}/3!$ for some θ between 0 and 1; that is, that the error lies between 0.001 33 and 0.001 63. We can conclude that $1.221\,33 < e^{0.2} < 1.221\,63$.

Exercise 4C

1   By discussing the remainder after n terms, establish the Taylor series for $\sin x$ and $\cos x$ given at the beginning of §4.

2   Use the first three non-zero terms of the Taylor series to calculate $\sin 0.3$, and show that the error is less than 3×10^{-7}.

3   What accuracy could you guarantee if the sum of the first ten terms of the series

$$1 + 1 + \frac{1}{2!} + \frac{1}{3!} + \ldots$$

is used to estimate the value of e?

4   (a) Use six terms (i.e. five non-zero terms) to calculate $\ln 1.3$ and $\ln 0.7$ approximately.

(b) Show that the remainder after six terms can be written as

$$-\frac{1}{6}\left(\frac{-x}{1 + \theta x}\right)^6, \quad \text{where } 0 < \theta < 1.$$

(c) Show that (b) gives the error in $\ln 1.3$ as calculated in (a) to lie between $+0.000\,025$ and $+0.000\,122$.

(d) Find an upper limit for the error in your answer for $\ln 0.7$.

5   Without discussion of the remainder terms or the range of convergence, obtain the following expansions:

(a) $\tan x = x + \frac{1}{3}x^3 + \frac{2}{15}x^5 + \ldots$ (b) $\sinh x = x + \frac{x^3}{3!} + \frac{x^5}{5!} + \ldots$

(c) $\tan^{-1} x = x - \frac{1}{3}x^3 + \frac{1}{5}x^5 - \ldots$

6   Obtain the first three non-zero terms of the power series for $\sqrt{(\cos x)}$ by using the binomial series expansion for

$$\left[1 + \left(-\frac{x^2}{2} + \frac{x^4}{24}\right)\right]^{1/2}.$$

7   Use known series to obtain Taylor series for the following:
  (a) $e^{-x^2/2}$, as far as the term in x^4;
  (b) $\ln(1 + \sin x)$, as far as the term in x^3;

  (c) $\sqrt{\left(\dfrac{1 + x}{1 - x}\right)}$, as far as the term in x^3 (*hint*: treat it as $(1 + x)^{1/2}(1 - x)^{-1/2}$);

  (d) $e^x \cos x$, as far as the term in x^4.

5. DERIVATION OF POWER SERIES BY INTEGRATION

Instead of using Taylor's theorem, the series for some of the elementary functions can be found by integration.

Example 2
Find the series for $\ln(1 + x)$ and discuss its convergence.

Solution
We begin with the finite geometric series,

$$1 - t + t^2 - t^3 + \ldots + (-t)^{n-1} = \frac{1 - (-t)^n}{1 - (-t)} = \frac{1}{1 + t} - \frac{(-t)^n}{1 + t}.$$

Integrate both sides from 0 to x (assuming $x > -1$):

$$x - \frac{x^2}{2} + \frac{x^3}{3} - \ldots + (-1)^{n-1}\frac{x^n}{n} = \ln(1 + x) - (-1)^n \int_0^x \frac{t^n}{1 + t}\, dt.$$

So
$$|\ln(1 + x) - S_n| = \left| \int_0^x \frac{t^n}{1 + t}\, dt \right|, \tag{1}$$

where
$$S_n = x - \frac{x^2}{2} + \frac{x^3}{3} - \ldots \text{ to } n \text{ terms.}$$

All that remains is for us to show that the right-hand side of equation (1) tends to zero as $n \to \infty$ when the fixed value of x lies in the range $-1 < x \le 1$. We set out the working for $0 < x \le 1$; the case where x is negative follows similar lines and is left to the reader.

If $x > 0$,
$$\int_0^x \frac{t^n}{1 + t}\, dt < \int_0^x \frac{t^n}{1}\, dt = \frac{x^{n+1}}{n + 1}.$$

Now $x^{n+1}/(n + 1) \to 0$ as $n \to \infty$ if $0 < x \le 1$, thus $\ln(1 + x) - S_n \to 0$ as $n \to \infty$.   □

Exercise 4D

1   Calculate the accuracy to which $S_n = 1 - \frac{1}{2} + \frac{1}{3} - \ldots$ with $n = 1000$ approximates to $\ln 2$ by examining $\int_0^1 \frac{t^n}{1 + t}\, dt$ and showing that

$$\frac{1}{2(n + 1)} < |\ln 2 - S_n| < \frac{1}{n + 1}.$$

2 Suppose $0 < x < c$, where c is some constant. Prove, by integrating the inequality

$$0 < e^t - 1 < e^c - 1$$

n times from 0 to x, that

$$0 < e^x - E_n(x) < (e^c - 1)\frac{x^n}{n!}$$

where

$$E_n(x) = 1 + x + \frac{x^2}{2!} + \ldots + \frac{x^n}{n!}.$$

Deduce that $E_n(x) \to e^x$ as $n \to \infty$, and carry out a similar proof for negative values of x.

3 (*Gregory's series*[*] for $\tan^{-1} x$). Prove that

$$\frac{1}{1 + t^2} = 1 - t^2 + t^4 - \ldots + (-1)^{n-1} t^{2n-1} + (-1)^n \frac{t^{2n}}{1 + t^2}.$$

Deduce that, if $-1 \leqslant x \leqslant 1$,

$$\tan^{-1} x = x - \frac{x^3}{3} + \frac{x^5}{5} - \ldots.$$

4 Setting $x = 1$ in Gregory's series gives

$$\tfrac{1}{4}\pi = 1 - \tfrac{1}{3} + \tfrac{1}{5} - \ldots$$

By considering $\int_0^1 \frac{t^{2n}}{1 + t^2} \, dt$, show that the sum of 1000 terms of this series differs from $\tfrac{1}{4}\pi$ by at least 2×10^{-4}. (In 1699, Abraham Sharp obtained π to 71 decimal places by substituting $x = 1/\sqrt{3}$ in Gregory's series.)

6. APPLICATIONS TO THE EVALUATION OF FUNCTIONS

How does your calculator work out $e^{0.2}$? How about $e^{-5.4}$? Long before you began this chapter, you must have thought about questions such as these. Given that the calculator has procedures for $+$, $-$, $\times$ and $\div$, how does it obtain e^x, $\ln x$, $\sin x$, or even just $\sqrt{x}$?

Your answer to the first question may well have been 'Find the sum of a suitable number of terms of the Taylor series with $x = 0.2$.' If the calculator rounds answers and displays six digits, how many terms of the series will it need to calculate to give $e^{0.2} = 1.221\,40$?

On the other hand, you might have said 'It uses an approximation related to the above series for e^x.' One such approximation is

$$e^x \approx \frac{(x + 3)^2 + 3}{(x - 3)^2 + 3}. \tag{1}$$

Approximation (1) becomes increasingly accurate as x gets smaller. For example, if $|x| < 0.05$, the approximation gives e^x correct to ten figures. However, direct substitution in (1) fails to give six correct figures once $|x| > 0.2$.

In principle, the Taylor series will give the value of e^x in all cases, as we have

* James Gregory published his theorem in 1671.

seen, but for values with $|x| > 1$ it becomes necessary to calculate a large number of terms, and the accumulated effect of rounding errors becomes serious.

Exercise 4E

1 Write and run a computer program which uses the series for e^x and obtains the value of e^x correct to six significant figures for any value of x in the range $-1 < x < 1$. Assume the computer works internally to 10 SF.

2 What is the maximum number of terms the program of question 1 will need to sum to achieve the required accuracy?

3 Use your program to find $e^{-5.4}$, and compare with the correct value. Modify your program so that the value of each term of the series is printed. Explain where the most significant errors are introduced.

4 (a) Verify that when $x = 0.2$, approximation (1) gives $e^{0.2}$ correct to 6 SF.
(b) Verify that by substituting $x = 0.1$ and squaring the result, the above approximation gives $e^{0.2}$ correct to 7 SF. Similarly, consider $((e^{0.5})^2)^2$.

5 Verify that substituting $x = 1$ in approximation (1) gives e correct to only 2 SF, whilst substituting $x = 2^{-6}$ in (1) and squaring the result six times gives e correct to 9 SF.

6 Try the following recipe on your calculator or computer: 'Divide x by 2 until the result is less than 0.025 (call the number of divisions n). Substitute the result in approximation (1). Square the result n times.'

7 Show that
$$\frac{(x+3)^2 + 3}{(x-3)^2 + 3} = 1 + x(1 - \tfrac{1}{2}x + \tfrac{1}{12}x^2)^{-1}.$$

Hence show that the expansion in ascending powers of x is identical to that of e^x as far as the terms in x^4. Show that the terms in x^5 differ by $\tfrac{1}{720}x^5$.

8 (a) If $\tan\theta = \tfrac{1}{5}$, use the double angle formula to find $\tan 2\theta$ and $\tan 4\theta$ as fractions, and hence show that $\tan(4\theta - \tfrac{1}{4}\pi) = \tfrac{1}{239}$.
(b) If $\tan\alpha = \tfrac{1}{4}$ and $\tan\beta = \tfrac{1}{20}$, find $\tan(3\alpha + \beta - \tfrac{1}{4}\pi)$ as a fraction.
(c) Deduce from (a) and (b) that

$$\tfrac{1}{4}\pi = 4\tan^{-1}\tfrac{1}{5} - \tan^{-1}\tfrac{1}{239} \qquad \text{(Machin)},$$
and
$$\tfrac{1}{4}\pi = 3\tan^{-1}\tfrac{1}{4} + \tan^{-1}\tfrac{1}{20} + \tan^{-1}\tfrac{1}{1985}. \quad \text{(Ferguson)}.$$

(d) Use Gregory's series with one of the relations in (c) to calculate π to 8 DP.

9 ln 3 cannot be calculated directly from the series for $\ln(1 + x)$. Compare the following three methods:
(a) Replace x by $-\tfrac{2}{3}$ in the series for $\ln(1 + x)$.
(b) Prove that $\ln\left(\dfrac{1+x}{1-x}\right) = 2(x + \tfrac{1}{3}x^3 + \tfrac{1}{5}x^5 + \ldots)$, and substitute $\tfrac{1}{2}$ for x.
(c) Take square roots repeatedly until the result is less than 1.001 (call the number of square roots n); subtract 1 from the result (call the answer t); calculate $t - \tfrac{1}{2}t^2$; double the result n times.

Miscellaneous exercise 4

1 Players A and B take turns in a game in which their respective probabilities of winning a turn are a and b. Find a relation between a and b which ensures that A and B have equal chances in the game. (A goes first.)

2 Prove that if $a + b = 1$, in question 1, then $a : b = 1 : \phi$ where ϕ is the 'golden ratio', $\frac{1}{2}(1 + \sqrt{5})$. Can such a game be realised in practice?

3 Find an expression for S_n, the sum to n terms of the series

$$\frac{x}{1 - x^2} + \frac{x^2}{1 - x^4} + \frac{x^4}{1 - x^8} + \ldots + \frac{x^{2^{r-1}}}{1 - x^{2^r}} + \ldots, \quad \text{where } |x| \neq 1.$$

Deduce that:

    (a) $S_n \to \dfrac{x}{1 - x}$ if $|x| < 1$ (b) $S_n \to \dfrac{x}{1 - x}$ if $|x| > 1$

4 Prove that $(r - \frac{1}{2})(r + \frac{1}{2}) < r^2 < (r - \frac{39}{80})(r + \frac{41}{80})$ for $r \geq 10$.

By inverting the inequalities and using partial fractions, prove that

$$\frac{80}{761} < \sum_{10}^{\infty} \frac{1}{r^2} < \frac{2}{19}.$$

Deduce that $\displaystyle\sum_{1}^{\infty} \frac{1}{r^2} = 1.645$ to 4 SF.

5 Prove that

$$2(\sqrt{(n + 1)} - \sqrt{n}) < \frac{1}{\sqrt{n}} < 2(\sqrt{n} - \sqrt{(n - 1)}) \quad \text{for } n \geq 1.$$

(You may find Figure 4 helpful.)

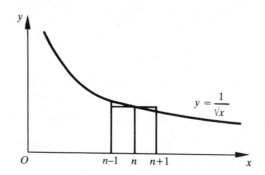

Figure 4

Deduce that $18 < \displaystyle\sum_{1}^{100} \frac{1}{\sqrt{r}} < 19.$

6 Interpret

$$\frac{1}{n}\left(\frac{1}{1 + 1/n} + \frac{1}{1 + 2/n} + \ldots + \frac{1}{2}\right)$$

as the sum of the areas of n rectangles under the graph of $y = 1/x$. Hence explain why

$$\lim_{n \to \infty}\left(\frac{1}{n + 1} + \frac{1}{n + 2} + \ldots + \frac{1}{2n}\right) = \int_{1}^{2} \frac{1}{x}\, dx = \ln 2.$$

7 The sum to n terms of the series $1 - \frac{1}{2} + \frac{1}{3} - \frac{1}{4} + \ldots$ is S_n. Prove that

$$S_{2n} = \frac{1}{n + 1} + \frac{1}{n + 2} + \ldots + \frac{1}{2n},$$

and deduce (using the result of question 6) that the sum to infinity of the series is $\ln 2$.

8 (a) Show that $\dfrac{d}{dx}(x \ln x - x) = \ln x$.

   (b) Use rectangle sums to show that

$$\int_1^n \ln x \, dx < \sum_2^n \ln r < \int_2^{n+1} \ln x \, dx.$$

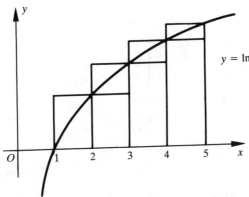

Figure 5

   (c) Use (b) to find limits between which $\ln 100!$ must lie.

   (d) Obtain closer limits by treating $\ln 100!$ as $\ln 10! + \sum_{11}^{100} \ln r$.

9 (a) Write down the first four terms of the series for $(1 - h)^{-1/2}$ and hence for $(1 - x^2)^{-1/2}$.

   (b) Integrate term by term to give the leading terms of the series for $\sin^{-1} x$.

   (c) Use a similar method to obtain the four leading terms of the series for $\sinh^{-1} x$.

   (d) Check (c) by taking $x = 0.4$.

10 Obtain the first three terms of a polynomial approximation to $\sqrt{\left(\dfrac{1 + 2x}{1 - 3x}\right)}$ for small x.

11 A telephone cable has a span of 40 metres and a sag of 1 metre (see Figure 6). Its equation can be written as $y = c \cosh(x/c)$.

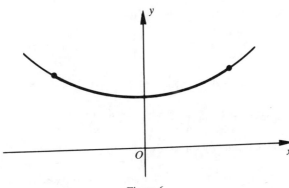

Figure 6

Show that c is a root of the equation $c + 1 = c \cosh(20/c)$, and use a quadratic approximation for $\cosh(20/c)$ to find an approximate value for c.

12 (a) Show that the total shaded area in Figure 7 is

$$(1 + \tfrac{1}{2} + \tfrac{1}{3} + \tfrac{1}{4} + \tfrac{1}{5}) - \ln 6.$$

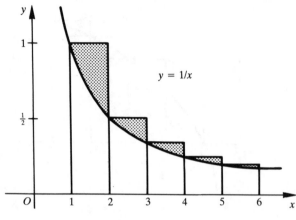

Figure 7

(b) Let $u_n = (1 + \tfrac{1}{2} + \ldots + 1/n) - \ln(n + 1)$.

Show that this gives an increasing sequence and $u_n < 1$ for all n, and hence that u_n tends to a limit γ as $n \to \infty$.

$\gamma = 0.577\,215\,6649$ to 10 DP; it is called Euler's constant after Leonhard Euler (1707–1783) who, with Maclaurin, investigated the properties of the harmonic series.

(c) If $v_n = (1 + \tfrac{1}{2} + \ldots + 1/n) - \ln n$, show that $v_n \to \gamma$ as $n \to \infty$.

(d) Show that $n > 25\,000 \Rightarrow 1 + \tfrac{1}{2} + \ldots + 1/n > 10$. (Compare §3.2.)

13 Evaluate u_n and v_n (from question 12) when $n = 2, 10, 100, 10\,000$.

14 (a) Prove by de Moivre's theorem that

$$\sin(2m + 1)\theta = \sin^{2m+1}\theta \left[\binom{2m+1}{1} \cot^{2m}\theta - \binom{2m+1}{3} \cot^{2m-2}\theta + \ldots \right].$$

(b) Prove that the roots of the equation

$$\binom{2m+1}{1}x^m - \binom{2m+1}{3}x^{m-1} + \ldots + (-1)^m = 0$$

are
$$\cot^2\left(\frac{k\pi}{2m+1}\right), \quad \text{where } k = 1, 2, 3, \ldots, m.$$

(c) Deduce that $\displaystyle\sum_1^m \cot^2\left(\frac{k\pi}{2m+1}\right) = \frac{m(2m-1)}{3}.$

(d) Use the inequality $\sin x < x < \tan x$ to prove that

$$\cot^2 x < \frac{1}{x^2} < 1 + \cot^2 x \quad \text{for } 0 < x < \tfrac{1}{2}\pi.$$

(e) Deduce that $\dfrac{m(2m-1)}{3} < \left(\dfrac{2m+1}{\pi}\right)^2 \sum\limits_1^m \dfrac{1}{k^2} < \dfrac{2m(m+1)}{3}$.

(f) Prove that $\sum\limits_1^\infty \dfrac{1}{r^2} = \tfrac{1}{6}\pi^2$.

15 What does the following algorithm calculate? Divide the modulus by 2 until the result is less than 0.005 (call the number of divisions n); call the result t; calculate $((t^2 - 6)^2 - 12)/24$; then perform the operation 'square, multiply by 2 and subtract 1' n times.

16 Given that n is a fixed positive integer, explain why $e^x > x^{n+1}/(n+1)!$ for all positive values of x. Deduce that $x^n/e^x \to 0$ as $x \to \infty$.

17 Let $\qquad\qquad S_n = x - \dfrac{x^3}{3!} + \dfrac{x^5}{5!} - \ldots$ to n terms.

If $x > 0$, show by repeated integration of the inequality $0 < t - \sin t$, where $0 < t > x$, that

$$S_{2m} < \sin x < S_{2m+1} \quad \text{for } m \geq 1.$$

Prove that as $m \to \infty$, S_{2m} and S_{2m+1} both tend to $\sin x$. Carry out a similar proof for negative values of x.

SUMMARY

An infinite series may converge, diverge, oscillate finitely or oscillate infinitely. When the sum of the first n terms, S_n, tends to a limit l as n tends to infinity, l is called the 'sum to infinity'.

Series may be proved to be convergent or divergent (i) by finding an explicit formula for S_n and examining its behaviour as n tends to infinity, or (ii) by comparison with a series whose convergence/divergence is known.

For a series of positive terms, if (for fixed k, m) $u_{n+1}/u_n < k < 1$ for all $n \geq m$, then $\sum\limits_1^\infty u_r$ is convergent (Exercise 4B, question 5).

An alternating series is convergent if (i) $u_n \to 0$ as $n \to \infty$, (ii) $0 < |u_{n+1}| < |u_n|$ for all $n \geq m$ (Exercise 4B, question 10).

Important series
(1) The geometric series:

$$\dfrac{a}{1-x} = a + ax + ax^2 + \ldots \quad \text{for } |x| < 1$$

(2) The harmonic series, $1 + \tfrac{1}{2} + \tfrac{1}{3} + \tfrac{1}{4} + \ldots$, diverges.

(3) The series $1 + \dfrac{1}{2^s} + \dfrac{1}{3^s} + \ldots$ converges if $s > 1$ and diverges if $0 < s \leq 1$.

(4) Taylor series:

$$e^x = 1 + x + \dfrac{x^2}{2!} + \dfrac{x^3}{3!} + \ldots \qquad \text{for all } x$$

$$\sin x = x - \frac{x^3}{3!} + \frac{x^5}{5!} - \ldots \qquad \text{for all } x$$

$$\cos x = 1 - \frac{x^2}{2!} + \frac{x^4}{4!} - \ldots \qquad \text{for all } x$$

$$\ln(1 + x) = x - \frac{x^2}{2!} + \frac{x^3}{3!} - \ldots \qquad \text{if } -1 < x \leqslant 1$$

$$(1 + x)^m = 1 + mx + \frac{m(m-1)}{2!} x^2 + \ldots \quad \text{if } -1 < x < 1, \text{ for any } m$$

$$\tan^{-1} x = x - \frac{x^3}{3} + \frac{x^5}{5} - \ldots \qquad \text{if } -1 \leqslant x \leqslant 1$$

Taylor's theorem

$$f(a + h) = f(a) + h f'(a) + \frac{h^2}{2} f''(a) + \ldots + \frac{h^{n+1}}{(n-1)!} f^{(n-1)}(a) + R_n,$$

where $R_n = \dfrac{h^n}{n!} f^{(n)}(a + \theta h)$ for some θ in the interval $0 < \theta < 1$.

5

Euler's relation

1. LIMITS OF COMPLEX SEQUENCES

The notions of limits of sequences and convergence of series are relevant to the world of complex numbers and we need to make only minor changes to the definitions of earlier chapters.

We must bear in mind that the complex field is not ordered: the relations $<$ and $>$ cannot be used between pairs of complex numbers. But the idea of modulus transfers easily from the real field to the complex field, and we can say that a sequence $z_1, z_2, z_3, \ldots$ tends to a limit l if for any chosen $k > 0$, there exists n_0 such that $|z_n - l| < k$ for all $n > n_0$. This requires z_n to lie within a circle of centre l and radius k for all $n > n_0$ (see Figure 1).

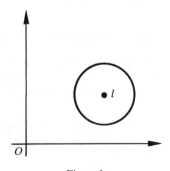

Figure 1

Figure 2 shows the first six terms of the sequence defined inductively by

$$z_1 = 1, \qquad z_{n+1} = \tfrac{1}{2}(1 + j)z_n + 1.$$

The points appear to be spiralling inwards and getting closer together.

If a limit exists, it is given by

$$l = \tfrac{1}{2}(1 + j)l + 1$$
$$\Rightarrow \quad l = \frac{2}{1 - j} = 1 + j.$$

We can then show that $\quad z_{n+1} - l = \tfrac{1}{2}(1 + j)(z_n - l)$

and hence that $\quad z_{n+1} - l = [\tfrac{1}{2}(1 + j)]^n (z_1 - l)$

and $\qquad |z_{n+1} - l| = \left(\dfrac{1}{\sqrt{2}}\right)^n |z_1 - l|,$

since
$$\left| \tfrac{1}{2}(1 + j) \right| = \frac{1}{\sqrt{2}}.$$

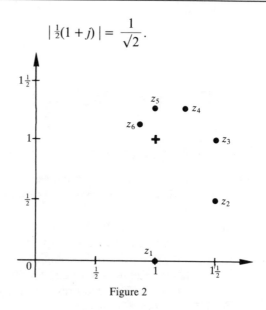

Figure 2

The convergence of the series is duly established.

1.1 The behaviour of z^n for $n = 1, 2, 3, \ldots$

Since $z = [r, \theta] \Rightarrow z^n = [r^n, n\theta]$, it is easy to see that the sequence $\{z^n\}$ diverges if $r = |z| > 1$ and converges if $|z| < 1$. If $|z| = 1$, the sequence converges only in the special case where $z = 1$; then $z^n = 1$ for all n, of course.

2. SERIES OF COMPLEX TERMS

It will not surprise you that the partial sums of the infinite geometric series

$$1 + z + z^2 + z^3 + \ldots$$

produce a diagram like Figure 2, spiralling inwards, if $|z| < 1$, and a diagram spiralling outwards if $|z| > 1$. Exercise 5A includes some examples of this kind. For more complicated series, convergence is less obvious.

Exercise 5A

1 Draw diagrams showing the first five terms of the sequences defined by:
   (a) $z_n = (1 + j)^n$ (b) $z_n = (\cos 1 + j \sin 1)^n$
   (c) $z_n = (0.8 - 0.5j)^n$ (d) $z_1 = 1, \quad z_{n+1} = 1 - \tfrac{1}{2}jz_n$
   (e) $z_1 = 1, \quad z_{n+1} = j/z_n + 1$

2 Which of the sequences in question 1 appear to converge? Suggest limits for the convergent sequences.

3 Prove that the points representing the terms of the sequence $z, z^2, z^3, \ldots$, where $|z| \neq 1$, lie on an equiangular spiral, and find its polar equation. (Take $z = [r, \theta]$ and use polar coordinates $[R, \phi]$.)

4 Prove that $z^n/n! \to 0$ for all z as $n \to \infty$.

5   Let $z_n = x_n + jy_n$, where x_n and y_n are real. Prove that

$$z_n \to a + jb \quad \Rightarrow \quad x_n \to a \text{ and } y_n \to b, \quad \text{where } a \text{ and } b \text{ are real.}$$

6   On Argand diagrams, plot points representing $S_1, S_2, \ldots, S_5$ for the geometric series $S_n = 1 + z + z^2 + \ldots + z^{n-1}$ when:

(a) $z = \tfrac{1}{2} + \tfrac{1}{2}j$ (b) $z = \tfrac{1}{2} - j$ (c) $z = j$ (d) $z = 0.6 + 0.8j$

Which of these series will converge as $n \to \infty$?

7   Show that the geometric series in question 6 converge if $|z| < 1$, and state the sum to infinity. Show that the sum to infinity in (a) is $(1 + j)$, and mark it on your diagram.

8   By substituting $z = \cos \theta + j \sin \theta$ in the geometric series, prove that

$$1 + \cos \theta + \cos 2\theta + \ldots + \cos(n-1)\theta = \tfrac{1}{2} \operatorname{cosec} \tfrac{1}{2}\theta [\sin \tfrac{1}{2}\theta + \sin(n - \tfrac{1}{2})\theta]$$

and find the sum of

$$\sin \theta + \sin 2\theta + \ldots + \sin(n-1)\theta.$$

9   Write down the sum of the infinite geometric series

$$1 + \frac{z}{2} + \frac{z^2}{4} + \frac{z^3}{8} + \ldots \quad \text{for } |z| < 2.$$

By putting $z = \cos \theta + j \sin \theta$ and taking the real part, show that the series

$$1 + \tfrac{1}{2} \cos \theta + \tfrac{1}{4} \cos 2\theta + \tfrac{1}{8} \cos 3\theta + \ldots$$

converges, with sum $(4 - 2 \cos \theta)/(5 - 4 \cos \theta)$.   [SMP]

10   If x is real and $|x| < 1$, $1 + 2x + 3x^2 + \ldots$ has sum to infinity $(1 - x)^{-2}$ (see Exercise 4A, question 11). For the complex series $1 + 2z + 3z^2 + \ldots$, simplify $(1 - z)^2 S_n$ and hence show that the series converges if $|z| < 1$.

11   If

$$S_n = 1 + z + \frac{z^2}{2!} + \ldots + \frac{z^{n-1}}{(n-1)!},$$

plot points representing $S_1, S_2, \ldots, S_5$ when (a) $z = \tfrac{1}{2}j$, and (b) $z = 1 + \tfrac{1}{2}j$.

3. THE EXPONENTIAL FUNCTION

So far, over the complex field we have met simple polynomials and rational functions such as $1 + z$ and $z^2/(1 + z)$, and we can deal with rational powers of z. We have not yet considered some of the other functions which have already been defined over the real field, such as $\ln x$, e^x, $\sin x$ and $\cosh x$.

We have defined $x \mapsto e^x$ as the inverse of $x \mapsto \ln x$, where

$$\ln x = \int_1^x \frac{1}{t} \, dt \quad (x > 0).$$

It is possible to extend this definition to the complex field, but since this involves an integral with complex limits and an integrand whose values are complex we shall not adopt this approach here. Instead we shall start with the fact that e^x has a Taylor series

$$1 + x + \frac{x^2}{2!} + \frac{x^3}{3!} + \ldots$$

which is valid for all real x.

To investigate what happens if we let x take complex values, define

$$S_n = 1 + z + \frac{z^2}{2!} + \frac{z^3}{3!} + \ldots + \frac{z^{n-1}}{(n-1)!}.$$

S_n is thus the sum of the first n terms of the exponential series.

First let $z = j$ and $n = 1, 2, 3, 4, 5, \ldots$. We find the following:

n	S_n
1	1
2	$1 + j$
3	$\frac{1}{2} + j$
4	$\frac{1}{2} + \frac{5}{6}j$
5	$\frac{13}{24} + \frac{5}{6}j$
⋮	⋮

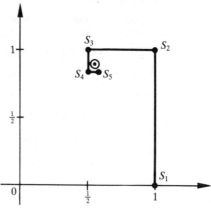

Figure 3

Next let $z = 1 + j$ and $n = 0, 1, 2, 3, 4, \ldots$. We obtain:

n	S_n
1	1
2	$2 + j$
3	$2 + 2j$
4	$1\frac{2}{3} + 2\frac{1}{3}j$
5	$1\frac{1}{2} + 2\frac{1}{3}j$
⋮	⋮

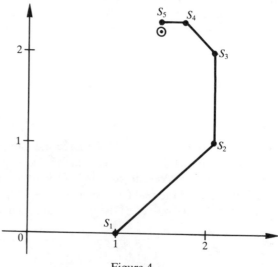

Figure 4

We can prove that as $n \to \infty$, S_n always tends to a finite complex value, whatever the value of z, so we can define the exponential function of z by the infinite series

$$e^z = 1 + z + \frac{z^2}{2!} + \frac{z^3}{3!} + \ldots . \qquad (1)$$

With this definition, the points representing S_n in Figure 3 home in on the point representing e^j. This is the limit of

$$1 + z + \frac{z^2}{2!} + \frac{z^3}{3!} + \ldots \quad \text{when } z = j,$$

i.e. the limit of

$$1 + j - \frac{1}{2!} + \frac{j}{3!} + \ldots$$

or

$$\left(1 - \frac{1}{2!} + \frac{1}{4!} - \ldots\right) + j\left(1 - \frac{1}{3!} + \frac{1}{5!} + \ldots\right).$$

We recognise these brackets as the familiar Taylor series for cos x and sin x, with x replaced by 1. Thus the limit is cos $1 + j$ sin 1, or $0.54 + 0.84j$. This is circled in Figure 3.

3.1 The exponential properties

Before proceeding any further, we must be sure that e^z does have exponential properties, that is to say (i) $e^0 = 1$, and (ii) $e^z e^w = e^{z+w}$.
  Now, from our definition,

$$e^0 = 1 + 0 + 0^2 + \ldots,$$

so we do have property (i). To investigate property (ii), we have to examine the product

$$\left(1 + z + \frac{z^2}{2!} + \frac{z^3}{3!} + \ldots\right)\left(1 + w + \frac{w^2}{2!} + \frac{w^3}{3!} + \ldots\right).$$

A full discussion of this is beyond the scope of this book. For the moment, we can get some idea by working with approximations to the third degree:

$$e^z e^w \approx \left(1 + z + \frac{z^2}{2!} + \frac{z^3}{3!}\right)\left(1 + w + \frac{w^2}{2!} + \frac{w^3}{3!}\right)$$

$$\approx 1 + z + w + \frac{z^2}{2!} + zw + \frac{w^2}{2!} + \frac{z^3}{3!} + \frac{z^2 w}{2!} + \frac{zw^2}{2!} + \frac{w^3}{3!}$$

$$= 1 + (z + w) + \frac{(z+w)^2}{2!} + \frac{(z+w)^3}{3!}$$

$$\approx e^{z+w}.$$

Thus property (ii) holds when dealing with approximations to the third degree. It works similarly with approximations of any higher degree.

4. EULER'S RELATION

Writing $z = x + yj$, we see that $e^z = e^x \times e^{yj}$. Now x is real, so we already know about the factor e^x. The factor e^{yj} can be interpreted by identifying yj with z in the defining series (1):

$$e^{yj} = 1 + yj + \frac{y^2 j^2}{2!} + \frac{y^3 j^3}{3!} + \ldots$$

$$= \left(1 - \frac{y^2}{2!} + \frac{y^4}{4!} - \ldots\right) + j\left(y - \frac{y^3}{3!} + \frac{y^5}{5!} - \ldots\right)$$

$$= \cos y + j \sin y.$$

It follows that $\qquad e^z = e^x(\cos y + j \sin y),$

that is, the complex number e^z has modulus e^x (which is positive for all real x) and argument y (within a multiple of 2π).

We are familiar with the relation

$$(\cos \theta + j \sin \theta)(\cos \phi + j \sin \phi) = \cos(\theta + \phi) + j \sin(\theta + \phi).$$

This is $\qquad f(\theta) \times f(\phi) = f(\theta + \phi), \quad$ where $f(\theta) = \cos \theta + j \sin \theta,$

which we may have recognised earlier as the essential property of an exponential function. Now we see indeed that

$$\cos \theta + j \sin \theta = e^{j\theta}.$$

This remarkable result is known as Euler's relation. Letting θ take certain values leads to some surprising results:

(i) $\theta = \pi$: $e^{j\pi} = -1$
(ii) $\theta = \pi/2$: $e^{j\pi/2} = j$
(iii) $\theta = 2\pi$: $e^{2j\pi} = 1$

Returning to Figure 4, since $S_n \to e^{1+j}$ and $e^j = \cos 1 + j \sin 1$, we see that the points $S_1,\ S_2,\ S_3,\ \ldots$ are converging on the point representing $e^1(\cos 1 + j \sin 1) \approx 1.47 + 2.29j$. This is circled in the diagram.

Example 1
Express e^{2+3j} in the form $a + bj$ to 3 SF.

Solution $\quad e^{2+3j} = e^2(\cos 3 + j \sin 3)$
$$\approx -7.32 + 1.04j. \qquad \square$$

Using Euler's relation, it is easy to prove de Moivre's theorem:

$$(\cos \theta + j \sin \theta)^n = (e^{j\theta})^n$$
$$= e^{jn\theta}$$
$$= \cos n\theta + j \sin n\theta.$$

Exercise 5B

1   Write the following in the form $a + bj$:
   (a) e^{2j} (b) $e^{3\pi j/4}$ (c) e^{3-j} (d) $e^{-j\theta}$
2   Express the following in the form $r\,e^{j\theta}$:
   (a) $4j$ (b) -7 (c) $1 + j\sqrt{3}$ (d) $-1 - j\sqrt{3}$

3   Find the modulus and argument of:
    (a) $7 e^{3\pi j/2}$ (b) e^j (c) e^{2+j} (d) $e^{2j\theta} + e^{2j\phi}$

4   Find the modulus and argument of:
    (a) $1 + e^{\theta j}$ (b) $1/(\sin \theta + j \cos \theta)$ (c) $(1 - e^{\theta j})/(1 + e^{\theta j})$

5   Show that e^z is a periodic function with period $2\pi j$.

6   On Argand diagrams, plot points representing the partial sums S_1, S_2, S_3, S_4, S_5 of
    the exponential series when:
    (a) $z = 2 - j$ (b) $z = 2j$ (c) $z = -1 + 2j$
    In each case, indicate also the point representing e^z.

7   (a) Explain why $|z_1 + z_2| \leqslant |z_1| + |z_2|$.
    (b) Write

$$1 + z + \frac{z^2}{2!} + \frac{z^3}{3!} + \ldots = 1 + z + \frac{z^2}{2!}\left(1 + \frac{z}{3} + \frac{z^2}{3 \times 4} + \ldots\right)$$

    and show that

$$\left| 1 + \frac{z}{3} + \frac{z^2}{3 \times 4} \cdots \right| \leqslant 1 + \frac{|z|}{3} + \frac{|z|^2}{3^2} \cdots$$

$$= \left(1 - \frac{|z|}{3}\right)^{-1} \qquad \text{if } |z| < 3.$$

    (c) Writing the exponential series as

$$1 + z + \frac{z^2}{2!} + \ldots + \frac{z^{n-1}}{(n-1)!} + R_n(z),$$

    use the method of (b) to find an upper bound for $|R_n(z)|$.
    (d) Show that the exponential series converges.

8   Use question 7(c) to show that the point corresponding to S_8 in question 6(c)
    will be within a distance 0.021 of the limit point.

9   Investigate the convergence of the series $z + \frac{1}{2}z^2 + \frac{1}{3}z^3 + \ldots$ for:
    (a) $z = \frac{1}{2} + \frac{1}{2}j$ (b) $z = \frac{1}{2} - j$ (c) $z = j$
    Show that the sum to infinity in (c) is equivalent to $-\ln(1 - z)$ if we assume that
    $\ln(r e^{j\theta}) = \ln r + j\theta$.
    Write the sum to infinity in (a) in the form $p + qj$.

10 Express in the form $p + qj$:
    (a) $\ln(2 e^{3j})$ (b) $\ln(3 + 4j)$ (c) $\ln(\cos \theta + j \sin \theta)$

11 Defining $\cosh z$ as $\frac{1}{2}(e^z + e^{-z})$, express in the form $p + qj$:
    (a) $\cosh(5j)$ (b) $\cosh(2 + 5j)$ (c) $\cosh(2\pi j)$

5. THE LINK BETWEEN THE CIRCULAR AND HYPERBOLIC FUNCTIONS

From $\cos \theta + j \sin \theta = e^{j\theta}$ and $\cos \theta - j \sin \theta = e^{-j\theta}$,

it follows that

$$\cos \theta = \tfrac{1}{2}(e^{j\theta} + e^{-j\theta}) \quad \text{and} \quad \sin \theta = \frac{1}{2j}(e^{j\theta} - e^{-j\theta}).$$

These exponential forms remind us of

$$\cosh u = \tfrac{1}{2}(e^u + e^{-u}) \quad \text{and} \quad \sinh u = \tfrac{1}{2}(e^u - e^{-u}).$$

We showed in Chapter 1 that

$$\cosh u \cosh v + \sinh u \sinh v = \tfrac{1}{4}(e^u + e^{-u})(e^v + e^{-v}) + \tfrac{1}{4}(e^u - e^{-u})(e^v - e^{-v})$$
$$= \tfrac{1}{2}(e^{u+v} + e^{-u-v})$$
$$= \cosh(u + v).$$

Writing in exponential form the corresponding expressions involving the circular functions,

$$\cos \theta \cos \phi + \sin \theta \sin \phi = \tfrac{1}{4}(e^{j\theta} + e^{-j\theta})(e^{j\phi} + e^{-j\phi}) + \frac{1}{4j^2}(e^{j\theta} - e^{-j\theta})(e^{j\phi} - e^{-j\phi})$$
$$= \tfrac{1}{2}(e^{j\theta - j\phi} + e^{-j\theta + j\phi})$$
$$= \cos(\theta - \phi).$$

This is in no sense a *proof*, since deriving the main ingredients of the working has depended heavily on the use of the addition formulae. But it does indicate why all the identities connecting the circular functions have counterparts in the world of hyperbolic functions. There are changes of sign whenever $\sin \theta \sin \phi$ or $\sin^2 \theta$ are involved; for then j^2 will come in, as it has done above.

A selection of the main properties are tabulated opposite.

Miscellaneous exercise 5

1 Simplify the product $(x - e^{\theta j})(x - e^{-\theta j})$.
   Write down the eight values of θ ($-\pi < \theta \leq \pi$) for which $x = e^{\theta j}$ is a solution of the equation $x^8 = 1$.
   Hence write $x^8 - 1$ as the product of two first-degree and three second-degree factors, all having real coefficients.

2 (a) Factorise $z^2 - 2z \cos \theta + 1$ into two linear factors.
   (b) Factorise $z^4 - 2z^2 \cos \theta + 1$ (i) into four linear factors, and (ii) into two quadratic factors with real coefficients.

3 Find an expression for the sum of the series

$$\sinh a + \sinh 2a + \sinh 3a + \ldots + \sinh na,$$

first in terms of exponential functions, then in a form involving only hyperbolic functions.
   Repeat this process for the series

$$\sin a + \sin 2a + \sin 3a + \ldots + \sin na.$$

Can you obtain the second result by an independent method which does not use complex numbers?

Circular functions	Hyperbolic functions
$\sin \theta = \frac{1}{2j}(e^{j\theta} - e^{-j\theta})$	$\sinh u = \frac{1}{2}(e^u - e^{-u})$
$\cos \theta = \frac{1}{2}(e^{j\theta} + e^{-j\theta})$	$\cosh u = \frac{1}{2}(e^u + e^{-u})$
$e^{j\theta} = \cos \theta + j \sin \theta$	$e^u = \cosh u + \sinh u$
$\sin(\theta + \phi) = \sin \theta \cos \phi + \cos \theta \sin \phi$	$\sinh(u + v) = \sinh u \cosh v + \cosh u \sinh v$
$\cos(\theta + \phi) = \cos \theta \cos \phi - \sin \theta \sin \phi$	$\cosh(u + v) = \cosh u \cosh v + \sinh u \sinh v$
$1 = \cos^2 \theta + \sin^2 \theta$	$1 = \cosh^2 u - \sinh^2 u$
$\sin 2\theta = 2 \sin \theta \cos \theta$	$\sinh 2u = 2 \sinh u \cosh u$
$\cos 2\theta = \cos^2 \theta - \sin^2 \theta$	$\cosh 2u = \cosh^2 u + \sinh^2 u$
$\quad = 2 \cos^2 \theta - 1$	$\quad = 2 \cosh^2 u - 1$
$\quad = 1 - 2 \sin^2 \theta$	$\quad = 1 + 2 \sinh^2 u$
$\dfrac{d}{dx}(\sin x) = \cos x$	$\dfrac{d}{dx}(\sinh x) = \cosh x$
$\dfrac{d}{dx}(\cos x) = -\sin x$	$\dfrac{d}{dx}(\cosh x) = \sinh x$
$\displaystyle\int \frac{1}{\sqrt{(1 - x^2)}} dx = \sin^{-1} x + k$	$\displaystyle\int \frac{1}{\sqrt{(1 + x^2)}} dx = \sinh^{-1} x + k$
$\qquad\qquad = -\cos^{-1} x + k'$	$\displaystyle\int \frac{1}{\sqrt{(x^2 - 1)}} dx = \cosh^{-1} x + k$
$(a \cos t, a \sin t)$ is a point on the circle $x^2 + y^2 = a^2$ for all t.	$(a \cosh t, a \sinh t)$ is a point on the rectangular hyperbola $x^2 - y^2 = a^2$ for all t.
$(a \cos t, b \sin t)$ is a point on the ellipse $\dfrac{x^2}{a^2} + \dfrac{y^2}{b^2} = 1$ for all t.	$(a \cosh t, b \sinh t)$ is a point on the hyperbola $\dfrac{x^2}{a^2} - \dfrac{y^2}{b^2} = 1$ for all t.

4 Criticise the following argument:

$$y = \cos\theta + j\sin\theta$$

$$\Rightarrow \quad \frac{dy}{d\theta} = -\sin\theta + j\cos\theta$$

$$= j(\cos\theta + j\sin\theta)$$

$$= jy.$$

Hence

$$\frac{1}{y}\frac{dy}{d\theta} = j,$$

giving on integration

$$\ln y = j\theta + k.$$

But $y = 1$ when $\theta = 0$, so $k = 0$ and $y = e^{j\theta}$.
This proves that $e^{j\theta} = \cos\theta + j\sin\theta$.

5 Since e^z has now been defined for complex z, there is no difficulty in extending the circular and hyperbolic functions over the domain of the complex number by defining:

$$\sin z = \frac{1}{2j}(e^{jz} - e^{-jz}) \qquad \cos z = \tfrac{1}{2}(e^{jz} + e^{-jz})$$

$$\sinh z = \tfrac{1}{2}(e^z - e^{-z}) \qquad \cosh z = \tfrac{1}{2}(e^z + e^{-z})$$

Using these definitions, show that:
  (a) $\cosh(z_1 + z_2) = \cosh z_1 \cosh z_2 + \sinh z_1 \sinh z_2$
  (b) $\cos z = \cosh(jz)$ and $\sin z = -j\sinh(jz)$
  (c) $\cos(z_1 + z_2) = \cos z_1 \cos z_2 - \sin z_1 \sin z_2$
  (d) $\cos z$ is a periodic function with period 2π, and $\cosh z$ is a periodic function with period $2\pi j$.
  (e) Show that if $z = a + bj$, where a and b are real, then

$$\cos z = \cos a \cosh b - j\sin a \sinh b.$$

  (f) Solve the equation $\cos z = 2$.

SUMMARY

The geometric series $1 + z + z^2 + z^3 + \ldots$ converges, with sum to infinity $(1 - z)^{-1}$, if the complex number z satisfies $|z| < 1$.

The series $1 + z + \dfrac{z^2}{2!} + \dfrac{z^3}{3!} + \ldots$ converges for all z, and its sum to infinity

defines e^z.

It follows that
and

$$e^z \times e^w = e^{z+w}$$
$$e^{j\theta} = \cos\theta + j\sin\theta.$$

6

Reduction formulae

1. THE BASIC IDEA

Some sequences of integrals can be evaluated by finding a difference equation (recurrence relation) connecting them. We illustrate this idea with an example.

Let $\qquad u_n = \int \tan^n x \, dx$ where n is a positive integer and $n \geq 2$.

Then $\qquad u_n = \int \tan^{n-2} x \tan^2 x \, dx$

$$= \int \tan^{n-2} x \, (\sec^2 x - 1) \, dx$$

$$= \int \tan^{n-2} x \sec^2 x \, dx - \int \tan^{n-2} x \, dx.$$

So $\qquad u_n = \dfrac{\tan^{n-1} x}{n-1} - u_{n-2} .$ $\qquad\qquad$ (1)

A relation like (1) above is called a *reduction formula*.

Example 1

Find $u_6 = \displaystyle\int_0^{\pi/4} \tan^6 x \, dx$.

Solution

$$u_6 = \left[\tfrac{1}{5} \tan^5 x \right]_0^{\pi/4} - u_4$$

$$= \tfrac{1}{5} - u_4$$

$$= \tfrac{1}{5} - (\tfrac{1}{3} - u_2)$$

$$= \tfrac{1}{5} - \tfrac{1}{3} + (1 - u_0).$$

But $\qquad u_0 = \displaystyle\int_0^{\pi/4} 1 \, dx = \tfrac{1}{4}\pi,$

so $\qquad u_6 = \tfrac{1}{5} - \tfrac{1}{3} + 1 - \tfrac{1}{4}\pi$

$\qquad\qquad = 0.0813 \quad$ to 3 SF. $\qquad\qquad$ $\square$

Example 2

Find a reduction formula for $u_n = \displaystyle\int \sin^n x \, dx$.

65

Solution

We write u_n as a product and use integration by parts:

$$u_n = \int \sin^{n-1} x \sin x \, dx$$

$$= \sin^{n-1} x \, (-\cos x) - \int (-\cos x) \times (n-1) \sin^{n-2} x \cos x \, dx$$

$$= \sin^{n-1} x \cos x + (n-1) \int \sin^{n-2} x \cos^2 x \, dx$$

$$= \sin^{n-1} x \cos x + (n-1) \int \sin^{n-2} x \, (1 - \sin^2 x) \, dx$$

$$= \sin^{n-1} x \cos x + (n-1)(u_{n-2} - u_n).$$

Solving this equation for u_n, we obtain

$$u_n = -\frac{1}{n} \sin^{n-1} x \cos x + \frac{n-1}{n} u_{n-2}.$$

By repeated use of this formula we can express u_n in terms of either u_1 or u_0.

The formula is especially useful for the definite integral $u_n = \int_0^{\pi/2} \sin^n x \, dx$,

since $\left[-\frac{1}{n} \sin^{n-1} x \cos x \right]_0^{\pi/2} = 0$, and so in this case $u_n = \frac{n-1}{n} u_{n-2}.$

(In fact, this applies if the limits of integration are any pair of multiples of $\frac{1}{2}\pi$.)

Thus, to evaluate $\int_0^{\pi/2} \sin^7 x \, dx$, we see that

$$u_7 = \tfrac{6}{7} u_5 = \tfrac{6}{7} \times \tfrac{4}{5} u_3 = \tfrac{6}{7} \times \tfrac{4}{5} \times \tfrac{2}{3} u_1 \quad \text{and} \quad u_1 = \int_0^{\pi/2} \sin x \, dx = 1,$$

so $\quad u_7 = \tfrac{16}{35}.$ $\qquad\qquad$ □

Exercise 6A

1 Use the reduction formulae in §1 to find:

(a) $\displaystyle\int \tan^4 x \, dx$ $\quad$ (b) $\displaystyle\int_0^{\pi/4} \tan^5 x \, dx$ $\quad$ (c) $\displaystyle\int_0^{\pi/2} \sin^6 x \, dx$

(d) $\displaystyle\int_0^{\pi} \sin^{11} x \, dx$

2 Find $\displaystyle\int_0^{\pi/2} \cos^7 x \, dx$ by starting with the substitution $y = \tfrac{1}{2}\pi - x$.

3 Use integration by parts to obtain a reduction formula for $u_n = \displaystyle\int \cos^n x \, dx$. Hence find $\displaystyle\int \cos^6 x \, dx$.

4 Find $\displaystyle\int_0^{\pi/4} \sin^4 x \, dx$.

5 Use the substitution $x = a \sin u$ to re-write $\displaystyle\int_0^a (a^2 - x^2)^{3/2} \, dx$, and hence evaluate the integral.

6 Write $u_n = \int \sec^n x\,.dx$ as $\int \sec^{n-2} x \sec^2 x \, dx$, and use integration by parts to find a reduction formula for u_n. Hence find u_4 and u_5.

7 Obtain a reduction formula for $u_n = \int x^n e^x \, dx$ and hence find u_5.

8 Obtain a reduction formula for $u_n = \int_1^e (\ln x)^n \, dx$ and hence find u_4.

9 Obtain reduction formulae for $\int \cosh^n x \, dx$ and $\int \sinh^n x \, dx$.

10 Use a suitable trigonometric substitution and a reduction formula to show that

$$\int_0^a \frac{1}{(a^2 + x^2)^3} \, dx = \frac{8 + 3\pi}{32a^5}.$$

11 Obtain a reduction formula for $\int x^n \cos x \, dx$. (Use integration by parts twice.)

2. REDUCTION FORMULAE WITH TWO PARAMETERS

To find an integral like $\int_0^{\pi/2} \sin^8 x \cos^6 x \, dx$, we could aim to reduce the powers of $\sin x$ or $\cos x$, or both.

We write

$$u_{m,n} = \int_0^{\pi/2} \sin^m x \cos^n x \, dx$$

$$= \int_0^{\pi/2} (\sin^m x \cos x) \times \cos^{n-1} x \, dx$$

$$= \left[\frac{1}{m+1} \sin^{m+1} x \cos^{n-1} x \right]_0^{\pi/2}$$

$$\quad - \int_0^{\pi/2} \frac{1}{m+1} \sin^{m+1} x \, (n-1) \cos^{n-2} x \, (-\sin x) \, dx$$

$$= \quad 0 \quad + \frac{n-1}{m+1} \int_0^{\pi/2} \sin^{m+2} x \cos^{n-2} x \, dx \qquad (2)$$

$$= \frac{n-1}{m+1} u_{m+2,n-2}.$$

So the example suggested originally, which is $u_{8,6}$, can be evaluated as follows:

$$u_{8,6} = \tfrac{5}{9} u_{10,4} = \tfrac{5}{9} \times \tfrac{3}{11} \times \tfrac{1}{13} u_{14,0}$$

$$= \tfrac{5}{9} \times \tfrac{3}{11} \times \tfrac{1}{13} \times \tfrac{13}{14} \times \tfrac{11}{12} \times \tfrac{9}{10} \times \tfrac{7}{8} \times \tfrac{5}{6} \times \tfrac{3}{4} \times \tfrac{1}{2} \times \tfrac{1}{2}\pi,$$

since $u_{14,0} = \int_0^{\pi/2} \sin^{14} x \, dx$ can be worked out by the reduction formula of §1.

Alternatively, $\int_0^{\pi/2} \sin^{m+2} x \cos^{n-2} x \, dx$ can be written as

$$\int_0^{\pi/2} \sin^m x \, (1 - \cos^2 x) \cos^{n-2} x \, dx \quad \text{or} \quad u_{m,n-2} - u_{m,n}.$$

Show that expression (2) above then leads to $u_{m,n} = \dfrac{n-1}{m+n} u_{m,n-2}$.

Now
$$u_{8,6} = \tfrac{5}{14} u_{8,4} = \tfrac{5}{14} \times \tfrac{3}{12} u_{8,2} = \tfrac{5}{14} \times \tfrac{3}{12} \times \tfrac{1}{10} u_{8,0}$$
$$= \tfrac{5}{14} \times \tfrac{3}{12} \times \tfrac{1}{10} \times \tfrac{7}{8} \times \tfrac{5}{6} \times \tfrac{3}{4} \times \tfrac{1}{2} \times \tfrac{1}{2}\pi,$$

which is equivalent to the answer obtained earlier.

Exercise 6B

1 (a) Evaluate $\displaystyle\int_0^{\pi/2} \sin^6 x \cos x \, dx$.

   (b) Use the second reduction formula of §2 to find $\displaystyle\int_0^{\pi/2} \sin^6 x \cos^7 x \, dx$.

2 If $u_{m,n} = \displaystyle\int_0^{\pi} \sin^m x \cos^n x \, dx$, show that $u_{m,n} = \dfrac{m-1}{m+n} u_{m-2,n}$.

3 Use the substitution $x = a \sin \theta$ to find $\displaystyle\int_0^a (a^2 - x^2)^{5/2} \, dx$ and $\displaystyle\int_0^a x^2 (a^2 - x^2)^{5/2} \, dx$.

4 (a) If $v_{m,n} = \displaystyle\int_0^1 x^m (1-x)^n \, dx$, show that $v_{m,n} = \dfrac{n}{m+1} v_{m+1,n-1}$.

   (b) Evaluate $\displaystyle\int_0^1 x^3 (1-x)^4 \, dx$ and $\displaystyle\int_0^1 x^{1/2} (1-x)^4 \, dx$.

5 If m and n are positive integers, use the reduction formula of question 4 to show that
$$v_{m,n} = \frac{m! \, n!}{(m+n+1)!}.$$

6 Show that for the integral of question 4(a), $v_{m,n} = \dfrac{m}{n+1} v_{m-1,n+1}$.

7 Investigate the effect of applying the substitution $x = \sin^2 \theta$ to the integral of question 4(a).

8 A family of probability density functions is given by
$$\phi(x) = k \, x^m \, (a - x)^n \quad \text{for } 0 \leqslant x \leqslant a.$$

Sketch the members of the family for which:
   (a) $m = 3, n = 0$ (b) $m = 2, n = 2$ (c) $m = 1, n = 3$ (d) $m = 3, n = 2$

Explain why
$$k = \frac{(m+n+1)!}{m! \, n! \, a^{m+n+1}}$$

and show that
$$\mu = \int_0^a x \, \phi(x) \, dx = \frac{(m+1)a}{m+n+2}.$$

9 For the probability model of question 8, find an expression for the variance, $\displaystyle\int_0^a x^2 \, \phi(x) \, dx - \mu^2$.

Miscellaneous exercise 6

1 In Exercise 6A, question 4 gives $I_1 = \displaystyle\int_0^{\pi/4} \sin^4 x \, dx = (3\pi - 8)/32$, while in question 10, $I_2 = \displaystyle\int_0^{\pi/4} \cos^4 x \, dx$ is found to equal $(3\pi + 8)/32$.

Explain independently why $I_2 - I_1 = \frac{1}{2}$ and $I_2 + I_1 = \int_0^{\pi/2} \sin^4 x \, dx = 3\pi/16$.

2   Use a reduction formula for $\int_0^t x^n e^{-x} \, dx$ to show that

$$e^t \int_0^t \frac{x^n}{n!} e^{-x} \, dx = e^t - \left(1 + t + \frac{t^2}{2!} + \ldots + \frac{t^n}{n!}\right).$$

Remembering that $x^n/n! \to 0$ as $n \to \infty$ for all x, deduce that the series

$$1 + t + \frac{t^2}{2!} + \ldots + \frac{t^n}{n!} + \ldots$$

converges to e^t for all t.

3   You are given that for the standardised normal probability function

$$\phi(x) = \frac{1}{\sqrt{(2\pi)}} e^{-x^2/2}, \quad \int_{-\infty}^{\infty} \phi(x) \, dx = 1 \quad \text{and} \quad \int_{-\infty}^{\infty} x\phi(x) \, dx = 0.$$

Find a reduction formula for $u_n = \int_{-\infty}^{\infty} x^n \, \phi(x) \, dx = 1$ and hence:

(a) prove that the variance $\int_{-\infty}^{\infty} x^2 \, \phi(x) \, dx = 1$;

(b) find $\int_{-\infty}^{\infty} x^3 \, \phi(x) \, dx$;

(c) find $\int_{-\infty}^{\infty} x^4 \, \phi(x) \, dx$.

4   For a uniform solid of revolution formed by rotating a curve about the y-axis (as in Figure 1), summing up for hollow cylindrical elements gives

$$\text{volume} = \int 2\pi xy \, dx$$

and   moment of inertia about the y-axis $= \int 2\pi\rho x^3 y \, dx$

(where ρ is the density).

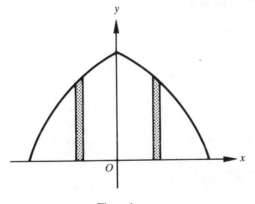

Figure 1

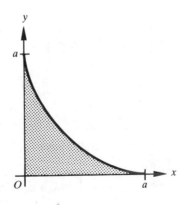

Figure 2

Work out these integrals

(a) for the hemisphere formed from

$$x = a \sin t, \quad y = a \cos t, \quad 0 \leqslant t \leqslant \tfrac{1}{2}\pi$$

(b) for the solid formed from the arc of the astroid given by

$$x = a \sin^3 t, \quad y = a \cos^3 t, \quad 0 < t < \tfrac{1}{2}\pi \quad \text{(see Figure 2)}.$$

5   The centre of mass of a lamina in the shape of Figure 2, bounded by the axes and the arc of question 4(b), has $\bar{x} = \bar{y}$ and

$$A\bar{x} = \int xy \, dx, \quad \text{where } A \text{ is the area.}$$

Find the centre of mass, and determine whether it lies within or outside the lamina.

6   For a probability model with density function $\phi(x) = k(1 - x^2)^n$, for $-1 \leqslant x \leqslant 1$;
(a) sketch graphs for $n = 1, 2, 3$;

(b) show that $\dfrac{1}{k} = 2 \times \dfrac{2}{3} \times \dfrac{4}{5} \times \ldots \times \dfrac{2n}{2n + 1}$;

(c) show that $\sigma^2 = \dfrac{1}{2n + 3}$.

(d) The model is 'standardised' by the transformation $x' = x/\sigma$, $y' = y\sigma$. Show that then

$$\frac{1}{y'} \frac{dy'}{dx'} = \frac{-2nx'}{2n + 3 - x'^2}$$

so that, for large n,

$$\frac{1}{y'} \frac{dy'}{dx'} \approx -x'.$$

(e) Show that $y = \dfrac{1}{\sqrt{(2\pi)}} e^{-x^2/2} \quad \Rightarrow \quad \dfrac{1}{y} \dfrac{dy}{dx} = -x$

and deduce that $k\sigma \approx 1/\sqrt{(2\pi)}$ for large n.
(f) Re-write the result of (e) as

$$\pi \approx (n + 1.5) \times \left[2 \times \frac{2}{3} \times \frac{4}{5} \times \ldots \times \frac{2n}{2n + 1} \right]^2$$

and test this with a computer.

SUMMARY

For $u_n = \displaystyle\int_0^{\pi/2} \sin^n x \, dx, \qquad u_n = \dfrac{n - 1}{n} u_{n-2}.$

The same reduction formula works for $\displaystyle\int_0^{\pi/2} \cos^n x \, dx.$

For $u_{m,n} = \displaystyle\int_0^{\pi/2} \sin^m x \cos^n x \, dx, \qquad u_{m,n} = \dfrac{n - 1}{m + n} u_{m,n-2} = \dfrac{m - 1}{m + n} u_{m-2,n}.$

All the formulae above apply when the limits of integration are any multiples of $\tfrac{1}{2}\pi$.

For $u_n = \displaystyle\int \tan^n x \, dx, \quad u_n = \dfrac{\tan^{n-1} x}{n - 1} - u_{n-2}.$

For $u_n = \displaystyle\int \sec^n x \, dx, \quad u_n = \dfrac{\sec^{n-2} x \tan x}{n - 1} + \dfrac{n - 2}{n - 1} u_{n-2}.$

In all these reduction formulae, the suffixes must be greater than or equal to zero.

7

Second-order differential equations

1. FOUNDATIONS

We assume in this book that the reader has met differential equations before and that it is understood that the solution of differential equations plays an important role in applied mathematics. One example will show the extent of the experience we shall assume.

Example 1
A ball is thrown vertically upwards, with initial speed 8 m s^{-1}. As well as the effect of gravity, air resistance causes a deceleration of $0.1v^2 \text{ m s}^{-2}$, where v is the velocity. Find how high the ball goes, and the time taken for it to rise to this height.

Solution
If, at time t, the height is y and the velocity v (in standard units), then we have

$$\text{acceleration} = \frac{dv}{dt} = -(10 + 0.1v^2),$$

taking $g = 10 \text{ m s}^{-2}$ for convenience.

Now $\qquad \dfrac{dt}{dv} = \dfrac{-1}{10 + 0.1v^2} = \dfrac{-10}{100 + v^2},$

giving $\qquad t = -\dfrac{10}{10} \tan^{-1} \dfrac{v}{10} + A, \quad$ where $A = \tan^{-1} 0.8,$

since $v = 8$ when $t = 0$.
   From this, $t = \tan^{-1} 0.8 \approx 0.675$ when $v = 0$. Re-writing the equations above we get

$$v = -10 \tan(t - A)$$

and hence, integrating, $\quad y = -10 \ln \sec(t - A) + B.$

The initial conditions, $y = 0$ when $t = 0$, give

$$B = 10 \ln \sec(-A)$$
$$= 5 \ln 1.64, \quad \text{since } \ln \sec A = \tfrac{1}{2} \ln(1 + \tan^2 A),$$

and this is the greatest height reached, since $y = B$ when $t = A$.
   The work so far can be illustrated by the solution curves of Figures 1 and 2 overleaf.

71

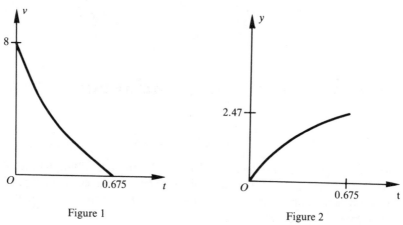

Figure 1   Figure 2

The final answer could also have been obtained directly, by seeking a differential equation connecting the velocity with the height. The chain rule gives

$$\frac{dv}{dt} = \frac{dv}{dy} \times \frac{dy}{dt} = \frac{dv}{dy} \times v,$$

so the original differential equation can be expressed as

$$v \frac{dv}{dy} = -(10 + 0.1v^2)$$

or

$$\frac{dy}{dv} = \frac{-10v}{100 + v^2}.$$

Integrating, we obtain

$$y = -5 \ln(100 + v^2) + C, \quad \text{where } C = 5 \ln 164,$$

since $y = 0$ when $v = 8$.

Then $v = 0$ when
$$y = -5 \ln 100 + 5 \ln 164$$
$$= 5 \ln 1.64.$$

When we have difficulty integrating a differential equation by exact methods, we can always fall back on a numerical method. A simple step-by-step solution (rounding each entry to 2 DP) of $\frac{dv}{dt} = -(10 + 0.1v^2)$ looks like this:

t	v	$\dfrac{dv}{dt} = -(10 + 0.1v^2)$	δv
0	8	− 16.4	− 1.64
0.1	6.36	− 14.04	− 1.40
0.2	4.96	− 12.46	− 1.25
0.3	3.71	− 11.38	− 1.14
0.4	2.57	− 10.66	− 1.07
0.5	1.50	− 10.23	− 1.02
0.6	0.48	− 10.02	− 1.00

For the final step, we take $\delta v = 0.48$ and $\dfrac{\delta v}{\delta y} = -10.02$, giving $\delta t \approx 0.048$, and the time to the highest point as 0.648 seconds (0.65 seconds to 2 DP).   □

1.1 Methods of exact solution

There exists a whole range of methods of solution, each appropriate for its own class of differential equations. It is important to realise, however, that even if all these methods are known, there remain very many equations which do not respond to any of them. Apart from the straightforward integration which sufficed in Example 1, two methods should already have been encountered (see, for example, *SMP Revised Advanced Mathematics 3*, Chapter 38). We illustrate these with worked examples.

Example 2: Separation of variables

Solve $\dfrac{dy}{dx} = (6x + 1)y^2$, given $y = 1$ when $x = 2$.

Solution
We can reverse the process of 'implicit differentiation' if we first write the equation in the form

$$\frac{1}{y^2}\frac{dy}{dx} = 6x + 1$$

This gives

$$-\frac{1}{y} = 3x^2 + x + A.$$

The initial conditions give $\quad -1 = 12 + 2 + A, \qquad$ so $A = -15$,

and the final answer is

$$-\frac{1}{y} = 3x^2 + x - 15. \qquad □$$

Example 3: Particular integral, complementary function method

Solve $\dfrac{dy}{dx} = 6x + 1 - 2y.$

Solution
This cannot be solved by separating the variables, but it pays to re-write the equation as

$$\frac{dy}{dx} + 2y = 6x + 1.$$

Now one simple solution has the form $y = Kx + L$. This is indeed a solution if $K + 2(Kx + L)$ can be made to come to $6x + 1$. This requires $K = 3$ and $L = -1$. So we have a *particular integral*, $y = 3x - 1$.

Now $\dfrac{dy}{dx} + 2y = 0$ when $y = A\,e^{-2x}$ whatever the value of A, and it is easily verified that $y = 3x - 1 + A\,e^{-2x}$ is a solution of the original differential equation, for

$$y = 3x - 1 + A\,e^{-2x} \quad \Rightarrow \quad \frac{dy}{dx} = 3 - 2A\,e^{-2x}$$

and
$$\frac{dy}{dx} + 2y = (3 - 2A\,e^{-2x}) + 2(3x - 1 + A\,e^{-2x})$$
$$= (3 + 6x - 2) + (-2A\,e^{-2x} + 2A\,e^{-2x})$$
$$= 6x + 1.$$

$A\,e^{-2x}$ is called the *complementary function*, and the method works because of the *linearity* of the differential equation.

In the check we have just written out, the terms contributed by the particular integral (PI) remain separate from the terms provided by the complementary function (CF). The total contribution is the sum of the two parts of the complete solution taken separately. This notion of linearity is illustrated further in the next section.

All the possible solutions are given by $y = 3x - 1 + A\,e^{-2x}$. Each value of A gives a solution curve; the solution curves fill the plane and no two curves intersect (see Figure 3).

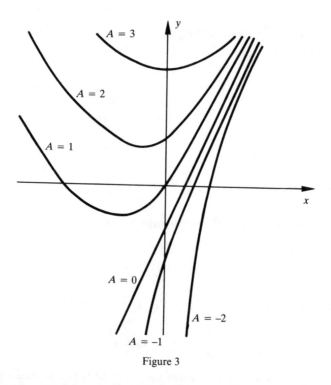

Figure 3

The central ideas of Example 3 will be important when we go on to consider *second-order* differential equations (ones containing second derivatives), and Exercise 7A is designed to clarify these issues.

1.2 Linearity

Example 4

Solve $\dfrac{dy}{dx} + y^2 = 4$.

Solution

Attempting to use the method of Example 3, we might note immediately that $y = 2$ and $y = -2$ are particular integrals, and find that $y = 1/(x - A)$ satisfies $\dfrac{dy}{dx} + y^2 = 0$ for all A. The temptation is to conclude that $y = 2 + 1/(x - A)$ is a solution of $\dfrac{dy}{dx} + y^2 = 4$.

However,

$$y = 2 + \frac{1}{x - A} \quad \Rightarrow \quad \frac{dy}{dx} + y^2 = -\frac{1}{(x - A)^2} + \left(2 + \frac{1}{x - A}\right)^2$$

$$= 4 + \frac{4}{x - A}.$$

The suggested function is not a solution of the differential equation, because y^2 is not a linear function of y.

On this occasion, separation of variables is feasible, and we obtain correct solutions

$$y = 2 \left(\frac{B e^{4x} + 1}{B e^{4x} - 1}\right),$$

with also the special case $y = 2$. ☐

Example 5

Solve $x^2 \dfrac{dy}{dx} - 3xy = x^3 + 8$.

Solution

This equation is linear in y; the powers of x do not affect this.

Substituting $y = x^2$ in $x^2 \dfrac{dy}{dx} - 3xy$ gives $2x^3 - 3x^3 = -x^3$.

Substituting $y = \dfrac{1}{x}$ in $x^2 \dfrac{dy}{dx} - 3xy$ gives $-1 - 3 = -4$.

It follows that if we substitute $y = -x^2 - 2/x$ we shall get $x^3 + 8$, so we have achieved a PI.

Moreover, $y = Ax^3$ is easily seen to give $x^2 \dfrac{dy}{dx} - 3xy = 0$, so we have achieved a CF also.

The complete solution is

$$y = -x^2 - \frac{2}{x} + Ax^3.$$

You should verify that this checks. ☐

We can write $$x^2 \frac{dy}{dx} - 3xy = x^3 + 8$$

in the form $$\left(x^2 \frac{d}{dx} - 3x \right) y = x^3 + 8,$$

or $L(y) = x^3 + 8,$ where L is the 'operator' $\left(x^2 \dfrac{d}{dx} - 3x \right).$

Then, for example, $L(\sin x) = x^2 \cos x - 3x \sin x$

and $L(e^{2x}) = 2x^2 e^{2x} - 3x e^{2x}.$

We formally define an operator L to be linear if

$$L(f + g) = L(f) + L(g) \quad \text{for any functions } f \text{ and } g.$$

Exercise 7A

1 Find values for K and L for which:

(a) $x = Kt + L$ is a solution of $\dfrac{dx}{dt} + 3x = 6t + 17$;

(b) $x = K e^t$ is a solution of $\dfrac{dx}{dt} - 4x = 6 e^t$;

(c) $x = K \sin t + L \cos t$ is a solution of $\dfrac{dx}{dt} + 2x = 3 \sin t.$

2 Write down the complementary functions for each of the differential equations in question 1, and hence the complete solutions.

3 Find particular integrals and complementary functions for:
   (a) $\dot{x} + 6x = 18$ (b) $\dot{x} + 6x = 18t - 3$
   (c) $\dot{x} + 10x = 3 e^{-t}$ (d) $\dot{x} + 10x = 17 \sin t + 32 \cos t$

   $\left(\dot{x} \text{ is used as a shorthand for } \dfrac{dx}{dt} . \right)$

4 Find the solutions of the equations in question 3 for which $x = 2$ when $t = 0$. In each case, sketch the solution curve.

5 (a) Find a PI for $\dfrac{dy}{dx} + xy = x^3$ of the form $y = Kx^2 + Lx + M.$

   (b) Solve $\dfrac{dy}{dx} + xy = 0$ by separating the variables.

   (c) Write down the complete solution of the differential equation in (a).

6 (a) Show that $y = x$ is a solution of $\dfrac{dy}{dx} + xy^2 = x^3 + 1.$

   (b) Show that $y = \dfrac{2}{x^2}$ is a solution of $\dfrac{dy}{dx} + xy^2 = 0.$

   (c) Is $y = x + \dfrac{2}{x^2}$ a solution of $\dfrac{dy}{dx} + xy^2 = x^3 + 1?$

7 (a) Show that $y = \dfrac{x^2}{3} + \dfrac{3}{x}$ is a solution of $x \dfrac{dy}{dx} + y = x^2.$ Find the general solution of this differential equation.

   (b) Show that $y = \dfrac{1}{3x + 1}$ is a solution of $x \dfrac{dy}{dx} + y = y^2.$ Find the general solution.

2. SECOND-ORDER EQUATIONS WITH CONSTANT COEFFICIENTS

We shall consider solutions of the equation $a\ddot{x} + b\dot{x} + cx = f(t)$ for different constants a, b, c and all sorts of functions $f(t)$. It is convenient to regard the independent variable as time (as it so often is in practical examples) and to use the dot notation for differentiation.

First we take an especially simple example.

Example 6
Solve $\ddot{x} + 5\dot{x} + 6x = 0$.

Solution
Our previous experience suggests that the solution might be exponential, so we try $x = e^{nt}$.

This is a solution if $\qquad n^2 e^{nt} + 5n e^{nt} + 6 e^{nt} = 0$.

This implies that $\qquad\qquad n^2 + 5n + 6 = 0,$ $\qquad\qquad\qquad$ (1)

so $\qquad\qquad\qquad\qquad n = -2 \text{ or } -3$.

Then $x = e^{-2t}$ is one solution, and $x = e^{-3t}$ is another. Since the original equation is linear, $x = A e^{-2t} + B e^{-3t}$ is also a solution, for all constant values of A and B. This must be *the* complete solution if we accept that this is unique and should contain two undetermined constants.

The last statement is true, but it may be more satisfactory to establish it directly. Starting again:

$$\ddot{x} + 5\dot{x} + 6x = 0$$
$$\ddot{x} + 3\dot{x} + 2\dot{x} + 6x = 0$$
$$\frac{d}{dt}(\dot{x} + 3x) + 2(\dot{x} + 3x) = 0$$
$$\dot{x} + 3x = C e^{-2t}.$$

This last equation has PI $A e^{-2t}$ (A is actually equal to C) and CF $B e^{-3t}$, so the complete solution is

$$x = A e^{-2t} + B e^{-3t}.$$

Here we have used the first-order technique twice in succession. $\qquad\qquad\square$

The key to Example 6 is the quadratic equation (1), known as the *auxiliary equation* of the differential equation. In the same way, the auxiliary equation of $\ddot{x} + a\dot{x} + bx = 0$ is $n^2 + an + b = 0$. Having established the method, answers may be obtained with little effort, as in the examples that follow.

Example 7
Solve $\ddot{x} - 100x = 0$.

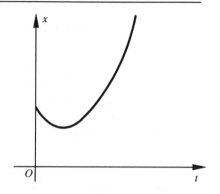

Figure 4

Solution
The auxiliary equation, $n^2 - 100 = 0$, gives $n \pm 10$. Hence the complete solution is $x = A\,e^{10t} + B\,e^{-10t}$; a typical solution curve is given in Figure 4. For large t, $x \approx A\,e^{10t}$. The behaviour for small t depends, of course, upon the relative values of A and B. ☐

It seems then that we have a straightforward extension of the familiar first-order situation. But consider the following example.

Example 8
In equilibrium, a 2 kg mass extends a spring by 0.098 m (see Figure 5). Describe the ensuing motion (neglecting air resistance and friction) if it is released from a point a small distance above the equilibrium position.

Solution
Assume that the tension is proportional to the extension (Hooke's law). Then when the mass is a distance x below the equilibrium position, $T = k(0.098 + x)$, and k is given by $2g = k \times 0.098$.

Figure 5

The equation of motion is

$$2g - T = 2\ddot{x},$$

so

$$-kx = 2\ddot{x}$$

and

$$\ddot{x} + 100x = 0.$$

This equation looks similar to that of Example 7, and yet we know that the motion is oscillatory, and hence that the solution (in real terms, anyway) is not exponential. The periodic nature of the motion suggests the use of the circular functions, and it is easily shown that $x = \sin 10t$ and $x = \cos 10t$ are solutions, and so $x = A \sin 10t + B \cos 10t$ is also a solution.

Now the method of the previous examples gives $x = C\,e^{10jt} + D\,e^{-10jt}$, and we may write this as

$$x = C(\cos 10t + j \sin 10t) + D(\cos 10t - j \sin 10t)$$
$$= (C + D) \cos 10t + (C - D)j \sin 10t,$$

if we recall the result $e^{j\theta} = \cos\theta + j \sin\theta$. Now we may write B for $C + D$ and A for $(C - D)j$, and so recover the earlier version of the solution. The solution curve is a sine wave, and we see that the different forms of motion given by differential equations of the type under discussion depend upon the nature of the roots of the auxiliary quadratic equation – real and distinct, real and equal, or complex. Exercise 7B should be completed before an attempt is made to summarise the possibilities. □

Exercise 7B

1 Find the values of n for which e^{nt} is a solution of:
    (a) $\ddot{x} - 6\dot{x} - 12x = 0$ (b) $\ddot{x} + 7\dot{x} + 10x = 0$
    (c) $\ddot{x} - 8\dot{x} + 11x = 0$ (d) $\ddot{x} + 6\dot{x} + 10x = 0$

2 Write down and solve the auxiliary equations of the following, and hence give the complete solutions:
    (a) $\ddot{x} + 9\dot{x} + 14x = 0$ (b) $\ddot{x} + 14\dot{x} + 9x = 0$

3 Solve $\ddot{x} + 3\dot{x} + 2x = 0$, given that $x = 4$ and $\dot{x} = 5$ when $t = 0$. Find t when $x = 0$, and sketch the graph of x against t for positive t.

4 Verify, by differentiation, that:
    (a) $x = 2 \sin 5t - 11 \cos 5t$ is a solution of $\ddot{x} + 25x = 0$.
    (b) $x = e^{-3t}(2 \sin 5t - 11 \cos 5t)$ is a solution of $\ddot{x} + 6\dot{x} + 34x = 0$.
Examine the auxiliary equations of each of these examples. Comment.

5 Find p and q if $x = e^{-pt} \sin qt$ satisfies $\ddot{x} + a\dot{x} + bx = 0$. Show that with these values, $x = e^{-pt} \cos qt$ is also a solution. State the condition on a and b for real solutions of this form to exist.

6 Solve:
    (a) $\ddot{x} + 6\dot{x} + 4x = 0$, if $x = 0$ and $\dot{x} = 5$ when $t = 0$
    (b) $\ddot{x} + 16x = 0$, if $x = 2$ and $\dot{x} = 3$ when $t = 0$
    (c) $\ddot{x} + 4\dot{x} + 13x = 0$, if $x = 1$ and $\dot{x} = 0$ when $t = 0$.
(Use the results of question 5.)

7 Sketch the solution curves for question 6.

8 The general solution of $\ddot{x} + 4\dot{x} + 13x = 0$ can be written

$$x = A\, e^{(-2+3j)t} + B\, e^{(-2+3j)t}.$$

Find A and B if $x = 1$ and $\dot{x} = 0$ when $t = 0$, and then show that this gives the same solution as that obtained in question 6(c).

3. SIMPLE HARMONIC MOTION

The solution of Example 8 suggests that the oscillations persist with constant amplitude, which is contrary to experimental evidence. Such idealised motion – sinusoidal oscillations with constant amplitude – is called *simple harmonic motion* (SHM for short). This simple model is of great importance and deserves detailed study, despite the fact that it does not closely represent the experimental evidence. (See, for example, *Mechanics and Vectors* in this series.)

SHM is characterised by a differential equation of the form $\ddot{x} + \omega^2 x = 0$, where ω is a positive constant. Solutions are then given by

$$x = A \sin \omega t + B \cos \omega t \tag{1}$$
$$= a \sin (\omega t + \epsilon), \tag{2}$$

where $a = \sqrt{(A^2 + B^2)}$, $\cos \epsilon = A/\sqrt{(A^2 + B^2)}$ and $\sin \epsilon = B/\sqrt{(A^2 + B^2)}$.
The *amplitude a* and *phase angle* ϵ depend upon the initial conditions. It is

easily seen that if form (1) of the solution is used, B is equal to the initial value of x, and $A\omega$ is the initial value of $\dot{x}$.

The distinctive feature of this type of oscillation is that the period $2\pi/\omega$ is independent of the initial conditions and hence of the amplitude of the oscillations. In Example 8, the period depends only upon the stiffness of the spring and the magnitude of the suspended mass.

3.1 Heavy damping

Consider a cube which is suspended by a spring in a tank containing a liquid and is moving vertically (see Figure 6). If x is its displacement from its equilibrium position at time t, the net force would be proportional to x if the liquid were not there, and for a spring of the right strength, Newton's laws might give

$$\ddot{x} = -10x.$$

As before, the negative sign indicates that when x is positive, the net force is negative, and vice versa.

But the liquid produces a force dependent upon the velocity $\dot{x}$, and we shall consider the simple and useful model in which this force is directly proportional to $\dot{x}$ and in the opposite direction to the velocity. For a liquid of suitable viscosity, we might have altogether

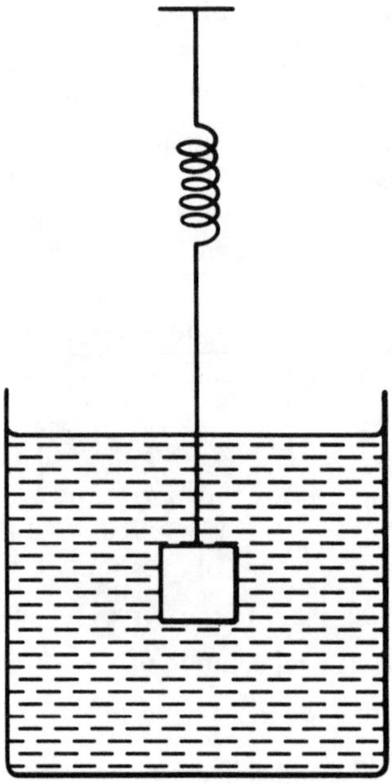

Figure 6

$$\ddot{x} = -10x - 7\dot{x},$$

i.e.

$$\ddot{x} + 7\dot{x} + 10x = 0.$$

The auxiliary equation, $n^2 + 7n + 10 = 0$, gives $n = -2$ or -5, so all possible solutions of this equation have the form

$$x = A\,e^{-2t} + B\,e^{-5t}.$$

With first-order differential equations, we have noted that the (single) constant in the general solution depends upon the initial conditions. With second-order differential equations, there are two aspects of the initial conditions: we can start with the body in any position and with any velocity.

Suppose $x = 0.2$ and $\dot{x} = 0.5$ when $t = 0$. Then $A + B = 0.2$, and since $\dot{x} = -2A\,e^{-2t} - 5B\,e^{-5t}$, we have also $-2A - 5B = 0.5$. Solving, we get $A = 0.5$ and $B = -0.3$, so

$$x = 0.5\,e^{-2t} - 0.3\,e^{-5t}.$$

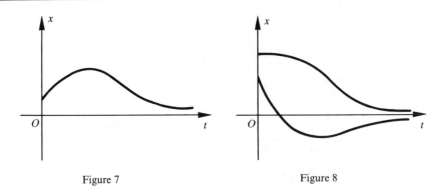

Figure 7   Figure 8

Figure 7 shows the solution curve. Figure 8 shows two other possible solution curves for the same differential equation, corresponding to different starting values. Because the starting values of the position and velocity are independent, it should come as no surprise that the general solution contains two arbitrary constants.

This differential equation describes the sort of motion we get in a thick, treacly fluid: the mass returns gradually towards its equilibrium position.

3.2 Light damping

With the same apparatus as in §3.1 but with a slightly less viscous liquid, the motion might be described by

$$\ddot{x} + 6\dot{x} + 10x = 0.$$

Now the auxiliary equation has roots $-3 + j$ and $-3 - j$, and the general solution may be written

$$x = A\, e^{(-3+j)t} + B\, e^{(-3-j)t}$$
or
$$x = e^{-3t}(A\, e^{jt} + B\, e^{-jt})$$
or again
$$x = e^{-3t}[A(\cos t + j \sin t) + B(\cos t - j \sin t)].$$

Finally, replacing $A + B$ by C and $(A - B)j$ by D, we have

$$x = C\, e^{-3t} \cos t + D\, e^{-3t} \sin t.$$

A real problem, with real starting values, must of course lead to a real solution. C and D will then be real, meaning that A and B in the earlier version of the solution are complex conjugates.

The solution curve looks like Figure 9 (overleaf). The oscillations are contained by the curves $x = \pm \sqrt{(C^2 + D^2)}\, e^{-3t}$, here shown dotted.

Complex numbers provide a useful catalyst, but it is quite possible to develop the theory without them. In particular, it is easily verified by differentiation that $x = e^{-3t} \cos t$ and $x = e^{-3t} \sin t$ satisfy the differential equation $\ddot{x} + 6\dot{x} + 10x = 0$. Another approach is taken in Chapter 10, where we shall also look into the case of critical damping, the watershed between light and

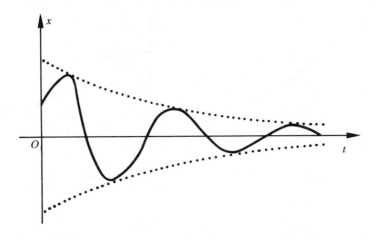

Figure 9

heavy damping, corresponding to a differential equation whose auxiliary equation has two equal roots.

Exercise 7C

1   Find the general solutions of:
    (a) $\ddot{x} - 8\dot{x} + 7x = 0$ (b) $\ddot{x} + 4\dot{x} + 7x = 0$ (c) $\ddot{x} - 8\dot{x} + 7x = 0$
    (d) $\ddot{x} + 6\dot{x} + 7x = 0$ (e) $2\ddot{x} + 5\dot{x} + 2x = 0$ (f) $\ddot{x} + 2\dot{x} + 17x = 0$

2   In each of the following cases, (i) find the solution subject to the initial conditions $x = 1$ and $\dot{x} = 0$ when $t = 0$, (ii) sketch the solution curve, and (iii) find approximately the minimum value of T if $|x| < 0.001$ for all $t > T$:
    (a) $\ddot{x} + 52\dot{x} + 100x = 0$ (b) $\ddot{x} + 29\dot{x} + 100x = 0$
    (c) $\ddot{x} + 16\dot{x} + 100x = 0$ (d) $\ddot{x} + 12\dot{x} + 100x = 0$

3   A 3 kg mass hangs in equilibrium on a spring, and extends it by 12 cm. If it is given a sharp downward blow of impulse 1.5 s N, derive a differential equation describing the motion. Find the position of the mass as a function of time, and write down the period and amplitude of the oscillation. Assume there are no damping forces.

4   Find the period and amplitude of oscillation of the mass in question 3 if it is set in motion 2 cm below the equilibrium position with velocity 1.0 m s^{-1} downwards. Is the spring extended throughout the subsequent motion?

5   Show that the maximum points on the graph of $x = e^{-kt} \sin \omega t$ lie on an exponential curve, and find its equation.

6   A simple pendulum is found to have a period of $\frac{1}{2}$ second, and the amplitude of the swings decreases by 50 per cent in 15 seconds. Assuming that the motion is described by $\ddot{\theta} + 2k\dot{\theta} + n^2\theta = 0$, find k and n.

7   Assuming no damping, the period of a simple pendulum is $2\pi\sqrt{(l/g)}$. In an experiment, l and the period are measured, and the formula is used to find g. What percentage error is involved in neglecting damping if the data of question 6 apply?

4. CONTROL MECHANISMS

The word 'automation' is often used to mean the automatic control of machinery. An early invention in this field was the centrifugal governor (see Figure 10). This can be used to keep a shaft rotating at almost constant angular velocity. If it rotates too fast, the masses A and B move outwards, raising the sleeve C and so compressing the spring a little. This movement may be used to regulate the input to the driving motor. In the diagram, it is suggested that this might be transmitted by a lever hinged at O. If the shaft slows down below the determined running speed, the spring extends and the motor is boosted.

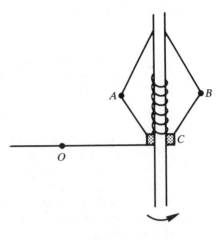

Figure 10

Control of the rate of flow of oil in a pipeline, the guidance system of a missile, and control of industrial machinery of all kinds present similar mathematical features. Another example is the way the eye and brain control the movement of the hand when one picks up a pin from a table.

With some modification of terminology, the block diagram shown in Figure 11 illustrates all these cases.

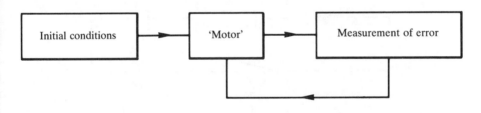

Figure 11

The modification of the operating conditions of the motor according to the results caused is called *feedback*; the whole process is akin to the (discrete) iterative procedures introduced elsewhere in the course. Whereas in discrete iterations the aim is to obtain the desired degree of accuracy with as few loops as possible, here we desire to conclude the approximating process as quickly as possible.

Consider a missile fired at a stationary target, as in Figure 12 (overleaf), and suppose that at time t the direction of flight makes a small angle θ with the line directly towards the target.

Figure 12

The angle θ is measured by some device in the nose of the missile, and a force proportional to θ is passed to the steering mechanism. This causes an angular acceleration $\ddot{\theta}$ proportional to the force, let us say, so that

$$\ddot{\theta} \propto \theta, \quad \text{i.e. } \ddot{\theta} = -\omega^2\theta,$$

if the feedback is always negative, meaning that it tends to reduce the error.

This is the equation of SHM, giving oscillations of constant amplitude. The missile turns towards the target but it has an angular velocity when it is momentarily pointing in the right direction, and it then develops an equal error in the opposite sense. The situation is then that of the proverbial drunk man trying to walk down the middle of the road and alternately hitting the hedges at either side of the road.

The solution of this problem, of course, is to have a damping device built into the design of the system. This brings us back to the mathematics of the previous section.

You will be able to think of many more situations described roughly by this same mathematical model. All can be simulated electrically by a simple circuit in which a capacitor, initially charged, discharges through an inductor and resistor in series (Figure 13).

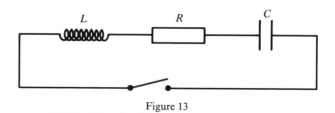

Figure 13

The resistor provides the damping, and if R is small we get an alternating current of decreasing amplitude. If R is large compared with L, the solution curve (as in Figure 8) is similar to that for the discharge of a capacitor through a non-inductive resistor.

5. FORCED OSCILLATIONS

We began this chapter by considering differential equations of the form

$$\ddot{x} + a\dot{x} + bx = f(t).$$

We have not yet progressed beyond examples where $f(t) = 0$. In circuit electricity, the more general case arises where an e.m.f. is applied to an LCR circuit; in mechanics, where there is an applied force which varies with time.

The particular integral, complementary function method is appropriate, and §§2 and 3 have explored the various forms the CF may take. Now we come to the PI and find that exactly the same technique applies as with first-order equations: we guess the form of the answer and find the constants by substitution. This presents no difficulty in the majority of practical examples, but there are some possible snags. A worked example demonstrates the technique.

Example 9
Solve $\ddot{x} + 4\dot{x} + 13x = \sin 2t$.

Solution
The CF is $e^{-2t}(A \sin 3t + B \cos 3t)$. To find a PI, suppose that $x = H \sin 2t + K \cos 2t$ is a solution. Then

$$- 4H \sin 2t - 4K \cos 2t + 8H \cos 2t - 8K \sin 2t$$
$$+ 13H \sin 2t + 13K \cos 2t = \sin 2t.$$

This implies that $\quad 9H - 8K = 1 \quad$ and $\quad 8H + 9K = 0,$

that is, $\qquad\qquad\qquad H = \frac{9}{145} \quad$ and $\quad K = -\frac{8}{145}.$

Hence $\qquad\qquad\qquad x = \frac{9}{145} \sin 2t - \frac{8}{145} \cos 2t$

is one solution, and

$$x = \tfrac{9}{145} \sin 2t - \tfrac{8}{145} \cos 2t + e^{-2t}(A \sin 3t + B \cos 3t)$$

is the complete solution. The proof that the final step is legitimate is given in Chapter 10. $\qquad\qquad\qquad\qquad\qquad\qquad\qquad\qquad\qquad\qquad\qquad\qquad$ $\square$

Exercise 7D

1   Find particular integrals of:
    (a) $\ddot{x} - 4x = 10$ (b) $\ddot{x} + 6x = e^{-2t}$ (c) $\ddot{x} + 6\dot{x} + 2x = t + 5$
    (d) $\ddot{x} - 3\dot{x} + x = 7t$ (e) $\ddot{x} + 5x = \sin 3t$ (f) $\ddot{x} + 2\dot{x} + 5x = \cos t$

2   Find the complete solutions of:
    (a) $\ddot{x} - 2\dot{x} - 3x = 15$ (b) $\ddot{x} - 9x = 4 e^t$ (c) $\ddot{x} + 9x = e^{3t}$
    (d) $\ddot{x} + 6\dot{x} + 5x = e^{-2t} + 10$ (e) $\ddot{x} - 3x = \cos 2t$
    (f) $\ddot{x} + 4x = \sin 3t + 5 \cos 3t$ (g) $2\ddot{x} + 5\dot{x} + 2x = \sin t$

3   Find a PI of $\ddot{x} + 2\dot{x} + 5x = e^{jt}$, then write down without further working a PI of $\ddot{x} + 2\dot{x} + 5x = e^{-jt}$. Hence check the answer to question 1(f), using the identity

$$\cos t = \tfrac{1}{2}(e^{jt} + e^{-jt}).$$

4   Use the method of question 3 to find PIs of:
    (a) $2\ddot{x} + 7\dot{x} + 3x = \sin 3t$ (b) $\ddot{x} + 10\dot{x} + 6x = 4 \cos 2t$

5   Find the solutions of the following differential equations with the given boundary conditions:
    (a) $\ddot{x} + x = 3$; $x = 2$ and $\dot{x} = 10$ when $t = 0$
    (b) $4\ddot{x} + x = 7$; $x = 4$ when $t = 0$ and $x = 1$ when $t = \pi$
    (c) $\ddot{x} + 2\dot{x} + 5x = \sin t$; $x = 1$ and $\dot{x} = 0$ when $t = 0$

6. FORMULATION OF DIFFERENTIAL EQUATIONS

Differential equations with constant coefficients form useful models for a wide variety of applications. Solving the equations should be a routine matter by now, but it is easy to lose sight of the basic structure of the mathematics while concentrating on setting up the equations. Experience is vital, as Exercise 7E will demonstrate.

Exercise 7E

1   A stone is dropped down a deep well. The effect of the well's atmosphere on the stone's motion (which is vertical) is to produce a retardation per unit mass proportional to its speed. If y is the distance fallen by the stone in time t, show that the equation of motion of the stone can be written in the form

$$\frac{d^2y}{dt^2} + k\frac{dy}{dt} = g, \quad \text{where } k \text{ is a constant.}$$

Solve this differential equation to obtain the relation between y, g, k and t, given that both y and $\frac{dy}{dt}$ are zero when t is zero.   [SMP]

2   A weather balloon of mass M kg floats in still air at a height of z_0 m and, if displaced from this level to a height z m, experiences a force tending to restore it to the equilibrium height, of amount $n^2(z - z_0)$ N. During any vertical motion there is assumed to be a resistance to relative motion of air and balloon equal to λMn N s m^{-1} times the relative vertical speed. In disturbed air there is a vertical air velocity $a \sin pt$ m s^{-1}, where $p = n/\sqrt{M}$. Set up an equation for the vertical motion of the balloon, and calculate this vertical motion for times well after the time of arrival at height z_0 m.   [SMP]

3   A uniform bar is heated at one end. If θ is the excess temperature of the surface of the bar over its surroundings at a distance x from the heated end, then $\frac{d^2\theta}{dx^2} = \mu^2\theta$, where μ is a constant. Obtain θ in terms of x, given that $\theta = \theta_0$ when $x = 0$, and $\theta \to 0$ as $x \to \infty$.

4   An Eskimo in the Arctic builds an igloo to save himself from being frozen to death when a blizzard sets in. Heat is generated in the igloo by the Eskimo's body, and there is a consequent rate of increase of the temperature θ in the igloo equal to k times the excess of his (fixed) body temperature T_1 above θ. Heat is also lost from the igloo by conduction, so that there is a rate of decrease of θ equal to $\frac{1}{6}k$ times the excess of θ above the outside temperature T. Write down a differential equation for θ.

At time $t = 0$ the temperature in the igloo is $-T_0$ °C, and the outside temperature T falls slowly according to the formula

$$T = -2T_0 + T_0 e^{-kt/6}.$$

Show that $\theta = A + B e^{-kt/6} + C e^{-7kt/6}$

where A, B and C are constants. Express A in terms of T_0 and T_1.   [SMP]

5 A deep-freeze cabinet stands in a small room; the deep-freeze compressor cools the interior of the cabinet, but warms the room; some of the heat in the room escapes to the outside air, and some penetrates into the cabinet. Let the various temperatures be as follows:

Room: T (variable)
Outside air: T_0 (fixed)
Cabinet: θ (variable)
Thermostat: θ_0 (fixed)

The relations between the temperatures are modelled as follows, with a, b, c and k all constants:

(i) T tends to decrease at rate $a(T - T_0)$ owing to loss to the outside air;
(ii) T tends to increase at rate $b(\theta - \theta_0)$ owing to the action of the compressor;
(iii) θ tends to decrease at rate $k(\theta - \theta_0)$ owing to the action of the compressor;
(iv) θ tends to increase at rate $c(T - \theta)$ owing to heat flow into the cabinet.

Set up a pair of differential equations for T and θ and reduce them to

$$\frac{d^2}{dt^2}(\theta - \theta_0) + (a + c + k)\frac{d}{dt}(\theta - \theta_0) + (ac + ak - bc)(\theta - \theta_0) = ac(T_0 - \theta_0).$$

If $ac + ak > bc$, find the temperature in the freezer after a long time. [SMP]

6 A man floats vertically in a swimming pool, with only a small portion of his head above the water. His breathing, by changing his volume, causes him to oscillate vertically. The pool's surface is at rest, apart from the slight disturbance caused by the man.

The man's breathing is described as follows. He has basic volume A_0 m³, and his breathing changes this to

$$A = A_0 + a \sin \omega t.$$

His head, near the waterline, is modelled by a cylinder of cross-sectional area $\frac{1}{36}$ m². He has mass 80 kg and his centre of mass does not move relative to his body as he breathes. Holding his breath, at volume A_0 m³, he would float in equilibrium with 3.6×10^{-2} m of his cylindrical head out of the water. The water has density 10^3 kg m⁻³ and air has negligible density. Take $g = 10$ (m s⁻²).

The water exerts three forces:

(i) an upthrust equal to the weight of water displaced;
(ii) a resistance equal to 20 kg times the man's acceleration;
(iii) a resistance equal to 200 kg s⁻¹ times his velocity.

Using as coordinate the height x (in metres) of the man's head which is above the water, show that the upthrust is

$$10^4 \left(A - \frac{x}{36}\right) \text{ newtons,}$$

and that $A_0 = 8.1 \times 10^{-2}$.

Set up the vertical equation of motion of the man, and find the general solution of this equation. [SMP]

7

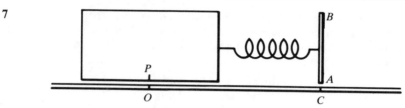

Figure 14

(*a*) A box of mass 2 kg runs on horizontal friction-free rails at right angles to a vertical plate *AB* which is held stationary at *C*. It is connected to the plate by a spring, and in the equilibrium position the point *P* on the box is over the point *O* on the rails. The box is pulled aside 0.05 m from the equilibrium position and released from rest. When in the subsequent motion *P* is *x* m from *O*, the force in the spring is $-8x$ newtons. If time is measured from the release of the mass, show that *x* is subsequently given by

$$x = a \cos \omega t.$$

State the values of *a* and *ω*.

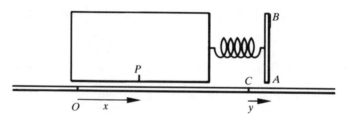

Figure 15

(*b*) The box is stopped at the equilibrium position and a fresh situation is now described. With the box initially stationary, but still free to move as before, the plate *AB* starts to oscillate on the rails about *C* in such a way that its displacement from *C* is $y = 3 \sin \frac{1}{2}\omega t$, where *ω* is the same as for the previous motion and *t* is measured from the commencement of the oscillation. If the force in the spring which tends to restore it to its natural length is 8 × (change in length) newtons, show that the equation of motion of the box is

$$\ddot{x} + 4x = 12 \sin \tfrac{1}{2}\omega t.$$

Solve this equation to find the relation between *x* and *t*, and indicate by a rough sketch the graph of *x* over the interval $0 \leqslant t \leqslant 6\pi$. [SMP]

Miscellaneous exercise 7

1 Show that $y = A\sqrt{(\cos x)}$ is a solution of the differential equation

$$y \frac{d^2y}{dx^2} + \left(\frac{dy}{dx}\right)^2 + \tfrac{1}{2}y^2 = 0,$$

whatever the value of the constant *A*. Show that $y = B\sqrt{(\sin x)}$ is also a solution for all values of the constant *B*. Explain why $y = A\sqrt{(\cos x)} + B\sqrt{(\sin x)}$ is not the general solution of the differential equation.

2 In a pathological investigation of the spread of infection in a culture, it is found that the time-rate at which the area of the infected parts spreads is directly proportional to the product of the infected area and the uninfected area. Initially, one half of the area is infected and it is found that the initial rate of spread is such that, if it remained constant thereafter, the culture would be completely infected in 24 hours. Set up a differential equation relating x, the infected proportion of the total area, to time t, and deduce that after 12 hours about 73 per cent of the culture is infected.

3 Find values of n for which $x = t^n$ is a solution of $t^2\ddot{x} - 7t\dot{x} + 12x = 0$. Hence solve
$$t^2\ddot{x} - 7t\dot{x} + 12x = 10t + 36.$$

Solve also
$$t^2\ddot{x} - 6t\dot{x} + 12x = \ln t.$$

4 Solve the equation $\dfrac{dy}{dx} - y \tan x = -4 \sin x$, with the condition that $y = 2$ when $x = 0$. For what values of x is this solution appropriate?   [SMP]

5 Find general solutions of:

(a) $\dfrac{dy}{dx} - \dfrac{(x + 1)y}{x} = 2x$ for $x > 0$ (b) $\dfrac{d^2y}{dx^2} + 4y = \cos x$ [SMP]

6 Find the solution of $\ddot{x} + x = \sin 2t$ for which both $\dot{x} = 0$ and $x = 0$ when $t = 0$. Find the maximum and minimum values of x and sketch the solution curve.

7 The differential equation $\ddot{x} + 6\dot{x} + 10x = 30 \sin 2t$ has a particular integral of the form $a \sin 2t + b \cos 2t$. Find a and b, and hence solve the equation completely, given that $x = 0$ when $t = 0$ and when $t = \frac{1}{2}\pi$.

Show, by sketching the graph, the nature of the solution between $t = 2n\pi$ and $t = 2(n + 1)\pi$, where n is a large positive integer, and give approximate values for the maximum and minimum of x over this interval.   [SMP]

8 A smooth straight hollow tube is rotating in a horizontal plane with constant angular velocity ω about a fixed point of itself (Figure 16). A small particle is released inside the tube at time $t = 0$. Initially it has zero velocity relative to the tube and is a distance a from the pivot. If it is a distance r from the pivot at time t, it can be shown that

$$\frac{d^2r}{dt^2} = \omega^2 r.$$

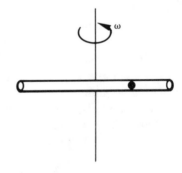

Figure 16

Find an expression giving r in terms of t.

9 A projectile is fired through a medium offering a resistance of $-k\dot{\mathbf{r}}$ per unit mass, where $\mathbf{r}$ is the position vector of the projectile at any instant. If the only other force experienced by the projectile is constant gravity, $\mathbf{g}$ per unit mass, show that the equation of motion of the projectile simplifies to

$$\ddot{\mathbf{r}} + k\dot{\mathbf{r}} = \mathbf{g}.$$

Treating this equation as a second-order linear differential equation with constant coefficients, find the complementary function and the particular integral. Hence write down the general solution of the differential equation.   [SMP]

10   A light elastic string AOB of unstretched length a has tension kx when extended by a length x. It is fixed at A and passes through a smooth fixed ring at O (where $OA = a$). A mass m is attached at B and moves in such a way that the string remains taut all the time.

Obtain a differential equation for $\mathbf{r}$, the vector $\mathbf{OB}$, and solve it. Describe the motion as fully as you can.

11   If $\omega \neq 10$, find the amplitude of the PI of $\ddot{x} + 100x = 7 \sin \omega t$, and draw a graph showing how this varies with ω.

12   The function satisfies the equation

$$f(x)\,f'''(x) = f''(x)$$

and also $f(0) = 1, f'(0) = 0$. Show that $f(x) = \cos 2x$ is *one* solution.

Show that $\dfrac{\mathrm{d}}{\mathrm{d}x} \left\{ \dfrac{f''(x)}{f(x)} \right\} = 0$

for any solution (where $f(x)$ is not 0). Deduce a second-order differential equation for $y = f(x)$.   [SMP]

SUMMARY

The particular integral, complementary function method is appropriate for solving *linear* differential equations. An especially simple and important subset consists of linear differential equations with constant coefficients.

For $\dot{x} + ax = f(t)$, the CF is the solution of $\dot{x} + ax = 0$, namely Ae^{-at}.

For $\ddot{x} + a\dot{x} + bx = g(t)$, the CF is the solution of $\ddot{x} + a\dot{x} + bx = 0$, and the nature of this depends upon whether the roots of the auxiliary equation $n^2 + an + b = 0$ are real or complex:

(1)   If the roots are real and distinct (α and β, say), the CF is $A\,e^{\alpha t} + B\,e^{\beta t}$.
(2)   If the roots are $\alpha \pm \beta j$, the CF is $e^{\alpha t}(A \cos \beta t + B \sin \beta t)$.

When $a = 0$ and $b > 0$ (case 2 with $\alpha = 0$), the differential equation describes *simple harmonic motion*.

When $a > 0$ and $a^2 < 4b$ (case 2 with $\alpha < 0$), the differential equation describes *damped simple harmonic motion*.

When $a > 0$, $b > 0$ and $a^2 > 4b$ (case 1 with $\alpha, \beta < 0$), the differential equation describes *heavy damping*.

The special case in which $a^2 = 4b$ corresponds to *critical damping*, and consideration of this is deferred to Chapter 10.

To find particular integrals, we are guided by the nature of $f(t)$ or $g(t)$: if these are polynomials we look for a polynomial PI, if exponential we look for an exponential PI, and so on.

8

Differential geometry

1. ARC LENGTH

Consider a spot on an oscilloscope screen for which the position at time t is given by

$$x = \sin 2t, \qquad y = 4\sqrt{2} \sin t.$$

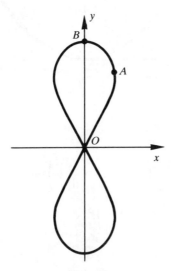

Figure 1

The path traced is a figure of eight (see Figure 1), the velocity vector is $\begin{bmatrix} 2\cos 2t \\ 4\sqrt{2}\cos t \end{bmatrix}$ and the speed at time t is

$$\sqrt{(4\cos^2 2t + 32\cos^2 t)}.$$

This can be written as
$$\sqrt{(4\cos^2 2t + 16(1 + \cos 2t))}$$
$$= \sqrt{(2\cos 2t + 4)^2}$$
$$= 2\cos 2t + 4.$$

We can use this to find the length of the path, since the speed is the rate of change of distance travelled.

The total length is $\quad 4 \times \text{arc } OAB = 4 \int_0^{\pi/2} (2\cos 2t + 4)\, \mathrm{d}t$
$$= 8\pi.$$

91

We use the letter s to denote arc length. Generalising what we have done above, we have

$$\frac{ds}{dt} = \sqrt{\left(\left(\frac{dx}{dt}\right)^2 + \left(\frac{dy}{dt}\right)^2\right)}. \tag{1}$$

This applies equally when x and y are functions of a parameter t which is not connected with time.

Example 1
Find the length of the parabola $y = x^2$ from (1, 1) to (3, 9).

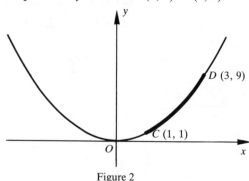

Figure 2

Solution

If we write $x = t$, then $y = t^2$.

$$\frac{ds}{dt} = \sqrt{\left(\left(\frac{dx}{dt}\right)^2 + \left(\frac{dy}{dt}\right)^2\right)} = \sqrt{(1 + 4t^2)}.$$

$$\text{Arc length } CD = \int_1^3 \sqrt{(1 + 4t^2)}\, dt$$

$$= \int \tfrac{1}{2} \cosh^2 u \, du \qquad (\text{putting } 2t = \sinh u)$$

$$= \int \tfrac{1}{4}(1 + \cosh 2u)\, du$$

$$= \left[\tfrac{1}{4}u + \tfrac{1}{8} \sinh 2u\right]_{\sinh^{-1} 2}^{\sinh^{-1} 6}$$

$$= 8.27. \qquad \qquad \square$$

When, as in this example, y is given as a function of x, there is no need to introduce a parameter. Formula (1) may be re-stated in the form

$$\frac{ds}{dx} = \sqrt{\left(1 + \left(\frac{dy}{dx}\right)^2\right)} \tag{2}$$

Figure 3 provides a helpful reminder. When x is increased by a small amount δx and y by δy, the change δs in the arc length is very close to the direct distance from P to Q.

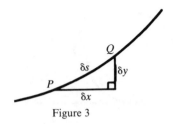

Figure 3

So $$(\delta s)^2 \approx (\delta x)^2 + (\delta y)^2,$$

giving $$\left(\frac{\delta s}{\delta x}\right)^2 \approx 1 + \left(\frac{\delta y}{\delta x}\right)^2 \quad \text{as well as} \quad \left(\frac{\delta s}{\delta t}\right)^2 \approx \left(\frac{\delta x}{\delta t}\right)^2 + \left(\frac{\delta y}{\delta t}\right)^2.$$

The limiting processes as δx and δt tend to zero are not easy to set out formally, but it will come as no surprise that they yield the exact results

$$\left(\frac{ds}{dx}\right)^2 = 1 + \left(\frac{dy}{dx}\right)^2 \quad \text{and} \quad \left(\frac{ds}{dt}\right)^2 = \left(\frac{dx}{dt}\right)^2 + \left(\frac{dy}{dt}\right)^2.$$

Exercise 8A

1 Write down the coordinates of A in Figure 1. Compare the arc length OA with the direct distance OA. Also compare the distances AB (a) along the curve, and (b) 'as the crow flies'.

2 (a) The velocity of a ball thrown through the air is given by $v = \begin{bmatrix} 20 \\ 12 - 10t \end{bmatrix}$, taking $g = 10 \text{ m s}^{-2}$ and neglecting air resistance. The ball hits the ground after 2.4 seconds. Write expressions for its speed at time t and the total distance travelled, and show that the substitution $u = (12 - 10t)/20$ gives the latter as

$$40 \int_{-0.6}^{0.6} \sqrt{(1 + u^2)} \, du.$$

(b) Use the further substitution $u = \sinh v$ to evaluate the distance.

3 Show that the arc length CD in Example 1 can be written as

$$\left[\tfrac{1}{4} \ln(2t + \sqrt{(1 + 4t^2)}) + \tfrac{1}{2} t \sqrt{(1 + 4t^2)} \right]_1^3,$$

and confirm the value given, using either the hyperbolic or the logarithmic form. Compare with the direct distance from $(1, 1)$ to $(3, 9)$.

4 Find the length of the curve $y = x^2 + 5$ from $(-1, 6)$ to $(1, 6)$.

5 Find the length of the curve $y = \cosh x$ from $x = 0$ to $x = 2$.

6 Express the length of the curve $y = e^x$ from $x = 0$ to $x = 1$ as an integral, and use Simpson's rule to find an approximate value.

7 Repeat question 6 for:
   (a) $y = 1/x$ from $x = 1$ to $x = 5$ (b) $y = \ln x$ from $x = 1$ to $x = e$

8 The path of a point on the rim of a wheel rolling along level ground is called a *cycloid*. It is given parametrically by

$$x = a(t + \sin t), \qquad y = a(1 + \cos t).$$

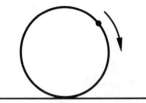

Figure 4

Sketch the path and find its length from $t = 0$ to $t = 2\pi$.

9   Find the distances travelled from $t = 0$ to $t = \frac{1}{2}\pi$ for:

(a) $x = a \sin t$, $y = a \cos t$

(b) $x = a \sin^2 t$, $y = a \cos^2 t$

(c) $x = a \sin^3 t$, $y = a \cos^3 t$

Sketch graphs to illustrate your answers.

10   Sketch the path given by

$$x = 3 \cos 2t, \qquad y = 4 \cos t$$

from $t = 0$ to $t = \pi$, and find the length of this arc.

2. POLAR COORDINATES

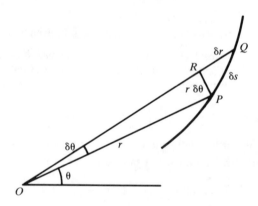

Figure 5

For curves defined in terms of polar coordinates, Figure 5 is the key diagram. Since we intend $\delta\theta$ to be a very small angle, it does not matter whether we regard PR as an arc of a circle centre O or as the perpendicular from P to OQ. In any case,

$$(\delta s)^2 \approx (\delta r)^2 + (r \, \delta\theta)^2,$$

and we obtain exact formulae

$$\left(\frac{ds}{d\theta}\right)^2 = \left(\frac{dr}{d\theta}\right)^2 + r^2 \quad \text{and} \quad \left(\frac{ds}{dt}\right)^2 = \left(\frac{dr}{dt}\right)^2 + \left(r \frac{d\theta}{dt}\right)^2.$$

Example 2
Sketch the spiral $r = a\theta$ and find its length from $\theta = 0$ to $\theta = 2\pi$.

Solution
Marking points where $\theta = 0, \frac{1}{2}\pi, \pi$, etc. soon gives Figure 6.

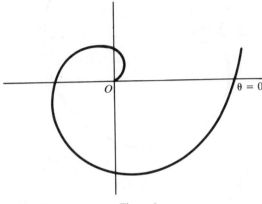

O

$\theta = 0$

Figure 6

The arc length is given by

$$\left(\frac{ds}{d\theta}\right)^2 = \left(\frac{dr}{d\theta}\right)^2 + r^2 = a^2(1 + \theta^2)$$

$$s = \int_0^{2\pi} a\sqrt{(1 + \theta^2)}\, d\theta$$

$$= a\left[\tfrac{1}{2}\sinh^{-1}\theta + \tfrac{1}{2}\theta\sqrt{(1 + \theta^2)}\right]_0^{2\pi}$$

$$= 21.3a. \qquad \square$$

Exercise 8B

1 If r and θ are functions of t, explain why

$$x = r\cos\theta \;\Rightarrow\; \dot{x} = \dot{r}\cos\theta - r\dot{\theta}\sin\theta.$$

Write down a similar expression for $\dot{y}$ and simplify $\dot{x}^2 + \dot{y}^2$. Comment.

2 Sketch the cardioid $r = a(1 - \cos\theta)$. Find the ratio of the lengths of the arc from $\theta = 0$ to $\theta = \frac{1}{2}\pi$ and the arc from $\theta = \frac{1}{2}\pi$ to $\theta = \pi$.

3 Sketch the spiral $r = e^{3\theta/4}$ and find the length of the arc from $\theta = 0$ to $\theta = \pi$.

4 Figure 7 (overleaf) is a sketch of $r = \cos^3 \frac{1}{3}\theta$. Find the total length of the curve and the length of the inner loop.

5 (a) Find the length of $r = \sqrt{3}\sec\theta$ from $\theta = 0$ to $\theta = \frac{1}{3}\pi$.
(b) Find the length of $r = 4\sin\theta$ from $\theta = 0$ to $\theta = \alpha$. Express each equation in Cartesian form using $\sin\theta = y/r$, $\cos\theta = x/r$, $r = \sqrt{(x^2 + y^2)}$, and hence check your arc lengths.

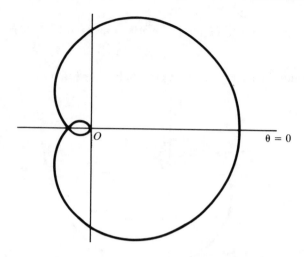

Figure 7

6 Sketch the graph of $r = \cos 2\theta$ for $\theta = 0$ to 2π. Find an approximate value for the length of each loop.

3. AREAS OF POLAR CURVES

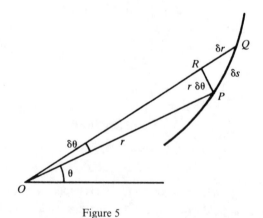

Figure 5

Figure 5, which is reproduced here, shows that the area of the sector OPQ bounded by the curve and the radial lines OP and OQ is approximately $\frac{1}{2}r^2 \, \delta\theta$. Areas of larger sectors are found from $\int \frac{1}{2}r^2 \, d\theta$.

Example 3
Find the ratio of the areas in the four quadrants bounded by the x- and y-axes and $r = a\theta$, $0 \leqslant \theta \leqslant 2\pi$ (see Figure 6).

Solution

The areas are
$$\int_0^{\pi/2} \tfrac{1}{2}a^2\theta^2 \, d\theta, \quad \int_{\pi/2}^{\pi} \tfrac{1}{2}a^2\theta^2 \, d\theta, \quad \text{etc.}$$

The first of these is
$$A_1 = \left[\tfrac{1}{6}a^2\theta^3 \right]_0^{\pi/2} = \tfrac{1}{48}a^2\pi^3.$$

The others are
$$A_1 \times (8 - 1), \quad A_1 \times (27 - 8) \quad \text{and} \quad A_1 \times (64 - 27).$$

The ratio of the areas is $1 : 7 : 19 : 37$. □

3.1 Use of limits

All the results used in this chapter so far have been plausible. There has been no attempt, though, to prove them in a rigorous way. Let us look more closely at the formula introduced in the previous paragraphs.

Figure 8(*a*) is drawn for a function which increases as the angle increases from θ to $\theta + \delta\theta$. Then arcs of circles centre O of radius r and $r + \delta r$ show that the area of the sector OPQ, denoted by δA, satisfies

$$\tfrac{1}{2}r^2 \, \delta\theta < \delta A < \tfrac{1}{2}(r + \delta r)^2 \, \delta\theta.$$

Dividing by $\delta\theta$, we get
$$\tfrac{1}{2}r^2 < \frac{\delta A}{\delta\theta} < \tfrac{1}{2}(r + \delta r)^2.$$

Now let $\delta\theta$ tend to zero. At the same time, δr and δA will tend to zero, and in the limit we find

$$\tfrac{1}{2}r^2 \leqslant \frac{dA}{d\theta} \leqslant \tfrac{1}{2}r^2.$$

Thus, $\dfrac{dA}{d\theta} = \tfrac{1}{2}r^2$ is an exact result.

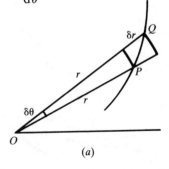 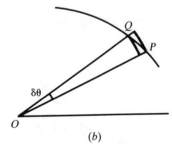

(*a*)   (*b*)

Figure 8

In Figure 8(*b*) r is a decreasing function of θ, and δr is negative. Now

$$\tfrac{1}{2}(r + \delta r)^2 \, \delta\theta < \delta A < \tfrac{1}{2}r^2 \, \delta\theta$$

$$\tfrac{1}{2}(r + \delta r)^2 < \frac{\delta A}{\delta\theta} < \tfrac{1}{2}r^2$$

$$\tfrac{1}{2}r^2 \leqslant \frac{dA}{d\theta} \leqslant \tfrac{1}{2}r^2.$$

Again, $\dfrac{\mathrm{d}A}{\mathrm{d}\theta} = \frac{1}{2}r^2$.

Any interval of θ can be divided into sub-intervals in each of which r is either increasing or decreasing throughout. The only special case is a circle centre O, when r is constant; the result is known to apply then. Thus

$$\frac{\mathrm{d}A}{\mathrm{d}\theta} = \tfrac{1}{2}r^2 \quad \text{or} \quad A = \int \tfrac{1}{2}r^2 \, \mathrm{d}\theta \quad \text{is proved.}$$

Similar arguments can be constructed for our other applications of calculus to geometry. We shall usually be content with the intuitive approach.

3.2 Angles

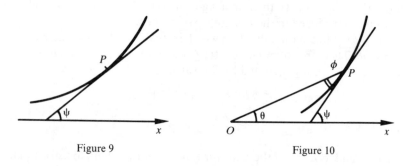

Figure 9   Figure 10

The direction of a curve at a point can be described by giving the angle between the tangent there and the x-axis. This is commonly written as ψ (see Figure 9) and we appreciate that

$$\tan \psi = \frac{\mathrm{d}y}{\mathrm{d}x}.$$

ψ is the limit of the angle marked in Figure 11 as $\delta x \to 0$.

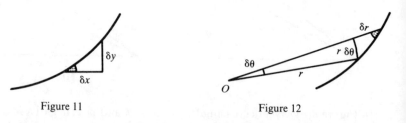

Figure 11   Figure 12

For polar graphs, we concentrate on the angle ϕ between radius and tangent (see Figure 10). It is the limit of the angle marked in Figure 12, and hence

$$\tan \phi = r \frac{\mathrm{d}\theta}{\mathrm{d}r} \quad \text{or} \quad \cot \phi = \frac{1}{r}\frac{\mathrm{d}r}{\mathrm{d}\theta}.$$

Figure 10 also shows that $\psi = \theta + \phi$.

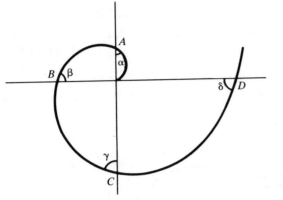

Figure 13

Example 4

Find the angles at which the spiral $r = a\theta$ crosses the x- and y-axes at A, B, C and D (Figure 13).

Solution

$$\cot \phi = \frac{1}{r}\frac{dr}{d\theta} = \frac{a}{a\theta} \implies \tan \phi = \theta.$$

Hence
$$\tan \alpha = \tfrac{1}{2}\pi, \quad \tan \beta = \pi, \quad \text{etc.;}$$
$$\alpha = 1.00 \text{ rad}, \quad \beta = 1.26 \text{ rad}, \quad \gamma = 1.36 \text{ rad}, \quad \delta = 1.41 \text{ rad}. \qquad \square$$

Exercise 8C

1 Find an expression for the angle ψ between the tangent at a general point and the x-axis for:

(a) $y = \tfrac{1}{2}x^2$ (b) $y = \ln \sec x$ $(-\tfrac{1}{2}\pi < x < \tfrac{1}{2}\pi)$

(c) $x = a(t + \sin t)$, $y = a(1 + \cos t)$ $(0 < t < \pi)$ (see Exercise 8A, question 8)

(d) $x = a \sin^n t$, $y = a \cos^n t$ $(n = 1, 2, 3)$ (see Exercise 8A, question 9)

2 (a) Show that for a general point P in the first quadrant on the hyperbola $y = 1/x$ (Figure 14), $\alpha = \beta$.

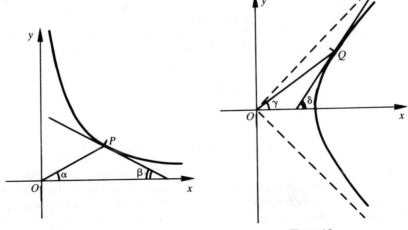

Figure 14   Figure 15

(b) Show that for a general point Q in the first quadrant on the hyperbola $x = \sec t$, $y = \tan t$ (Figure 15), $\gamma + \delta = \tfrac{1}{2}\pi$.

3   Repeat question 2(b) using the parametric representation $x = \cosh u$, $y = \sinh u$.

4   (a) Show that for $r = e^{3\theta/4}$, the angle ϕ is the same at all points. For this reason, it, and all other curves with equations of the form $r = a\,e^{k\theta}$, are called equiangular spirals.

  (b) Find the area of the sector bounded by $r = e^{3\theta/4}$, $\theta = 0$ and $\theta = 1$.

5   Find the total area of the cardioid $r = a(1 - \cos\theta)$, and show that the angle ϕ at a general point P is equal to $\frac{1}{2}\theta$ for $0 < \theta < 2\pi$ (see Figure 16).

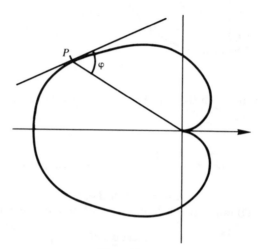

Figure 16

6   (a) Find the angles at which $r = \cos^3\frac{1}{3}\theta$ (Figure 7) crosses $\theta = \frac{1}{2}\pi$ and $\theta = \pi$, and obtain a general formula for ϕ in terms of θ.

  (b) Find the area of the sector bounded by $r = \cos^3\frac{1}{3}\theta$, $\theta = \alpha$ and $\theta = \beta$ for (i) $\alpha = 0$, $\beta = \frac{3}{2}\pi$, and (ii) $\alpha = 0$, $\beta = \pi$. Hence find the area of the inner loop.

7   For $r = \cos 2\theta$ (see Exercise 8B, question 6), find the area of each loop, and show that $\phi = \pi - \tan^{-1}(1/2\sqrt{3})$ when $\theta = \frac{1}{6}\pi$.

8   By plotting a few points, sketch the ellipse $3/r = 1 - \frac{1}{2}\cos\theta$, and the branch of the hyperbola $8/r = 1 + 2\cos\theta$ for $-\frac{2}{3}\pi < \theta < \frac{2}{3}\pi$. Show that they meet at $[4, \frac{1}{3}\pi]$ and $[4, -\frac{1}{3}\pi]$. Find the angle at which the curves meet.

9   Apply the formal methods to find (i) the area bounded by the graphs and $\theta = 0$, $\theta = \alpha$, and (ii) the angle ϕ when $\theta = \alpha$ for:

  (a) $r = \sqrt{3}\sec\theta$ (b) $r = 4\sin\theta$

  Explain the results (see Exercise 8B, question 5).

4. RADIUS OF CURVATURE

When a particle moves in a vertical plane along the surface of a bowl (see Figure 17), it has an acceleration component towards the 'inside' of the curve. If the curve is part of a circle, it is well known that the acceleration component equals v^2/r, where v is the speed and r the radius of the circle. The corresponding result for a general curve is v^2/ρ, where ρ is the radius of the circle that fits the curve best at the point concerned.

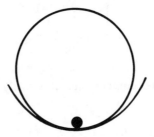

Figure 17

This definition is hopelessly vague. How do we choose the 'best fit'? Following the procedure used in Taylor approximations, we select the circle with the same y-value, same gradient and same rate of change of gradient (second derivative) at the point.

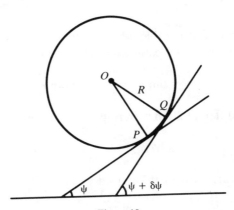

Figure 18

Since OP and OQ in Figure 18 are perpendicular to the tangents at P and Q, and the angle between these tangents is $\delta\psi$, it follows that angle $POQ = \delta\psi$. Also

$$\text{arc length } PQ = \delta s = R\,\delta\psi, \quad \text{giving} \quad R = \frac{\delta s}{\delta\psi}.$$

Accordingly, we define the *radius of curvature* ρ for any curve as $\dfrac{\mathrm{d}s}{\mathrm{d}\psi}$.

Now $\quad \dfrac{\mathrm{d}y}{\mathrm{d}x} = \tan\psi \quad \Rightarrow \quad \dfrac{\mathrm{d}^2y}{\mathrm{d}x^2} = \sec^2\psi\,\dfrac{\mathrm{d}\psi}{\mathrm{d}x}$ (by the chain rule)

$$= (1 + \tan^2\psi)\,\frac{\mathrm{d}\psi}{\mathrm{d}s} \times \frac{\mathrm{d}s}{\mathrm{d}x}$$

$$= \left(1 + \left(\frac{\mathrm{d}y}{\mathrm{d}x}\right)^2\right)\frac{1}{\rho} \times \sqrt{\left(1 + \left(\frac{\mathrm{d}y}{\mathrm{d}x}\right)^2\right)}.$$

Hence

$$\rho = \frac{\left[1 + \left(\dfrac{dy}{dx}\right)^2\right]^{3/2}}{\dfrac{d^2y}{dx^2}}.$$

Although the formula looks cumbersome, it is easily applied.

Example 5
Find the radius of curvature of $y = 12/x$ at $A\ (4, 3)$.

Solution

$$\frac{dy}{dx} = -\frac{12}{x^2} = -\tfrac{3}{4} \text{ at } A; \qquad \frac{d^2y}{dx^2} = \frac{24}{x^3} = \tfrac{3}{8} \text{ at } A.$$

$$\rho = (1 + \tfrac{9}{16})^{3/2}/\tfrac{3}{8}$$
$$= \tfrac{125}{24}.$$

An alternative formula applicable when a curve is described by Cartesian coordinates given in terms of a parameter t is found in a similar way:

$$\frac{dy}{dx} = \tan \psi \quad \Rightarrow \quad \frac{\dot{y}}{\dot{x}} = \tan \psi$$

(dots representing differentiation with respect to t, as usual)

$$\Rightarrow \quad \frac{\dot{x}\ddot{y} - \ddot{x}\dot{y}}{\dot{x}^2} = \sec^2\psi\ \dot{\psi},$$

using the quotient rule for the left-hand side,

$$\Rightarrow \quad \frac{\dot{x}\ddot{y} - \ddot{x}\dot{y}}{\dot{x}^2} = \left(1 + \frac{\dot{y}^2}{\dot{x}^2}\right) \frac{d\psi}{ds} \dot{s}$$

$$\Rightarrow \quad \dot{x}\ddot{y} - \ddot{x}\dot{y} = (\dot{x}^2 + \dot{y}^2)^{3/2}/\rho, \qquad \text{since } \dot{s} = \sqrt{(\dot{x}^2 + \dot{y}^2)}$$

$$\Rightarrow \quad \rho = \frac{(\dot{x}^2 + \dot{y}^2)^{3/2}}{\dot{x}\ddot{y} - \ddot{x}\dot{y}}.$$

Yet another formula applies to polar equations; this is given in Exercise 8D, question 8. In simple cases, though, the radius of curvature may be found by dividing $\dfrac{ds}{d\theta}$ by $\dfrac{d\psi}{d\theta}$.

4.1 Curvature and centre of curvature

The Greek letter κ is used to denote the *curvature*, defined as the reciprocal of ρ. Clearly, a curve which bends sharply at a point will have a large curvature there.

Another term often used is the *centre of curvature* at a point P: this is the centre C of the circle of radius ρ which gives a good fit to the curve at P (see Figure 19).

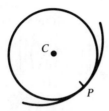

Figure 19

Exercise 8D

1 Find a formula for ρ in terms of x or t for the curves in Exercise 8C, question 1(*a*), (*b*) and (*c*).

2 Find the radius of curvature of $y = 1/x$ at $(1, 1)$ and that of $x^2 - y^2 = 1$ at $(1, 0)$ (see Exercise 8C, questions 2 and 3). Explain the connection between your answers.

3 Find the curvature of $y = \cosh x$, (*a*) when $x = 0$, and (*b*) when $x = 2$. Repeat for $y = \sinh x$.

4 Find the radius of curvature of:
   (*a*) $y = \sin x$ where $x = 1.2$ (*b*) $y = 2 \sin x$ where $x = 1.2$
   (*c*) $y = \sin 2x$ where $x = 0.6$

5 Find the radius of curvature of the ellipse $x = 5 \cos t, y = 3 \sin t$ at the points where $t = 0, \frac{1}{4}\pi, \frac{1}{2}\pi$.

6 For the spiral $r = e^{3\theta/4}$, show that $\dfrac{d\psi}{d\theta} = 1$ and $\dfrac{ds}{d\psi} = \frac{5}{4}r$.

7 For the spiral $r = a\theta$, show that

$$\frac{d\psi}{d\theta} = \frac{2 + \theta^2}{1 + \theta^2},$$

and deduce a formula for ρ. Show that $\rho \approx r$ when r is large.

8 Using $\quad \psi = \theta + \phi = \theta + \cot^{-1}\left(\dfrac{1}{r}\dfrac{dr}{d\theta}\right) = \theta + \frac{1}{2}\pi - \tan^{-1}\left(\dfrac{1}{r}\dfrac{dr}{d\theta}\right),$

show that $\rho = \dfrac{(r^2 + r'^2)^{3/2}}{r^2 + 2r'^2 - rr''}$, where $r' = \dfrac{dr}{d\theta}$ and $r'' = \dfrac{d^2r}{d\theta^2}$.

9 Use the formula from question 8 to find the radius of curvature of the hyperbola $\dfrac{6}{r} = 1 + 2 \cos \theta$ at the point $[3, \frac{1}{3}\pi]$.

10 Check question 9, given that it is equivalent to finding the radius of curvature of $x = -2 \cosh u, y = 2\sqrt{3} \sinh u$ at the point where $\cosh u = \frac{5}{4}, \sinh u = \frac{3}{4}$.

11 Find ρ at the general point of the cardioid $r = a(1 - \cos \theta)$.

12 Find the radius of curvature of the cycloid $x = a(t - \sin t), y = a(1 + \cos t)$ for $t = 0, \frac{1}{2}\pi, \pi$.
   Explain your first answer.

13   Find the maximum and minimum points of $y = x^3 - 12x$. Are these the points where the curvature is greatest?

5. SIGNS

From the formula

$$\rho = \frac{\left[1 + \left(\dfrac{dy}{dx}\right)^2\right]^{3/2}}{\dfrac{d^2y}{dx^2}},$$

we see that a negative value will be obtained whenever $\dfrac{d^2y}{dx^2}$ is negative. No other significance attaches to a negative radius of curvature.

More care must be taken with arc length formulae. From $\dot{s}^2 = \dot{x}^2 + \dot{y}^2$, we have written $\dot{s} = \sqrt{(\dot{x}^2 + \dot{y}^2)}$. Taking the positive square root is correct if we wish s to increase as t increases. Now consider the astroid $x = a \sin^3 t$, $y = a \cos^3 t$. Taking values of t from 0 to 2π, we get Figure 20.

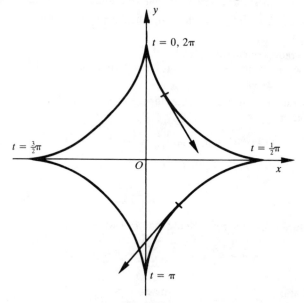

Figure 20

$$\dot{s} = \sqrt{(9a^2 \sin^4 t \cos^2 t + 9a^2 \sin^2 t \cos^4 t)}$$
$$= \sqrt{(9a^2 \sin^2 t \cos^2 t)}.$$

It is tempting to write

$$s = \int_0^{2\pi} 3a \sin t \cos t \, dt$$

for the length of the whole curve. But this gives

$$\left[\tfrac{3}{2}a \sin^2 t\right]_0^{2\pi} = 0,$$

which is not helpful.

The correct procedure is to use $\dot{s} = 3a \sin t \cos t$ in the first and third quadrants and $\dot{s} = -3a \sin t \cos t$ in the other quadrants. Obviously, we can also invoke symmetry and say:

$$\text{total length} = 4 \times \left[\tfrac{3}{2}a \sin^2 t \right]_0^{\pi/2} = 6a.$$

Similar problems arise with angles. For the astroid, $\tan \psi = -\cot t$; when $0 < t < \tfrac{1}{2}\pi$, we can deduce that $\psi = t - \tfrac{1}{2}\pi$, the diagram showing that ψ goes from $-\tfrac{1}{2}\pi$ to 0 in this interval. In the fourth quadrant, ψ goes from $-\pi$ to $-\tfrac{1}{2}\pi$ as t goes from $\tfrac{1}{2}\pi$ to π; now $\psi = t - \tfrac{3}{2}\pi$. Checking one's inferences from a diagram is always sensible.

Miscellaneous exercise 8

1   Show that the length of that part of the parabola $y = x^2 - 1$ which lies below the x-axis is $\sqrt{5} + \tfrac{1}{2} \sinh^{-1} 2$.   [SMP]

2   Find the points of intersection of the curves

$$\frac{1}{r} = 1 + \cos \theta \quad \text{and} \quad \frac{3}{r} = 1 - \cos \theta.$$

Show that the curves intersect at right angles.   [SMP]

3   Draw the curves whose polar equations are

$$4r = 3a \sec \theta \quad \text{and} \quad r = a(\cos \theta + 1)$$

for $0 \le \theta \le \pi$. Determine the value of θ at the point of intersection, and the angle between the curves there.   [SMP]

4   Show that the tangent to the spiral given by the polar equation

$$r = a\theta, \quad a > 0, \quad 0 < \theta < \tfrac{1}{2}\pi$$

makes an angle $\psi = \theta + \tan^{-1} \theta$

with the line $\theta = 0$. Hence show that the radius of curvature, defined as $\dfrac{ds}{d\psi}$, is given

by $$\rho = \frac{(a^2 + r^2)^{3/2}}{2a^2 + r^2}.$$ [SMP]

5   Sketch the curve given parametrically by

$$\mathbf{r} = a \begin{bmatrix} \cos \theta \\ \tfrac{1}{2} \sin \theta \end{bmatrix}, \quad 0 \le \theta \le \pi.$$

Calculate the curvature at the point $\theta = \tfrac{1}{2}\pi$, and find the centre of curvature for this point.   [SMP]

6   The curve $r = a \sin^3 \tfrac{1}{3}\theta$ for $0 \le \theta \le 3\pi$ is sketched in Figure 21 (overleaf). Show that

$$\frac{dx}{d\theta} = a \sin^2 \tfrac{1}{3}\theta \cos \tfrac{4}{3}\theta$$

at any point P on the curve. Use this and a similar expression for $\dfrac{dy}{d\theta}$ to show that the

tangent at P makes an angle $\tfrac{4}{3}\theta$ with the x-axis.

By using the formula $$\kappa = \frac{d\psi}{ds},$$

or otherwise, calculate the radius of curvature of the curve at P (in terms of a and θ).

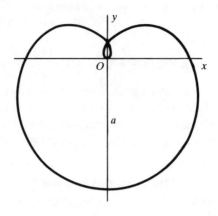

Figure 21

7 For a point half-way along a spoke of a wheel rolling along level ground,

$$x = at - \tfrac{1}{2}a \sin t, \qquad y = a - \tfrac{1}{2}a \cos t.$$

Find an integral for the length of the path between $t = 0$ and $t = 2\pi$, and obtain an approximate value.

8 Repeat question 7 for the ellipse

$$x = 5 \cos t, \qquad y = 3 \sin t.$$

Compare your answer with the length of a circle of radius 4.

9 Find the area of the loop of $r = \cos^3 3\theta$ between $\theta = -\tfrac{1}{6}\pi$ and $\theta = \tfrac{1}{6}\pi$. (*Hint*: put $u = 3\theta$ in the integral and use a reduction formula.)

10 Compare the answer to question 9 with the area of the loop of $r = \cos^2 4\theta$ between $\theta = -\tfrac{1}{8}\pi$ and $\theta = \tfrac{1}{8}\pi$.

11 (*a*) Show that $y = \ln(e^u - 1) - \ln(e^u + 1) \Rightarrow \dfrac{dy}{du} = \dfrac{1}{\sinh u}$.

   (*b*) Calculate the length of the curve $y = e^x$ from $x = 0$ to $x = 1$ to 5 SF.
(*Hint*: you will find the substitution $x = \ln \sinh u$ and (*a*) helpful.)
Compare with Exercise 8A, question 6.

SUMMARY

Arc length

$$\dot{s} = \sqrt{(\dot{x}^2 + \dot{y}^2)}$$

$$\frac{ds}{dx} = \sqrt{\left(1 + \left(\frac{dy}{dx}\right)^2\right)}$$

$$\frac{ds}{d\theta} = \sqrt{\left(r^2 + \left(\frac{dr}{d\theta}\right)^2\right)}$$

Area of a polar curve

$$A = \int \tfrac{1}{2}r^2 \, d\theta$$

Angles
$$\tan \psi = \frac{dy}{dx} = \frac{\dot{y}}{\dot{x}},$$

where ψ is the angle between the tangent and the x-axis.

$$\cot \phi = \frac{1}{r}\frac{dr}{d\theta},$$

where ϕ is the angle between the tangent and the radial line.

$$\psi = \theta + \phi$$

Curvature and radius of curvature

$$\rho = \frac{1}{\kappa} = \frac{(\dot{x}^2 + \dot{y}^2)^{3/2}}{\dot{x}\ddot{y} - \ddot{x}\dot{y}} = \frac{\left[1 + \left(\dfrac{dy}{dx}\right)^2\right]^{3/2}}{\dfrac{d^2y}{dx^2}},$$

Also,
$$\rho = \frac{ds}{d\theta} \div \frac{d\psi}{d\theta} = \frac{(r^2 + r'^2)^{3/2}}{r^2 + 2r'^2 - rr''},$$

where
$$r' = \frac{dr}{d\theta} \quad \text{and} \quad r'' = \frac{d^2r}{d\theta^2}.$$

9

Improper integrals and limits of sequences

To keep Chapter 3 to a reasonable length, these two aspects were deferred. They both concern limits but otherwise have nothing in common. It is convenient to place them both in this chapter.

1. IMPROPER INTEGRALS

Example 1

Consider $\displaystyle\int_{-2}^{3} \frac{1}{x}\,dx.$

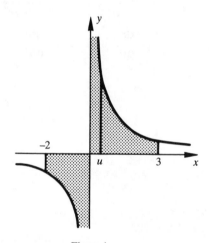

Figure 1

It is tempting to write

$$\int_{-2}^{3} \frac{1}{x}\,dx = \left[\ln |x|\right]_{-2}^{3}$$
$$= \ln 3 - \ln 2$$
$$\approx 0.41.$$

You will have expected a snag, and this is revealed by a graph (Figure 1): the integrand is not defined at one point in the domain. Note also that

$$\int_{u}^{3} \frac{1}{x}\,dx = \ln 3 - \ln u$$

and this tends to infinity as $u \to 0$. The answer 0.41 can only be defended as the result of combining an infinitely large negative contribution with a slightly larger positive contribution. We do not accept juggling with infinity in this way (it would lead to terrible paradoxes!), so no meaning is assigned to the integral.

□

Example 2

Consider $\int_{-1}^{8} x^{-2/3} \, dx$.

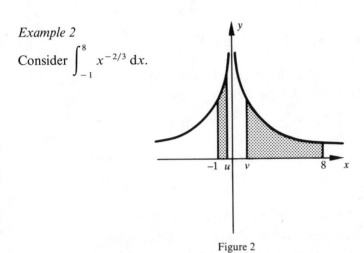

Figure 2

The way forward has been demonstrated in Example 1. We can evaluate $\int_{-1}^{u} x^{-2/3} \, dx$ and $\int_{v}^{8} x^{-2/3} \, dx$, and see whether they tend to limits as u tends to 0 from below and v tends to 0 from above (see Figure 2).

$$\int_{-1}^{u} x^{-2/3} \, dx = 3u^{1/3} + 3 \to 3 \quad \text{as } u \to 0^{-}$$

and

$$\int_{v}^{8} x^{-2/3} \, dx = 6 - 3v^{1/3} \to 6 \quad \text{as } v \to 0^{+}.$$

This time the integral is acceptable, and having conducted the above limiting processes, we can write

$$\int_{-1}^{8} x^{-2/3} \, dx = 3 + 6 = 9.$$

□

Example 3

Consider $\int_{0}^{\infty} x \, e^{-x} \, dx$.

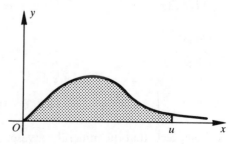

Figure 3

As in the last two examples, we are dealing with an unbounded region, and the correct way to proceed is as follows:

$$\int_0^u x\, e^{-x}\, dx = \left[-x\, e^{-x} - e^{-x} \right]_0^u = -u\, e^{-u} - e^{-u} + 1$$
$$\rightarrow 1 \quad \text{as } u \rightarrow \infty.$$

It is now admissible to write $\int_0^\infty x\, e^{-x}\, dx = 1$.   □

You have probably used such integrals before, maybe in connection with probability density functions. If we write

$$\int_0^\infty x\, e^{-x}\, dx = \left[-x\, e^{-x} - e^{-x} \right]_0^\infty = 1,$$

it is only legitimate as a formal shorthand for the limiting process.

Definitions

The integral $\int_a^b f(x)\, dx$ is said to be *improper* whenever

  (i) $f(x)$ is not defined at one or more points of the domain, or
  (ii) the range of integration is infinite, i.e. $a = -\infty$ or $b = \infty$.

Improper integrals can be investigated as in §1. When the appropriate limits exist, the integral is said to be *convergent*. Otherwise, the integral is meaningless.

1.1 Comparison methods

Where it is easy to find integral functions, as in all three examples so far studied, there is no difficulty in deciding whether or not an improper integral converges. In other cases, such decisions can often be made without actually carrying out the full working, which may be complicated.

Example 4
Decide whether the following converge:

(a) $\int_1^4 \dfrac{\sqrt{x+3}}{\sqrt{(x-1)}}\, dx,$ (b) $\int_1^\infty \dfrac{\sqrt{x}}{x+1}\, dx$

Solution

(a) Near $x = 1$, $\dfrac{\sqrt{x+3}}{\sqrt{(x-1)}} \approx \dfrac{4}{\sqrt{(x-1)}}.$

Now $\int_u^a \dfrac{4}{\sqrt{(x-1)}}\, dx = \left[8\sqrt{(x-1)} \right]_u^a \rightarrow 8\sqrt{(a-1)} \quad \text{as } u \rightarrow 1.$

This suggests that the integral converges, and also suggests how to construct a proof:

$$0 < \int_u^4 \frac{\sqrt{x}+3}{\sqrt{(x-1)}}\,dx < \int_u^4 \frac{\sqrt{4}+3}{\sqrt{(x-1)}}\,dx = \int_u^4 \frac{5}{\sqrt{(x-1)}}\,dx$$

$$= \left[10\sqrt{(x-1)}\right]_u^4$$
$$= 10(\sqrt{3} - \sqrt{(u-1)})$$
$$\to 10\sqrt{3} \quad \text{as } u \to 1,$$

and so $\int_u^4 \frac{\sqrt{x}+3}{\sqrt{(x-1)}}\,dx$ tends to a limit less than $10\sqrt{3}$.

(b) For large x, $\frac{\sqrt{x}}{x+1} \approx \frac{1}{\sqrt{x}}$.

Since $\int_a^u \frac{1}{\sqrt{x}}\,dx = 2(\sqrt{u} - \sqrt{a}) \to \infty \quad \text{as } u \to \infty,$

it looks as if $\int_1^\infty \frac{\sqrt{x}}{x+1}\,dx$ does not converge. This is easily proved:

$$\int_1^u \frac{\sqrt{x}}{x+1}\,dx > \int_1^u \frac{\sqrt{x}}{x+x}\,dx = \int_1^u \frac{1}{2\sqrt{x}}\,dx = \sqrt{u}-1 \to \infty \quad \text{as } u \to \infty. \qquad \square$$

Exercise 9A

Find the values of the integrals in questions 1, 2 and 3, where they exist.

1 (a) $\int_0^4 \frac{1}{x^2}\,dx$ (b) $\int_0^4 \frac{1}{\sqrt{x}}\,dx$ (c) $\int_0^4 \frac{1}{(x-1)^2}\,dx$

   (d) $\int_0^4 \frac{1}{x-2}\,dx$ (e) $\int_0^4 \frac{1}{\sqrt{(16-x^2)}}\,dx$ (f) $\int_0^{\pi/2} \tan x\,dx$

2 (a) $\int_4^\infty \frac{1}{x^2}\,dx$ (b) $\int_4^\infty \frac{1}{\sqrt{x}}\,dx$ (c) $\int_4^\infty \frac{1}{(x-1)^2}\,dx$

   (d) $\int_4^\infty \frac{1}{x-2}\,dx$ (e) $\int_4^\infty \frac{1}{16+x^2}\,dx$ (f) $\int_4^\infty \frac{1}{\sqrt{(16+x^2)}}\,dx$

3 (a) $\int_0^\infty \frac{12}{(2x-3)^2}\,dx$ (b) $\int_0^1 \ln x\,dx$ (c) $\int_0^1 x \ln x\,dx$

   (d) $\int_0^\infty x\,e^{-x^2}\,dx$ (e) $\int_1^5 \frac{x}{\sqrt{(x-1)}}\,dx$ (f) $\int_1^\infty \frac{1}{x^2}\sin\left(\frac{1}{x}\right)\,dx$

4 Investigate whether the following integrals are convergent by comparing them with simpler integrals. (There is no need to evaluate those that do exist.)

   (a) $\int_1^5 \frac{\sqrt{x}}{x-1}\,dx$ (b) $\int_0^\pi \frac{\sin x}{x^2}\,dx$ (c) $\int_0^\infty \frac{1}{1+x^3}\,dx$

   (d) $\int_0^\pi \frac{1}{\sqrt{(\sin x)}}\,dx$ (e) $\int_0^{\pi/2} \ln \sin x\,dx$ (f) $\int_0^1 \frac{1}{\sinh x}\,dx$ (g) $\int_1^\infty \frac{1}{\sinh x}\,dx$

5   The period, t hours, between gas leaks being reported in a particular locality is
modelled by the probability density function

$$\phi(t) = k \exp(-t/20), \quad \text{for } t > 0.$$

(a) Find the value of k so that $\displaystyle\int_0^\infty \phi(t)\,dt = 1$.

(b) Find the mean interval $\displaystyle\int_0^\infty t\,\phi(t)\,dt$.

6   If $\sec\theta = \cosh u$ with $u > 0$ and $0 < \theta < \frac{1}{2}\pi$, express (a) $\tan\theta$ and (b) $\dfrac{d\theta}{du}$ in terms
of u.

Hence, or otherwise, evaluate $\displaystyle\int_0^\infty \frac{1}{\cosh u}\,du.$ [SMP]

2. CONVERGENCE OF SEQUENCES

In the introduction to Chapter 3, you were asked to consider the sequence
defined inductively by

$$x_1 = 1, \qquad x_{i+1} = \sqrt{(2/x_i)}.$$

A little numerical work soon convinces us that the sequence converges. The task
we now set ourselves is to see how to forecast the speed of convergence.

If a limit l exists, we understand that it must satisfy the equation

$$l = \sqrt{(2/l)}, \quad \text{giving} \quad l = \sqrt[3]{2}.$$

We shall now define a new sequence by $e_i = x_i - l$: for each x-term, this gives
the distance from the limit or 'error'. We expect the error sequence to tend to 0.
Before going on, let us tabulate some terms:

i	x_i	e_i	e_{i+1}/e_i
1	1	-0.2599	-0.59
2	1.4142	0.1543	-0.46
3	1.1892	-0.0707	-0.52
4	1.2968	0.0369	-0.49
5	1.2420	-0.0181	-0.51
6	1.2691	0.0091	—

The e-sequence alternates, with the absolute value approximately halving each
time. The fourth column has been included in the table to emphasise this. An
algebraic explanation can be given.

If $x_{i+1} = \sqrt{(2/x_i)}$ and $e_i = x_i - l$ for all i, and where $l = \sqrt[3]{2}$,

then
$$x_{i+1}^2 = 2/x_i$$

$$\Rightarrow \qquad x_{i+1}^2 - l^2 = \frac{2}{x_i} - l^2$$

$$\Rightarrow \quad (x_{i+1} - l)(x_{i+1} + l) = \frac{2 - l^2 x_i}{x_i} = \frac{l^3 - l^2 x_i}{x_i}$$

$$\Rightarrow \qquad e_{i+1}(x_{i+1} + l) = -\frac{l^2 e_i}{x_i}$$

$$\Rightarrow \qquad \frac{e_{i+1}}{e_i} = -\frac{l^2}{x_i(x_{i+1} + l)}.$$

Now when x_i and x_{i+1} are both close to l, this relation shows that $e_{i+1} \approx -\frac{1}{2}e_i$, as expected.

Let us carry out a similar analysis for the sequence defined by

$$x_1 = 1, \qquad x_{i+1} = 2/x_i^2.$$

Again, if a limit l exists it will be $\sqrt[3]{2}$.

$$x_{i+1} - l = \frac{2}{x_i^2} - l = \frac{l^3 - lx_i^2}{x_i^2} = \frac{l(l + x_i)(l - x_i)}{x_i^2}$$

giving
$$\frac{e_{i+1}}{e_i} = -\frac{l(l + x_i)}{x_i^2}, \quad \text{where } e_i = x_i - l.$$

Now
$$x_i \approx l \quad \Rightarrow \quad -\frac{l(l + x_i)}{x_i^2} \approx -2,$$

meaning that even if one term of the sequence is close to $\sqrt[3]{2}$, the next will be about twice as far away. The sequence cannot converge on l.

Here is the table for the first six terms:

i	x_i	e_i	e_{i+1}/e_i
1	1	-0.2599	-2.85
2	2	0.7401	-1.03
3	0.5	-0.7599	-8.87
4	8	6.7401	-0.18
5	0.0313	-1.2287	-1666
6	2048	2046	—

2.1 Graphical representation of a sequence

The idea of representing a sequence defined iteratively by a 'cobweb' diagram will probably be familiar. Figure 4 (overleaf) shows how the first sequence from the previous section is generated by moving horizontally from the curve

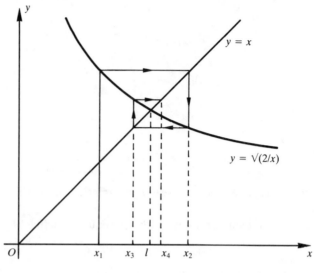

Figure 4

$y = \sqrt{(2/x)}$ to the line $y = x$, then vertically back to the curve. The iteration causes a spiral inwards to the point of intersection where $x = l$, the limit of the sequence.

Similar diagrams (Figure 5) show that the way a sequence converges depends upon the gradient of the curve close to the point of intersection.

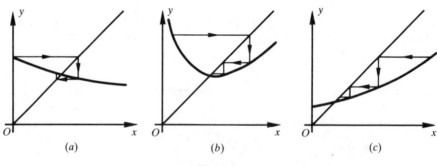

Figure 5

For Figure 4,

$$y = \sqrt{2}\, x^{-1/2} \quad \Rightarrow \quad \frac{dy}{dx} = -\frac{1}{\sqrt{2}} x^{-3/2} = -\tfrac{1}{2} \quad \text{when } x = 2^{1/3}.$$

Figure 6, which is an enlargement of part of Figure 4, shows the relevance of this.

$$AM = x_2 - l = e_2, \qquad LM = MB = l - x_3 = -e_3,$$

$$\Rightarrow \quad \text{gradient of curve at } L \approx -\frac{LM}{AM} = \frac{e_3}{e_2}.$$

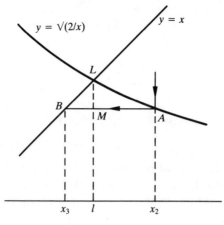

Figure 6

A similar diagram can be drawn for each stage of the sequence generation.

We find that $x_{i+1} = f(x_i)$ gives a convergent sequence, with a suitable starting value, if $-1 < f'(x) < 1$ at the point of intersection of $y = x$ with $y = f(x)$. The smaller the value of $|f'(x)|$ at this point, the more rapid will be the convergence.

Exercise 9B

1   With sketch graphs of $y = x$ and $y = 2/x^2$, illustrate the divergence of the second sequence of §2.

2   For the sequence defined by $x_1 = 2$, $x_{i+1} = 1 + 1/x_i$:
    (a) find the possible limit by solving $l = 1 + 1/l$;
    (b) draw up a table as in §2 to show the first six terms and their corresponding 'errors' (a computer program is simple to write and will be useful for later questions too);
    (c) draw a diagram like Figure 4;
    (d) calculate $f'(l)$.

3   Carry out investigations like question 2 for:
    (a) $x_1 = 1$, $x_{i+1} = \sqrt{(x_i + 1)}$
    (b) $x_1 = 1$, $x_{i+1} = \frac{1}{5}(x_i^2 + 3)$
    (c) $x_1 = 1$, $x_{i+1} = 3/(x_i - 4)$

4   Use your diagrams from questions 2 and 3 to discuss what would happen in each case if other values of x_1 were chosen.

5   Show that for the sequence in question 2, $e_{i+1}/e_i = -1/(lx_i)$, where $l = 1 + 1/l$. What light does this throw on the convergence process?

6   For each of the sequences in question 3, express e_{i+1}/e_i in a simple form.

7   Investigate numerically, graphically and algebraically the convergence of the sequences defined by:
    (a) $x_1 = 2$, $x_{i+1} = (x_i + 10)/(x_i + 1)$ (b) $x_1 = 2$, $x_{i+1} = \frac{1}{2}(x_i + 10/x_i)$

8   Investigate the sequences defined by:
    (a) $x_1 = 1$, $x_{i+1} = \frac{1}{4}(x_i^2 + 4)$ (b) $x_1 = 3$, $x_{i+1} = \frac{1}{4}(x_i^2 + 4)$

9 Investigate the sequences defined by:

(a) $x_1 = \frac{1}{2}$, $x_{i+1} = 1/(1 - x_i)$ (b) $x_1 = 1$, $x_{i+1} = 4/(2 - x_i)$
(c) $x_1 = 5$, $x_{i+1} = 2 - 2/x_i$

3. PROOF

Let us look more closely at the possible sequences resulting from $x_{i+1} = \frac{1}{5}(x_i^2 + 3)$ (see Exercise 9B, question 3(b)). You may have found that

$$e_{i+1}/e_i = \tfrac{1}{5}(x_i + l),$$

where l is the smaller root of the equation $l^2 - 5l + 3 = 0$, which is approximately 0.7. We can use this relation to *prove* that the sequence converges to l for all sensible positive starting values as well as giving some indication of the speed of convergence.

Firstly, we note that e_{i+1} will have the same sign as e_i. In other words, if we start above l, all members of the sequence will be greater than l; similarly, if $0 < x_1 < l$, then $x_n < l$ for all n.

If $x_1 > 5 - l$, $e_{i+1}/e_i > l$ and the terms of the error sequence increase; the sequence diverges, i.e. $x_n \to \infty$.

If $l < x_1 < 5 - l$, the error sequence tends to 0 ever more rapidly. With $x_1 = 1$ for example (as in Exercise 9B, question 3),

$$e_{i+1}/e_i = \tfrac{1}{5}(x_i + l) < 0.36 \quad \text{for all } i,$$

so we can calculate how many terms to take to guarantee some desired degree of accuracy. More generally, if $l < x_1 < 5 - l$, we can choose k such that $\frac{1}{5}(x_1 + l) < k < 1$. Then $e_{i+1} < ke_i$, giving $e_n < k^{n-1}e_1$. Hence $e_n \to 0$ and $x_n \to l$ as $n \to \infty$.

If $0 < x_1 < l$, $e_{i+1}/e_i < \frac{2}{5}l < 0.3$ for all i, and again convergence is proved.

3.1 Complex sequences

The observant reader will have noticed that the ideas of the last two sections have already been employed in an *ad hoc* manner with a sequence of complex numbers in the first section of Chapter 5. Look back at this example now.

If we write $e_i = z_i - l$, the points on an Argand diagram representing a sequence will progressively approach the limiting point if

$$|e_{i+1}| < k|e_i|,$$

where k is a real number for which $0 < k < 1$. This is just one way of proving convergence with complex numbers. Another is illustrated now.

Example 5
Investigate the convergence of the series

$$S_n = z - \frac{z^2}{2} + \frac{z^3}{3} - \ldots + (-1)^{n-1}\frac{z^n}{n} \quad \text{as } n \to \infty, \text{ if } |z| < 1.$$

Solution

In this case,
$$e_i = (-1)^i \left[\frac{z^{i+1}}{i+1} - \frac{z^{i+2}}{i+2} + \frac{z^{i+3}}{i+3} - \cdots \right]$$

and
$$|e_i| \leqslant |z|^i \left[\frac{|z|}{i+1} + \frac{|z|^2}{i+2} + \frac{|z|^3}{i+3} + \cdots \right]$$

At this stage we are using the result $|z_1 + z_2| \leqslant |z_1| + |z_2|$ extensively; note that all the signs on the right-hand side must be positive. The proof then follows similar lines to those in Chapter 4:

$$|e_i| < |z|^i [\, |z| + |z|^2 + |z|^3 + \cdots \,]$$

$$= |z|^i \times \frac{|z|}{1 - |z|}.$$

But $|z| < 1$, so $|z|^i \to 0$ as $i \to \infty$. Thus $|e_i| \to 0$, and S_i tends to a limit. $\qquad \square$

4. SECOND-ORDER CONVERGENCE

The iteration $x_{i+1} = \frac{1}{2}(x_i + 10/x_i)$ – see Exercise 9B, question 7 – is an example of Heron's method of finding square roots, in this case $\sqrt{10}$. The method, discovered 2000 years ago, is equivalent to the Newton–Raphson method applied to $x^2 - 10 = 0$, for

$$x_{i+1} = x_i - \frac{x_i^2 - 10}{2x_i} \quad \Rightarrow \quad x_{i+1} = \frac{1}{2}\left(x_i + \frac{10}{x_i} \right).$$

For this sequence,

$$x_{i+1} - \sqrt{10} = \frac{x_i^2 - 2\sqrt{10}\,x_i + 10}{2x_i} = \frac{(x_i - \sqrt{10})^2}{2x_i},$$

i.e.
$$e_{i+1} = \frac{e_i^2}{2x_i}. \qquad (1)$$

If $e_i = 0.1$ at some stage,
$$e_{i+1} \approx \frac{0.1^2}{2\sqrt{10}} < 0.002$$

and
$$e_{i+2} < \frac{0.002^2}{2\sqrt{10}} < 10^{-6}.$$

The existence of the square in (1) ensures extremely rapid convergence once we get well within range. This is an example of *second-order convergence*. Our previous examples, in which e_i appeared unsquared in expressions for e_{i+1}, represent first-order convergence.

Suppose we are misguided enough to carry out this iteration with $x_1 = 10$. Then we could compute the table overleaf.

i	x_i	e_i
1	10	6.84
2	5.5	2.34
3	3.65909091	0.497
4	3.19600508	3.37×10^{-2}
5	3.16246562	1.78×10^{-4}
6	3.16227766	4.66×10^{-9}

When relation (1) is written in the form $e_{i+1} = (e_i/2x_i)e_i$, we see that however large x_1 may be, the error is more than halved in each early stage (since $e_i < x_i$). From the time that the error becomes less than 1, the convergence is as rapid as we predicted above.

Also $f(x) = \frac{1}{2}(x + 10/x) \Rightarrow f'(x) = \frac{1}{2}(1 - 10/x^2) \Rightarrow f'(\sqrt{10}) = 0.$

Since the graph of $y = f(x)$ has zero gradient where it crosses $y = x$, we have ideal conditions for rapid convergence when considered from a geometrical standpoint (see Figure 7).

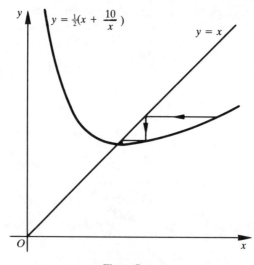

Figure 7

4.1 The Newton–Raphson method

We now show that the Newton–Raphson method always gives second-order convergence.

The formula for solving $f(x) = 0$ is

$$x_{i+1} = x_i - \frac{f(x_i)}{f'(x_i)}.$$

Now

$$y = x - \frac{f(x)}{f'(x)}$$

$$\Rightarrow \quad \frac{dy}{dx} = 1 - \frac{\{f'(x)\}^2 - f(x) f''(x)}{\{f'(x)\}^2}$$

$$= 0 \quad \text{when } f(x) = 0.$$

This shows that the zero gradient in our last example was no fluke.
  Furthermore,

$$x_{i+1} = x_i - \frac{f(x_i)}{f'(x_i)}$$

$$\Rightarrow \quad x_{i+1} - l = (x_i - l) - \frac{f(x_i)}{f'(x_i)}$$

$$\Rightarrow \quad e_{i+1} = e_i - \frac{f(l + e_i)}{f'(l + e_i)} = \frac{e_i f'(l + e_i) - f(l + e_i)}{f'(l + e_i)}$$

$$\Rightarrow \quad e_{i+1} = \frac{e_i\{f'(l) + e_i f''(l) + \dots\} - \{f(l) + e_i f'(l) + \frac{1}{2}e_i^2 f''(l) + \dots\}}{f'(l + e_i)}$$

When $f(l) = 0$, the leading term on the right-hand side contains e_i^2, the hallmark of second-order convergence.

Exercise 9C

1   In Exercise 9B, questions 2 and 5, it transpired that for $x_{i+1} = 1 + 1/x_i$, then $e_{i+1}/e_i = -1/(lx_i)$ and $l \approx 1.62$. Show that the sequence converges to l for all possible positive values of x_1.

2   Prove that $x_1 = 2$, $x_{i+1} = (x_i + 10)/(x_i + 1)$ gives first-order convergence.

3   Given that $x_{i+1} = x_i(2 - x_i)$, prove that the sequence converges if $0 < x_1 < 2$. What is the order of convergence?

4   Prove that $x_1 = 2$, $x_{i+1} = x_i - (x_i^3 - 6)/(3x_i^2)$ gives second-order convergence.

5   For the Fibonacci sequence defined by

$$u_1 = 1, \quad u_2 = 1, \quad u_{i+1} = u_i + u_{i-1},$$

write down $u_3, u_4, u_5, \dots, u_{10}$.
  Prove that the ratio of consecutive terms, $v_i = u_i/u_{i-1}$, tends to $\frac{1}{2}(1 + \sqrt{5})$ as $i \to \infty$.

6   Given $z_1 = 1$, $z_{i+1} = \frac{1}{2}(1 + j) + j/z_i$, find z_2 and z_3 and show the corresponding points on an Argand diagram. Prove that the sequence has first-order convergence with limit $1 + j$.

7   Given $z_1 = 1$, $z_{i+1} = \frac{1}{2}z_i + j/z_i$, find z_2 and z_3. Show that the sequence has second-order convergence with limit $1 + j$.

8   Given that $x_1 = 1$, $x_{i+1} = (x_i + 2)/(x_i + 1)$, show that

$$x_{i+1}^2 - 2 = -(x_i^2 - 2)/(x_i + 1)^2.$$

Discuss the convergence of the sequence.

9   The sequence $\{x_n\}$ is defined by

$$x_{n+1} = \frac{x_n + 5}{x_n + 1}, \qquad n = 1, 2, 3, \ldots$$

By setting $x_n = e_n + \sqrt{5}$, or otherwise, prove that if $x_1 > \sqrt{5}$, then $x_{2n+1} > \sqrt{5}$, and $x_{2n} < \sqrt{5}$, for all n.

Prove further that, in this case:

(a) $x_{2n+1} < x_{2n-1}$ (b) $x_{2n} > x_{2n-2}$ (c) $x_n \to \sqrt{5}$ as $n \to \infty$ [SMP]

10   A sequence $\{u_n\}$ is defined by the relation $u_{n+1} = 1 + 2/u_n$, with $u_1 = 1$. Calculate u_6 as a rational number and guess the value of the limit p of the sequence as n tends to infinity.

Prove

$$\frac{u_{n+2} - p}{u_n - p} = \frac{1}{u_n + p}$$

and hence prove that $u_n \to p$ as $n \to \infty$.

Construct a flow diagram to find the smallest value of n for which $|u_n - p| < 10^{-10}$.   [SMP]

11   Investigate the sequences defined by:

(a) $z_1 = 1, \quad z_{i+1} = 1 - \frac{1}{2}jz_i$ (b) $z_1 = 1, \quad z_{i+1} = 1 + j/z_i$

Miscellaneous exercise 9

1   (a) Show that $\displaystyle\int_0^\infty \frac{1}{1 + x^3}\,dx$, exists, and that its value is less than 1.5.

(b) Can you demonstrate a smaller upper bound for the integral?

(c) Write the integrand in the form

$$\frac{A}{1 + x} + \frac{Bx + C}{\frac{3}{4} + (\frac{1}{2} - x)^2}$$

and hence show that the integral has the value $2\pi/(3\sqrt{3})$.

2   In Exercise 9A, question 4(e), it was shown that $I = \displaystyle\int_0^{\pi/2} \ln \sin x \, dx$ exists.

(a) By putting $x = \frac{1}{2}\pi - u$, show that $\displaystyle\int_0^{\pi/2} \ln \cos x \, dx = I$.

(b) By putting $x = \frac{1}{2}v$, show that $\displaystyle\int_0^{\pi/2} \ln \sin 2x \, dx = I$.

(c) Deduce from (a) and (b) that $I = -\frac{1}{2}\pi \ln 2$.

3   Explain what it means to say that the integral $\displaystyle\int_0^1 x^{-1/2} \, dx$ *converges* (despite the fact that $x^{-1/2}$ tends to infinity as x tends to zero). Explain also what is meant by $\displaystyle\int_1^\infty x^{-\alpha} \, dx$, and state the range of values of α for which this integral converges.

Sketch graphs (on the same diagram) which show clearly why

$$\frac{2}{\pi}\theta \leqslant \sin \theta \leqslant \theta \quad \text{for } 0 \leqslant \theta \leqslant \tfrac{1}{2}\pi.$$

Deduce that $\displaystyle\int_0^{\pi/2} \frac{d\theta}{\sqrt{(\sin \theta)}}$

converges and lies between $(2\pi)^{1/2}$ and π.

Make the substitution $x = -\ln \sin \theta$ to show that

$$\int_0^\infty \frac{dx}{\sqrt{(\sinh x)}}$$

converges and find bounds between which it lies. [SMP]

4 Evaluate the integral $\int_0^\infty \frac{e^{-t}\,dt}{(1 + e^{-2t})^{1/2}}$,

showing that it exists. [SMP]

5 Prove that $\sinh^{-1} x = \ln\{x + \sqrt{(1 + x^2)}\}$.

Show that $\sinh^{-1} x - \ln x \to \ln 2 \quad \text{as } x \to \infty$.

Hence prove that the integral

$$\int_1^\infty \left\{ \frac{1}{(1 + x^2)^{1/2}} - \frac{1}{x} \right\} dx$$

exists, and find its value. [SMP]

6 Sketch a graph of the function $y = \tanh x$ which shows clearly the behaviour of y at $x = 0$ and as $x \to \infty$.

Show by using the substitution $x = \sinh u$ or otherwise that

$$\int_0^\infty \frac{dx}{(1 + x^2)^{3/2}} = 1.$$

Let $\qquad I_n = \int_0^\infty \frac{dx}{(1 + x^2)^{n + 1/2}} \qquad (n = 1, 2, 3, \ldots).$

By integrating by parts show that

$$I_n = (2n + 1)(I_n - I_{n+1}).$$

Hence obtain the reduction formula

$$I_n = \frac{2n - 2}{2n - 1} I_{n-1}.$$

Deduce that the integral $\qquad \int_0^\infty \frac{dx}{(1 + x^2)^{7/2}} = 1$

exists, and find its value. [SMP]

7 Write down the first four terms of the power series of the function $(1 + x)^{-1}$, for small x.

The periodic function $f(x)$ is defined by the equations

$$f(x) = \begin{cases} 1 & (0 \leqslant x < a) \\ -1 & (a \leqslant x < 2a) \end{cases}$$

$$f(x + 2a) = f(x) \qquad \text{for all } x.$$

Sketch the graph of $f(x)$ for $0 \leqslant x \leqslant 6a$. Show that

$$\int_0^{2na} e^{-kx} f(x)\,dx = \frac{1}{k}(1 - 2e^{-ak} + 2e^{-2ak} - \ldots - 2e^{-(2n-1)ak} + e^{-2nak}).$$

Deduce that if $k > 0$ the integral $\int_0^\infty e^{-kx} f(x)\,dx$ is convergent. (*Hint*: put $e^{-ak} = t$.)

Show further that this integral then has the value

$$\int_0^\infty e^{-kx} f(x)\,dx = \frac{1}{k}\tanh\frac{ak}{2}.$$ [SMP]

8   Given that $x_n = \dfrac{x_{n-1} + x_{n-2}}{2}$ for $n \geqslant 3$,

and $x_1 = 1$, $x_2 = 2$, prove, by induction or otherwise, that $x_n - x_{n-1} = (-\tfrac{1}{2})^{n-2}$. Obtain x_n in terms of n, and hence find the limit of the sequence.

9   If $x_1, x_2 > 0$ and $x_n = \sqrt{(x_{n-1}x_{n-2})}$ for $n \geqslant 3$,

prove that $x_n \to x_1^{1/3} x_2^{2/3}$ as $n \to \infty$.

10   A sequence $\{u_n\}$ is defined by

$$u_1 = \sin x \qquad (0 < x < \tfrac{1}{2}\pi),$$
$$u_2 = \sin u_1, \quad u_3 = \sin u_2, \quad \dots, \quad u_{r+1} = \sin(u_r), \quad \dots.$$

Prove that the terms of the sequence are positive and decreasing, and find $\lim_{n \to \infty} u_n$. Prove also that $u_n > (2/\pi)^n x$.
     [SMP]

11   Investigate sequences defined by $x_{i+1} = c - c/x_i$ for different starting values when (a) $c = 1$, (b) $c = 2$, (c) $c = 3$, and (d) $c = 4$.

12   Repeat question 11 for $x_{i+1} = cx_i(1 - x_i)$, taking starting values between 0 and 1.

13   Let $\{z_n\}$ be the sequence of numbers defined by

$$z_{n+1} = \frac{z_n + a}{z_n + 1}, \qquad z_1 = 1.$$

Assuming that z_n has a limit Z, prove that $Z = \pm\sqrt{a}$.

In the case where $a = j$, plot the complex numbers z_1, z_2, z_3 on a diagram, using a scale of 10 cm = 1 unit.

Evaluate $\sqrt{j}$, which is that complex number in the first quadrant whose square is j, and plot it on your diagram.   [SMP]

14   (a) Evaluate $z_n = (1 + j/n)^n$ for $n = 1, 2, 3, 4, 5$. Does the sequence appear to be converging?

(b) Use a binomial expansion to show that $z_n \approx e^j = \cos 1 + j \sin 1$ for large n.

15   Let S_n equal the sum of n terms of the series $z - \dfrac{z^2}{2} + \dfrac{z^3}{3} - \dots$

(a) Show that the sequence converges when $z = j$ and find the limit. Is this the same as $\ln(1 + z)$ when $z = j$?

(b) Repeat (a) for $z = \tfrac{1}{2}j$.

SUMMARY

Improper integrals

When $\displaystyle\int_a^b f(x)\,\mathrm{d}x$ is not represented by the area of a bounded region, either because (i) $a = -\infty$ or $b = \infty$ or both, or because (ii) the integrand tends to infinity at some point in the domain, care must be taken to establish the convergence of the integral. This usually involves a limiting process.

Limits of sequences

The convergence of a sequence of real numbers $\{x_n\}$ can be investigated

    (i) numerically, in which case a short computer program is helpful,

    (ii) geometrically, by means of diagrams like Figure 5, or

    (iii) algebraically, by reference to a relation connecting e_{i+1} and e_i, where $e_i = x_i - l$ and l is the anticipated limit.

The convergence of a sequence of complex numbers can be probed by either of methods (i) and (iii) above.

10

Differential equations and substitution

1. INTRODUCTION

The most useful general method for tackling integrals which cannot be dealt with by inspection is the method of substitution, the idea being to transform a complicated integral into a much simpler one. Examples 1 and 2 show how a substitution may also help to solve a differential equation.

Example 1
Solve $\dot{x} + 5x = e^{-5t}$.

Solution
Here the CF is $A\,e^{-5t}$, so it is no use trying to find a PI of the form $K\,e^{-5t}$. Since e^{-5t} is clearly a key ingredient of the solution, we write $x = u\,e^{-5t}$ and eliminate x in favour of the new variable u, remembering to treat u as a function of t.

The product rule gives $\qquad \dot{x} = \dot{u}\,e^{-5t} - 5u\,e^{-5t}$

and hence
$$\dot{x} + 5x = e^{-5t}$$
$$\Rightarrow \quad (\dot{u}\,e^{-5t} - 5u\,e^{-5t}) + 5u\,e^{-5t} = e^{-5t}$$
$$\Rightarrow \qquad\qquad \dot{u}\,e^{-5t} = e^{-5t}$$
$$\Rightarrow \qquad\qquad \dot{u} = 1$$
$$\Rightarrow \qquad\qquad u = t + A$$
$$\Rightarrow \qquad\qquad x = t\,e^{-5t} + A\,e^{-5t} \qquad\qquad \square$$

Example 2
Use the substitution $x = u \cos 10t$ to simplify and solve the simple harmonic motion equation $\ddot{x} + 100x = 0$.

Solution

Now
$$x = u \cos 10t$$
$$\Rightarrow \quad \dot{x} = \dot{u} \cos 10t - 10u \sin 10t$$
$$\Rightarrow \quad \ddot{x} = \ddot{u} \cos 10t - 10\dot{u} \sin 10t - 10\dot{u} \sin 10t - 100u \cos 10t.$$

The differential equation now becomes
$$\ddot{u} \cos 10t - 20\dot{u}\, sin\, 10t = 0,$$

giving $\qquad \dfrac{\ddot{u}}{\dot{u}} = 20 \tan 10t$

$$\Rightarrow \quad \ln \dot{u} = 2 \ln \sec 10t + A$$
$$\Rightarrow \quad \dot{u} = B \sec^2 10t, \qquad\qquad \text{where } B = e^A$$
$$\Rightarrow \quad u = \frac{B}{10} \tan 10t + C$$
$$\Rightarrow \quad x = D \sin 10t + C \cos 10t, \quad \text{where } D = B/10$$

This confirms the result of Chapter 7 without using complex numbers. □

1.1 Review of the PI, CF method

For the differential equation $\ddot{x} + 5\dot{x} + 6x = 18t + 21$, we can easily obtain $x = 3t + 1$ as a PI. How do we justify our standard method for proceeding from here to the general solution?

We shall use the substitution $x = u + (3t + 1)$, for which $\dot{x} = \dot{u} + 3$ and $\ddot{x} = \ddot{u}$. The equation becomes

$$\ddot{u} + 5(\dot{u} + 3) + 6(u + 3t + 1) = 18t + 21,$$

which simplifies to $\qquad\qquad \ddot{u} + 5\dot{u} + 6u = 0.$

The solution of this, $A\,e^{-2t} + B\,e^{-3t}$, is by definition the CF of the original differential equation. So all possible solutions are given by adding the CF to the PI.

This approach is successful whenever the differential equation is *linear*, so that the contributions from the PI do not become entwined with the terms involving u and its derivatives. Example 3 shows how it fails if the equation is not linear.

Example 3
Show that $x = 3 + 1/t$ is a PI for $\dot{x} + x^2 = 9 + 6/t$. Find whether the substitution $x = u + (3 + 1/t)$ helps to find other solutions.

Solution
$$x = 3 + 1/t \;\Rightarrow\; \dot{x} = -1/t^2 \;\Rightarrow\; \dot{x} + x^2 = -1/t^2 + (3 + 1/t)^2$$
$$= 9 + 6/t.$$

$x = u + 3 + 1/t$ transforms $\dot{x} + x^2 = 9 + 6/t$ to

$$(\dot{u} - 1/t^2) + u^2 + 2u(3 + 1/t) + (3 + 1/t)^2 = 9 + 6t,$$

i.e. $\qquad\qquad \dot{u} + u^2 + 2u(3 + 1/t) = 0.$

This is worse than the original equation! □

Exercise 10A

1   Use the substitution $x = u\,e^{-4t}$ to simplify:
   (a) $\dot{x} + 4x = 10\,e^t$ (b) $\dot{x} + 4x = 3\,e^{-4t}$
   Obtain the complete solution in each case. Comment.

2 (a) For the equation $\ddot{x} + 5\dot{x} + 6x = 0$, show that the substitution $x = u\,e^{-2t}$ gives $\ddot{u} + \dot{u} = 0$, and so $\dot{u} + u = A$. Hence show that $x = A\,e^{-2t} + B\,e^{-3t}$.
   (b) Show that the substitution $x = v\,e^{-3t}$ leads to the same solution.

3 Apply the substitution $x = u\,e^{-3t}$ to obtain a differential equation in u from the equation $\ddot{x} + 6\dot{x} + 10x = 0$. Comment on your result.

4 Obtain the general solution of $\ddot{x} + 6\dot{x} + 9x = 0$ by using the substitution $x = u\,e^{-3t}$.

5 Obtain PIs for the following equations by first using the substitutions given:
   (a) $\ddot{x} + 5\dot{x} + 6x = e^{-2t}$, $\quad x = u\,e^{-2t}$
   (b) $\ddot{x} + 100x = \cos 10t$, $\quad x = u \sin 10t$
   (c) $\ddot{x} + 6\dot{x} + 9x = 4\,e^{-3t}$, $\quad x = u\,e^{-3t}$
   (d) $\ddot{x} + 6\dot{x} + 9x = (4t + 5)\,e^{-3t}$, $\quad x = u\,e^{-3t}$

6 Demonstrate that the substitution $x = u \cos 10t$ is *not* helpful in solving $\ddot{x} + 100x = \cos 10t$.

2. CRITICAL DAMPING

We shall now tie up some of the loose ends from Chapter 7. We showed that $\ddot{x} + 6\dot{x} + 16x = 0$ gives an oscillation whose amplitude decreases exponentially, while $\ddot{x} + 10\dot{x} + 16x = 0$ is over-damped and there are no oscillations. The first example has an auxiliary equation with complex roots, while the second has an auxiliary equation with two distinct real roots.

$\ddot{x} + 8\dot{x} + 16x = 0$ has an auxiliary equation with equal roots, and represents what we call *critical damping*. Clearly $x = A\,e^{-4t}$ is a solution, but we are looking for two independent solutions, giving a general solution with two arbitrary constants.

You can quickly show that the substitution $x = u\,e^{-4t}$ reduces the equation to

$$\ddot{u}\,e^{-4t} = 0, \quad \text{i.e.} \quad \ddot{u} = 0.$$

Integration is now easy: $\quad \dot{u} = B \;\Rightarrow\; u = A + Bt.$

The final solution is $\quad x = A\,e^{-4t} + Bt\,e^{-4t}.$

In control mechanisms, it is desirable to 'damp down' the motion quickly. For $\ddot{x} + 6\dot{x} + 16x = 0$, the solution is

$$x = e^{-3t}\,(A \cos \sqrt{7}\,t + B \sin \sqrt{7}\,t),$$

and the factor e^{-3t} decides how quickly the oscillations die away.

For $\ddot{x} + 10\dot{x} + 16x = 0$, the solution is $x = A\,e^{-2t} + B\,e^{-8t}$, and the e^{-2t} term is dominant when t is large.

For $\ddot{x} + 8\dot{x} + 16x = 0$, the solution is $x = A\,e^{-4t} + Bt\,e^{-4t}$, and the factor e^{-4t} ensures rapid attenuation in spite of the extra factor of t in the second term.

To sum up, $\ddot{x} + a\dot{x} + bx = 0$, with b fixed gives:
   (i) damped oscillations if $a^2 < 4b$ (the *larger* the value of a, the quicker the motion dies away);
   (ii) over-damping if $a^2 > 4b$ (the *smaller* the value of a, the quicker the motion dies away);
   (iii) critical damping if $a^2 = 4b$ (this gives the most rapid attenuation).

3. RESONANCE

Example 4

Solve $\ddot{x} + 9x = 5 \cos 4t$.

Solution
This describes an undamped oscillatory system with a periodic forcing term. The solution is easily found to be

$$x = -\tfrac{5}{7} \cos 4t + A \cos 3t + B \sin 3t,$$

a linear combination of an oscillation with the *natural frequency* of the system and an oscillation with the *forcing frequency*.   □

Example 5
Solve $\ddot{x} + 9x = 5 \cos 3t$.

Solution
Here the forcing frequency is exactly equal to the natural frequency. The CF is still $A \cos 3t + B \sin 3t$, but the PI must take a more complicated form.

To find this, we might try the substitution $x = u \cos 3t$ or alternatively $x = u \sin 3t$. You may have discovered, with surprise perhaps, that the latter is effective but the former is not.

$$x = u \sin 3t \quad \Rightarrow \quad \dot{x} = \dot{u} \sin 3t + 3u \cos 3t$$
$$\Rightarrow \quad \ddot{x} = \ddot{u} \sin 3t + 6\dot{u} \cos 3t - 9u \sin 3t.$$

So $\qquad \ddot{x} + 9x = 5 \cos 3t \quad \Rightarrow \quad \ddot{u} \sin 3t + 6\dot{u} \cos 3t = 5 \cos 3t.$

We now see that $u = \tfrac{5}{6}t$ is a solution, since it gives $\dot{u} = \tfrac{5}{6}$ and $\ddot{u} = 0$. It follows that $x = \tfrac{5}{6}t \sin 3t$ is a PI.

The complete solution is

$$x = \tfrac{5}{6}t \sin 3t + A \cos 3t + B \sin 3t;$$

Figure 1 (overleaf) is a sketch of a solution curve.   □

This is the phenomenon called *resonance*. It is used in the design of oscillators (e.g. for radio transmitters) and signal generators. The forcing voltage is supplied by *positive feedback*, part of the output of the circuit being channelled back to provide an input of precisely the required frequency and phase. Mechanical resonance is also well known, though the designer's aim is usually to avoid resonance if possible. Bridges and tall buildings may have natural frequencies, and disaster can result if high winds produce oscillatory forces with these frequencies. Less seriously, the body of a car may vibrate at certain speeds, and the shock absorbers may have the opposite of the desired effect if a series of ruts is met and the spacing of the ruts is unfortunate; this would be like giving a pendulum a helping tap every time it passes the vertical position. Sound waves provide other examples of resonance, the most startling being that a wine glass can be shattered by playing a musical note of the right frequency.

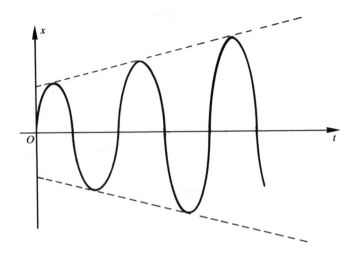

Figure 1

Example 6
Solve $\ddot{x} + 9x = \cos 2.8t$.

Solution
In this example, the forcing frequency is close to the resonant frequency. If $\dot{x} = 0$ and $x = 0$ when $t = 0$, the solution is

$$x = 0.86 \cos 2.8t - 0.86 \cos 3t,$$

and this can be written $x = 1.72 \sin 0.1t \sin 2.9t$.

The solution can be regarded as an oscillation with frequency $2.9/(2\pi)$ with slowly changing amplitude $1.72 \sin 0.1t$. The rhythmic fluctuations of amplitude are called *beats*, and are of notable use in tuning pianos and organs (see Figure 2).

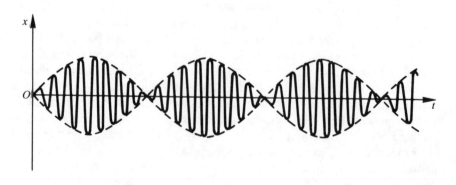

Figure 2

4. EXAMPLES SUMMARISED

It is worth collecting together all our evidence from the text examples and from Exercise 10A.

$$\ddot{x} + 6\dot{x} + 9x = 0 \qquad \Rightarrow \qquad x = A\,e^{-3t} + Bt\,e^{-3t}$$
$$\dot{x} + 4x = 3\,e^{-4t} \quad \text{has PI} \quad x = 3t\,e^{-4t}$$
$$\ddot{x} + 5\dot{x} + 6x = e^{-2t} \quad \text{has PI} \quad x = t\,e^{-2t}$$
$$\ddot{x} + 9x = 5\cos 3t \quad \text{has PI} \quad x = \tfrac{5}{6}t\sin 3t$$
$$\ddot{x} + 6\dot{x} + 9x = 4\,e^{-3t} \quad \text{has PI} \quad x = 2t^2\,e^{-3t}$$

The message seems to be this: if difficulties are encountered in obtaining either a CF or a PI, try introducing an extra factor of t.

Example 7
Solve $\ddot{x} + 7\dot{x} + 12x = 5\,e^{-4t}$.

Solution
The CF is $A\,e^{-3t} + B\,e^{-4t}$, since $n^2 + 7n + 12 = 0 \Rightarrow n = -3$ or -4. We can find a PI by putting $x = u\,e^{-4t}$, but it will be quicker to put $x = Kt\,e^{-4t}$ and try to find a suitable value of K.

$$x = Kt\,e^{-4t}$$
$$\Rightarrow \dot{x} = -4Kt\,e^{-4t} + K\,e^{-4t}$$
$$\Rightarrow \ddot{x} = 16Kt\,e^{-4t} - 8K\,e^{-4t}.$$

$\ddot{x} + 7\dot{x} + 12x = 5\,e^{-4t}$ is satisfied if

$$(16Kt - 8K) + 7(-4Kt + K) + 12Kt = 5, \quad \text{i.e. if } K = -5.$$

The complete solution is

$$x = -5t\,e^{-4t} + A\,e^{-3t} + B\,e^{-4t}. \qquad \square$$

Exercise 10B

1 Find the complete solutions of:
   (a) $\ddot{x} + 4\dot{x} + 3x = 10$ (b) $\ddot{x} + 4\dot{x} + 5x = 10$
   (c) $\ddot{x} + 4\dot{x} + 4x = 10$ (d) $\ddot{x} + 4\dot{x} + 4x = 10t + 12$

2 If $x = Kt\,e^{-2t}$, find expressions for $\dot{x}$ and $\ddot{x}$. Hence find PIs for:
   (a) $\dot{x} + 2x = 12\,e^{-2t}$ (b) $\ddot{x} + 7\dot{x} + 10x = 12\,e^{-2t}$
   (c) $\ddot{x} + \dot{x} - 2x = 12\,e^{-2t}$
   Find the complete solution in each case.

3 Find K if $x = Kt^2\,e^{-2t}$ is a solution of $\ddot{x} + 4\dot{x} + 4x = 5\,e^{-2t}$.

4 Find a PI for $\ddot{x} + x = 3\,e^{jt}$, then write down a PI for $\ddot{x} + x = 3\,e^{-jt}$. Hence obtain a PI for $\ddot{x} + x = 6\cos t$, using the results $\cos t = \tfrac{1}{2}(e^{jt} + e^{-jt})$ and $\sin t = \dfrac{1}{2j}(e^{jt} - e^{-jt})$.

5 Find the complete solutions of:
   (a) $\ddot{x} + 6\dot{x} + 5x = e^{-2t}$ (b) $\ddot{x} + 6\dot{x} + 5x = 2\,e^{-t}$
   (c) $\ddot{x} + 10\dot{x} + 25x = 2\,e^{-t}$ (d) $\ddot{x} + 10\dot{x} + 25x = e^{-5t}$
   (e) $\ddot{x} + 6\dot{x} + 5x = 3\sin t$ (f) $\ddot{x} + x = 3\sin t$

6   If $\dot{x} + 3x = 10\,e^{-3t}$ and $x = 1$ when $t = 0$, find (a) an expression for x in terms of t, and (b) the maximum value of x for positive t. Sketch the solution curve.

7   Repeat question 6 given that:
  (a) $4\ddot{x} + 5\dot{x} + x = 0$ and $x = 1$, $\dot{x} = 2$ when $t = 0$
  (b) $4\ddot{x} + 4\dot{x} + x = 0$ and $x = 1$, $\dot{x} = 2$ when $t = 0$.

5. DIFFERENTIAL EQUATIONS ASSOCIATED WITH ELECTRICAL CIRCUITS

Mention has already been made of electrical circuits containing inductance (L), resistance (R) and capacitance (C).

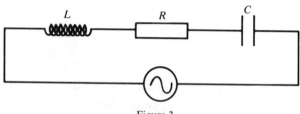

Figure 3

In Figure 3, the applied voltage v will equal the sum of the voltages across the three elements, which the laws of physics give as $L\dfrac{di}{dt}$, Ri and q/C. Since the current i is dq/dt (the rate of charge on the capacitor), we can differentiate the equation

$$L\frac{di}{dt} + Ri + \frac{q}{C} = v$$

to give

$$L\frac{d^2i}{dt^2} + R\frac{di}{dt} + \frac{1}{C}i = \frac{dv}{dt}.$$

With an alternating voltage, we should have the kind of differential equation considered extensively in this chapter and in Chapter 7. For example, $\ddot{x} + 4\dot{x} + 13x = \sin 2t$ was found to have the complete solution

$$x = \tfrac{9}{145}\sin 2t - \tfrac{8}{145}\cos 2t + e^{-2t}(A\sin 3t + B\cos 3t).$$

The terms of the CF are *transient* – they become negligibly small after the first few seconds – and we are left with the PI – the *steady-state solution*. It comes as no surprise that an alternating voltage should cause an alternating current of the same frequency. The analysis requires both a sine and cosine term in the PI, and this means that the current is out of phase with the applied voltage.

5.1 Resonant frequency with damped simple harmonic motion

A slight generalisation of the example in the last section is

$$\ddot{x} + 4\dot{x} + 13x = \sin \omega t.$$

We shall only concern ourselves with the PI, and this will be of the form $x = H \sin \omega t + K \cos \omega t$, representing a wave with amplitude $\sqrt{(H^2 + K^2)}$.

Substituting in the equation gives

$$(13 - \omega^2)H - 4\omega K = 1, \qquad 4\omega H + (13 - \omega^2)K = 0.$$

Squaring and adding, we get

$$[(13 - \omega^2)^2 + 16\omega^2](H^2 + K^2) = 1,$$

so the amplitude is
$$\frac{1}{\sqrt{[(13 - \omega^2)^2 + 16\omega^2]}}.$$

Treating this as a function of ω, we get a graph like Figure 4, with a maximum point at the resonant frequency. Introducing a damping term is seen to result in the amplitude being finite at the resonant frequency, but it can, nevertheless, be very large if the damping constant is sufficiently small. This is the situation desired in a radio oscillator, when a graph with a high narrow peak is obtained.

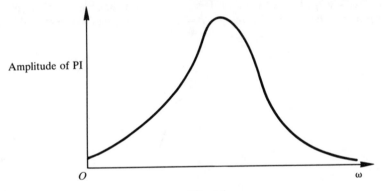

Figure 4

Exercise 10C

1 (a) Show that in the example of §5.1, the resonant frequency is found by minimising $\omega^4 - 10\omega^2 + 169$.

   (b) Show that the resonant frequency is $\sqrt{5}/(2\pi)$.

2 (a) If $\ddot{x} + a\dot{x} + bx = 0$, express the natural frequency in terms of a and b.

   (b) If $\ddot{x} + a\dot{x} + bx = c \sin \omega t$, express the resonant frequency in terms of a and b, and show that this is approximately equal to the natural frequency if a is small.

3 An alternating e.m.f. $E_0 \sin \omega t$ is applied to a circuit with inductance L, resistance R and capacitance C, all in series. The current i then satisfies the differential equation

$$L\frac{d^2i}{dt^2} + R\frac{di}{dt} + \frac{1}{C}i = E_0\omega \cos \omega t.$$

Show that the steady-state current has amplitude

$$A = \frac{E_0}{\sqrt{\left[\left(\dfrac{1}{\omega C} - \omega L\right)^2 + R^2\right]}}$$

We wish to investigate the way the magnitude of the current depends upon ω.

(a) For what value of ω is $(1/(\omega C) - \omega L)^2$ a minimum?

(b) What is the corresponding value of the current amplitude?

(c) If $f(\omega) = 1/(\omega C) - \omega L$, and $f(\alpha) = 0$, find $f'(\alpha)$, and sketch the graph of $f(\omega)$ for positive ω.

(d) Find the resonant frequency of the circuit if $R = 2\,\Omega$, $L = 3$ H, $C = 5\,\mu$F.

(e) With the same axes, sketch the graph of A against ω in the following cases:

(i) $R = 2\,\Omega$, $L = 3$ H, $C = 5\,\mu$F.

(ii) $R = 5\,\Omega$, $L = 3$ H, $C = 5\,\mu$F.

(iii) $R = 2\,\Omega$, $L = 6$ H, $C = 2.5\,\mu$F.

4   The humped graph of question 3(e) demonstrates the use of the circuit for selecting one frequency while rejecting others. Explain how to choose values for the components to give a highly selective circuit tuned to a given frequency. Is there any limit to the selectivity obtainable?

5   If the response (the amplitude of the steady-state current given an applied voltage of fixed amplitude) at ω_1 and ω_2 is half the response at the resonant frequency Ω, show that $\omega_1 - \omega_2 \approx \sqrt{3}R/L$ (see Figure 5). Does this suggest that the selectivity of the circuit is independent of C? Express $\omega_1 - \omega_2$ as a percentage of Ω using the data of question 3(e).

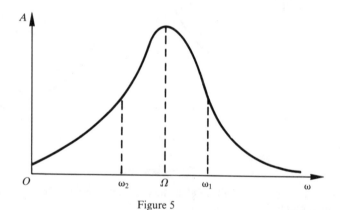

Figure 5

6   A tall metal chimney is capable of oscillating in a wind. Only the upper part of the chimney is exposed to the wind, and a steady force F_0 applied at the top of the chimney produces a deflection Z_0 there. The mass of the upper part of the chimney is m_0.

The oscillation produced by the wind is modelled by the equation

$$m_0 \ddot{z} + \frac{F_0 z}{Z_0} = F,$$

where z is the actual displacement and F the wind force. It is assumed that $F = cV^2 \cos(kVt)$, where c and k are constants, and V is the wind speed.

At what wind speed does resonance occur? For this wind speed, solve the equation with initial conditions that the chimney is at rest and undeflected when $t = 0$.[SMP]

7   Two cars are travelling in the fast lane of the M4, G being the gap between them. The

one behind is trying to maintain the gap G at a constant value equal to l, but is finding it difficult to achieve this exactly, owing to the various lags in the responses of himself and his car to the changes in the speed of the car in front. In fact, G is varying with time t according to the equation

$$\alpha^2 \frac{d^2G}{dt^2} + G = l(1 + \alpha \sin t), \quad \text{where } \alpha \text{ is a constant.}$$

Explain why
(a) disaster threatens if the value of α is too close to unity;
(b) the progress is probably very uncomfortable for passengers if α is small.

[SMP]

Miscellaneous exercise 10

1   The function y satisfies the differential equation

$$x^2 \frac{dy}{dx} + 2y^2 = 3xy$$

for $x > 0$, and $y = 1$ when $x = 1$. Use the substitution $y = 1/z$ to reduce the equation to

$$x^2 \frac{dz}{dx} + 3xz = 2.$$

Hence find y.   [SMP]

2   Use the substitution $y = 1/z^{1/2}$ to reduce

$$x^3 \frac{dy}{dx} = 2x^2y + y^3$$

to a linear equation for z, and solve this equation for $x \geqslant 0$ given that $y = \frac{1}{2}$ when $x = 1$. Sketch the graph of your solution.   [SMP]

3   Use the substitution $y = \ln u$ to reduce the equation

$$\frac{dy}{dx} = e^{-y} + x^{-1}, \qquad x > 0,$$

to the linear equation $x \dfrac{du}{dx} = u + x$. Hence solve for y, given that $y = 1$ when $x = 1$. Show that this particular solution is valid only for $x > e^{-e}$.   [SMP]

4   If $y = f(x)$ and $x = e^t$, show that $\dfrac{dy}{dx} = e^{-t} \dfrac{dy}{dt}$ and find an expression for $\dfrac{d^2y}{dx^2}$ in terms of t, $\dfrac{dy}{dt}$ and $\dfrac{d^2y}{dt^2}$.

By using the substitution $x = e^t$, or otherwise, find the general solution (for $x > 0$) of the differential equation

$$x^2 \frac{d^2y}{dx^2} + 3x \frac{dy}{dx} - 3y = 0.$$ [SMP]

5   An electrical circuit consists of a battery of e.m.f. E, a switch, an inductance L, a resistance R and a capacitance C, all in series. Initially the capacitor is discharged. Find a differential equation for the current i at time t after the switch is closed, and the critical value of R (in terms of L and C) if the current is to be non-oscillatory.

6

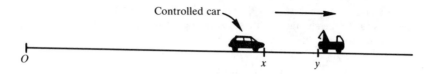

Figure 6

An automatic control of a car is being tested on a motorway. The front of the controlled car is a distance x from O along the motorway, and the back of the vehicle in front is a distance y from O (as in Figure 6). The control on an earlier model set the relation between the acceleration $\ddot{x}$ and the gap $y - x$ so that

$$\ddot{x} = \alpha\,(y - x - L)/L,$$

where α and L are constants. If the version now being tested also makes an allowance for the speed $\dot{y}$ of the vehicle in front, and further increases the acceleration by a term which is proportional to the excess of $\dot{y}$ over a standard speed V, show that its motion satisfies the equation

$$\ddot{x} + \alpha\frac{x}{L} = \alpha\frac{y}{L} + \beta\frac{\dot{y}}{V} - (\alpha + \beta),$$

where β is a constant. Verify that this equation has a steady-state solution in which both vehicles move with a constant speed V separated by a constant gap L.

(a) In a safety test, both vehicles are moving at a steady speed V with gap L when the leading vehicle stops dead. Taking $\alpha = \beta$, find an expression for the separation of the vehicles at a time t later. Deduce that a crash is avoided only if $\alpha > V^2/3L$.

(b) In another test, the leading vehicle moves with a speed which fluctuates about the steady-state value, so that

$$y = L + Vt + b\cos\omega t,$$

where b is a small constant length. Simplify the equation for x to the form

$$\ddot{x} + \frac{\alpha x}{L} = f(t).$$

What value of ω is likely to cause problems with the control? Give reasons for your answer.   [SMP]

7 (a) Solve the equation $\dfrac{dw}{dx} + \dfrac{3w}{x} = 0$ for $x > 0$.

(b) Solve the equation $\dfrac{dy}{dx} + y^2 = 1$ for $x > 0$ (A)

with the condition $y = 0$ when $x = 1$.
    Verify that the equation

$$\frac{dy}{dx} + y^2 = \frac{3}{4x^2} \quad \text{for } x > 0   \tag{B}$$

has two solutions of the form $y = c/x$, neither of which satisfies $y = 0$ when $x = 1$.

Make the substitution
$$y = \frac{1}{z}\frac{dz}{dx} + \frac{3}{2x}$$

in equation (B) to obtain an equation for z, and solve this equation. Hence find a solution of equation (B) which has $y = 0$ when $x = 1$.   [SMP]

8   (a) The functions x and y satisfy the simultaneous differential equations

$$\left.\begin{array}{l} \dot{x} = y - 4x \\ \dot{y} = -4x \end{array}\right\}$$

and the boundary conditions $x = 0$ and $y = 1$ when $t = 0$. Show, by differentiating the first equation, that

$$\ddot{x} + 4\dot{x} + 4x = 0.$$

Hence solve for both x and y in terms of t.

  (b) The functions u and v satisfy the simultaneous differential equations

$$\left.\begin{array}{l} \dot{u} = -u^2 - uv - \tfrac{1}{2}v^2 \\ \dot{v} = -\tfrac{1}{2}v^2 - uv \end{array}\right\}$$

for $t \geq 0$, and the boundary conditions $u = 0$ and $v = 1$ when $t = 0$. Let $w = u + v$. Find a differential equation for w and show that

$$w = (1 + t)^{-1}.$$

Hence show that $\dot{v} + (1 + t)^{-1}v = \tfrac{1}{2}v^2.$

By making the substitution $v = 1/z$, find a linear equation for z, and solve it so as to find v and u in terms of t for $t < e^2 - 1$.

SUMMARY

Critical damping
$\ddot{x} + a\dot{x} + bx = 0$ represents critical damping if $a^2 = 4b$. Then the auxiliary equation $n^2 + an + b = 0$ has a repeated root, α say, and the general solution is $A\,e^{\alpha t} + Bt\,e^{\alpha t}$.

Finding the particular integrals
If the complementary function of $\ddot{x} + a\dot{x} + bx = f(t)$ contains a term of the same kind as $f(t)$, one should try to find a PI with an extra factor of t. (For examples, see §4.)

Electrical circuits
Currents in electrical circuits containing inductance, capacitance and resistance satisfy second-order linear differential equations with constant coefficients.

11

Complex-number geometry

Since addition of complex numbers corresponds to addition of vectors, in the Argand diagram, all proofs in vector geometry can be expressed just as well in terms of complex numbers. But since multiplication of complex numbers corresponds to rotation and enlargement, we have altogether a tool with considerable scope. We will demonstrate this now, starting with the simplest ideas.

1. LINES AND CIRCLES

The locus in the complex plane satisfying the equation $|z| = 5$ is clearly a circle with centre the origin and radius 5.

In much the same way as we have seen that the graph of $(y - 4) = (x - 3)^2$ is the parabola $y = x^2$ translated by $\begin{bmatrix} 3 \\ 4 \end{bmatrix}$, so $|z - a| = 5$ is the image of the previous circle after the translation $z \mapsto z + a$. Here a can be any complex number.

Another way of looking at this is to interpret $z - a$ as the displacement from A (the point corresponding to a) to P (the point representing z). This is like the vector statement $\mathbf{AB} = \mathbf{b} - \mathbf{a}$. Thus $|z - a| = 5$ is the locus of points P at a distance 5 from the fixed point A (see Figure 1).

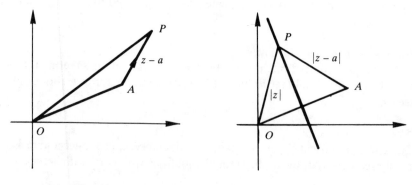

Figure 1   Figure 2

In the same way, we can interpret $|z| = |z - a|$ as the set of points such that $OP = AP$, i.e. the perpendicular bisector of OA (see Figure 2); also $|z - a| = |z - b|$ describes the perpendicular bisector of AB, where B is the point representing the complex number b.

136

Any circle or line has a simple equation involving the modulus function. Less usefully, we can employ the argument function to describe loci; $\arg(z - a)$ gives the direction of AP in Figure 1. Figures 3, 4 and 5 illustrate simple cases. Notice that the line segment OA in Figure 5 is *not* part of the locus; for a point on this segment, the vectors OP and AP are in opposite directions.

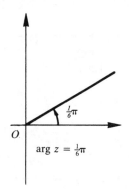

$\arg z = \frac{1}{6}\pi$

Figure 3

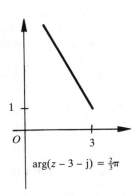

$\arg(z - 3 - j) = \frac{2}{3}\pi$

Figure 4

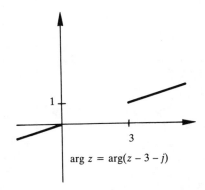

$\arg z = \arg(z - 3 - j)$

Figure 5

1.1 Simple transformations

Translation $z \mapsto z + (2 + 4j)$ is obviously a translation, as we have observed.

Rotation $z \mapsto e^{j\theta} z$ is a rotation through an angle θ about the origin.

Enlargement $z \mapsto kz$ is an enlargement, scale factor k, centre the origin, if k is real.

Reflection in the real axis $z \mapsto z^*$ maps $a + bj$ onto $a - bj$, and so reflects in the x-axis.

1.2 Combined transformations

Example 1
Identify the single transformations given by:
(a) $z \mapsto jz - 2$ (b) $z \mapsto jz^*$

Solution
(a) The 90° rotation $z \mapsto jz$ is followed by the translation $z \mapsto z - 2$. We have a 90° rotation about some centre to be determined.

Now the invariant point of the transformation is given by $z = jz - 2$; that is,

$$z = \frac{-2}{1-j} = \frac{-2(1+j)}{(1-j)(1+j)} = -1 - j.$$

As a check, we can note that under $z \mapsto jz - 2$,

$$-j \mapsto j(-j) - 2 = -1, \quad -1 \mapsto -j - 2, \quad -2 - j \mapsto -1 - 2j,$$
$$-1 - 2j \mapsto -j,$$

i.e. $A \mapsto B \mapsto C \mapsto D \mapsto A$ in Figure 6.

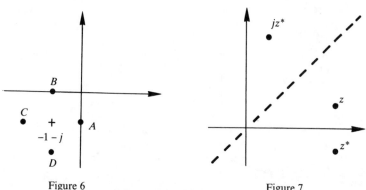

Figure 6   Figure 7

(b) $z \mapsto jz^*$ is the reflection $z \mapsto z^*$ followed by the 90° rotation $z \mapsto jz$. Since $a + bj \mapsto a - bj \mapsto b + aj$, we have a reflection in the line $y = x$; that is, $|z - 1| = |z - j|$. See Figure 7.   □

We can write a wide range of plane transformations as combinations of the basic ones from §1.1.

Exercise 11A

1   Illustrate the loci in the complex plane given by these equations:
(a) $|z + 2| = 3$ (b) $|z - 2 - 5j| = 1$ (c) $|z + 3 - 4j| = 5$
(d) $|z + 2| = |z - 2 - 5j|$ (e) $|z - 2 - 5j| = |z + 3 - 4j|$
(f) $\arg(z + 2) = \tfrac{1}{4}\pi$ (g) $\arg(z + 2) = \arg(z - 2 - 5j)$

2 Show the images of the flag in Figure 8 under each of the following transformations:

(a) $z \mapsto z + 3 + 4j$ (b) $z \mapsto (3 + 4j)z$

(c) $z \mapsto (3 + 4j)z^*$ (d) $z \mapsto (3 + 4j)z + (2 - 6j)$

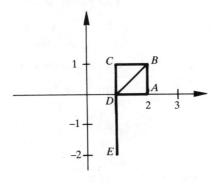

Figure 8

3 Notice that **OB′** = 5**OB** in question 2(c). Deduce that this transformation is a reflection in the line OB together with an enlargement with centre O.

4 What is the invariant point in question 2(d)? Describe the transformation.

5 Find the equations of the images of the line $|z| = |z - 2 + 3j|$ and the circle $|z - 1 + 5j| = 2$ under (a) the translation $z \mapsto z + 4 + j$, (b) the reflection $z \mapsto z^*$, and (c) the rotation $z \mapsto -jz$.

2. FURTHER LOCI

2.1 Expression in parametric form

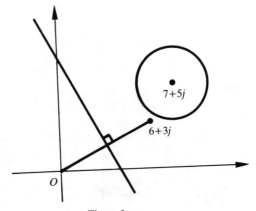

Figure 9

Note that the line $|z| = |z - 6 - 3j|$ (see Figure 9) can be written in terms of a real parameter t as

$$z = (3 + 1\tfrac{1}{2}j) + t(-1 + 2j)$$

and the circle $|z - 7 - 5j| = 2$ as

$$z = 7 + 5j + 2\,e^{j\alpha}.$$

Similarly, the lines $x = 2$ and $y = 9$ can be written as

$$z = 2 + tj \quad \text{and} \quad z = t + 9j.$$

2.2 Cartesian representation of loci

Writing $z = x + yj$, we can convert equations of loci into Cartesian form. For example,

$$
\begin{aligned}
& |z| = |z - 6 - 3j| \\
\Rightarrow\quad & |x + yj| = |x + yj - 6 - 3j| \\
\Rightarrow\quad & |x + yj| = |(x - 6) + (y - 3)j| \\
\Rightarrow\quad & \sqrt{(x^2 + y^2)} = \sqrt{[(x - 6)^2 + (y - 3)^2]} \\
\Rightarrow\quad & x^2 + y^2 = x^2 - 12x + 36 + y^2 - 6y + 9 \\
\Rightarrow\quad & 4x + 2y = 15.
\end{aligned}
$$

This is, as we expected, the line through $(3, 1\tfrac{1}{2})$ with gradient -2.

2.3 Apollonius circles

At first sight, $2|z| = |z - 6 - 3j|$ is similar to the example in §2.2. But if we interpret this as $2OP = AP$ and construct points on the locus using compasses with a table of values starting as follows, we get the points of Figure 10, and joining them up gives a closed loop which looks as if it might be a circle.

OP	2.5	3	3.5	4
AP	5	6	7	8

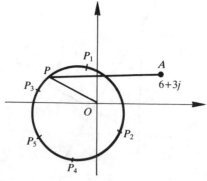

Figure 10

The algebraic method gives

$$2\sqrt{(x^2 + y^2)} = \sqrt{[(x - 6)^2 + (y - 3)^2]}$$

$$4(x^2 + y^2) = x^2 - 12x + 36 + y^2 - 6y + 9$$
$$x^2 + y^2 + 4x + 2y = 15$$
$$(x + 2)^2 + (y + 1)^2 = 20.$$

This is indeed a circle: one with centre $(-2, -1)$ and radius $\sqrt{20}$.

$AP = k\,BP$ or $|z - a| = k\,|z - b|$ gives a circle whenever $k \neq 1$. The locus was known 2000 years ago, long before complex numbers were invented.

Example 2
Interpret the locus $|z - j| = 3\,|z - 4 - 9j|$.

Solution

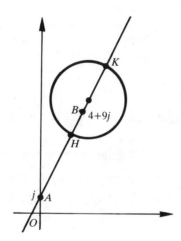

Figure 11

See Figure 11. If H and K divide AB internally and externally in the ratio $3 : 1$, then the locus is a circle on HK as diameter.

H is $3 + 7j$ and K is $6 + 13j$, so the circle has centre $4\frac{1}{2} + 10j$ and radius $\sqrt{[(1\frac{1}{2})^2 + 3^2]} = \sqrt{11\frac{1}{4}}$.   □

Example 3
Interpret the locus $|z + 3| + |z - 3| = 10$.

Solution
See Figure 12 (overleaf). This is the locus of P such that $AP + PB = 10$. It can be constructed from a table of values and it may well be familiar that it is an ellipse with A and B as foci. The algebraic proof is rather lengthy:

$$|x + yj + 3| + |x + yj - 3| = 10$$
$$\Rightarrow \qquad \sqrt{[(x + 3)^2 + y^2]} = 10 - \sqrt{[(x - 3)^2 + y^2]}$$
$$\Rightarrow \qquad (x + 3)^2 + y^2 = 100 - 20\sqrt{[(x - 3)^2 + y^2]} + (x - 3)^2 + y^2$$
$$\Rightarrow \qquad 20\sqrt{[(x - 3)^2 + y^2]} = 100 - 12x$$
$$\Rightarrow \qquad 400(x^2 - 6x + 9 + y^2) = 10\,000 - 2400x + 144x^2$$
$$\Rightarrow \qquad 256x^2 + 400y^2 = 6400$$
$$\Rightarrow \qquad 16x^2 + 25y^2 = 400.$$

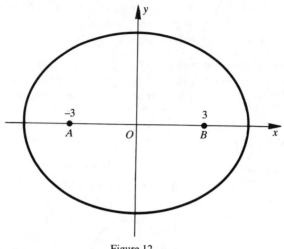

Figure 12

This is an ellipse cutting the axes at (5, 0), (− 5, 0), (0, 4) and (0, − 4).   ☐

Exercise 11B

1   Express in parametric form each part of Figure 13. For example, the 'tail' is

$$z = 30 + t(-5 + 3j), \qquad 0 \leqslant t \leqslant 2.$$

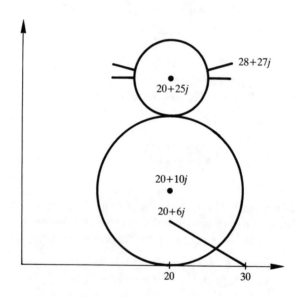

Figure 13

2   Express in Cartesian form:
   (a) $|z| = 5$ (b) $|z - 2 - j| = 3$
   (c) $|z| = |z - 2 - j|$ (d) $3|z| = |z - 2 - j|$

3 Find the centre and radius of the following circles:

(a) $|z| = 2|z - 3j|$ (b) $\left| \dfrac{z + 4}{z - 8j} \right| = \tfrac{1}{3}$ (c) $\left| 2 - \dfrac{5}{z} \right| = 1$

4 Interpret the following loci:

(a) $z + z^* = 6$ (b) $z - z^* = 4j$ (c) $z^* - z = 4j$ (d) $zz^* = 4$

5 Show that $|z + 3| - |z - 3| = 4 \Rightarrow 5x^2 - 4y^2 = 20.$

Sketch the locus, and explain the restriction $x > 0$.

3. THE TRANSFORMATION $z \mapsto 1/z$

This is a transformation with unexpected properties. If $z = [r, \theta]$, then $1/z = [1/r, -\theta]$, so all points outside the circle $|z| = 1$ map onto points inside the circle, and vice versa (see Figure 14).

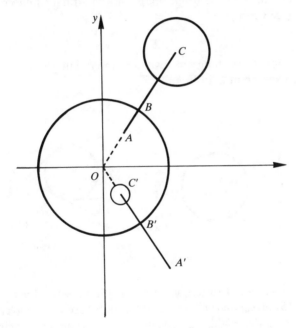

Figure 14

The half-line of which ABC is a part maps onto its reflection in the x-axis. But does the circle centre C map onto a circle? If $w = 1/z$, then

$$|z - c| = k \quad \text{is equivalent to} \quad \left| \frac{1}{w} - c \right| = k$$

$$\Rightarrow \quad \left| \frac{1 - cw}{w} \right| = k$$

$$\Rightarrow \quad |c| \times \left| \frac{1}{c} - w \right| = k|w|$$

$$\Rightarrow \qquad \left| w - \frac{1}{c} \right| = \frac{k}{|c|} \times |w|$$

This is an Apollonius circle unless $k = |c|$. In this special case, the circle passes through the origin and the image is a straight line. Since the function is self-inverse, a straight line not through the origin maps onto a circle through the origin.

To sum up, under the transformation $z \mapsto 1/z$:

(i) the origin has no image;

(ii) for the circle $|z| = 1$, the transformation is equivalent to reflection in the real axis;

(iii) a circle radius k with centre the origin maps onto a circle radius $1/k$ with the same centre;

(iv) the half-line $\theta = \alpha$ maps onto the half-line $\theta = -\alpha$;

(v) a circle through the origin maps onto a straight line not through the origin, and vice versa.

Example 4

How many circles touching the two non-intersecting circles can be drawn through the fixed point O in Figure 15?

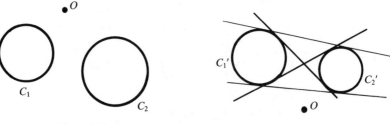

Figure 15   Figure 16

Solution

Figure 16 shows Figure 15 after the transformation $z \mapsto 1/z$. Every circle through O in Figure 15 corresponds to a straight line in Figure 16. If two circles touch in the first diagram, that is they have a single point in common, their images must clearly touch. So we want to know how many straight lines in Figure 16 touch both the circles C_1' and C_2'. There are four.

It might have been the case that O lay on one (or even two) of the common tangents in Figure 16. This corresponds to O lying on one (or two) of the common tangents in Figure 15. The number of possible circles is then reduced accordingly. □

3.1 Inversion

$z \mapsto k^2/z^*$ is similar to the transformation of the last section, but now the circle $|z| = k$ is invariant and each point of the plane has the same argument as its

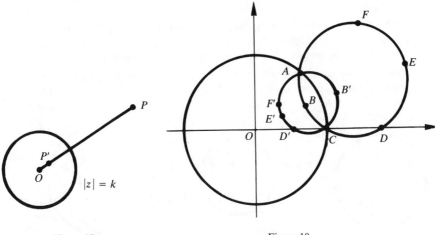

Figure 17   Figure 18

image (see Figure 17). Figure 18 shows six points on a circle and their positions on the image circle.

Exercise 11C

1 Find the images of A, B, C, D, E and F in Figure 19 under the transformation $z \mapsto 4/z^*$ and draw a diagram showing the images of all the lines, and also the circle.

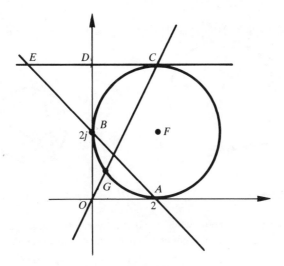

Figure 19

2 Find the image of the Apollonius circle $|z - 4j| = 4|z + 1|$ under the transformation $z \mapsto 1/z$ by writing $z = 1/w$ and simplifying.

3 Repeat question 2 for the circle $|z - 3 + 4j| = 5$.

4 Under an inversion, what is special about the images of two parallel lines not through the origin?

5 (*a*) Show that the image of the centre of a circle not through the origin is not the centre of the image circle.

   (*b*) Sketch the images of a circle through *O* and its centre.

6 Under an inversion, centre *O*, do the points inside the circles of Figure 20 map onto points inside or outside the image circles?

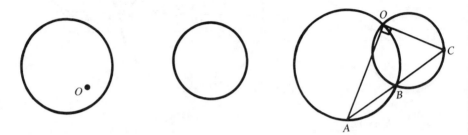

Figure 20   Figure 21

7 In Figure 21, *B* is any point on the hypotenuse of the right-angled triangle *OAC*. Show the images of all parts of the diagram under an inversion centre *O*, and hence show that the circles *OAB* and *OBC* intersect at right angles.

8 In Figure 22, the circles intersect at *O* and *P*, and the common tangents are *AB* and *CD*. Show by inversion that the circles *ABO* and *CDO* touch at *O*.

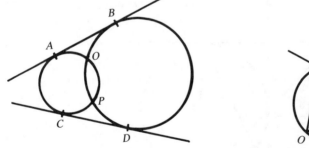

Figure 22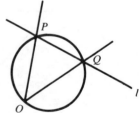

                                             Figure 23

9 In Figure 23, *O* is a fixed point, while *P* and *Q* are variable points on a fixed line *l* such that the angle *POQ* is always equal to *α*, a fixed angle. Show that all the circles *OPQ* touch a fixed circle.

4. GEOMETRY USING COMPLEX NUMBERS

As indicated earlier, geometrical properties of complex numbers can be used to explore properties of configurations.

Example 5
Triangle ABC in Figure 24 is equilateral. Given that A and B represent $1 + j$ and $3 + 2j$, find the complex number represented by C.

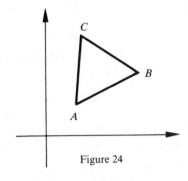

Figure 24

Solution
In this example and the next, and in Exercise 11D, we write a, b etc. as the complex numbers represented by A, B, etc.

Then
$$\mathbf{AB} = b - a \quad \text{and} \quad \mathbf{AC} = c - a.$$

A rotation of $\frac{1}{3}\pi$ about A maps B onto C, so
$$c - a = e^{\pi j/3}(b - a).$$

It follows that
$$c = 1 + j + (\tfrac{1}{2} + \tfrac{1}{2}\sqrt{3}\,j)(2 + j)$$
$$= (2 - \tfrac{1}{2}\sqrt{3}) + (1\tfrac{1}{2} + \sqrt{3})j. \qquad \square$$

Example 6
In Figure 25, A and B are the fixed points representing $z = a$ and $z = -a$ (where a is real). P is a variable point in the half-plane $y \geqslant 0$, and $APTS$ and $BPUV$ are squares. Draw the diagram with three different choices for P, and join V to S each time. What do you notice?

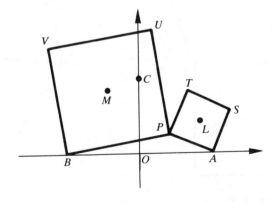

Figure 25

Solution
BP corresponds to $p + a$, so **BV** corresponds to $j(p + a)$.

Hence
$$v = -a + j(p + a).$$

Similarly, $s = a - j(p - a).$

It follows that $\frac{1}{2}v + \frac{1}{2}s = ja,$

meaning that whatever point P is chosen, the mid-point of VS is C, on the y-axis with $OC = OA = OB$.   □

Exercise 11D

1   The square $ABCD$ is drawn with A and B representing $1 + j$ and $6 + 2j$. Find the complex numbers represented by C and D. (There are two possible answers.)

2   Show that the triangle with vertices $a + b$, $a + b\omega$ and $a + b\omega^2$ is equilateral, where $\omega = e^{2\pi j/3}$, one of the cube roots of 1.

3   The triangle ABC is equilateral. Show that $a + b\omega + c\omega^2 = 0$ or $a + b\omega^2 + c\omega = 0$.

4   Show that if the centres of the squares in Figure 25 are L and M, then

$$l = \tfrac{1}{2}(1 + j)a + \tfrac{1}{2}(1 - j)p,$$

and find a similar expression for m. Deduce that OL is equal and perpendicular to OM.

5   In Figure 26, ABC is any triangle and P, Q and R are the centres of squares drawn outwardly on the three sides. Show that $PQ = CR$ and that PQ is perpendicular to CR.

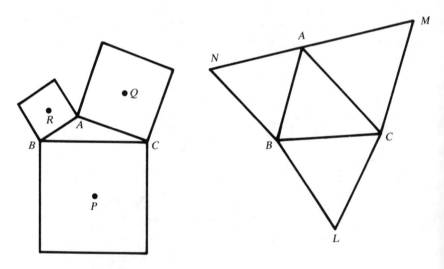

Figure 26   Figure 27

6   In Figure 27, equilateral triangles are drawn outwards from the sides of triangle ABC. Show that $AL = BM = CN$.

7   (*Napoleon's theorem*) Show that the centres of the equilateral triangles in Figure 27 themselves form an equilateral triangle, whatever the shape of triangle ABC.

Miscellaneous exercise 11

1 Show that the points representing $2 + j$, $5 + 5j$ and $6 + 4j$ are three vertices of a rhombus, and find the fourth vertex.

2 Show that it is impossible to choose three points in a plane with integer coordinates to form the vertices of an equilateral triangle.

3 Show that a rotation of 90° about (1, 0) may be written as $z \mapsto 1 + j(z - 1)$. Write a 90° rotation about (0, 2) in a similar way and deduce that the first rotation followed by the second is equivalent to a 180° rotation about some fixed point. Find the coordinates of this point.

4 As in question 3, find the invariant point of the single transformation that is equivalent to a 90° rotation about (1, 0) followed by a 180° rotation about (0, 2).

5 Show that the centre C of the single rotation equivalent to a 120° rotation about B followed by a 120° rotation about A is given by

$$a + b\omega + c\omega^2 = 0.$$

6 Show that $\arg(z - a) - \arg(z - b) = \alpha$ in Figure 28.

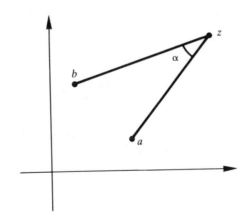

Figure 28

Sketch the loci:
(a) $\arg(z - 3 - j) - \arg(z) = \frac{1}{2}\pi$ (b) $\arg(z - 3 - j) - \arg(z) = -\frac{1}{2}\pi$
(c) $\arg(z - 3 - j) - \arg(z) = \pi$

7 Interpret the loci:
(a) $|z| + |z - 6 - 8j| = 10$ (b) $|z| - |z - 6 - 8j| = 10$
(c) $\arg(z) = \arg(z - 6 - 8j)$ (d) $\arg(z) = \arg(z - 6 - 8j) + \pi$

8 Interpret the loci:
(a) $|z| = |z - 6 - 8j|$ (b) $|z| = 4|z - 6 - 8j|$
(c) $|z| + |z - 6 - 8j| = 12$ (d) $\arg(z) - \arg(z - 6 - 8j) = \frac{1}{3}\pi$
(e) $\arg(z) + \arg(z - 6 - 8j) = 0$

9　Show that if $z = a + bj$, then $zz^* = a^2 + b^2 = |z|^2$. Writing

$$2|z| = |z - 6 - 3j| \quad \text{as} \quad 4zz^* = (z - 6 - 3j)(z^* - 6 + 3j),$$

show that the equation can be written as

$$(z + 2 + j)(z^* + 2 - j) = 20 \quad \text{or} \quad |z + 2 + j| = \sqrt{20}.$$

Compare with the working of §2.3.

10　Using the method of question 9, show that $|z + 8| = 2|z + 2|$ may be reduced to $zz^* = 16$. Describe the locus. Investigate in this way the locus $|z - j| = 3|z - 4 - 9j|$.

11　The origin is at the circumcentre of triangle ABC.
(a) Explain why the point representing $b + c$ forms a rhombus with O, B and C.
(b) Show that the point representing $a + b + c$ lies on the altitude of the triangle through A.
(c) Explain why $a + b + c$ represents the orthocentre of the triangle.

12　Squares are drawn outwardly on the sides AB, BC, CD and DA of a quadrilateral. The centres of these squares are P, Q, R and S respectively. Show that $PR = QS$ and that PR is perpendicular to QS.

SUMMARY

Transformations

$z \mapsto z + a$ is a translation.

$z \mapsto e^{j\theta} z$ is a rotation about the origin.

$z \mapsto kz$ is an enlargement, centre the origin, if k is real.

$z \mapsto z^*$ is a reflection in the x-axis.

$z \mapsto 1/z^*$ is an inversion. Under an inversion, lines through O map onto themselves; other lines map onto circles through O, and vice versa; circles not through O map onto circles.

Loci

$|z - a| = k$ is a circle, centre a, radius k.

$|z - a| = |z - b|$ is a line, the perpendicular bisector of AB.

$|z - a| = k|z - b|$ is an Apollonius circle if $k \neq 1$.

$\arg(z - a) = \alpha$ is the half-line through a in the direction α.

12

Partial differentiation

So far we have restricted our differentiation and integration to functions of one variable. For example, we have set up simple business models expressing the manufacturing costs of a factory as a function of the output, and the demand for a product as a function of the price. In practice, life is much more complicated: demand depends upon advertising, rival companies' pricing and marketing policies, weather maybe, seasonal factors, and so on.

We shall now look at functions of two variables. This will indicate how to proceed with functions of three or more variables.

With functions of a single variable, we find it helpful to refer to graphs – curves drawn in two dimensions. The corresponding geometrical entity for a function of two variables is a *surface* in *three dimensions*. To help us visualise such a surface, we commonly draw contour maps.

As a simple example, take the volume of a cylinder, $V = \pi r^2 h$. Figure 1 shows combinations of r and h for which $V = 10, 20, 30$ cm^3. Imagine that the rh-plane is horizontal and that there is a vertical V-axis. The surface contains the r- and h-axes at zero height and rises as we move away from the axes.

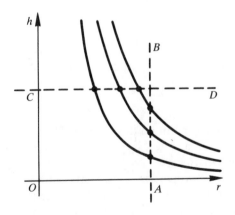

Figure 1

The contours are produced by taking horizontal sections through the surface. Now think about all the cylinders with radius 3 cm, represented by the section through the surface made by the plane $r = 3$ (indicated by AB on the contour map). Since V is a linear function of h ($V = 9\pi h$), the section is a straight line, and the intervals along AB cut off by the contours are equal in length.

151

On the other hand, for fixed h, V is a quadratic function of R, and the section through the surface indicated by CD is parabolic. As one moves to the right along CD, the contours get closer together, showing that the section through the surface is becoming steeper.

1. TANGENT PLANES

A straightforward exercise with functions of one variable is to find the equation of the tangent at a point to the corresponding graph. In three dimensions, we find the *tangent plane* to a surface.

Example 1

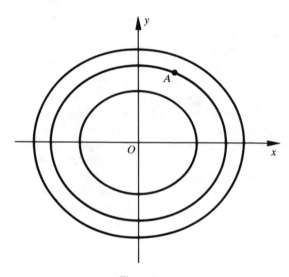

Figure 2

Figure 2 shows contours of the paraboloid $z = 3x^2 + 4y^2 + 1$. Find the equation of the tangent plane at $(1, 2, 20)$.

Solution
Check that A $(1, 2, 20)$ is a point on this surface. The section in the plane $y = 2$ has equation $z = 3x^2 + 17$, and at A its gradient is 6. Similarly, the section in the plane $x = 1$ has gradient 16 at A.

A plane with these properties must have an equation of the form $z = 6x + 16y + k$. For it to pass through $(1, 2, 20)$, we require $20 = 6 + 32 + k$, i.e. $k = -18$. So the tangent plane to $z = 3x^2 + 4y^2 + 1$ at $(1, 2, 20)$ has equation $z = 6x + 16y - 18$. □

1.1 Partial derivatives

We use the notation $\dfrac{\partial z}{\partial x}$ for the derivative of z with respect to x when y is kept constant, and this is called a *partial derivative*.

Thus $\qquad\qquad\qquad z = 3x^2 + 4y^2 + 1$

$$\Rightarrow \quad \frac{\partial z}{\partial x} = 6x \quad \text{and} \quad \frac{\partial z}{\partial y} = 8y$$

$$\Rightarrow \quad \frac{\partial z}{\partial x} = 6 \quad \text{and} \quad \frac{\partial z}{\partial y} = 16 \quad \text{at } (1, 2, 20).$$

Example 2

Find the equation of the tangent plane to

$$z = 2x^2 - 3xy + 5y^2 - 16 \quad \text{at } (3, 2, 4).$$

Solution

$$\frac{\partial z}{\partial x} = 4x - 3y \quad \text{and} \quad \frac{\partial z}{\partial y} = -3x + 10y,$$

so when $x = 3$ and $y = 2$,

$$\frac{\partial z}{\partial x} = 6 \quad \text{and} \quad \frac{\partial z}{\partial y} = 11.$$

The tangent plane is $z = 6x + 11y + k$, where $4 = 18 + 22 + k$, so $k = -36$. $\square$

Exercise 12A

1 Find the equations of the tangent planes to the following surfaces at the given points:
   (a) $z = 5x^2 - y^2$, at $(2, 4, 4)$ (b) $z = \sqrt{x} + \sqrt{y}$, at $(4, 1, 3)$
   (c) $z = x^2 + xy + y^3$, at $(3, -1, 5)$ (d) $z = x/y$, at $(6, 2, 3)$

2 Give expressions for the partial derivatives $\dfrac{\partial z}{\partial x}$ and $\dfrac{\partial z}{\partial y}$ if:
   (a) $z = \sin(x + 5y)$ (b) $z = x^p y^q$ (c) $z = y/(x^2 + y^2)$
   (d) $z = \tan^{-1}(y/x)$

3 After a stone has been dropped into a pond, the height of the water surface (z) depends on the time after the stone enters the water (t) and the distance from the point of impact (r). Sketch graphs illustrating the variation of z with t for constant r, and of z with r for a given t. Describe the significance of $\dfrac{\partial z}{\partial t}$ and $\dfrac{\partial z}{\partial r}$.

4 The lift L on an aircraft depends on its speed v and the density ρ of the air. What are measured by $\dfrac{\partial L}{\partial v}$ and $\dfrac{\partial L}{\partial \rho}$?

5 Second partial derivatives are defined in the obvious way. Find $\dfrac{\partial^2 z}{\partial x^2}$ and $\dfrac{\partial^2 z}{\partial y^2}$ for each of the surfaces in question 1.

6 (a) For $z = x^3 + 2xy^2 + y^3$, complete the following table:

x	y	z	$\dfrac{\partial z}{\partial x}$	$\dfrac{\partial z}{\partial y}$
3	1			
3.2	1			
3	1.1			
3.2	1.1			

Explain how your entries are connected.

(b) Find the values of $\dfrac{\partial^2 z}{\partial x^2}$ and $\dfrac{\partial^2 z}{\partial y^2}$ for the function in (a) when $x = 3$ and $y = 1$,

and also of $\dfrac{\partial^2 z}{\partial x\,\partial y}$ $\left(\text{defined as } \dfrac{\partial}{\partial x}\left(\dfrac{\partial z}{\partial y}\right)\right)$ and $\dfrac{\partial^2 z}{\partial y\,\partial x}$. Show the connections between

these and your entries in the last two columns of the table.

7 Repeat question 6 for a surface of your own choice.

8 (a) Interpret $\dfrac{\partial^2 z}{\partial x\,\partial y}$ and $\dfrac{\partial^2 z}{\partial y\,\partial x}$ in terms of the gradients of sections through a surface.

(b) If $A\,(x, y, z)$ and $B\,(x + \delta x, y + \delta y, z + \delta z)$ lie on the surface, explain (with reference to questions 6 and 7) why you would expect

$$\delta z \approx \frac{\partial z}{\partial x}\,\delta x + \frac{\partial z}{\partial y}\,\delta y, \quad \text{where } \frac{\partial z}{\partial x} \text{ and } \frac{\partial z}{\partial y} \text{ are evaluated at } A.$$

2. TANGENTS AND TANGENT PLANES; INCREMENT NOTATION

The fact that Q and R are very close in Figure 3 if the increment δx is small is expressed by the statement

$$\delta y \approx \frac{\mathrm{d}y}{\mathrm{d}x}\,\delta x. \tag{1}$$

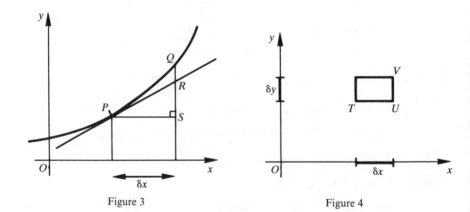

Figure 3   Figure 4

In just the same way, in three dimensions we find that

$$\delta z \approx \frac{\partial z}{\partial x}\,\delta x + \frac{\partial z}{\partial y}\,\delta y. \tag{2}$$

In (1), the gradient $\dfrac{\mathrm{d}y}{\mathrm{d}x}$ is understood to be that at P. Similarly in (2), when we move from T to U in the domain, the z-value on the surface increases by approximately $\dfrac{\partial z}{\partial x}\,\delta x$, the partial derivative being evaluated for the point corresponding to T. If we then move in the domain from U to V, there is a further increase in z, approximately equal to $\dfrac{\partial z}{\partial y}\,\delta y$. Here the partial derivative should strictly be evaluated at U, but for well-behaved functions this will not be very different from its value at T. So altogether the increment in z when x is increased by δx and y by δy satisfies

$$\delta z \approx \frac{\partial z}{\partial x}\,\delta x + \frac{\partial z}{\partial y}\,\delta y.$$

2.1 Small errors

Example 3
The radius and height of a cylinder are measured as 4.0 cm and 10.0 cm, but these measurements may be up to 0.1 cm in error. Estimate the maximum possible error in the volume calculated from these measurements.

Solution
Since $V = \pi r^2 h$, $\qquad \dfrac{\partial V}{\partial r} = 2\pi rh \quad \text{and} \quad \dfrac{\partial V}{\partial h} = \pi r^2.$

Now $$\delta V \approx \frac{\partial V}{\partial r}\,\delta r + \frac{\partial V}{\partial h}\,\delta h$$

gives
$$\begin{aligned}
\delta V &\approx 80\pi\,\delta r + 16\pi\,\delta h \\
&= 9.6\pi \qquad \text{when } \delta r = \delta h = 0.1 \\
&= 30.2 \text{ cm}^3 \quad \text{(to 3 SF)}.
\end{aligned}$$

Of course, it is as easy to calculate that

$$\begin{array}{lll}
r = 4.0, & h = 10.0 & \Rightarrow \quad V = 502.7 \\
r = 4.1, & h = 10.1 & \Rightarrow \quad V = 533.4 \\
r = 3.9, & h = 9.9 & \Rightarrow \quad V = 473.1,
\end{array}$$

and

showing that the calculated volume might be up to 30.7 cm³ out in one direction and 29.6 cm³ out in the other.

However, it is illuminating to write

$$\delta V \approx 2\pi rh\,\delta r + \pi r^2\,\delta h$$

and divide each term by V or $\pi r^2 h$.

We then have
$$\frac{\delta V}{V} \approx 2\,\frac{\delta r}{r} + \frac{\delta h}{h}\,,$$

and multiplying by 100 we get

$$(\% \text{ error in } V) \approx 2(\% \text{ error in } r) + (\% \text{ error in } h).$$

Such results give us quick ways of estimating the consequences of experimental error for subsequent calculations. $\qquad\qquad\qquad\qquad\qquad\qquad\qquad\square$

Exercise 12B

1 (a) If $z = 5x^2y^3$, what would be the approximate percentage error consequent on a 3% error in x and a 1.4% error in y?

    (b) Repeat (a) for $z = 5x^2/y^3$ if both x and y are over-estimated.

    (c) Repeat (b) if x is over-estimated and y is under-estimated.

2 Explain why $\dfrac{\partial V}{\partial r}$ in Example 3 gives the curved surface area of the cylinder and $\dfrac{\partial V}{\partial h}$ gives the area of one end.

3 The total surface area of a cylinder of radius r and height h is denoted by S. Obtain the result

$$\delta S \approx 2\pi(h + 2r)\, \delta r + 2\pi r\, \delta h.$$

A particular cylinder has its radius and height measured as 2.0 cm and 3.0 cm, both measurements being to the nearest 0.1 cm. Use the above approximation to estimate the maximum error in the surface area calculated from these measurements.

    Check by an independent method.

4 A driver covers the 200 km between two towns in two hours, and estimates his average speed as 100 km h^{-1}. If there may be an error of up to 4 km in his value for the distance, and one of up to five minutes in the time, by how much might his estimate of the average speed be in error? Which of the two inaccuracies could have the greater effect?

5 If a value of z is calculated from measurements x and y with the aid of the formula $z = x^p/y^q$, and x and y are liable to proportional errors of $u\%$ and $v\%$ respectively, find a simple expression which gives approximately the largest possible proportional error in z.

6 Percentage errors are added when numbers are multiplied or divided. If x and y are positive, what can you say about the percentage error in $3x + 5y$ if there is a 2% error in x and a 3% error in y?

7 For $z = \sqrt{(x^2 + y^2)}$, obtain an approximate expression for δz in terms of δx and δy. Explain how your answer relates to the question of calculating the length of the hypotenuse of a right-angled triangle from measurements of the other two sides.

3. FUNCTION NOTATION AND TAYLOR APPROXIMATIONS

Result (1) in §2, $\delta y \approx \dfrac{\mathrm{d}y}{\mathrm{d}x}\, \delta x$, is often expressed in function notation. It then takes the familiar form

$$f(a + h) - f(a) \approx h f'(a)$$

or
$$f(a + h) \approx f(a) + h f'(a) \tag{3}$$

For a function of two variables, result (2) can be written as

$$f(a + h,\ b + k) \approx f(a, b) + h f_x(a, b) + k f_y(a, b). \tag{4}$$

It will be noticed that the suffix x is used for partial differentiation with respect to x, and similarly $f_y(a, b)$ denotes the value of $\dfrac{\partial z}{\partial y}$ when $x = a$ and $y = b$.

We refer to these as *first* (or *linear*) *Taylor approximations*. Better fits are given, in both two and three dimensions, by second Taylor approximations (which involve second derivatives).

For functions of one variable, we are familiar with

$$f(a + h) \approx f(a) + h f'(a) + \tfrac{1}{2}h^2 f''(a).$$

This represents a parabola with the same y-value, the same gradient and the same curvature as the graph of $y = f(x)$ at the point where $x = a$. Incidentally, the quadratic term shows that the graph has

a minimum point when $f'(a) = 0,$ $f''(a) > 0,$
a maximum point when $f'(a) = 0,$ $f''(a) < 0.$

For functions of two variables, we achieve a good fit with

$$f(a + h, b + k) \approx f(a, b) + h f_x(a, b) + k f_y(a, b)$$
$$+ \tfrac{1}{2}h^2 f_{xx}(a, b) + hk f_{xy}(a, b) + \tfrac{1}{2}k^2 f_{yy}(a, b).$$

The meaning of $f_{xx}(a, b)$ is obvious: the rate of change of gradient of the section through the surface made by the plane $y = b$. On the other hand, $f_{xy}(a, b)$, the value of $\dfrac{\partial}{\partial x}\left(\dfrac{\partial z}{\partial y}\right)$ when $x = a$, $y = b$, is harder to interpret.

Imagine lots of different sections perpendicular to the x-axis, corresponding to lines in the domain as in Figure 5. Each section has a gradient $\dfrac{\partial z}{\partial y}$ when $y = b$, and for a well-behaved surface these will change continuously as x changes through values close to a. The term $f_{xy}(a, b)$ represents the rate of change with x of the gradient $\dfrac{\partial z}{\partial y}$. It turns out that $f_{yx}(a, b)$ has the same value, but this is not at all apparent from a geometrical viewpoint.

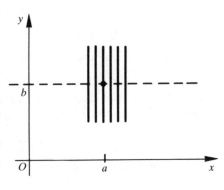

Figure 5

3.1 Algebraic approaches

The justification for the first Taylor approximation given in §2 could be written more abstractly as follows:

$$f(a + h, b + k) - f(a, b) = f(a + h, b + k) - f(a + h, b) + f(a + h, b) - f(a, b)$$
$$\approx k f_y(a + h, b) + h f_x(a, b) \quad \text{if } h \text{ and } k \text{ are small}$$
$$\approx k f_y(a, b) + h f_x(a, b).$$

It is easy to extend this to functions of three or more variables.

Similarly,

$$f_y(a, b) = \lim_{k \to 0} \left[\frac{f(a, b + k) - f(a, b)}{k} \right]$$

and

$$f_{xy}(a, b) = \lim_{h \to 0} \frac{1}{h} \left[\lim_{k \to 0} \left\{ \frac{f(a+h, b+k) - f(a+h, b)}{k} \right\} \right.$$

$$\left. - \lim_{k \to 0} \left\{ \frac{f(a, b+k) - f(a, b)}{k} \right\} \right]$$

$$= \lim_{h \to 0, \, k \to 0} \left\{ \frac{1}{hk} [f(a+h, b+k) - f(a+h, b) - f(a, b+k) + f(a, b)] \right\}.$$

Usually it makes no difference how we make h and k both tend to zero – first one and then the other, or both together in some specified way. So we are interested in the square bracket in our final expression. This is equal to

$$[f(a+h, b+k) - f(a, b+k) - f(a+h, b) + f(a, b)].$$

We soon conclude that $\qquad f_{xy}(a, b) = f_{yx}(a, b).$

3.2 Maxima and minima

The statements in §3 about maxima and minima for curves in two dimensions were carefully worded. You will recall that the possibility that $f''(a) = 0$ complicates matters, and the third type of stationary point, a point of inflexion, must be borne in mind. Consider the following statements:

$$f'(a) = 0, \quad f''(a) > 0 \quad \Rightarrow \quad \text{stationary point is a minimum.}$$

Stationary point is a point of inflexion $\quad \Rightarrow \quad f'(a) = 0, \quad f''(a) = 0.$

Both of these are true, but neither implication sign can be reversed. In each case, $f(x) = x^4$ would provide a simple counter-example.

In three dimensions, life is even more complicated.

Example 4
Describe the shape near the origin of the surfaces:
  (a) $z = x^2 + 5xy + 4y^2$ (b) $z = x^2 + 4xy + 5y^2$
  (c) $z = x^2 + 4xy + 4y^2$

Solution
In (a), the sections through the origin perpendicular to the x-axis and the y-axis are described by $z = 4y^2$ and $z = x^2$. Both are U-shaped parabolas. But the origin is not a minimum point as one might suppose.

Writing $z = x^2 + 5xy + 4y^2 = (x + y)(x + 4y)$, we see that the contour map consists of hyperbolas with asymptotes $x + y = 0$ and $x + 4y = 0$, the special case $x = 0$ giving a pair of lines.

The origin is a *saddle point*, like a 'pass' or 'col' in a mountain range. In Figure 6, A and B are below O, while C and D are on slopes above O.

Figures 7 and 8 are contour maps for (b) and (c). In the first, z cannot be negative, and for positive z the contours are ellipses; the origin is a minimum

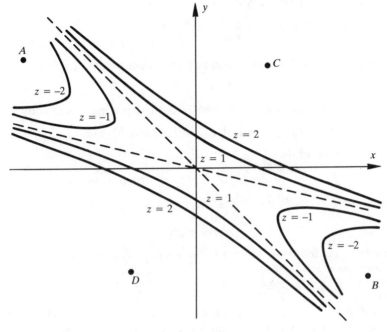

Figure 6

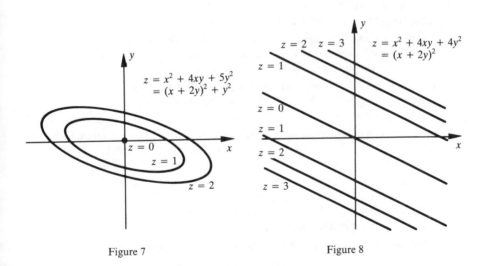

Figure 7   Figure 8

point. The contours in (c) are parallel lines, and the surface is a level cylinder with parabolic cross-section.   □

Clearly, the behaviour of $z = ax^2 + bxy + cy^2$ depends upon the value of the discriminant $b^2 - 4ac$.

Returning to the second Taylor approximation,

$$f(a + h, b + k) \approx f(a, b) + h f_x(a, b) + k f_y(a, b)$$
$$+ \tfrac{1}{2}h^2 f_{xx}(a, b) + hk f_{xy}(a, b) + \tfrac{1}{2}k^2 f_{yy}(a, b),$$

a *necessary* condition for a maximum or a minimum point at (a, b) is

$$f_x(a, b) = f_y(a, b) = 0.$$

If the second partial derivatives are non-zero, there is a maximum point if

$$f_{xx}(a, b) < 0 \quad \text{and} \quad [f_{xy}(a, b)]^2 < f_{xx}(a, b) f_{yy}(a, b)$$

and a minimum point if

$$f_{xx}(a, b) > 0 \quad \text{and} \quad [f_{xy}(a, b)]^2 < f_{xx}(a, b) f_{yy}(a, b).$$

As before, these are *sufficient*, but *not necessary*, conditions.

Exercise 12C

1   For each of the following, decide whether $x = 0$, $y = 0$ gives a maximum point, a minimum point or a saddle point:

    (a) $z = 4 + x^2 + 3xy - 5y^2$ (b) $z = 4 - x^2 + 3xy - 5y^2$
    (c) $z = 4 + x^2 - 3xy + 5y^2$ (d) $z = 4 + x^2 - 5xy + 3y^2$

    For each saddle point, give one point of the surface below $(0, 0, 4)$ and one above.

2   For $f(x, y) = \sqrt{(x + 2y)}$, find $f_x(5, 2)$, $f_y(5, 2)$, $f_{xx}(5, 2)$, $f_{xy}(5, 2)$, $f_{yx}(5, 2)$ and $f_{yy}(5, 2)$.

3   Repeat question 2 for:

    (a) $f(x, y) = \sqrt{(x^2 - 4y^2)}$ (b) $f(x, y) = \sqrt{(xy^2 - 4)}$

4   For $f(x, y) = xy^2$, find the first and second partial derivatives where $x = 2$, $y = 3$, and hence write down a second Taylor approximation for $f(2 + h, 3 + k)$.
    Check by expanding $(2 + h)(3 + k)^2$.

5   Find second Taylor approximations for $f(2 + h, 3 + k)$ when:

    (a) $f(x, y) = y^2/(1 + x)$ (b) $f(x, y) = (y + x)/(y - x)$
    (c) $f(x, y) = x(x^2 - y^2)^{-1}$

6   Show that one of the following has a minimum point and one a maximum point. Find these points.

    (a) $z = x^2 - 4xy + 5y^2 - 6x$ (b) $z = -x^2 - 2xy - 3y^2 + 6x + 2y + 5$

7   For the surface $z = 2x^4 + 4xy + y^2$:

    (a) show that the origin is a saddle point;
    (b) show that $(1, -2, -2)$ is a minimum point;
    (c) find the other minimum point.

8   Show that, for positive x and y, every section through the surface

$$z = \frac{(x + 3)(x + 3y)(y + 8)}{xy}$$

perpendicular to the y-axis has a minimum point, as does every section perpendicular to the x-axis. Find the minimum point of the surface.

9   Show that for the surface $z = f(x, y) = x^2y + 4x + 2y^2$:

    (a) the section in the plane $y = 6$ is a parabola with minimum point where $x = -\tfrac{1}{3}$;
    (b) all sections perpendicular to the y-axis (except in the plane $y = 0$) have

maximum or minimum points which satisfy $xy = -2$;

(c) all sections perpendicular to the x-axis have minimum points which satisfy $y = -\frac{1}{4}x^2$;

(d) $(2, -1, 6)$ is a saddle point of the surface.

Can you visualise the surface with the aid of Figure 9?

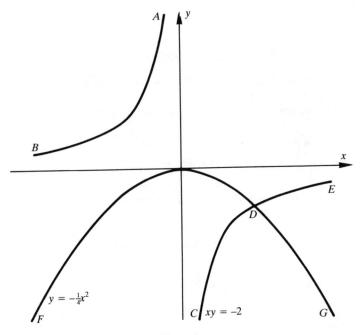

Figure 9

Miscellaneous exercise 12

1   Find the equation of the tangent plane to the surface S_1 given by

$$40 - z^2 = 5(x + y)$$

at the point P $(2, 1, 5)$.

The surface S_2 given by $z = x^2 + y^2$

cuts S_1 in the curve C. Find the direction of the tangent to C at P, by considering the intersection of the tangent planes to S_1 and S_2.   [SMP]

2   A function $z = f(x, y)$ is defined for $y \geq 0$ by

$$\frac{\partial z}{\partial x} = 2xy, \quad \frac{\partial z}{\partial y} = x^2, \quad f(0, 0) = 2.$$

Find $f(x, y)$ and sketch the contours $z = 4$ and $z = 2$. Sketch the intersections of the surface $z = f(x, y)$ with the planes $x = 2$ and $y = 1$.   [SMP]

3   Readings of atmospheric pressure at three ground-level weather stations with map coordinates $(0, 0)$, $(1, 1)$ and $(-1, 2)$ are $p(0, 0) = 1005$, $p(1, 1) = 1010$ and $p(-1, 2) = 995$, where the unit of length is 10^5 m and that of pressure is 10^2 N m^{-2}.

Calculate the coefficients in the local linear approximation

$$p(x, y) = p(0, 0) + \alpha x + \beta y$$

and hence estimate $\dfrac{\partial p}{\partial x}$ and $\dfrac{\partial p}{\partial y}$ at $(0, 0)$.

At what point on the circle $x^2 + y^2 = 4$ is the pressure greatest, according to this approximation?   [SMP]

4 A function is defined by

$$f(x, y) = \frac{x^2 - y^4}{x^2 + y^2} \quad \text{(except when } x = y = 0).$$

Draw a diagram which shows clearly the sets of points at which:
  (a) $f(x, y) = 1$ (b) $f(x, y) = 0$
Can $f(0, 0)$ be given a value which makes the function continuous at $(0, 0)$? Give reasons.   [SMP]

5 A function is defined by

$$f(x, y) = \frac{x^2 + y^2 - x}{(x^2 + y^2)^{1/2}} \quad \text{for } (x, y) \neq (0, 0).$$

By transforming to polar coordinates r, θ, show that the equation of the contour $f(x, y) = 0$ is $r = \cos\theta$.

Find the polar equation of the contour $f(x, y) = 1$, and sketch both contours.

Does $f(x, y)$ tend to a unique value as x and y both tend to zero? Give reasons for your answer.   [SMP]

6 The formula $$\cos A = \frac{b^2 + c^2 - a^2}{2bc}$$

is used to calculate the angle A of a triangle ABC, given the lengths of its sides. Assuming that c is known exactly, but that errors δa and δb are made in measuring the lengths of a and b, use a linear approximation to estimate the error δA in the calculated value of A.

Two points A and B are marked 4 inches apart on a piece of paper. A student attempts to construct a right-angled triangle ABC by measuring lengths of 3 inches from A and 5 inches from B, and marking the point of intersection C. Assuming that he can measure each of these two lengths correct to $\frac{1}{16}$ inch, show that the angle he constructs at A will be within ± 2.4 degrees of a right angle.   [SMP]

7 A surveyor wishes to calculate the distance d of an object A from the point P. He makes measurements of the angles α and β from the ends of a baseline PQ whose length is known to be exactly l (see Figure 10). Show that

$$d = \frac{l \sin\beta}{\sin(\beta - \alpha)}.$$

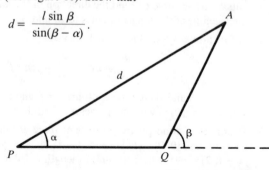

Figure 10

Find the maximum percentage error in d due to 1% errors in α and β when the measured values of α and β are $\frac{1}{6}\pi$ and $\frac{1}{3}\pi$ respectively.   [SMP]

8   A differentiable function $f(x, y)$ satisfies the equations

$$x\frac{\partial f}{\partial x} + y\frac{\partial f}{\partial y} = 3f \quad \text{and} \quad \frac{\partial f}{\partial x} + \frac{\partial f}{\partial y} = 0.$$

Given that $f(2, 1) = 1$, find the values of $\dfrac{\partial f}{\partial x}$ and $\dfrac{\partial f}{\partial y}$ at the point $(2, 1)$. Hence find an approximation to $f(x, y)$ in the form

$$f(x, y) \approx a + bx + cy$$

where a, b and c are constants which you should specify, when $|x - 2|$ and $|y - 1|$ are small.

Find constants α, β, γ such that

$$f(x, y) = (\alpha x + \beta y)^\gamma$$

is a solution of the original equations which satisfies $f(2, 1) = 1$.   [SMP]

SUMMARY

The derivative of $z = f(x, y)$ with respect to x, keeping y constant, is written $\dfrac{\partial z}{\partial x}$ or $f_x(x, y)$.

$$\frac{\partial^2 z}{\partial x^2} = \frac{\partial}{\partial x}\left(\frac{\partial z}{\partial x}\right) = f_{xx}(x, y); \qquad \frac{\partial^2 z}{\partial x\,\partial y} = \frac{\partial}{\partial x}\left(\frac{\partial z}{\partial y}\right) = f_{xy}(x, y)$$

Tangent plane
The tangent plane to the surface $z = f(x, y)$ at the point P where $x = a$, $y = b$, is given by

$$z = mx + ny + k,$$

where $m = f_x(a, b)$, $n = f_y(a, b)$, and k is chosen so that the coordinates of P satisfy the equation of the plane.

Taylor approximations
The linear (first) approximation is

$$\delta z \approx \frac{\partial z}{\partial x}\,\delta x + \frac{\partial z}{\partial y}\,\delta y,$$

which is equivalent to

$$f(a + h, b + k) \approx f(a, b) + h f_x(a, b) + k f_y(a, b).$$

The second-degree approximation is

$$f(a + h, b + k) \approx f(a, b) + h f_x(a, b) + k f_y(a, b)$$
$$+ \tfrac{1}{2}h^2 f_{xx}(a, b) + hk f_{xy}(a, b) + \tfrac{1}{2}k^2 f_{yy}(a, b).$$

Maximum and minimum points

A surface has a *maximum point* where $x = a$ and $y = b$ if

$$f_x(a, b) = 0, \quad f_y(a, b) = 0, \quad f_{xx}(a, b) < 0,$$

and
$$[f_{xy}(a, b)]^2 < f_{xx}(a, b) f_{yy}(a, b).$$

There is a *minimum point* if the same conditions hold except that

$$f_{xx}(a, b) > 0.$$

There is a *saddle point* if

$$f_x(a, b) = 0, \quad f_y(a, b) = 0$$

and
$$[f_{xy}(a, b)]^2 > f_{xx}(a, b) f_{yy}(a, b).$$

13

Double integrals

1. VOLUMES

We have applied differentiation to functions of two variables, so now let us do the same with integration. This will give us the volume under a surface.

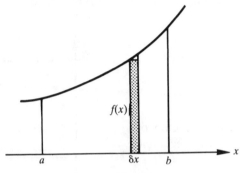

Figure 1

When finding the area under a curve, we divided it up into many narrow strips, a typical one having an area of approximately $f(x) \, \delta x$. The standard limiting process shows that the sum of the areas of all the strips is given exactly by $\int_a^b f(x) \, dx$.

For the volume under a surface, we divide the domain into small regions (mostly rectangular – see Figure 2) and imagine a matchstick rising from each little region to the required surface. The task is to add up the volumes of all the matchstick elements.

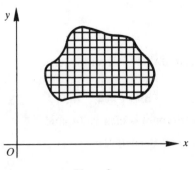

Figure 2

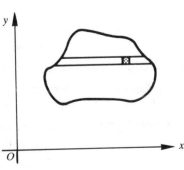

Figure 3

165

We shall carve up the domain into strips parallel to the x-axis and find the volume for each strip. The second stage will be to sum the volumes of the strips.

In the first stage, we want the limit of $\sum_x f(x, y)\, \delta x\, \delta y$, and we appreciate that y is to remain constant for the moment. We shall obviously require $[\int f(x, y)\, dx]\, \delta y$, and it is not difficult to see that the integral gives the area of one face of the slice between y and $y + \delta y$. Hence the expression given is approximately the volume of the slice, as we hoped. To complete the job, we integrate with respect to y. We write the whole volume as $\int [\int f(x, y)\, dx]\, dy$ or, more usually, without the brackets, as $\iint f(x, y)\, dx\, dy$.

Example 1

Find $V = \displaystyle\int_3^4 \int_0^3 (2x + 3y + 5)\, dx\, dy$.

Solution

It is always helpful to draw a diagram of the domain. Here it is the rectangle shown in Figure 4.

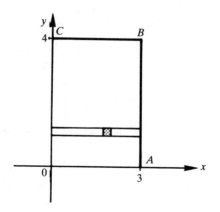

Figure 4

Now
$$V = \int_0^4 \left[x^2 + 3xy + 5x \right]_0^3 dy$$
$$= \int_0^4 (9 + 9y + 15)\, dy$$
$$= \left[9y + 4.5y^2 + 15y \right]_0^4$$
$$= 168.$$

We have found the volume under a plane, and there is a simple check.

If $x = 0$ and $y = 0$, then $z = 5$; if $x = 3$ and $y = 0$, then $x = 11$;
if $x = 0$ and $y = 4$, then $z = 17$; if $x = 3$ and $y = 4$, then $z = 23$.

From these figures, the average z over the domain is clearly 14, and
$$V = (\text{area of base}) \times (\text{average height})$$
$$= 12 \times 14$$
$$= 168.$$

Each section perpendicular to the y-axis is a trapezium; and the typical one in Figure 5 has area $(3y + 8) \times 3 = 9y + 24$, the result of the first integration above.   □

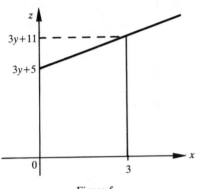

Figure 5   Figure 6

Example 2
Find the volume under $z = 2x + 3y + 5$ for the domain shown in Figure 6.

Solution
The complication compared with Example 1 is that here all the strips have different starting values for x. The equation of OB is $y = \frac{4}{3}x$, i.e. $x = \frac{3}{4}y$.

Now
$$V = \int_0^4 \int_{3y/4}^3 (2x + 3y + 5)\,\mathrm{d}x\,\mathrm{d}y$$

$$= \int_0^4 \left[x^2 + 3xy + 5x \right]_{3y/4}^3 \mathrm{d}y$$

$$= \int_0^4 (24 + 9y) - (\tfrac{9}{16}y^2 + \tfrac{9}{4}y^2 + \tfrac{15}{4}y)\,\mathrm{d}y$$

$$= \left[24y + \tfrac{9}{2}y^2 - \tfrac{3}{16}y^3 - \tfrac{3}{4}y^3 - \tfrac{15}{8}y^2 \right]_0^4$$

$$= 96 + 72 - 12 - 48 - 30$$

$$= 78.$$

$V = $ (area of base) $\times$ (average height) now gives $6 \times \frac{1}{3}(5 + 11 + 23) = 78$ as a check.   □

There is no logical or practical reason for integrating with respect to x first. Figure 7 (overleaf) enables us to write the volume for Example 2 as

$$\int_0^3 \int_0^{4x/3} (2x + 3y + 5)\,\mathrm{d}y\,\mathrm{d}x.$$

Notice that the limits for the second integral will always be numbers. If the first integral is with respect to y, its limits may be functions of x, and vice versa.

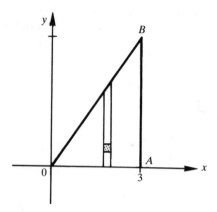

Figure 7

Exercise 13A

1 Use a double integral to find the volume under $z = 4x - 5y + 21$ for each of the domains in Figure 8. In each case, find the z-value corresponding to the centre of the domain, and hence check the volume.

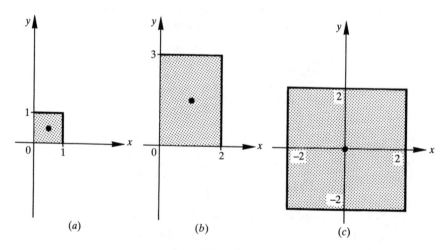

Figure 8

2 Find the volumes under the surfaces (i) $z = 3x^2 + 2xy + y^2 + 10$, and (ii) $z = (x - 2)^2/(y + 3)^2$ for each of the domains in Figure 8. Check your answers.

3 Check that the same answers are obtained for Examples 1 and 2 if the integrations are carried out with respect to y first.

4 Explain why $\displaystyle\int_0^2 \int_0^x (4x - 5y + 21)\,dy\,dx$ gives the volume under $z = 4x - 5y + 21$ for the domain in Figure 9.

Evaluate the double integral and check your answer.

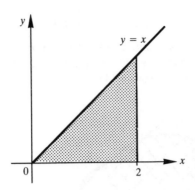

Figure 9

5 If the volume in question 4 is written in the form $\int_{0}^{2}\int\int (4x - 5y + 21)\, dx\, dy$, what should be the limits for the inner integral? Check that this double integral gives the same answer as before.

6 Find $\int_{1}^{2}\int_{1}^{3-y} (3x^2 + 4xy + 6y^2)\, dx\, dy$, and illustrate the domain on a diagram. Carry out a rough check.

7 Repeat question 6 for:

(a) $\int_{1}^{3}\int_{-x}^{x} (x^2 - y^2 + 10)\, dy\, dx$ (b) $\int_{1}^{3}\int_{-y}^{y} (x^2 - y^2 + 10)\, dx\, dy$

8 Find $\int\int (x + y)\, dx\, dy$ for each of the domains shown in Figure 10. Check the answer for (b) by reversing the order of integration.

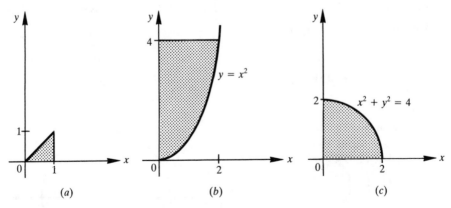

(a)   (b)   (c)

Figure 10

9 Draw diagrams of the domains for each of these integrals, and then write down equivalent integrals with the order of integration changed:

(a) $\int_{1}^{2}\int_{1}^{x} z\, dy\, dx$ (b) $\int_{0}^{1}\int_{y}^{\sqrt{y}} (x^2 + y^2)\, dx\, dy$ (c) $\int_{0}^{1}\int_{0}^{y} e^{-y^2}\, dx\, dy$

Evaluate (b) in whichever form you prefer. Can either form be used to evaluate (c)?

2. POLAR COORDINATES

Sometimes it pays to use polar coordinates rather than Cartesians, and divide the domain into elements by means of circles centre the origin and half-lines radiating out from O (see Figure 11).

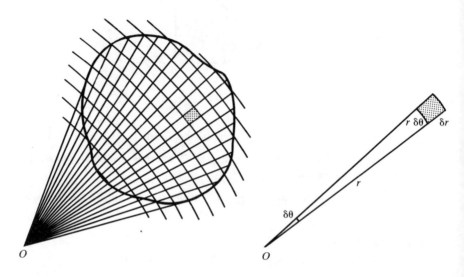

Figure 11

Then a typical matchstick will have volume approximately $zr \, \delta\theta \, \delta r$, and the total volume will be given exactly by $\iint zr \, d\theta \, dr$ (with suitable limits). Note the extra factor of r which comes in.

Example 3
Find the volume of the paraboloid $z = 4 - x^2 - y^2$ cut off by the xy-plane.

Solution
The domain is the circle of Figure 12, and it is natural to use polar coordinates. Then $z = 4 - r^2$, and

$$V = \int_0^2 \int_0^{2\pi} (4 - r^2) r \, d\theta \, dr$$

$$= 2\pi \left[2r^2 - \tfrac{1}{4} r^4 \right]_0^2$$

$$= 8\pi.$$

$\square$

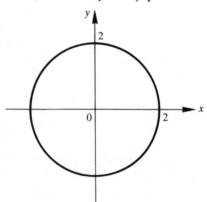

Figure 12

Example 4

Find $I = \int_0^1 \int_y^1 \sqrt{(x^2 + y^2)} \, dx \, dy$.

Solution

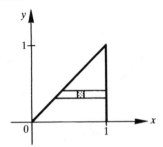

Figure 13

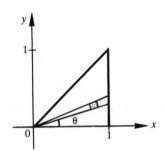

Figure 14

Although the domain (Figure 13) is simply described in Cartesian terms, the integrand is much simpler in polar form. When expressing the double integral in polar coordinates, we must decide whether to sum up first for different r's, keeping θ constant, or vice versa. It is undoubtedly easier to refer to Figure 14 and write

$$I = \int_0^{\pi/4} \int_0^{\sec\theta} r \times r \, dr \, d\theta,$$

giving $$I = \int_0^{\pi/4} \tfrac{1}{3} \sec^3 \theta \, d\theta.$$

This is a standard type of integral (see Chapter 6), and it can be shown that

$$I = \tfrac{1}{6}\sqrt{2} + \tfrac{1}{6} \ln(\sqrt{2} + 1) = 0.383 \quad \text{(to 3 SF)}. \qquad \square$$

Exercise 13B

1 Use polar coordinates to find $\iint xy \, dx \, dy$, where the domain is the first quadrant of the unit circle.

2 Use polar coordinates to find $\int_0^1 \int_0^{1-x} \dfrac{1}{\sqrt{(x^2 + y^2)}} \, dy \, dx$.

3 A circular cylinder of radius $\tfrac{1}{2}a$ is bored through a sphere of radius a in such a way that there is a plane of symmetry as in Figure 15. Find the volume of the part that is removed.

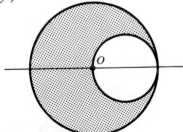

Figure 15

4 Find the volumes under the following surfaces if, in each case, the domain is the first
quadrant of the unit circle. Where it is convenient, do each calculation twice, first in
Cartesian and then in polar coordinates. Otherwise, just use polars.

(a) $z = x + 2y$ (b) $z = x\sqrt{y}$
(c) $z = 1/\sqrt{(x^2 + y^2 + 1)}$ (d) $z = 1 - \sqrt{(x^2 + y^2)}$

5 Show that the volume of the cap of a
sphere of radius a cut off by a plane
which is a distance b from the centre of
the sphere (Figure 16) is given by

$$V = \int_0^{2\pi} \int_0^{\sqrt{(a^2 - b^2)}} r\,[\sqrt{(a^2 - r^2)} - b]\,dr\,d\theta.$$

Evaluate this integral, and check by an
independent method.

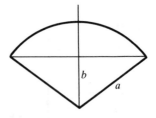

Figure 16

3. APPLICATIONS TO PROBABILITY

Double (and triple) integrals have many uses. For the moment we confine
ourselves to just one of these.

Suppose that each member of a given statistical population consists of values
of a *pair* of random variables, x and y (for example, the height and weight of
people in a country). The related frequency or probability function is then said
to be *bivariate*; we are interested here in the case where the variables x and y are
'continuous', so that the domain is a region of the xy-plane.

By analogy with the single-variable case, we need to represent the probabilities in the continuous bivariate case by a probability density function in
both the variables: thus we define a function $\phi(x, y)$ which gives the *probability
density* at any point (x, y), that is, the probability per unit area at this point. The
density graph will be the surface $z = \phi(x, y)$, and volumes over specified regions
of the domain will give the appropriate probabilities.

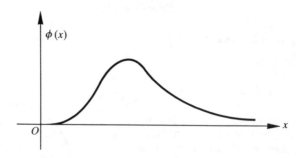

Figure 17

With probability density functions of a single variable x (see Figure 17), we
require that

(i) $\phi(x)$ is non-negative throughout the domain, and

(ii) $\int \phi(x)\,dx$ over the whole domain equals 1.

Similarly, for $\phi(x, y)$ to be a bivariate probability density function, we must have

(i) $\phi(x, y) \geq 0$ for all (x, y) in the domain, and

(ii) $\iint \phi(x, y) \, dx \, dy = 1$, where the double integral is taken over the complete domain.

With one variable, we define $\mu = \int x \, \phi(x) \, dx$ and $\sigma^2 = \int (x - \mu)^2 \, \phi(x) \, dx$; similar ideas can be introduced for bivariate models.

Example 5
Candidates who take two examinations score marks X and Y, where both X and Y may take values from 0 to 100. The distribution of the marks is modelled by a probability density function $\phi(x, y) = k(x + 2y)$, the integral marks being replaced by *real* numbers x and y. Find (*a*) the value of k, (*b*) the proportion of the candidates scoring less than half marks, and (*c*) the expected value of the total mark $(x + y)$.

Solution
(*a*) k is found from $\displaystyle\int_0^{100} \int_0^{100} k(x + 2y) \, dx \, dy = 1$. We find $k = \frac{2}{3} \times 10^{-6}$ (see Exercise 13C, question 1).

(*b*) We want $\displaystyle\iint k(x + 2y) \, dx \, dy$ over the triangle OAB of Figure 18, i.e. $\displaystyle\int_0^{100} \int_0^{100-y} k(x + 2y) \, dx \, dy$. The answer is $\frac{1}{3}$, which is reasonable since in this simple model high marks are more likely than low ones.

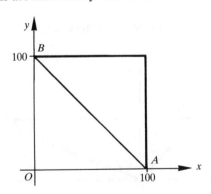

Figure 18

(*c*) The expected total is $\displaystyle\int_0^{100} \int_0^{100} (x + y) \, \phi(x, y) \, dx \, dy$,

i.e. $\displaystyle k \int_0^{100} \int_0^{100} (x^2 + 3xy + 2y^2) \, dx \, dy$.

This comes to 117, again a plausible answer.   □

Exercise 13C

1 Carry out the integrations for Example 5 and check the answers.

2 For the model of Example 5, find:
   (*a*) the probability that $x < 20$;
   (*b*) the probability that $50 < y < 60$;
   (*c*) the probability that $x + y < 80$;
   (*d*) the probability that $100 < x + y < 120$;
   (*e*) the expected value of x, i.e. $\iint x\,\phi(x, y)\,dx\,dy$;
   (*f*) the expected value of y;
   (*g*) the expected value of $(y - x)$.

3 Repeat Example 5(*a*) and question 2(*a*) and (*b*) for $\phi(x, y) = kxy^2(100 - x)(100 - y)$, with the same domain.

4 Show that for a bivariate distribution, the expected value of $x + y$ is the sum of the expected value of x and the expected value of y.

5 Show that if x and y are independent and have probability density functions $f(x)$ and $g(y)$, with expected values m and n, then the bivariate distribution is given by $\phi(x, y) = f(x)\, g(y)$ and the expected value of xy is mn.

6 If x and y are independent variates with normal probability density functions

$$\frac{1}{\sqrt{(2\pi)}} e^{-x^2/2} \quad \text{and} \quad \frac{1}{\sqrt{(2\pi)}} e^{-y^2/2},$$

find the probability that $x^2 + y^2 \leqslant a^2$.
Verify that this probability tends to 1 as $a \to \infty$.

Miscellaneous exercise 13

1 Evaluate $\iint (x + y)^{1/2}\,dS$ over the triangular region S shown in Figure 19.

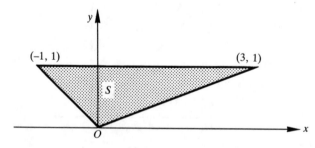

Figure 19

2 Evaluate $\iint_S x^2 y^3\,dx\,dy$, where S is the region bounded by the lines $y = \pm\sqrt{3}x$, $y = a$. Find the value of $\iint_S x^3 y^2\,dx\,dy$.   [SMP]

3 Sketch the region of integration of the double integral

$$\int_0^4 dy \int_{y^2/4}^y \frac{y}{\{(4-x)(4x-y^2)\}^{1/2}} \, dx.$$

By changing the order of integration, or otherwise, show that the integral has value $\frac{16}{3}$.
[SMP]

4 Sketch the curve defined by the equation $y^2 + 2y - x^2 = 0$.

Show that the integral of the function $1/\{x(y+1)^2\}$ over the finite region bounded by this curve and by the lines $y = 0$ and $x = 1$ can be written as the double integral

$$\int_0^1 dx \int_0^{g(x)} \frac{dy}{x(y+1)^2},$$

where you must give an expression for $g(x)$.

Prove that the integral exists and evaluate it, given that

$$\int \frac{dx}{x\sqrt{(1+x^2)}} = \ln\{x/(1+\sqrt{(1+x^2)})\}. \qquad \text{[SMP]}$$

5 Part of the hull of a submerged vessel is a flat hatch, the shape of which is bounded by the curves

$$y = \frac{2}{a}(a^2 - x^2) \quad \text{and} \quad y = 0.$$

The hatch is hinged along the edge $y = 0$. The total thrust on the hatch due to the water pressure P is the double integral $F = \iint P \, dx \, dy$, evaluated over the hatch. The water pressure at a depth h is $P = \rho g h$, where ρ is the density of the water and g is the gravitational acceleration.

Evaluate the integrals

$$\iint dx \, dy, \qquad \iint y \, dx \, dy, \qquad \iint y^2 \, dx \, dy$$

over the hatch. Use these results to calculate the thrust F when the hatch is in a vertical plane, and the hinged edge is horizontal and at the lowest point, at a depth $L > 2a$ (see Figure 20).

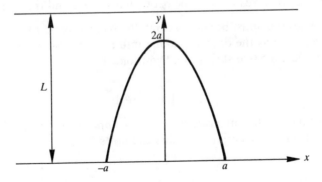

Figure 20

Calculate also the moment $M = \iint Py \, dx \, dy$ of the thrust about the hinge.
[SMP]

6 When a lamina is held vertically in a fluid, the thrust on one side of the lamina is $\iint \rho y \, d\sigma$, where y measures depth below the surface, ρ is a constant, and the integral is taken over the submerged portion of the lamina. Find the thrust in the following cases.

(*a*) The lamina is a right-angled triangle OAB (with $OA = b$ and $AB = a$) with the vertex O at the surface of the fluid, OA vertical and AB horizontal (Figure 21(*a*)).

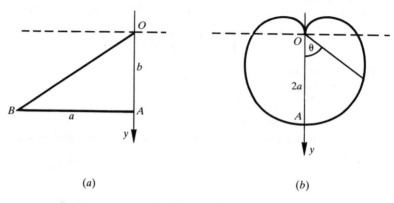

(*a*)   (*b*)

Figure 21

(*b*) The lamina is in the shape of the cardioid

$$r = a(1 + \cos \theta)$$

and is held, with initial line OA vertically downwards, partially immersed with the water level through O (Figure 21(*b*)).

(You may quote the reduction formula for $\int_0^{\pi/2} \cos^n x \, dx$.)   [SMP]

SUMMARY

$V = \iint z \, dx \, dy$ gives the volume between a surface and the xy-plane. The limits of integration must be chosen carefully to correspond to the *region* of the xy-plane required as the domain, taking into account the order in which it is decided to effect the two stages of integration.

In polar coordinates,

$$V = \iint zr \, d\theta \, dr.$$

Double (and triple) integrals have many applications in probability and mechanics; Chapter 16 contains further examples.

14

Conformal transformations of the complex plane

1. TRANSFORMATION DIAGRAMS

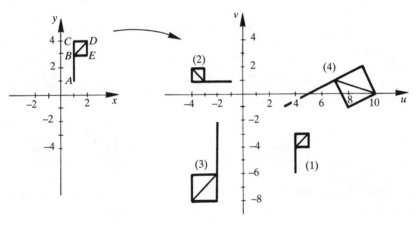

Figure 1

Figure 1 shows a flag and its image under the following transformations of the complex plane:

   (i) the translation $z \mapsto z + (3 - 7j)$
   (ii) the rotation $z \mapsto jz$
   (iii) the enlargement $z \mapsto -2z$
   (iv) the enlargement and rotation $z \mapsto (1 - 2j)z$.

For (iv) we can proceed like this:

$$
\begin{aligned}
1 + j &\mapsto (1 - 2j)(1 + j) = 3 - j \\
1 + 3j &\mapsto (1 - 2j)(1 + 3j) = 7 + j \\
1 + 4j &\mapsto (1 - 2j)(1 + 4j) = 9 + 2j \\
2 + 4j &\mapsto (1 - 2j)(2 + 4j) = 10 \\
2 + 3j &\mapsto (1 - 2j)(2 + 3j) = 8 - j
\end{aligned}
$$

In all these transformations, discussed in Chapter 11, straight lines map onto straight lines, and the image flags are all similar to the original flag.

In this chapter we consider more general transformations and take as our main example the function $z \mapsto z^2$.

177

Now
$$1+j \mapsto (1+j)^2 = \quad 2j$$
$$1+3j \mapsto (1+3j)^2 = -8+6j$$
$$1+4j \mapsto (1+4j)^2 = -15+8j.$$

Work out the images of $(2+4j)$ and $(2+3j)$, and so complete a diagram of the image flag in Figure 2.

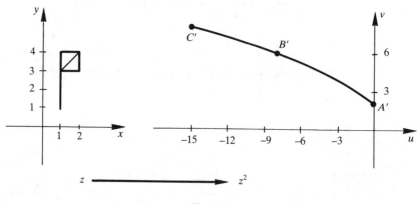

Figure 2

It is clear that A', B' and C' do not lie on a straight line, so we can expect the images of the line segments CD, DE, etc. to be curved also. Let us see how to investigate these.

A general point in the domain corresponds to $(x+yj)$, and we denote its image by $(u+vj)$.

Then
$$x + yj \mapsto (x+yj)^2 = (x^2-y^2) + 2xyj,$$

so
$$\left.\begin{array}{l} u = x^2 - y^2 \\ v = 2xy \end{array}\right\}$$

The flagpole ABC forms part of the line $x = 1$. For points on this line,
$$\left.\begin{array}{l} u = 1 - y^2 \\ v = 2y \end{array}\right\}$$

These equations describe the curve in the range plane of which $A'B'C'$ is a part, y acting here as a parameter. Eliminating y, we obtain the equation $u = 1 - \frac{1}{4}v^2$.

Where does the graph of $u = 1 - \frac{1}{4}v^2$ cross the u- and v-axes? Sketch the complete graph.

Exercise 14A

Questions 1 to 4 all refer to Figure 2 and to the transformation $z \mapsto z^2$.

1   Write down parametric equations for the image curves of (a) $x = 2$, (b) $y = 4$, and (c) $y = 3$, and eliminate the parameter in each case to give the uv-equation.

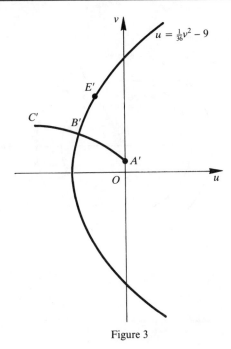

Figure 3

2 (a) Find the gradients of $u = 1 - \frac{1}{4}v^2$ and $u = \frac{1}{36}v^2 - 9$ at B' (Figure 3). What can you deduce?

   (b) Find the gradients of the relevant image curves at C' and E'. Comment.

3 BD has equation $y = x + 2$. Show that for its image,

$$\left.\begin{array}{l} u = -4x - 4 \\ v = 2x^2 + 4x \end{array}\right\}$$

Now calculate $\dfrac{du}{dx}$ and $\dfrac{dv}{dx}$ when $x = 1$, and deduce that $\begin{bmatrix} -1 \\ 2 \end{bmatrix}$ is a vector in the direction of the tangent at B' to the image curve $B'D'$.

Find the angle between $\begin{bmatrix} -1 \\ 2 \end{bmatrix}$ and $\begin{bmatrix} 1 \\ 3 \end{bmatrix}$, and comment.

4 Investigate the angles at D' as in question 3.

5 Find the images of the points A, B, C, D and E of the flag in Figure 2 under the transformation $z \mapsto 12/z$. Draw the image flag. Investigate the angle between the arcs $B'C'$ and $C'D'$.

6 Find the image of the flag in Figure 4 (overleaf) (formed from parts of $r = 3$, $r = 4$, $\theta = \pi/3$ and $\theta = \pi/4$) under the transformations (a) $z \mapsto z^2$, and (b) $z \mapsto 12/z$.

7 (a) Draw the image of the 'A' in Figure 5 (overleaf) under the transformation $z \mapsto \frac{1}{5}z^2$.

   (b) Show that the image of the line $y = 2x - 1$ is given by

$$\left.\begin{array}{l} u = \frac{1}{5}(-3x^2 + 4x - 1) \\ v = \frac{1}{5}(4x^2 - 2x) \end{array}\right\}$$

   (c) Show that the tangent at Q' to the image of PQR is in the direction of the vector

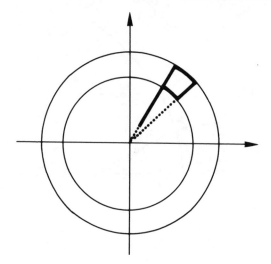

Figure 4

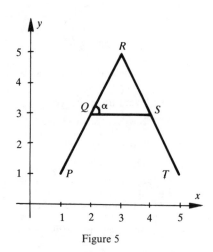

Figure 5

$\begin{bmatrix} -4 \\ 7 \end{bmatrix}$, and that the tangent at Q' to the image of QS is in the direction of $\begin{bmatrix} 2 \\ 3 \end{bmatrix}$.

(*d*) Verify that the angle between these two vectors is equal to α.

8 Find the image of the 'A' in Figure 5 under the transformation $z \mapsto \frac{1}{5}(z^2 + 2z)$ and investigate the angles of this image.

2. ORTHOGONAL FAMILIES

The transformations of §1 and Exercise 14A deform the complex plane and any objects drawn on the plane, yet apparently *angles* are unchanged. In particular, the lines parallel to the coordinate axes, $x = c$ and $y = k$, map onto orthogonal families of curves, i.e. curves in which each member of one family meets every member of the other at right angles. We prove this for two simple examples.

Example 1
For $z \mapsto z^2$, $u = x^2 - y^2$ and $v = 2xy$.

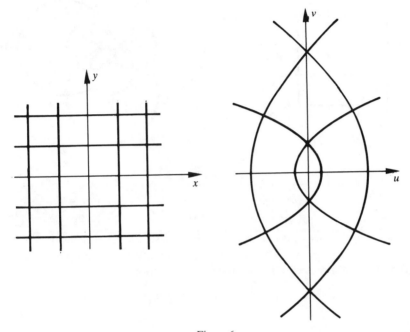

Figure 6

For the uv-curve corresponding to $x = c$, a tangent vector is

$$\begin{bmatrix} \partial u / \partial y \\ \partial v / \partial y \end{bmatrix} = \begin{bmatrix} -2y \\ 2x \end{bmatrix} = \begin{bmatrix} -2k \\ 2c \end{bmatrix} \quad \text{at the point corresponding to } x = c, \, y = k.$$

Similarly, for the image of $y = k$, a tangent vector is

$$\begin{bmatrix} \partial u / \partial x \\ \partial v / \partial x \end{bmatrix} = \begin{bmatrix} 2c \\ 2k \end{bmatrix} \quad \text{at this point.}$$

By inspection, these are perpendicular. ☐

Example 2　　　　　　　　　　　$z \mapsto 12/z$

In Chapter 11, we showed that this maps lines not through the origin into circles through the origin.

The line $x = c$ maps onto a circle with centre on the u-axis, while $y = k$ maps onto a circle with centre on the v-axis. These circles are orthogonal at the origin and consequently, by symmetry, at their other point of intersection also (see figure 7, overleaf). ☐

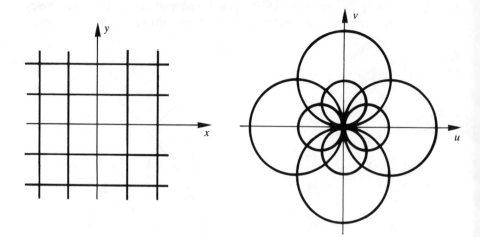

Figure 7

2.1 The derivative, $f'(z)$

Examples 1 and 2 provide two very special cases of a general result which is surprisingly easy to prove. This involves the derivative of a complex function. For functions of a real variable we have the definition

$$f'(a) = \lim_{b \to a} \left(\frac{f(b) - f(a)}{b - a} \right),$$

provided that the limit exists. We shall take the same definition for functions from $\mathbb{C}$ to $\mathbb{C}$.

For the squaring function $f: x \mapsto x^2$, we had

$$f'(a) = \lim_{b \to a} \left(\frac{b^2 - a^2}{b - a} \right) = \lim_{b \to a} (b + a) = 2a.$$

Now this working is just as relevant when a and b are complex numbers; the only question we must ask is what it all signifies.

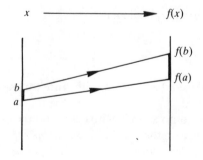

Figure 8

With real variables we can interpret it in terms of number lines (see Figure 8).
$\dfrac{f(b) - f(a)}{b - a}$ is the *average scale factor* over the interval $[a, b]$; its limit is the *local scale factor* at $x = a$.

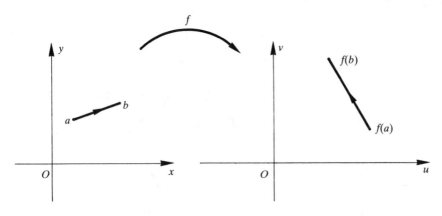

Figure 9

With complex variables, the picture is as shown in Figure 9. The complex number $b - a$ is represented by the displacement from a to b, and $f(b) - f(a)$ by the displacement in the codomain from $f(a)$ to $f(b)$. The first displacement is transformed into the second by a spiral similarity – that is, an enlargement and rotation. Now the transformation of spiral similarity in the complex plane has been shown to correspond to multiplication by a complex number, whose modulus gives the enlargement factor and whose argument the angle of rotation. In our example, this complex number is

$$\frac{f(b) - f(a)}{b - a}$$

which we call the 'average scale factor' of the transformation between a and b.

Notice the likeness and the differences between this and the real case. The algebraic expression for the average scale factor is precisely the same as for functions from $\mathbb{R}$ to $\mathbb{R}$, and therefore all the rules for calculation will carry over directly from the real to the complex situation. On the other hand, the term 'scale factor' is now given a new significance. In geographers' parlance, the scale of a map is a ratio of lengths, and therefore essentially a positive real number. We have already gone beyond this in describing the scale of a decreasing function from $\mathbb{R}$ to $\mathbb{R}$ as a negative number; and we are now defining the scale of a mapping as a complex number, which indicates not only a ratio of lengths (the modulus) but also an angle of rotation (the argument). Notice that we can no longer speak of the scale factor 'over the interval $[a, b]$', for in the complex field we have no inequality relation so that it is meaningless to write $\{z: a \leqslant z \leqslant b\}$ when a and b are complex numbers.

For the squaring function, whenever b is close to a, the average scale factor

$(b + a)$ is approximately equal to the derivative $2a$. If a number of different displacements of small modulus are made from a, these are all enlarged in approximately the same ratio and rotated through approximately the same angle, so that locally the function preserves shapes and merely changes size and orientation.

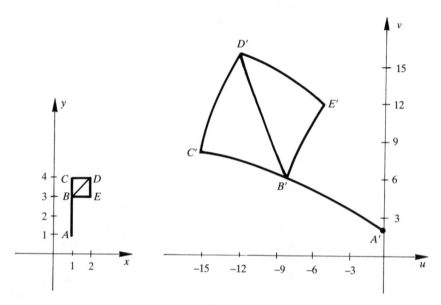

Figure 10

Since $\qquad f(z) = z^2 \ \Rightarrow \ f'(z) = 2z, \qquad f'(1 + j) = 2 + 2j.$

$|2 + 2j| = \sqrt{8}$ and $\arg(2 + 2j) = \frac{1}{4}\pi$, so that at A the flagpole in Figure 10 is enlarged by a factor of $\sqrt{8}$ and rotated through $\frac{1}{4}\pi$.

Similarly, $f'(1 + 3j) = 2 + 6j$, so at B the local transformation is an enlargement with scale factor $\sqrt{40}$ and rotation through $\tan^{-1} 3$.

Transformations which preserve shape locally in this way are said to be *conformal*. The argument used above can be applied generally to show that:

> Any differentiable function from $\mathbb{C}$ to $\mathbb{C}$ effects a conformal transformation of the complex plane at any point where the derivative is non-zero.

The reason for excluding points where the derivative is zero is that at such points the local 'first-order' transformation is a shrinkage to a point; the second-order distortions of the transformation therefore become significant, and the property of approximate preservation of shape is lost.

2.2 Differentiability

Working from first principles, we can verify that such functions as $z \mapsto z^3$, $z \mapsto 1/z$ and $z \mapsto (z + 3j)/(2z - 1)$ are differentiable at all points at which they are defined.

Simple examples of non-differentiable functions exist too, for example $z \mapsto z^*$ (Figure 11).

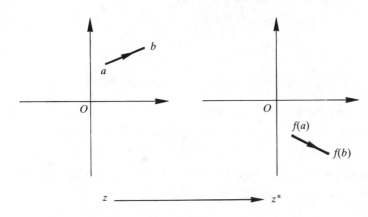

Figure 11

If $\arg(b - a) = \theta$, then $\dfrac{f(b) - f(a)}{b - a}$ is the complex number $[1, -2\theta]$, and this varies for different directions of the displacement $(b - a)$. There is no local scale factor. Here we have a conformal transformation (reflection in the real axis) represented by a non-differentiable function.

Exercise 14B

1   For the function f: $z \mapsto 12/z$, find the modulus and argument of $f'(1 + j)$, $f'(1 + 3j)$ and $f'(2 + 4j)$. Interpret your answers in terms of Figure 7.

2   For each of the following functions find the modulus of $f'(6 + 4j)$, and hence estimate the area of the image of the lantern $ABCD$ in Figure 12:
   (a) f: $z \mapsto z^2 - 6z + 5$
   (b) f: $z \mapsto jz + 26/z$

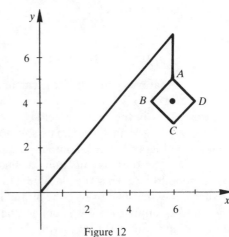

Figure 12

3   What is the image of $1 + j$ under the function $f: z \mapsto 1/z$? Make an accurate drawing of a region $ABCD$ bounded by arcs, centre O, and segments of radii surrounding the point $1 + j$ in the z-plane, and of its image $A'B'C'D'$ in the w-plane.

State the value of the derivative $f'(1 + j)$, and describe its significance in terms of your diagram.

4   Show that (a) $z \mapsto 2z + z^*$ is a one-way stretch, and (b) $z \mapsto 3z + z^*$ is a two-way stretch. Are these conformal transformations?

5   Explain why, for the transformation $f: z \mapsto e^z$,

$$\left. \begin{array}{l} u = e^x \cos y \\ v = e^x \sin y \end{array} \right\}$$

Show that the image of the line $x = 1$ is a circle, and that the image of $y = 1$ is a half-line from the origin.

Draw the image of the flag in Figure 2.

6   For the function in question 5, show the image of the square bounded by $x = b$, $x = -b$, $y = b$ and $y = -b$, where b is small. Explain why $f'(0) = 1$.

Simplify $\dfrac{f(a + h) - f(a)}{h}$ and explain why its limit is e^a as h tends to zero from any direction in the complex plane.

7   Show that the function $f: z \mapsto \dfrac{z - 2j}{jz + 1}, \quad z \neq j,$

is differentiable, and find its derived function.

8   Show that $z \mapsto z^{1/2}$ is a function if the codomain is limited to the half-plane above $v = 0$ plus half the u-axis.

Show that $x = u^2 - v^2$ and give a relation connecting y, u and v. Draw the images of the lines $x = 2, 1, 0, -1, -2$ and $y = 2, 1, 0, -1, -2$.

Draw the images of the flags in Figures 2 and 4.

Investigate from first principles the derivative of the function and check that this is consistent with your diagrams.

9   Are the usual map projections used by geographers conformal transformations from the globe to the plane?

3. THE NEWTON–RAPHSON PROCESS

We notice that many results in the calculus of real functions have counterparts in the world of complex numbers. We now ask whether equations can be solved approximately in the complex field by the Newton–Raphson method.

Suppose $z = a$ is an approximate solution of the equation $f(z) = 0$. This means that P (see Figure 13) maps onto a point of the w-plane close to the origin.

If f is a continuous function, a small displacement in the z-plane will correspond to some small displacement in the w-plane. We would like to move P in such a way that P' moves to the origin. But the ratio of small displacements of this kind is approximately equal to the derivative $f'(a)$, assuming that f is differentiable. Since $\mathbf{P'O} = -f(a)$, the required displacement in the z-plane is

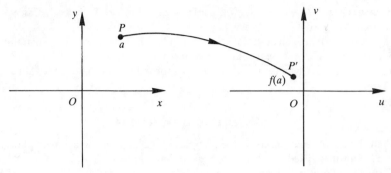

Figure 13

$- f(a)/f'(a)$, and a better approximation to the solution of $f(z) = 0$ is

$$a - \frac{f(a)}{f'(a)}.$$

This is the familiar formula.

Exercise 14C

1 Derive the Newton–Raphson formula for solving a real equation $f(x) = 0$ with the help of a number-line diagram.

2 What are the limitations of the Newton–Raphson process for real functions? Are there similar restrictions on its use in the complex field?

3 Show that $3 + 5j$ is a close approximation to a root of $z^3 - 2z + 200 = 0$, and find a closer one.

4 Show that $2 - j$ is an approximate solution of $z^3 + 5jz^2 - 20 = 0$, and find a closer one.

5 Write a computer program to carry out three stages of the Newton–Raphson process on the equation of question 4 or an equation of your own choice.

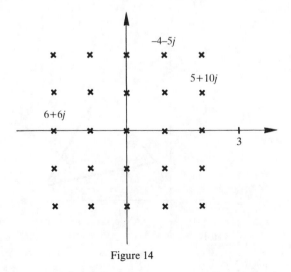

Figure 14

6   Given $f(z) = z^3 - (3 + j)z + (8 + 4j)$, explain why $|f(z)| > 8$ if $|z| = 3$. Can you be sure that $|f(z)| > 0$ if $|z| > 3$?

   Work out $f(z)$ for each of the lattice points in Figure 14 on page 187. (Treat this as a cooperative exercise or use a computer program.)

   Use the Newton–Raphson method to find approximations to the three solutions of $f(z) = 0$.

Miscellaneous exercise 14

1   Find the set of fixed points of the mapping $z \mapsto z^4 + jz$ of the complex plane into itself. Plot these fixed points on an Argand diagram.

   (A 'fixed point' of a mapping is a point that maps to itself.)   [SMP]

2   The complex number $z = x + jy$ corresponds to the vector $\begin{bmatrix} x \\ y \end{bmatrix}$.

   A transformation **T** of the complex plane is given by

$$\mathbf{T}: z \mapsto az + cz^*,$$

where $a = \alpha + j\beta$ and $c = \gamma + j\delta$ are complex numbers. Find a 2×2 matrix **A** such that **T** corresponds to the mapping

$$\begin{bmatrix} x \\ y \end{bmatrix} \mapsto \mathbf{A} \begin{bmatrix} x \\ y \end{bmatrix}.$$

State a condition on **A** which determines whether or not **T** has an inverse. Use it to show that **T** has an inverse if $|a| \neq |c|$.   [SMP]

3   Copy the diagram of the complex plane (Figure 15), and give clearly the geometrical significance of

$$\arg\left(\frac{z_3 - z_1}{z_3 - z_2}\right).$$

On separate diagrams, mark in the set of all points which satisfy:

(a) $\arg\left(\dfrac{z - j}{z + 1}\right) = \pi$ (b) $\arg\left(\dfrac{z - j}{z + 1}\right) = 0$ (c) $\arg\left(\dfrac{z - j}{z + 1}\right) = \tfrac{1}{2}\pi$

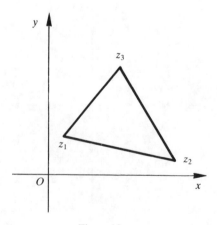

Figure 15   [SMP]

4   The equation $$w = \left(\frac{z+j}{z-1}\right)$$

defines a transformation of the complex plane. Find the sets of points in the z-plane which map into:

(a) the unit circle $| w | = 1$;
(b) the circle $| w | = 2$;
(c) the line $\arg w = \tfrac{1}{2}\pi$.

Sketch each of these sets of points on diagrams of the complex z-plane.   [SMP]

5   A complex number $w = u + jv$ satisfies the equation $e^w = z$. Show that

$$u = \ln | z |, \qquad v = \arg z + 2n\pi$$

for some integer n.

If $z = 1 + jt$ where t is real, express u and v in terms of t (if $-\pi < v \leqslant \pi$).

Plot the points corresponding to $t = 0, 1$ on a diagram of the uv-plane. What happens to v when t is very large? Sketch the locus of W.   [SMP]

6   The curve PQ in Figure 16 is a quarter-circle. Write down a parametric form for points z on the curve PQ in terms of a real parameter, giving the range of values of the parameter.

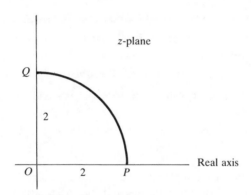

Figure 16

Draw a diagram of the image of the path $OPQO$ under the transformation $w = z^2$. Sketch also a path starting at Q which is mapped into one complete circuit of the circle $| w | = 4$ in the w-plane.   [SMP]

7   Sketch the locus W given by $| z - 1 - j | = 1$.

Show that the mapping $z \mapsto jz^*$ corresponds to a single reflection. Deduce that, under the mapping $f: z \mapsto jz^* - 1$, W is mapped onto the locus given by $| z - j | = 1$.

By considering the expression $1/(f(z))^*$, or otherwise, find the image of W under the mapping $g: z \mapsto -1/(jz + 1)$. Draw a sketch of this image, and show on your sketch the part of the image that corresponds to the part of W for which $\operatorname{Im} z \leqslant \operatorname{Re} z$.   [SMP]

8   Give a geometrical interpretation of

$$\arg\left(\frac{z_1 - z}{z_2 - z}\right),$$

where z_1, z_2 and z are complex numbers, represented by points P_1, P_2 and P in the complex plane.

Show that the curve S in the complex plane given by

$$\arg\left(\frac{3 + j\sqrt{3} - z}{1 - z}\right) = \tfrac{1}{6}\pi$$

consists of part of a circle through the origin. Draw the circle in the complex plane, and show which part of it corresponds to S.

Show that the centre C of the circle lies on the line $\operatorname{Re} z = \tfrac{1}{2}$ and also on the line given by

$$z = \tfrac{1}{2}(3 + j\sqrt{3}) + jt(3 + j\sqrt{3}) \quad \text{for real } t.$$

Find C, and verify that the radius of the circle is $\sqrt{7}$.   [SMP]

9 The real part of e^z is $e^x \cos y$, where $z = x + jy$. Write down the imaginary part of e^z and give similar expressions for the real and imaginary parts of e^{-z}.

The complex hyperbolic function $z \mapsto \sinh z$ is defined by the formula

$$\sinh z = \tfrac{1}{2}(e^z - e^{-z}).$$

Show that $\sinh z$ is a periodic function of period $2\pi j$. Show also that the real and imaginary parts of $\sinh z$ are given by the formula

$$\sinh z = \sinh x \cos y + j \cosh x \sin y.$$

Deduce that the image of the line $\operatorname{Im} z = \tfrac{1}{4}\pi$ under the transformation $z \mapsto w$ where $w = \sinh z$ is part of the curve

$$v^2 - u^2 = \tfrac{1}{2}, \quad \text{if } w = u + jv.$$

Draw a sketch of the w-plane showing this image, and also the image of the line $\operatorname{Re} z = 1$.   [SMP]

10 Let C be a curve in the complex plane with parametric equations

$$x = f(t), \quad y = g(t) \qquad (a \leqslant t \leqslant b)$$

and let C' be the image of C under the transformation of the complex plane $w \geqslant e^z$, where $z = x + jy$. Write down the real and imaginary parts of w in terms of x and y. Deduce that the length of C' can be written

$$\int_a^b e^x \, (\dot{x}^2 + \dot{y}^2)^{1/2} \, dt.$$

If C is the straight line segment

$$x = t, \quad y = \tfrac{1}{2}\pi t \qquad (0 \leqslant t \leqslant 1),$$

mark on a diagram for w the images of the points $t = 0, \tfrac{1}{2}, 1$ on C. Hence draw a rough sketch of C'. Show that the length of C' is $(e - 1) \sqrt{(1 + \tfrac{1}{4}\pi^2)}$.   [SMP]

11 Sketch the locus S given by $|z - j| = \sqrt{2}$.

Use the fact that $|w|^2 = ww^*$ to show that if $|z - j| = \sqrt{2}$ then

$$zz^* + zj - z^*j - 1 = 0.$$

Deduce that if z represents a point on S then so does $1/z$.

By multiplying top and bottom by $(z + j)^*$, prove that if z represents a point on S then

$$\frac{(1/z) + j}{z + j} = \frac{2}{|z + j|^2}.$$

What does this tell you about the geometric configuration of the points corresponding to z, $1/z$ and $-j$?   [SMP]

SUMMARY

A function $z \mapsto f(z)$ corresponds to a transformation of the complex plane. If f is differentiable, the transformation is conformal; in other words, angles are unchanged and the local transformation is a spiral similarity. The modulus of $f'(z)$ is the scale factor, and the argument is the angle of rotation.

The Newton–Raphson process holds for complex numbers: if a is an approximate solution of the equation $f(z) = 0$, then

$$a - \frac{f(a)}{f'(a)}$$

is usually a better approximation.

15

Jacobians

1. LOCAL DISTORTIONS

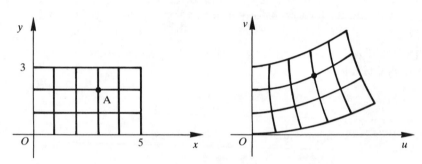

Figure 1

Figure 1 shows a diagram of a rectangular plate, and the same plate distorted under externally applied loading. Situations of this kind pose two important problems:

(i) What shape does the plate then assume?

(ii) What internal stresses are set up in the plate?

To answer such questions calls for difficult analysis; in this section we shall build up some of the mathematical equipment which can be used to handle this.

It will be recognised that this is essentially a transformation problem: a point (x, y) of the plate moves to a new position (u, v). We may therefore describe the geometry in function terms, writing

$$f: (x, y) \mapsto (u, v).$$

Once this function has been determined, the first of our two problems is answered.

The second problem, however, forces us to look more closely at the local transformation around the point (x, y). It should be noted that if the whole plate were subjected to a direct isometry, such as translation

$$(x, y) \mapsto (x + a, \ y + b),$$

then no internal stresses at all would be created.

As a simple example, take the transformation of the plate given by

$$\left. \begin{array}{l} u = \ x + \ \frac{1}{2}y \\ v = \frac{1}{2}x + 1\frac{1}{2}y \end{array} \right\}$$

192

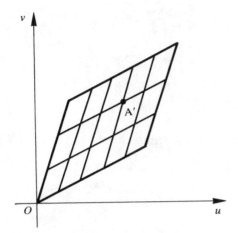

Figure 2

Here every part of the plate is deformed in the same way (see Figure 2), and this is characterised by the matrix $\begin{bmatrix} 1 & \frac{1}{2} \\ \frac{1}{2} & 1\frac{1}{2} \end{bmatrix}$.

The transformation
$$\left. \begin{array}{l} u = x - \frac{1}{20}xy \\ v = y + \frac{1}{10}xy \end{array} \right\}$$

on the other hand, gives a variable distortion. Check that $(5, 0) \mapsto (5, 0)$, $(5,3) \mapsto (4.25, 4.5)$ and $(3, 2) \mapsto (2.7, 2.6)$. The complete image is shown in Figure 3.

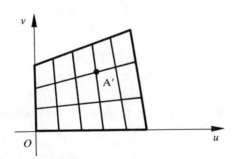

Figure 3

To describe the stresses set up at A', say, we need to look at the distortion in the region immediately surrounding this point.

Now the image of $y = 2$ is given by
$$\left. \begin{array}{l} u = x - \frac{1}{10}x \\ v = 2 + \frac{1}{5}x \end{array} \right\},$$

hence $$\frac{du}{dx} = 0.9 \quad \text{and} \quad \frac{dv}{dx} = 0.2.$$

A small displacement $\begin{bmatrix} \delta x \\ 0 \end{bmatrix}$ is mapped onto $\begin{bmatrix} 0.9\ \delta x \\ 0.2\ \delta x \end{bmatrix}$. Similarly, a small

displacement $\begin{bmatrix} 0 \\ \delta y \end{bmatrix}$ is mapped onto $\begin{bmatrix} -0.15\ \delta y \\ 1.3\ \delta y \end{bmatrix}$.

What is the image of a small displacement $\begin{bmatrix} \delta x \\ \delta y \end{bmatrix}$ from A? We have here only a
slight extension of the work we undertook when dealing with functions from $\mathbb{C}$
to $\mathbb{C}$.

Exercise 15A

1 Draw the images of the rectangular plate in Figure 1 together with the grid marked on
   it under the following transformations:

   $(a) \quad \begin{aligned} u &= x + \tfrac{1}{10}y \\ v &= \tfrac{1}{5}x + y \end{aligned}\Big\} \qquad (b) \quad \begin{aligned} u &= x + \tfrac{1}{10}y^2 \\ v &= y + \tfrac{1}{20}x^2 \end{aligned}\Big\} \qquad (c) \quad \begin{aligned} u &= x - \tfrac{1}{10}xy \\ v &= y - \tfrac{1}{20}xy \end{aligned}\Big\}$

   For each transformation, investigate the distortion of the region around the image of
   (3, 2).

2 Show that the image of the line $x = 5$ in question 1(b) is given by
   $u = 5 + 0.1(v - 1.25)^2$ and find the uv-equation of the image of $y = 3$.

3 Explain why the distortion around A' in Figure 3 can be described by the matrix
   $\begin{bmatrix} 0.9 & -0.15 \\ 0.2 & 1.3 \end{bmatrix}$, and use your answers to question 1 to write down the relevant
   matrices for those three transformations.

4 For the transformation of the first quadrant given by

   $$u = xy, \qquad v = y/x,$$

   show that the inverse transformation is given by

   $$x = \sqrt{(u/v)}, \qquad y = \sqrt{(uv)}.$$

   Draw separate diagrams showing the images in the uv-plane of the lines $x = 1, 2, 3$
   and $y = 1, 2, 3$, and the curves in the xy-plane corresponding to $u = 1, 2, 3$ and
   $v = 1, 2, 3$.
   Find matrices as in question 3 to describe the distortion of the region round $x = 2$,
   $y = 3$ in the transformation $(x, y) \mapsto (u, v)$ and the distortion of the region around
   $u = 6, v = 1.5$ in the inverse transformation. Comment on your answers.

2 THE JACOBIAN MATRIX

In §1 we considered the equations

$$\begin{aligned} u &= x - \tfrac{1}{20}xy \\ v &= y + \tfrac{1}{10}xy \end{aligned}\Bigg\}.$$

When we kept y constant and differentiated with respect to x, we were in fact carrying out partial differentiation, although the notation was not necessary because we were focusing on one particular point. Now we shall generalise.

Since
$$\frac{\partial u}{\partial x} = 1 - \tfrac{1}{20}y \quad \text{and} \quad \frac{\partial v}{\partial x} = \tfrac{1}{10}y,$$

the vector $\begin{bmatrix} \delta x \\ 0 \end{bmatrix}$ at the point (x, y) maps approximately onto the vector

$\begin{bmatrix} 1 - \tfrac{1}{20}y \\ \tfrac{1}{10}y \end{bmatrix} \delta x$ in the uv-plane.

Also,
$$\frac{\partial u}{\partial y} = -\tfrac{1}{20}x \quad \text{and} \quad \frac{\partial v}{\partial y} = 1 + \tfrac{1}{10}x,$$

and the vector $\begin{bmatrix} 0 \\ \delta y \end{bmatrix}$ at (x, y) maps approximately onto $\begin{bmatrix} -\tfrac{1}{20}x \\ 1 + \tfrac{1}{10}x \end{bmatrix} \delta y.$

Moreover, $\begin{bmatrix} \delta x \\ \delta y \end{bmatrix} = \begin{bmatrix} \delta x \\ 0 \end{bmatrix} + \begin{bmatrix} 0 \\ \delta y \end{bmatrix}$, and this general displacement maps onto

$$\begin{bmatrix} 1 - \tfrac{1}{20}y \\ \tfrac{1}{10}y \end{bmatrix} \delta x + \begin{bmatrix} -\tfrac{1}{20}x \\ 1 + \tfrac{1}{10}x \end{bmatrix} \delta y = \begin{bmatrix} 1 - \tfrac{1}{20}y & -\tfrac{1}{20}x \\ \tfrac{1}{10}y & 1 + \tfrac{1}{10}x \end{bmatrix} \begin{bmatrix} \delta x \\ \delta y \end{bmatrix}.$$

This 2×2 matrix fulfils the role of a 'local scale factor'. We may think of it as the derivative of the function mapping $\begin{bmatrix} x \\ y \end{bmatrix}$ onto $\begin{bmatrix} u \\ v \end{bmatrix}$. In general, this matrix is given by

$$\begin{bmatrix} \dfrac{\partial u}{\partial x} & \dfrac{\partial u}{\partial y} \\ \dfrac{\partial v}{\partial x} & \dfrac{\partial v}{\partial y} \end{bmatrix}.$$

It is usually denoted by the symbol $\dfrac{\partial(u, v)}{\partial(x, y)}$ and called the *Jacobian matrix*, after Carl Jacobi (1804–1851).

2.1 Alternative derivation

In Chapter 12 we saw that if u is a function of two variables x and y, then

$$\delta u \approx \frac{\partial u}{\partial x} \delta x + \frac{\partial u}{\partial y} \delta y.$$

Here we have also
$$\delta v \approx \frac{\partial v}{\partial x} \delta x + \frac{\partial v}{\partial y} \delta y.$$

Combining these two relations gives

$$
\begin{bmatrix} \delta u \\ \delta v \end{bmatrix} \approx \begin{bmatrix} \dfrac{\partial u}{\partial x} & \dfrac{\partial u}{\partial y} \\ \dfrac{\partial v}{\partial x} & \dfrac{\partial v}{\partial y} \end{bmatrix} \begin{bmatrix} \delta x \\ \delta y \end{bmatrix},
$$

which is another way of expressing the result just obtained.

2.2 Properties

(i) The determinant of the Jacobian matrix, which we shall denote by $\left| \dfrac{\partial(u, v)}{\partial(x, y)} \right|$, measures the ratio in which areas are magnified locally by the transformation. It will play an important role when we explore double integrals further, in Chapter 16.

(ii) If an inverse transformation $(u, v) \mapsto (x, y)$ exists, its local scale factor $\dfrac{\partial(x, y)}{\partial(u, v)}$ must be the inverse of $\dfrac{\partial(u, v)}{\partial(x, y)}$. This result may have been suggested by Exercise 15A, question 4.

You might have wondered whether there is a simple connection between $\dfrac{\partial x}{\partial u}$, the leading element in the first of these Jacobians, and $\dfrac{\partial u}{\partial x}$, the leading element in the other: after all, $\dfrac{dx}{dy}$ is the reciprocal of $\dfrac{dy}{dx}$. A moment's reflection shows that none is expected: in calculating $\dfrac{\partial x}{\partial u}$ we are keeping v constant, while $\dfrac{\partial u}{\partial x}$ is found keeping y constant. A complicated connection does exist, in that one Jacobian matrix is the inverse of the other.

(iii) *Combined transformations* Since the Jacobian matrix describes the first-order transformation, such transformations can be combined by the usual process of matrix multiplication. Suppose, for example, that a differentiable function maps (x, y) onto (u, v), and that a second differentiable function maps (u, v) onto (s, t). Then the local distortions will be described by the first-order approximations

$$
\begin{bmatrix} \delta s \\ \delta t \end{bmatrix} \approx \begin{bmatrix} \dfrac{\partial s}{\partial u} & \dfrac{\partial s}{\partial v} \\ \dfrac{\partial t}{\partial u} & \dfrac{\partial t}{\partial v} \end{bmatrix} \begin{bmatrix} \delta u \\ \delta v \end{bmatrix} \quad \text{and} \quad \begin{bmatrix} \delta u \\ \delta v \end{bmatrix} \approx \begin{bmatrix} \dfrac{\partial u}{\partial x} & \dfrac{\partial u}{\partial y} \\ \dfrac{\partial v}{\partial x} & \dfrac{\partial v}{\partial y} \end{bmatrix} \begin{bmatrix} \delta x \\ \delta y \end{bmatrix}.
$$

so that

$$
\begin{bmatrix} \delta s \\ \delta t \end{bmatrix} \approx \begin{bmatrix} \dfrac{\partial s}{\partial u} & \dfrac{\partial s}{\partial v} \\ \dfrac{\partial t}{\partial u} & \dfrac{\partial t}{\partial v} \end{bmatrix} \begin{bmatrix} \dfrac{\partial u}{\partial x} & \dfrac{\partial u}{\partial y} \\ \dfrac{\partial v}{\partial x} & \dfrac{\partial v}{\partial y} \end{bmatrix} \begin{bmatrix} \delta x \\ \delta y \end{bmatrix}.
$$

But the transformation which effects the composite mapping $(x, y) \mapsto (s, t)$ yields the local approximation

$$
\begin{bmatrix} \delta s \\ \delta t \end{bmatrix} \approx \begin{bmatrix} \dfrac{\partial s}{\partial x} & \dfrac{\partial s}{\partial y} \\[2mm] \dfrac{\partial t}{\partial x} & \dfrac{\partial t}{\partial y} \end{bmatrix} \begin{bmatrix} \delta x \\ \delta y \end{bmatrix}.
$$

It follows that, in the notation of Jacobian matrices,

$$
\frac{\partial(s, t)}{\partial(x, y)} = \frac{\partial(s, t)}{\partial(u, v)} \times \frac{\partial(u, v)}{\partial(x, y)}.
$$

It is natural to call this the *chain rule* for functions $\mathbb{R}^2$ to $\mathbb{R}^2$. The order of the two matrices on the right is, of course, important.

From the chain rule we can derive four equations for the individual partial derivatives. For example,

$$
\frac{\partial s}{\partial x} = \frac{\partial s}{\partial u}\frac{\partial u}{\partial x} + \frac{\partial s}{\partial v}\frac{\partial v}{\partial x}.
$$

3. FUNCTIONS MAPPING $\mathbb{R}^m$ TO $\mathbb{R}^n$

The ideas of §2 can be extended immediately to transformations of spaces of higher dimensions, and those from $\mathbb{R}^3$ to $\mathbb{R}^3$ are of special importance. Moreover, the domain and codomain do not need to have the same dimension.

Exercise 15B

1   Write down in terms of x and y the Jacobian matrices for each of the transformations in Exercise 15A, question 1.

2   (a) Find the image of the flag in Figure 4 under the transformation

$$u = xy, \qquad v = y/x.$$

(b) Use $\mathbf{J} = \dfrac{\partial(u, v)}{\partial(x, y)}$ to describe the local transformation of the regions around B and D.

(c) Find the value of the determinant of $\mathbf{J}$ at $x = 1\frac{1}{2}$, $y = 3\frac{1}{2}$.

(d) Show by integration that the area of the image of $BCDE$ is $7 \ln 2$. Compare with your answer to (c).

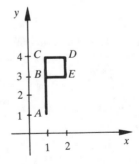

Figure 4

3   Given $x = \sqrt{(u/v)}$, $y = \sqrt{(uv)}$, write down the matrix $\mathbf{J}' = \dfrac{\partial(x, y)}{\partial(u, v)}$. Show that this is the inverse of the matrix $\mathbf{J}$ in question 2.

4   Find in terms of x and y both $\dfrac{\partial(u, v)}{\partial(x, y)}$ and $\dfrac{\partial(x, y)}{\partial(u, v)}$ for the function defined by $u = x + y$, $v = \sqrt{(xy)}$.

5 Draw the image of the flag of Figure 4 under the transformation

$$u = x^2 + y^2, \qquad v = 2xy.$$

Find the approximate area of $B'C'D'E'$ by using the value of the determinant of $\dfrac{\partial(u, v)}{\partial(x, y)}$ at $(1\frac{1}{2}, 3\frac{1}{2})$.

6 For the function $z \mapsto z^2$ mapping $x + yj$ onto $u + vj$, we have

$$u = x^2 - y^2, \qquad v = 2xy.$$

Repeat question 5 for this transformation.

How do you recognise that the Jacobian matrix is that of a spiral similarity? Why would you expect this?

7 Prove that the function $u = x - y$, $v = xy$ maps the first quadrant one-to-one onto the half-plane above the u-axis. Draw in the codomain a number of loci $x = $ constant and $y = $ constant. Calculate $\dfrac{\partial(u, v)}{\partial(x, y)}$, and show in detail how this describes the local transformation at the points $x = 1, y = 1$; $x = 2, y = 2$; $x = 1, y = 2$.

Use the Jacobian matrix to find the partial derivatives for the inverse function mapping (u, v) onto (x, y), and then calculate these partial derivatives by an independent method.

8 Verify the chain rule connecting the Jacobian matrices for the functions defined by

$$\left.\begin{array}{l} u = xy^3 \\ v = x^3 y \end{array}\right\} \quad \text{and} \quad \left.\begin{array}{l} s = \sqrt{(uv)} \\ t = u - v \end{array}\right\}$$

9 For the function transforming polar to Cartesian coordinates,

$$x = r \cos \theta, \qquad r \sin \theta,$$

find $\dfrac{\partial(x, y)}{\partial(r, \theta)}$ and its determinant.

From $r = \sqrt{(x^2 + y^2)}$ and $\theta = \tan^{-1}(y/x)$, find $\dfrac{\partial(r, \theta)}{\partial(x, y)}$ and its determinant.

10 When r is increased by δr, keeping θ constant (see Figure 5), x is increased by $\delta r \cos \theta$. This shows geometrically that $\dfrac{\partial x}{\partial r} = \cos \theta$. Show in a similar way that

$$\frac{\partial x}{\partial \theta} = -r \sin \theta.$$

Use Figure 6 to show that $\dfrac{\partial r}{\partial x} = \cos \theta$ and $\dfrac{\partial \theta}{\partial x} = -(\sin \theta)/r$.

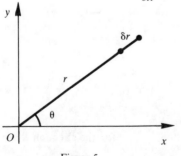

Figure 5

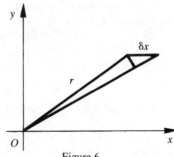

Figure 6

11 Devise a generalisation of the Newton–Raphson process and use it to improve on $x = 3$, $y = 5$ as an approximate solution to the equations

$$\left.\begin{array}{r} x^2 + 3xy - y^2 - 30 = 0 \\ 2x^2 - xy + 5y^2 - 130 = 0 \end{array}\right\}$$

12 Regarding each of the following as functions $(x, y) \mapsto (u, v)$, find the Jacobian matrix $\dfrac{\partial(u, v)}{\partial(x, y)}$:

(a) $z \mapsto z^3$ (b) $z \mapsto e^z$ (c) $z \mapsto 1/z$ (d) $z \mapsto 3z + z^*$

In each of the first three parts, find the real and imaginary parts of $f'(z)$.

13 For the function $f: z \mapsto z^{1/2}$ (with suitable choice of domain and codomain), find the matrix $\dfrac{\partial(x, y)}{\partial(u, v)}$ in terms of u and v, and deduce $\dfrac{\partial(u, v)}{\partial(x, y)}$. Hence give an expression for $\dfrac{\partial u}{\partial x}$.

Obtain $\dfrac{\partial u}{\partial x}$ independently from $f'(z) = \tfrac{1}{2} z^{-1/2}$.

14 Given that f is differentiable, use the fact that the local transformation for the function $z \mapsto f(z)$ mapping $x + yj$ to $u + vj$ is a spiral similarity to show that

$$\frac{\partial u}{\partial x} = \frac{\partial v}{\partial y} \quad \text{and} \quad \frac{\partial u}{\partial y} = - \frac{\partial v}{\partial x}.$$

These are known as the *Cauchy–Riemann equations*.

15 Given that $u + vj = f(x + yj)$, show that (if f is differentiable),

$$\frac{\partial u}{\partial x} + \frac{\partial v}{\partial x} j = f'(x + yj) \quad \text{and} \quad \frac{\partial u}{\partial y} + \frac{\partial v}{\partial y} j = f'(x + yj) \times j.$$

Deduce the Cauchy–Riemann equations.

Miscellaneous exercise 15

1 A mapping from $\mathbb{R}^2$ to $\mathbb{R}^2$ is defined by

$$\left.\begin{array}{r} u = x^2 - y^2 \\ v = 2xy \end{array}\right\}$$

Calculate the Jacobian matrix $\mathbf{J}$ such that

$$\begin{bmatrix} \delta u \\ \delta v \end{bmatrix} = \mathbf{J} \begin{bmatrix} \delta x \\ \delta y \end{bmatrix}.$$

Use $\mathbf{J}$ to state the rotation and enlargement which the mapping produces on any small triangle near the point $(1, 1)$.   [SMP]

2 On a Mercator chart, the point with longitude θ and latitude λ is represented by coordinates

$$x = \theta, \qquad y = \ln(\sec \lambda + \tan \lambda).$$

On a stereographic chart, the same point is represented by coordinates

$$u = 2(\sec \lambda + \tan \lambda) \sin \theta, \qquad v = 2(\sec \lambda + \tan \lambda) \cos \theta.$$

Calculate the Jacobian matrices for the mappings $(\theta, \lambda) \mapsto (x, y)$ and $(\theta, \lambda) \mapsto (u, v)$. Deduce the matrices for the mappings $(x, y) \mapsto (\theta, \lambda)$ and $(x, y) \mapsto (u, v)$.

Show that this last matrix can be put into the form

$$f(\lambda) \begin{bmatrix} \cos\theta & \sin\theta \\ -\sin\theta & \cos\theta \end{bmatrix},$$

and state what this implies about the geometrical nature of the local transformation at any point.   [SMP]

3 Variables u and v are functions of x, y. It is desired to find a point $x = a$, $y = b$ at which $u = v = 1$. Show that if $x = x_1$, $y = y_1$, are first approximations to the coordinates of this point, then the errors $\delta x = a - x_1$, $\delta y = b - y_1$, satisfy

$$\begin{bmatrix} 1 - u_1 \\ 1 - v_1 \end{bmatrix} = \mathbf{J}_1 \begin{bmatrix} \delta x \\ \delta y \end{bmatrix},$$

where u_1, v_1 are the values of u, v at (x_1, y_1) and $\mathbf{J}_1$ is the value of the Jacobian matrix

$$\mathbf{J} = \frac{\partial(u, v)}{\partial(x, y)} \quad \text{at } (x_1, y_1).$$

If $\qquad\qquad u = x + \dfrac{x}{x^2 + y^2}, \qquad v = y - \dfrac{y}{x^2 + y^2},$

calculate the value of $\mathbf{J}$ at the point $(1, 2)$ and show that it is a scalar multiple of $\begin{bmatrix} 7 & -1 \\ 1 & 7 \end{bmatrix}$. Taking $x_1 = 1$, $y_1 = 2$ as a first approximation to (a, b), use the above formula to calculate a second approximation.   [SMP]

4 Cartesian coordinates are given in terms of three-dimensional polar coordinates by

$$\left. \begin{array}{l} x = r\sin\theta\cos\phi \\ y = r\sin\theta\sin\phi \\ z = r\cos\theta \end{array} \right\},$$

Find $\dfrac{\partial(x, y, z)}{\partial(r, \theta, \phi)}$ and show that its determinant is equal to $r^2\sin\theta$.

5 If u is the real part of $f(x + yj)$, where f is a differentiable function mapping $\mathbb{C}$ to $\mathbb{C}$, use the Cauchy–Riemann equations to show that

$$\frac{\partial^2 u}{\partial x^2} + \frac{\partial^2 u}{\partial y^2} = 0.$$

Illustrate by choosing several particular functions f.

SUMMARY

For a transformation from $\mathbb{R}^2$ to $\mathbb{R}^2$ given by $u = f(x, y)$, $v = g(x, y)$, the local scale factor is the Jacobian matrix,

$$\frac{\partial(u, v)}{\partial(x, y)} = \begin{bmatrix} \dfrac{\partial u}{\partial x} & \dfrac{\partial u}{\partial y} \\ \dfrac{\partial v}{\partial x} & \dfrac{\partial v}{\partial y} \end{bmatrix}.$$

Its determinant gives the local area scale factor.

For the inverse transformation, the Jacobian matrix $\dfrac{\partial(x, y)}{\partial(u, v)}$ is the inverse of $\dfrac{\partial(u, v)}{\partial(x, y)}$.

For a combined transformation $(x, y) \mapsto (u, v) \mapsto (s, t)$, the Jacobian matrices satisfy the chain rule

$$\frac{\partial(s, t)}{\partial(x, y)} = \frac{\partial(s, t)}{\partial(u, v)} \times \frac{\partial(u, v)}{\partial(x, y)} .$$

For a complex transformation $x + yj = z \mapsto w = u + vj$ given by a differentiable function $w = f(z)$, the Cauchy–Riemann equations hold:

$$\frac{\partial u}{\partial x} = \frac{\partial v}{\partial y} , \qquad \frac{\partial u}{\partial y} = - \frac{\partial v}{\partial x} .$$

16

Triple integrals and substitution

1. APPLICATIONS TO MECHANICS

1.1 Centres of mass

It may be recalled that the definition of the centre of mass G of a set of particles of mass m_i at points with position vectors $\mathbf{r}_i$ is given by

$$(\Sigma m_i) \, \bar{\mathbf{r}} = \Sigma(m_i \mathbf{r}_i).$$

The x-coordinate of G is therefore given by $M\bar{x} = \Sigma m_i x_i$ where $M = \Sigma m_i$, a formula reminiscent of that for the mean of a statistical sample. With continuous distributions of matter, the necessary summation is effected by integration, and often we can get away with using a single variable.

Example 1
Find the centre of mass of a uniform solid hemisphere of radius a.

Solution
Let the density be ρ. With the hemisphere in the position shown in Figure 1, the shaded portion represents a disc of volume δV, and

$$\delta V \approx \pi y^2 \, \delta x,$$
$$\delta m \approx \pi y^2 \, \delta x \times \rho.$$

The disc contributes a 'moment' of approximately

$$\pi y^2 \, \delta x \times \rho \times x$$

to the sum we require, and the usual limiting process yields an exact total

$$\int \pi y^2 \rho x \, dx.$$

Figure 1

Since $y^2 = a^2 - x^2$, we get $\quad M\bar{x} = \displaystyle\int_0^a \pi \rho x(a^2 - x^2) \, dx,$

giving $\qquad \frac{2}{3}\pi a^3 \rho \bar{x} = \pi \rho \left[-\frac{1}{4}(a^2 - x^2)^2 \right]_0^a = \frac{1}{4}\pi \rho a^4.$

Thus $\qquad\qquad\qquad \bar{x} = \frac{3}{8}a.$

Since by symmetry the centre of mass lies on the *x*-axis, we have located its position precisely. ☐

With more complicated shapes, it may be desirable to use a double integral.

Example 2
Find the centre of mass of a uniform lamina bounded by the arcs of $y = 3\sqrt{x}$ and $y = \frac{3}{8}x^2$ (see Figure 2).

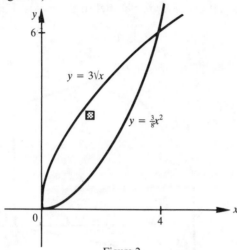

Figure 2

Solution
This time we shall take a small rectangular element, δx by δy, and integrate first with respect to *y* and then with respect to *x*.

The total area
$$A = \int_0^4 \int_{3x^2/8}^{3\sqrt{x}} 1 \, dy \, dx = 8,$$

so the total mass $= 8\rho$, where ρ is the mass per unit area. For the element, $\delta m = \rho \, \delta x \, \delta y$, and its moment about the *y*-axis is approximately $\rho \, \delta x \, \delta y \times x$.

Then
$$M\bar{x} = \int_0^4 \int_{3x^2/8}^{3\sqrt{x}} \rho x \, dy \, dx = \tfrac{72}{5}\rho$$

and hence
$$\bar{x} = \tfrac{9}{5}.$$

Evaluating the double integrals is a routine matter and the working is left to the reader (see Exercise 16A, question 1).

To complete this example we need $\bar{y}$. This is, of course, defined by
$$M\bar{y} = \Sigma m_i y_i,$$

and we get
$$8\rho\bar{y} = \int_0^4 \int_{3x^2/8}^{3\sqrt{x}} \pi y \, dy \, dx = \tfrac{108}{5}\rho,$$

giving
$$\bar{y} = \tfrac{27}{10}.$$ ☐

1.2 Triple integrals

Example 2 is two-dimensional. For non-symmetrical shapes in three dimensions, we shall require triple integrals. In principle this is no more difficult, though getting the right limits of integration may not be straightforward.

Example 3
The top face of the wedge $OABCDE$ in Figure 3 is formed by the plane $z = 5 - 2x - y$, and AD and BE are parallel to the z-axis. Find its volume and centre of mass.

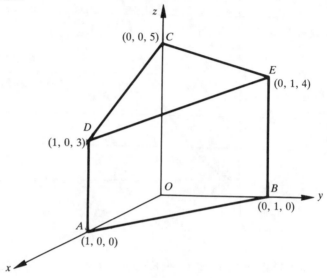

Figure 3

Solution
Take a small cuboid δx by δy by δz with one vertex at (x, y, z). Its volume is $\delta x \, \delta y \, \delta z$ and the total volume is

$$V = \int_0^1 \int_0^{1-x} \int_0^{5-2x-y} 1 \, dz \, dy \, dx.$$

This equals

$$\int_0^1 \int_0^{1-x} (5 - 2x - y) \, dy \, dx,$$

and we would have been happy to write down the volume in this form at the outset. Its value is 2.

The triple-integral form is easier to comprehend when we look for the centre of mass. Then

$$V\bar{x} = \iiint x \, dz \, dy \, dx, \quad V\bar{y} = \iiint y \, dz \, dy \, dx, \quad \text{and} \quad V\bar{z} = \iiint z \, dz \, dy \, dx,$$

In each case the limits of integration are the same as for V. Where the density is uniform, it will always cancel, and here it has been omitted.   □

1.3 Moments of inertia

The moment of inertia of a set of particles about an axis is defined as $\Sigma m_i s_i^2$, where s_i is the distance of the particle of mass m_i from the axis. Once again, continuous distributions of matter mean that integration is required for the summation, and whereas moments of inertia of uniform rods, discs and spheres can be obtained by simple integrals (see Exercise 16A, question 10), double and triple integrals will be needed for more complicated bodies.

Thus for the wedge of Example 3, the cuboid element has moment of inertia $\rho \, \delta x \, \delta y \, \delta z \, (y^2 + z^2)$ about the x-axis (more or less: in fact, points of the cuboid other than one edge are a tiny bit further than $\sqrt{(y^2 + z^2)}$ from the x-axis).

The total moment of inertia is given exactly by

$$\iiint \rho(y^2 + z^2) \ dz \ dy \ dx,$$

with the same limits of integration as before.

Exercise 16A

1 For Example 2,
  (*a*) evaluate the double integrals;
  (*b*) show how $\bar{y}$ can be calculated by a single integration if strips are taken parallel to the x-axis;
  (*c*) show how $\bar{y}$ can be calculated by a single integration if strips are taken parallel to the y-axis.

2 A uniform lamina has the shape shown in Figure 4. Find its area and the coordinates of its centre of mass.

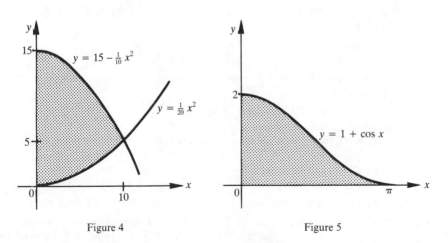

Figure 4   Figure 5

3 Find $\bar{x}$ and $\bar{y}$ for a uniform lamina bounded by the coordinate axes and $y = 1 + \cos x$ (as in Figure 5).

4 Show that in Example 3, $\bar{x} = \frac{5}{16}$ and $\bar{y} = \frac{1}{3}$. Find $\bar{z}$.

5 (a) Explain why for a uniform sector of radius a and angle 2α as in Figure 6(a),

$$a^2 \alpha \bar{x} = 2 \int_0^{a\sin\alpha} \int_{y\cot\alpha}^{\sqrt{(a^2-y^2)}} x \, dx \, dy.$$

Find $\bar{x}$ in terms of a and α.

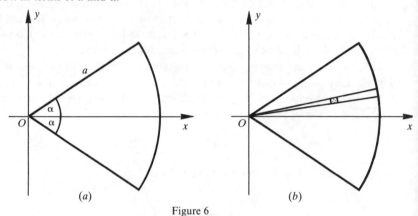

Figure 6

(b) Use Figure 6(b) to show that for the same lamina,

$$a^2 \alpha \bar{x} = \int \int r^2 \cos\theta \, dr \, d\theta$$

with suitable limits of integration. Show that this yields the same answer.

6 With domain the cuboid with faces $x = 0$, $y = 0$, $z = 0$, $x = 1$, $y = 2$ and $z = 3$, evaluate:

(a) $\iiint (x + y + z) \, dx \, dy \, dz$ (b) $\iiint (x^2 + y^2) \, dx \, dy \, dz$

7 Repeat question 6 if the domain is the tetrahedron with vertices $(0, 0, 0)$, $(2, 0, 0)$, $(0, 2, 0)$ and $(0, 0, 2)$.

8 A uniform solid is bounded by the planes $x = 0$, $y = 0$, $z = 0$, $x = 3$, $y = 2$ and $z = 4x - y + 5$. Find its volume, and $\bar{x}$, $\bar{y}$ and $\bar{z}$.

9 If in question 8 the top surface, instead of being $z = 4x - y + 5$ is $z = -x^2 + y^2 + 10$, find $\bar{x}$.

10 Derive the formulae for the moments of inertia of
    (a) a uniform rod about a perpendicular axis through its centre;
    (b) a thin uniform disc about an axis through its centre, perpendicular to its plane;
    (c) a uniform sphere about a diameter.
In each case, with suitably chosen elements, a single integral will suffice.

11 Find the moments of inertia about the z-axis of the solids in questions 8 and 9.

12 Write down an expression for the perpendicular distance from (p, q) to the line $ax + by + c = 0$. Hence show that the moment of inertia about AC of a uniform plate $ABCD$ 3 m by 6 m (as in Figure 7) is given by

$$\rho \int_0^6 \int_0^3 \frac{(2x - y)^2}{5} \, dx \, dy,$$

where ρ is the mass per unit area. Evaluate the integral.

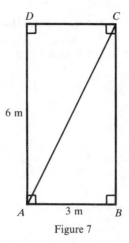

Figure 7

13 Show that the point of the line $\begin{bmatrix} x \\ y \\ z \end{bmatrix} = t \begin{bmatrix} 1 \\ 1 \\ 1 \end{bmatrix}$ closest to (p, q, r) has $t = \frac{1}{3}(p + q + r)$.

Hence find the moment of inertia about a diagonal of the uniform unit cube with edges parallel to the coordinate axes and $(0, 0, 0)$, $(1, 1, 1)$ as opposite vertices.

2. SUBSTITUTION IN DOUBLE INTEGRALS

The method of substitution is the most powerful way of tackling integrals of one variable when the answer cannot be found directly. Before seeing how this can be extended to double and triple integrals, let us look at a geometrical explanation of the familiar procedure.

For $\displaystyle\int_0^2 \sqrt{(1 + x^2)}\, dx$, we use the substitution $x = \sinh u$. Then $\sqrt{(1 + x^2)} = \cosh u$.

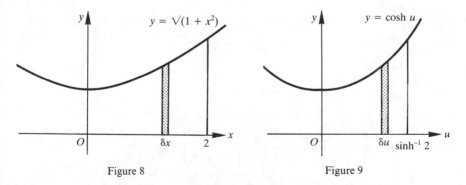

Figure 8   Figure 9

The shaded rectangles in Figures 8 and 9 have the same height, but they do not have the same area, since $\delta x \neq \delta u$. The connection between these small lengths is given by the *linear scale factor* $\dfrac{dx}{du}$, for $\delta x \approx \dfrac{dx}{du}\,\delta u$. This explains why the extra factor $\dfrac{dx}{du}$ must be introduced as a vital part of the substitution process.

Formally, we replace the dx in the integral by $\dfrac{dx}{du}\,du$.

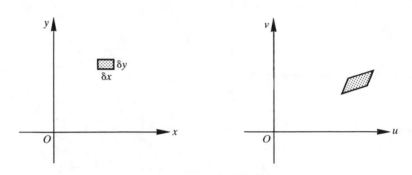

Figure 10

For double integrals, we may wish to replace variables x and y by new variables u and v, where x and y are separate functions of u and v. A matchstick with base a rectangle with sides δx and δy is replaced by a matchstick with a parallelogram base in the uv-plane (see Figure 10).

Now the local scale factor is given by the Jacobian $\dfrac{\partial(x,\,y)}{\partial(u,\,v)}$, and the local *area* scale factor is its *determinant*.

For double integrals, the appropriate formal equivalent of the familiar 'replace dx by $\dfrac{dx}{du}\,du$' is 'replace $dx\,dy$ by $\left|\dfrac{\partial(x,\,y)}{\partial(u,\,v)}\right|\,du\,dv$'. Note the use of the vertical lines to signify the determinant.

Example 4

Find $\displaystyle\iint e^{(y-x)/(y+x)}\,dx\,dy$, where the domain is the triangle bounded by $x = 0$, $y = 0$ and $x + y = 1$ (see Figure 11).

Solution

Put
$$y + x = u \quad \text{and} \quad y - x = v,$$
so that
$$x = \tfrac{1}{2}(u - v) \quad \text{and} \quad y = \tfrac{1}{2}(u + v).$$

Then
$$\left|\frac{\partial(x,\,y)}{\partial(u,\,v)}\right| = \begin{vmatrix} \tfrac{1}{2} & -\tfrac{1}{2} \\ \tfrac{1}{2} & \tfrac{1}{2} \end{vmatrix} = \tfrac{1}{2},$$

and the integral reduces to $\displaystyle\iint e^{v/u} \times \tfrac{1}{2}\,dv\,du$.

It pays to add up for v first, equivalent to taking strips parallel to $x + y = 1$.

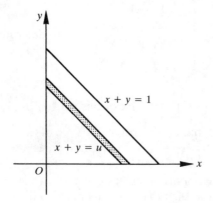

Figure 11

Now for $y = 0$, $v = -u$, while for $x = 0$, $v = u$. This gives us the limits of integration, and the rest is straightforward:

$$\int_0^1 \int_{-u}^u \tfrac{1}{2} e^{v/u} \, dv \, du = \int_0^1 \left[\tfrac{1}{2} u \, e^{v/u} \right]_{-u}^u \, du$$

$$= \int_0^1 \tfrac{1}{2} u(e - e^{-1}) \, du$$

$$= \tfrac{1}{4}(e - e^{-1}). \qquad \square$$

Example 5
Find the area of the region bounded by arcs of the four parabolas $y^2 = x$, $y^2 = 4x$, $x^2 = y$ and $x^2 = 9y$ (see Figure 12).

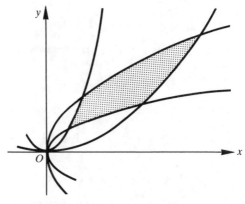

Figure 12

Solution
This can be answered by elementary methods, of course, but it is instructive (and easier) to use the substitution $u = y^2/x$, $v = x^2/y$. Then the region in the uv-plane is a rectangle bounded by $u = 1$, $u = 4$, $v = 1$ and $v = 9$.

The form of the substitution is such that it is easy to find $\dfrac{\partial(u, v)}{\partial(x, y)}$. We get

$$\frac{\partial(u, v)}{\partial(x, y)} = \begin{bmatrix} -\dfrac{y^2}{x^2} & \dfrac{2y}{x} \\ \dfrac{2x}{y} & -\dfrac{x^2}{y^2} \end{bmatrix}, \quad \text{with determinant } -3.$$

We can obtain $\dfrac{\partial(x, y)}{\partial(u, v)}$ as the inverse of this matrix, but in fact we only need to realise that its determinant is the reciprocal, $-\frac{1}{3}$, of the previous determinant. If the transformation $(x, y) \mapsto (u, v)$ multiplies areas by 3, the inverse transformation multiplies areas by $\frac{1}{3}$. The negative signs imply a reflection or change of sense, but this is unimportant here: we might just as well have chosen to write $u = x^2/y$, $v = y^2/x$, and then the determinants would have been positive.

So the required area $= \displaystyle\iint dx\, dy = \int_1^9 \int_1^4 \tfrac{1}{3}\, du\, dv = 8.$ □

2.1 The Cartesian-to-polar transformation

The link between the ideas of the last section and previous work involving polar coordinates is illuminating.

From
$$x = r \cos \theta, \qquad y = r \sin \theta,$$

$$\left| \frac{\partial(x, y)}{\partial(r, \theta)} \right| = \begin{vmatrix} \cos \theta & -r \sin \theta \\ \sin \theta & r \cos \theta \end{vmatrix} = r(\cos^2 \theta + \sin^2 \theta) = r.$$

If we write $\displaystyle\iint f(x, y)\, dx\, dy$ in terms of polars, therefore, we must replace $dx\, dy$ by $r\, dr\, d\theta$. The extra factor of r was explained by an independent method in Chapter 13.

Exercise 16B

1   (a) For $u = y + x$, $v = y - x$, evaluate $\left| \dfrac{\partial(u, v)}{\partial(x, y)} \right|$. Compare with the determinant in Example 4.

(b) For $u = y^2/x$, $v = x^2/y$, show that $x = u^{1/3}v^{2/3}$, $y = u^{2/3}v^{1/3}$, and deduce the value of $\left| \dfrac{\partial(x, y)}{\partial(u, v)} \right|$. Compare with Example 5.

2   Under the transformation $z \mapsto z^2$, the flag in Figure 13 maps onto the flag in Figure 14 (see Chapter 14, §1). Here $u = x^2 - y^2$, $v = 2xy$.

Work out $\left| \dfrac{\partial(u, v)}{\partial(x, y)} \right|$, and hence express the area of the second flag, $\displaystyle\iint du\, dv$,

in the form $\displaystyle\int_3^4 \int_1^2 f(x, y)\, dx\, dy$. Find the area.

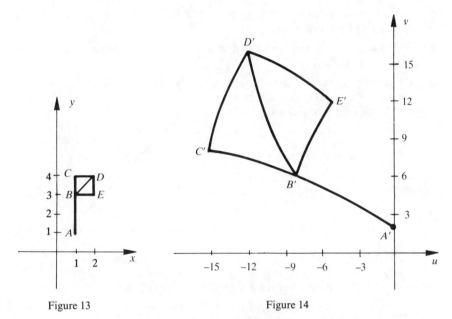

Figure 13   Figure 14

3   Use substitutions to find $\iint xy\, dx\, dy$ with each of the domains given in Figure 15.

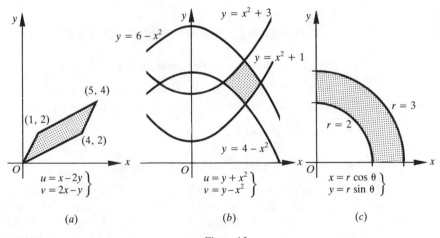

Figure 15

4   Find the area bounded by the four curves $2y = x^3$, $4y = x^3$, $5x = y^3$ and $8x = y^3$.

5   Find $\displaystyle\iint \frac{(x^2 + y^2)^2}{x^2 y^2}\, dx\, dy$ over the region common to the circles $x^2 + y^2 = ax$ and $x^2 + y^2 = by$ by putting $u = (x^2 + y^2)/x$, $v = (x^2 + y^2)/y$.

6   Find the area and the x-coordinate of the centre of mass of a uniform lamina in the shape of the shaded region of Figure 15(b).

7   A hollow hemispherical shell is formed by rotating Figure 15(c) about the

x-axis. Find its volume, centre of mass and moment of inertia about the x-axis, assuming uniform density ρ.

8 Find the centre of mass of a uniform lamina in the shape of the cardioid $r = a(1 + \cos\theta)$.

9 A bivariate probability density function has the form $\phi(x, y) = k\,e^{-3(x+y)^2}$, with domain the triangle of Figure 16. Find k.

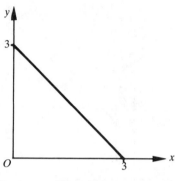

Figure 16

10 Find $\displaystyle\iint (x + y)\, dx\, dy$ over the first quadrant of the ellipse

$$\frac{x^2}{a^2} + \frac{y^2}{b^2} = 1$$

(*a*) directly, and (*b*) using the substitution $x = ar\cos\theta$, $y = br\sin\theta$.

3. POLAR COORDINATES IN THREE DIMENSIONS

3.1 Cylindrical polar coordinates

In three dimensions, we often use (r, θ, z) — polar coordinates in the xy-plane together with a z-coordinate. Obviously, in a triple integral we shall replace $dx\,dy\,dz$ by $r\,dr\,d\theta\,dz$.

3.2 Spherical polar coordinates

Genuine three-dimensional polar coordinates consist of the distance from the origin and two angles. To describe where to point a telescope we might give the angle down from the vertical and a bearing, i.e. an angle in the horizontal plane.

In Figure 17, P has coordinates $[r, \theta, \phi]$, where $r = OP$, θ is the angle between OP and the z-axis, N is the foot of the perpendicular from P to the xy-plane, and ϕ is the angle between ON and the x-axis. We see that $ON = r\sin\theta$, and so

$$x = r\sin\theta\cos\phi, \quad y = r\sin\theta\sin\phi \quad \text{and} \quad z = r\cos\theta.$$

The Jacobian is

$$\frac{\partial(x, y, z)}{\partial(r, \theta, \phi)} = \begin{bmatrix} \sin\theta\cos\phi & r\cos\theta\cos\phi & -r\sin\theta\sin\phi \\ \sin\theta\sin\phi & r\cos\theta\sin\phi & r\sin\theta\cos\phi \\ \cos\theta & -r\sin\theta & 0 \end{bmatrix}$$

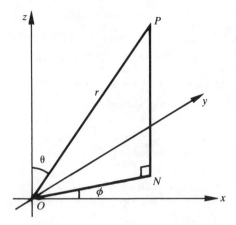

Figure 17

This has determinant $r^2 \sin \theta$, and so in a triple integral we need to use $r^2 \sin \theta \, dr \, d\theta \, d\phi$ in place of $dx \, dy \, dz$.

The factor $r^2 \sin \theta$ can be obtained geometrically with reference to Figure 17:

if r is increased by δr, keeping θ and ϕ constant, P moves a distance δr;

if θ is increased by $\delta\theta$, keeping r and ϕ constant, P moves a distance $r \, \delta\theta$;

if ϕ is increased by $\delta\phi$, keeping r and θ constant, P moves a distance $ON \, \delta\phi = r \sin \theta \, \delta\phi$.

These displacements are mutually perpendicular at P, and form edges of a solid element of volume approximately $r^2 \sin \theta \, \delta r \, \delta\theta \, \delta\phi$.

Example 6

Find the centre of mass of the hemi-sphere of radius a, centre the origin, where $z \geq 0$ (see Figure 18).

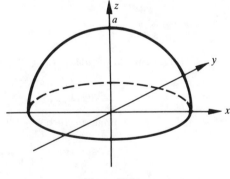

Figure 18

Solution

$$V\rho\bar{z} = \iiint \rho z \, dx \, dy \, dz$$

gives $\quad \frac{2}{3}\pi a^3 \bar{z} = \int_0^{2\pi} \int_0^{\pi/2} \int_0^a r \cos \theta \times r^2 \sin \theta \, dr \, d\theta \, d\phi,$

and this quickly yields the standard result $\bar{z} = \frac{3}{8}a$. $\square$

Exercise 16C

1   Verify that the Jacobian in §3.2 has determinant $r^2 \sin \theta$.

2   Carry out the integration in Example 6 and show that $\bar{z} = \frac{3}{8}a$.

3   Find $\displaystyle\int\int\int xyz \, dx \, dy \, dz$ over the octant of the unit sphere $x^2 + y^2 + z^2 \leqslant 1$ for which $x \geqslant 0$, $y \geqslant 0$, $z \geqslant 0$, (a) by using Cartesian coordinates, and (b) by using spherical polars.

4   Use cylindrical polar coordinates to find the volume, centre of mass and moment of inertia about the z-axis for the portion of the sphere $x^2 + y^2 + z^2 \leqslant a^2$ for which $z \geqslant 0$ and $x^2 + y^2 \leqslant b^2$ (where $a > b$).

5   A circular disc of radius b is rotated through half a revolution about a line in its plane distance a from its centre (where $a > b$). The uniform density is ρ.

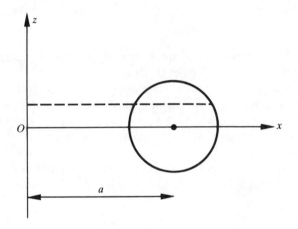

Figure 19

(a) Show that the mass M may be calculated from

$$\int_{-b}^{b} \int_{a-\sqrt{(b^2-z^2)}}^{a+\sqrt{(b^2-z^2)}} \int_{-\pi/2}^{\pi/2} \pi r \, d\theta \, dr \, dz,$$

and the centre of mass is then given by $\bar{x}$, where

$$M\bar{x} = \int\int\int \rho(r \cos \theta) \, r \, d\theta \, dr \, dz,$$

with the same limits.

(b) Evaluate M and $\bar{x}$.

6   A bracelet with a heart-shaped cross-section has the form of the solid generated by rotating the cardioid

$$r = a(1 - \cos \theta), \qquad (0 \leqslant \theta < 2\pi)$$

about the axis $x = 6a$ in its plane (see Figure 20). Calculate the (heart-shaped) cross-sectional area of the bracelet. Show that the volume of the bracelet is given by the double integral

$$V = \int\int 2\pi(6a - r \cos \theta)\, r\, dr\, d\theta$$

evaluated over a suitable region, and hence evaluate V.

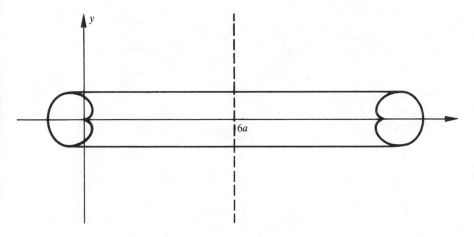

Figure 20   [SMP]

7   (a) Use the substitution $u = x + y + z$, $v = x + 2y + 3z$, $w = x + 3y + 8z$ to find the
volume of the parallelepiped with faces $x + y + z = 2$, $x + y + z = 4$, $x + 2y + 3z = 5$,
$x + 2y + 3z = 9$, $x + 3y + 8z = 7$ and $x + 3y + 8z = 11$.

    (b) Show that $z = \frac{1}{3}(u - 2v + w)$, and hence find $\iiint z\, dx\, dy\, dz$ with the
parallel piped as domain.

    (c) Use a simple method to check (a) and (b).

8   Use whichever method you think simplest to find the area of the parallelogram
bounded by the lines $2x + 3y = 4$, $2x + 3y = 10$, $5x - y = 2$ and $5x - y = 7$.

4. TWO IMPORTANT APPLICATIONS

We end with two results of crucial value in applied mathematics.

4.1 The normal probability curve

Figure 21 (overleaf) shows two vertical sections of the infinite symmetrical
surface $z = e^{-(x^2 + y^2)/2}$. We shall find the volume of this hill in two ways.

Using polars:
$$V = \int_0^\infty \int_0^{2\pi} e^{-r^2/2}\, r\, d\theta\, dr$$
$$= 2\pi \int_0^\infty r\, e^{-r^2/2}\, dr$$
$$= 2\pi \left[-e^{-r^2/2} \right]_0^\infty$$
$$= 2\pi.$$

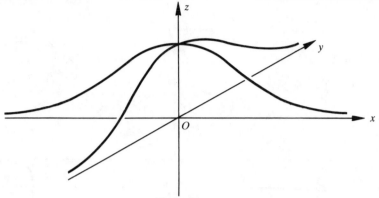

Figure 21

Using Cartesians:
$$V = \int_{-\infty}^{\infty} \int_{-\infty}^{\infty} e^{-x^2/2} \times e^{-y^2/2} \, dx \, dy$$
$$= \int_{-\infty}^{\infty} e^{-x^2/2} \, dx \times \int_{-\infty}^{\infty} e^{-y^2/2} \, dy$$
$$= A^2,$$

where A = total area under the graph of $e^{-x^2/2}$. It follows that $A = \sqrt{(2\pi)}$, a result which is probably well known to the reader but impossible to obtain by elementary means.

The explanation above sweeps under the carpet all problems about convergence, and assumes that the infinite integrals behave well. It is more convincing to construct a proof along the lines advocated in Chapters 3 and 9.

Now we shall consider finite domains, as shown in Figure 22.

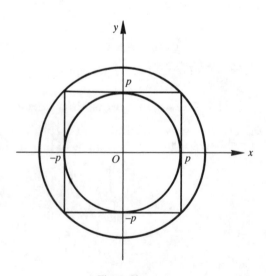

Figure 22

The portion of the hill with the square as base has volume A'^2, where $A' = \int_{-p}^{p} e^{-x^2/2} \, dx$. The cylindrical portions have radii p and $\sqrt{2}p$ and volumes $2\pi(1 - e^{-p^2/2})$ and $2\pi(1 - e^{-p^2})$.

Consequently, $2\pi(1 - e^{-p^2/2}) < A'^2 < 2\pi(1 - e^{-p^2})$.

At this stage we can let p tend to infinity. Then

$$2\pi \leq \lim_{p \to \infty} \left\{ \int_{-p}^{p} e^{-x^2/2} \, dx \right\}^2 \leq 2\pi,$$

so that $\int_{-p}^{p} e^{-x^2/2} \, dx \to \sqrt{(2\pi)}$ as $p \to \infty$.

4.2 Centres of gravity

Two particles of mass m_1 and m_2 and a distance d apart attract each other with a gravitational force of Gm_1m_2/d^2, where G is a constant. With this as an axiom, we can find by integration the gravitational effects of extended bodies of different shapes. Take first a uniform rod of length l and density ρ per unit length, and consider its attraction on a point mass m_1 at a distance d from its centre, as in Figure 23.

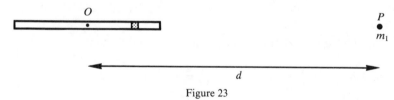

Figure 23

An element of length δx at a distance x from O contributes a force of approximately $Gm_1(\rho \, \delta x)/(d - x)^2$, and the total force is exactly

$$Gm_1\rho \int_{-l/2}^{l/2} \frac{1}{(d - x)^2} \, dx = Gm_1\rho \left[\frac{1}{d - \frac{1}{2}l} - \frac{1}{d + \frac{1}{2}l} \right]$$

$$= \frac{Gm_1m_2}{d^2 - \frac{1}{4}l^2}, \quad \text{where } m_2 = \rho l.$$

This is equivalent to the force provided by a particle of mass m_2 at a distance $\sqrt{(d^2 - \frac{1}{4}l^2)}$ from P. In this case, the centre of gravity does not coincide with the centre of mass.

Let us repeat this, but with a uniform sphere of radius a instead of the rod. The component of the force provided by the element in Figure 24 (overleaf) in the direction PO is approximately

$$\frac{Gm_1\rho \, \delta x \, \delta y \, \delta z}{R^2} \cos \alpha.$$

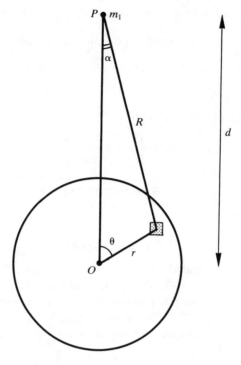

Figure 24

It is essential to use polar coordinates. Then the total force is

$$\int_0^{2\pi} \int_0^\pi \int_0^a \frac{Gm_1\rho r^2 \sin\theta \cos\alpha}{R^2} \, dr \, d\theta \, d\phi.$$

When we note that

$$r \cos\theta + R \cos\alpha = d \quad \text{and} \quad R^2 = d^2 + r^2 - 2dr \cos\theta,$$

the integral becomes

$$2\pi Gm_1\rho \int_0^a \int_0^\pi \frac{r^2 \sin\theta \, (d - r \cos\theta)}{(d^2 + r^2 - 2dr \cos\theta)^{3/2}} \, d\theta \, dr.$$

The integral with respect to ϕ is trivial, and we have disposed of it. Then it pays to integrate with respect to θ using the substitution $u = d^2 + r^2 - 2dr \cos\theta$. For, treating r as a constant,

$$\int_0^\pi \frac{\sin\theta \, (d - r \cos\theta)}{(d^2 + r^2 - 2dr \cos\theta)^{3/2}} \, d\theta = \int_{(d-r)^2}^{(d+r)^2} \frac{u + d^2 - r^2}{4d^2 r u^{3/2}} \, du$$

$$= \frac{1}{4d^2 r} \int_{(d-r)^2}^{(d+r)^2} \{u^{-1/2} + (d^2 - r^2) \, u^{-3/2}\} \, du$$

$$= \frac{1}{2d^2 r} \left[u^{1/2} + (d^2 - r^2) \, u^{-1/2} \right]_{(d-r)^2}^{(d+r)^2}$$

$$= \frac{1}{2d^2r}\{(d+r)-(d-r)-(d-r)+(d+r)\},$$

(assuming $d>r$)

$$= \frac{2}{d^2}.$$

Finally,   the total force $= 2\pi Gm_1\rho \int_0^a \frac{2r^2}{d^2}\,dr$

$$= \frac{Gm_1m_2}{d^2}, \quad \text{since } m_2 = \tfrac{4}{3}\pi a^3\rho.$$

This means that the sphere behaves exactly like a particle of the same mass at its centre; in other words, the centre of gravity is at the geometrical centre. The example of the rod shows that this result, although often used without question, should not be taken for granted. Of course, when we consider the weight of a rod near the surface of the earth, i.e. the gravitational force between the earth and the rod, d (in our notation) is vastly greater than l, and the centre of gravity is to all intents and purposes at the geometrical centre.

Finally, look back at the stage in the working for the sphere where it was assumed that $d>r$. If, instead, $d<r$, then

$$u^{1/2} = \{(d-r)^2\}^{1/2} = -(d-r) \quad \text{when } u = (d-r)^2.$$

The integral now equals

$$\frac{1}{2d^2r}\{(d+r)-(d-r)+(d-r)-(d+r)\} = 0.$$

The interpretation of this is not obvious. It means that the gravitational forces due to a thin spherical shell on a point mass inside the shell cancel out (see Figure 25), a surprising result of importance in electrostatics as well, where the inverse square law also holds and the working is almost identical.

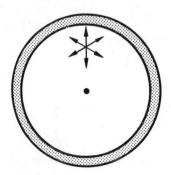

Figure 25

All of this means that if you go down a mine, your weight decreases a little, as it does when you climb a mountain.

Miscellaneous exercise 16

1   Describe the region D defined by

$$x^2 + y^2 \leqslant a^2, \qquad 0 \leqslant z \leqslant b.$$

Evaluate the triple integral $\qquad \iiint_D x^2 \, dV.$ [SMP]

2   Coordinates u, v in the region $x > 0$, $y > 0$ are related to the Cartesian coordinates by the equations

$$\left. \begin{array}{l} u = x^2 - y^2 \\ v = x^2 + y^2 \end{array} \right\}$$

Sketch the region D of the xy-plane bounded by the curves $u = 0$, $u = 1$, $v = 1$ and $v = 4$.

Evaluate $\qquad \iint_D xy^3 \, dx \, dy.$ [SMP]

3   A solid of uniform density occupies the region R given by x, y, $z > 0$, $x + y + z < 3$ and $x + y < 1$. Sketch the solid, and calculate its volume V.

The distance of the centroid of the solid from the plane $x = 0$ is given by

$$\bar{x} = \frac{1}{V} \iiint_R x \, dx \, dy \, dz.$$

Calculate $\bar{x}$.   [SMP]

4   Find

$$\frac{\partial(u, v)}{\partial(x, y)},$$

where $u = y \, e^x$ and $v = y \, e^{-x}$.

Draw a sketch showing the bounded region D enclosed by the curves

$$y = 2 \, e^{-x}, \quad y = 4 \, e^{-x}, \quad y = \tfrac{1}{2} \, e^x \quad \text{and} \quad y = 2 \, e^x.$$

Show that the area of D is given by

$$\iint \frac{du \, dv}{2\sqrt{u}\sqrt{v}}$$

evaluated over an appropriate region, and deduce that it is equal to $2(\sqrt{2} - 1)$.

Find the y-coordinate of the centre of mass of D.   [SMP]

5   A solid object consists of the interior of the sphere $x^2 + y^2 + z^2 = a^2$ with the portion lying inside the cylinder $x^2 + y^2 = b^2$ removed (where $0 < b < a$). Find a function $f(r)$ so that the volume of the object is given by

$$\int_{r=b}^{a} \int_{\theta=0}^{2\pi} \int_{z=-f(r)}^{f(r)} r \, dz \, d\theta \, dr.$$

Evaluate this integral.

Show that, if the object has uniform density and mass M, then its moment of inertia about the z-axis is

$$\tfrac{1}{5}M(2a^2 + 3b^2).$$

Discuss the significance of the limiting values of this expression as $b \to a$, and as $b \to 0$.   [SMP]

6   The boundary of an elliptically-shaped flat disc is defined relative to suitable coordinate axes OX and OY by the curve

$$\frac{x^2}{a^2} + \frac{9y^2}{4a^2} = 1.$$

The disc has a mass per unit area which varies in accordance with the formula

$$m = m_0 \left(1 - \frac{x^2}{a^2} - \frac{9y^2}{4a^2}\right).$$

Coordinates r and θ are defined by the equations

$$x = ar \cos \theta, \qquad y = \tfrac{2}{3}ar \sin \theta.$$

Determine the Jacobian matrix $\dfrac{\partial(x, y)}{\partial(r, \theta)}$. Deduce that the total mass of the disc is

$$M = \tfrac{2}{3}m_0 \, a^2 \int_0^{2\pi} d\theta \int_0^1 r(1 - r^2) \, dr.$$

Calculate M. Calculate also the moment of inertia about the axis OY in terms of M and a. [SMP]

SUMMARY

Centre of mass $\qquad\qquad V\bar{x} = \iiint x \, dx \, dy \, dz$

$\bar{y}$ and $\bar{z}$ are found similarly.

Moment of inertia
The moment of inertia about the z-axis is given by

$$\iiint \rho \, (x^2 + y^2) \, dx \, dy \, dz.$$

Substitution in triple integrals

Replace $dx \, dy \, dz$ by $\left| \dfrac{\partial(x, y, z)}{\partial(u, v, w)} \right| du \, dv \, dw,$

the determinant of the Jacobian being the local volume scale factor.

Coordinate systems in three dimensions
Cylindrical polars (r, θ, z): $\qquad x = r \cos \theta$
$\qquad\qquad\qquad\qquad\qquad\qquad\quad y = r \sin \theta$

$$\left| \frac{\partial(x, y)}{\partial(r, \theta)} \right| = r$$

Spherical polars (r, θ, ϕ): $\qquad x = r \sin \theta \cos \phi$
$\qquad\qquad\qquad\qquad\qquad\qquad\quad y = r \sin \theta \sin \phi$
$\qquad\qquad\qquad\qquad\qquad\qquad\quad z = r \cos \theta$

$$\left| \frac{\partial(x, y, z)}{\partial(r, \theta, \phi)} \right| = r^2 \sin \theta$$

Answers, hints and comments on the exercises

Exercise 1A

1 (*a*) $\sinh 2x$ (*b*) $\cosh 2x$ (*c*) 1   (*d*) $\cosh(a + b)$ (*e*) $\cosh 2x$
(*f*) $\cosh 2x$
These results are similar to the formulae for the circular functions, though sometimes the signs are different.

2 See §2.

3 $\dfrac{\mathrm{d}}{\mathrm{d}x}(\sinh x) = \cosh x;$ $\dfrac{\mathrm{d}}{\mathrm{d}x}(\cosh x) = \sinh x$
The graph of $y = \sinh x$ has a positive gradient everywhere, and the minimum gradient is 1, at the origin.

Exercise 1B

1 $\displaystyle\int \sinh x \, \mathrm{d}x = \cosh x + k;$ $\displaystyle\int \cosh x \, \mathrm{d}x = \sinh x + k$

2 $\cosh 2 - 1 = 2.76;$ $\sinh 2 = 3.63$

3 (*a*) e^a
   (*b*) $(\cosh a + \sinh a)(\cosh b + \sinh b) = e^a \times e^b = e^{a+b} = \cosh(a + b) + \sinh(a + b)$
   (*c*) True, since $(e^a)^n = e^{na}$.
   (*d*) $(\cos a + j \sin a)(\cos b + j \sin b) = \cos(a + b) + j \sin(a + b);$
      $(\cos a + j \sin a)^n = \cos na + j \sin na$

4 (*b*) $\cos \theta = \pm\frac{20}{29}$ (*c*) $\cosh u = \sqrt{(1 + \sinh^2 u)} = \frac{29}{20}$ (*d*) $\sinh u = \pm\frac{12}{5}$

5

x	-1	-0.5	0	0.5	1
$\cos^{-1} x$	3.14	2.09	1.57	1.05	0

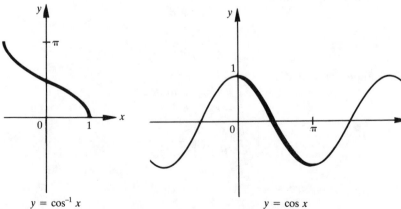

$y = \cos^{-1} x$ $y = \cos x$

6 The range is from $-\frac{1}{2}\pi$ to $\frac{1}{2}\pi$.

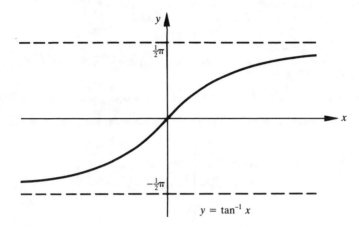

$y = \tan^{-1} x$

7 (a) $\cosh u = \sqrt{5}, \quad e^u = 2 + \sqrt{5}, \quad u = \ln(2 + \sqrt{5})$
(b) $\cosh v = 3, \quad \sinh v = \sqrt{8}, \quad v = \ln(3 + \sqrt{8})$
   Note that in both (a) and (b) it is correct to take the positive square root.
   (c) The proofs follow the procedures used in (a) and (b).

8 (a) $\displaystyle\int \frac{1}{\sqrt{(1 + x^2)}}\,dx = \int 1\,du = u + k = \sinh^{-1} x + k$

(b) $\displaystyle\int \frac{1}{\sqrt{(1 + x^2)}}\,dx = \int \sec\theta\,d\theta = \ln(\sec\theta + \tan\theta) + k$
$$= \ln(x + \sqrt{(x^2 + 1)}) + k$$

9 $x = a\cosh u$ and $x = a\sec\theta$ lead to
$$I = \cosh^{-1}(x/a) + k = \ln\left(\frac{x + \sqrt{(x^2 - a^2)}}{a}\right) + k.$$

10 $\displaystyle\frac{1}{x + \sqrt{(1 + x^2)}} \times \left(1 + \frac{x}{\sqrt{(1 + x^2)}}\right)$; simplifies to $\displaystyle\frac{1}{\sqrt{(1 + x^2)}}$.

Questions 8 and 10 provide alternative proofs of the second result of question 7(c).

11 0.589, 2.13. A table of values such as the one below is useful in suggesting sensible
starting values if a calculator (or tables) is used, but the question is best answered
with the help of a computer or programmable calculator.

x	0	1	2	3
$\cosh x$	1	1.54	3.76	10.1
$2x$	0	2	4	6

12 $\displaystyle\int \sinh^2 x\,dx = \int \tfrac{1}{2}(\cosh 2x - 1)\,dx = \tfrac{1}{4}\sinh 2x - \tfrac{1}{2}x + k,$ or

$\displaystyle\int \sinh^2 x\,dx = \int (\tfrac{1}{2}(e^x - e^{-x}))^2\,dx = \int \tfrac{1}{4}(e^{2x} - 2 + e^{-2x})\,dx$
$$= \tfrac{1}{8}(e^{2x} - 4x - e^{-2x}) + k;$$

$\displaystyle\int \cosh^2 x\,dx = \int \tfrac{1}{4}\sinh 2x + \tfrac{1}{2}x + k = \tfrac{1}{8}(e^{2x} + 4x - e^{-2x}) + k$

13   (a) This is because cosh $u > 0$ for all u and $\cosh^2 u - \sinh^2 u = 1$.

    (b) $FP^2 = (\sqrt{2} - \cosh u)^2 + \sinh^2 u$

$$= (2 - 2\sqrt{2} \cosh u + \cosh^2 u) + (\cosh^2 u - 1)$$
$$= 1 - 2\sqrt{2} \cosh u + 2 \cosh^2 u$$
$$= (1 - \sqrt{2} \cosh u)^2.$$

So $FP = \sqrt{2} \cosh u - 1$, this being the positive square root since cosh $u > 1$. Similarly, $F'P = \sqrt{2} \cosh u + 1$.

    (c) Area $= \displaystyle\int y \, dx = \int \sinh^2 t \, dt$, putting $x = \cosh t$ and $y = \sinh t$. The limits of integration are 0 and u. Triangle OPN has area

$$\tfrac{1}{2} \sinh u \cosh u = \tfrac{1}{4} \sinh 2u.$$

The area of the 'sector' OAP is therefore

$$\tfrac{1}{4} \sinh 2u - \left[\tfrac{1}{4} \sinh 2t - \tfrac{1}{2}t \right]_0^u = \tfrac{1}{2}u.$$

Exercise 1C

1   The method of Exercise 1B, question 5, demonstrated again in §3, achieves the desired result quickly.

2   (a) $\ln(4 + \sqrt{17})$ (b) $\ln(2 + \sqrt{3})$ (c) $\ln(-2 + \sqrt{5})$ (d) $\ln(1.5 + \sqrt{1.25})$

3   Since $[-x + \sqrt{(1 + x^2)}][x + \sqrt{(1 + x^2)}] = -x^2 + 1 + x^2 = 1$,

$$\ln[-x + \sqrt{(1 + x^2)}] = \ln[x + \sqrt{(1 + x^2)}]^{-1} = -\ln[x + \sqrt{(1 + x^2)}].$$

This is equivalent to saying that $\sinh^{-1}$ is an odd function, i.e. that $\sinh^{-1}(-x) = -\sinh^{-1} x$.

4   (a) $2 \cosh 2x$ (b) $\tfrac{1}{2} \sinh(\tfrac{1}{2} x + 3)$ (c) $\sinh x + x \cosh x$ (d) $\dfrac{3}{\sqrt{(1 + 9x^2)}}$

    (e) $\dfrac{1}{\sqrt{[(x + 5)^2 - 1]}}$ (f) $\dfrac{1}{2\sqrt{(\tfrac{1}{4}x^2 - 1)}}$ or $\dfrac{1}{\sqrt{(x^2 - 4)}}$ (g) $\dfrac{-1}{x\sqrt{(1 + x^2)}}$

5   (a) 0.392   (b) 0.771   (c) 2.09   (d) 0.539

6   This shows how to deal with negative limits. Notice also that $\ln(x + \sqrt{(x^2 - 1)})$ is undefined when x is negative.

7   (a) $\left[\sinh^{-1}\left(\dfrac{x + 2}{3} \right) \right]_0^1 = 0.256$ (b) $\left[\sinh^{-1}(x + 2) \right]_2^3 = 0.218$

    (c) $\left[\cosh^{-1}\left(\dfrac{x + 2}{3} \right) \right]_2^3 = 0.303$

8   (a) 1.41   (b) $x = \sinh u$ leads to an answer of 1.15   (c) 2.69

9   (a) $\left[\sin^{-1}\left(\dfrac{x - 2}{3} \right) \right]_0^1 = 0.390$ (b) $\left[\tan^{-1}(x + 2) \right]_0^1 = 0.142$ (c) $6 \ln \tfrac{6}{5} = 1.09$

10   (a) $x \cosh x - \sinh x + k$ (b) $x \sinh^{-1} x - \sqrt{(1 + x^2)} + k$

Miscellaneous exercise 1

1 $2 \cosh 2x$; $2 \cosh^2 x + 2 \sinh^2 x$.
These are equal, as expected. Differentiating again, we get $4 \sinh 2x$ and $8 \sinh x \cosh x$.

2 $\tanh 2x = \dfrac{2 \tanh x}{1 + \tanh^2 x}$; $\dfrac{d}{dx}(\tanh x) = \dfrac{1}{\cosh^2 x} = \operatorname{sech}^2 x$;

$\displaystyle\int \tanh x \, dx = \ln \cosh x + k$

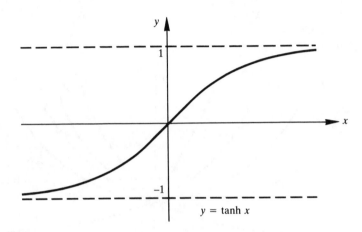

$y = \tanh x$

3 $y = \tanh^{-1} x \;\Rightarrow\; x = 1 - \dfrac{2}{e^{2y} + 1} \;\Rightarrow\; e^{2y} + 1 = \dfrac{2}{1 - x}$

$$\Rightarrow \qquad y = \tfrac{1}{2} \ln\left(\frac{1 + x}{1 - x}\right).$$

Note that this is an odd function, as expected.

4 Here is yet another way of proving a result we have already obtained by three different methods.

5 $y = A \sin nx + B \cos nx \;\Rightarrow\; \dfrac{d^2 y}{dx^2} = -n^2 y$

6 $\sinh x \approx x + \dfrac{x^3}{3!} + \dfrac{x^5}{5!} + \ldots + \dfrac{x^{2n-1}}{(2n-1)!}$;

$\cosh x \approx 1 + \dfrac{x^2}{2!} + \dfrac{x^4}{4!} + \ldots + \dfrac{x^{2n}}{(2n)!}$

7 $(1 + x^2)^{-1/2} \approx 1 - \tfrac{1}{2}x^2 + \tfrac{3}{8}x^4$ (binomial series)

$\Rightarrow\; \sinh^{-1} x \approx x - \tfrac{1}{6}x^3 + \tfrac{3}{40}x^5$.

There is no constant of integration, since $\sinh^{-1} 0 = 0$.

8 If $x/2^n$ is small enough, the first two terms of the Taylor series will give an excellent approximation to $\cosh(x/2^n)$. Then repeated use of the cosh $2u$ formula gives in turn $\cosh(x/2^{n-1})$, $\cosh(x/2^{n-2})$, ..., $\cosh x$.

9   In BBC Basic, a simple program is

```
10   INPUT X
20   N = 0
30   X = MOD(X)
40   REPEAT
50   X = X/2
60   N = N + 1
70   UNTIL X < 0.005
80   Y = 1 + X * X/2
90   FOR I = 1 TO N
100  Y = 2 * Y * Y − 1
110  NEXT I
120  PRINT Y
```

10

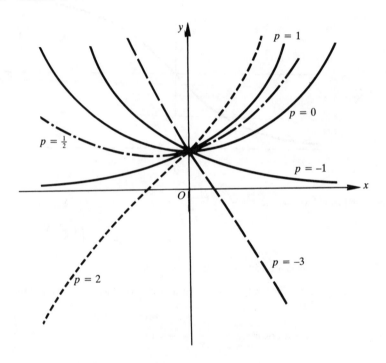

$p = 0$ gives a catenary; $p = 1$ and $p = -1$ give exponential curves; $p = 2$ gives a graph with gradient 2 at $(0, 1)$ and a point of inflexion on the x-axis; while $p = -2$ is the reflection of this in the y-axis. And so on.

11   (a) $3 \cosh x + 4 \sinh x = \sqrt{7} \left(\dfrac{3}{\sqrt{7}} \cosh x + \dfrac{4}{\sqrt{7}} \sinh x \right)$

$$= \sqrt{7} \left(\sinh \alpha \cosh x + \cosh \alpha \sinh x \right)$$

(where $\sinh \alpha = 3/\sqrt{7}$ and $\cosh \alpha = 4/\sqrt{7}$)

$$= \sqrt{7} \sinh(x + \alpha);$$

$$x = \sinh^{-1}\left(\frac{10}{\sqrt{7}}\right) - \sinh^{-1}\left(\frac{3}{\sqrt{7}}\right) = \ln\left(\frac{10 + \sqrt{107}}{7}\right) = 1.067$$

(b) $3.5u - 0.5u^{-1} = 10$ where $u = e^{-x}$

$\Rightarrow$ $7u^2 - 20u - 1 = 0$

$\Rightarrow$ $u = \dfrac{10 + \sqrt{107}}{7}$ (we take the positive square root because we require $u > 0$.)

$\Rightarrow$ $x = \ln\left(\dfrac{10 + \sqrt{107}}{7}\right)$,   as in (a).

12 (a) 0.310, -2.51 (b) 1.67,   0.529

13 This is an improper integral since the integrand is undefined when $x = 0$. With the definition of Chapter 9, however, we may write

$$I = \lim_{\alpha \to 0} \int_\alpha^1 \frac{1}{\sqrt{((x+2)^2 - 4)}} dx = \lim_{\alpha \to 0} \left[\cosh^{-1}\left(\frac{x+2}{2}\right)\right]_\alpha^1 = 0.962.$$

14 The substitution reduces the integral to $-\dfrac{1}{a}\displaystyle\int \frac{1}{\sqrt{(1+u^2)}} du$;

$$\frac{d}{dx}\left[\sinh^{-1}\left(\frac{a}{x}\right)\right] = \frac{1}{\sqrt{\left(1 + \frac{a^2}{x^2}\right)}} \times -\frac{a}{x^2} = \frac{-a}{x\sqrt{(x^2 + a^2)}}, \quad \text{as expected.}$$

15 $y = \dfrac{1}{\cosh x}$ $\Rightarrow$ $\dfrac{dy}{dx} = \dfrac{\sinh x}{\cosh^2 x}$ $\Rightarrow$ $\dfrac{d^2y}{dx^2} = \dfrac{\cosh^2 x - 2\sinh^2 x}{\cosh^3 x}$

$$= \frac{1 - \sinh^2 x}{\cosh^3 x}$$

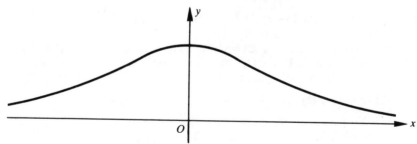

$\dfrac{d^2y}{dx^2} = 0$ when $x = \sinh^{-1}(\pm 1)$
$= \ln(1 + \sqrt{2})$ or $\ln(-1 + \sqrt{2})$
$= \pm\ln(1 + \sqrt{2})$

16 P lies on the right-hand branch of the hyperbola for all t. The area of $\mathcal{R}$ is $\frac{1}{2}u$ (see Exercise 1B, question 13). The transformation maps U onto the point V with parameter $(u + \alpha)$, and the arc AU onto the arc UV. The matrix has determinant 1 so the sector OUV also has area $\frac{1}{2}u$.

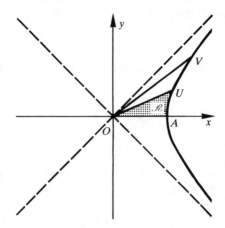

17 Since cosh $x = \sqrt{((\cosh 2x + 1)/2)}$, the algorithm is:

'Add 1, divide by 2, square root repeatedly until the result is less than 1.001 (call the number of occasions n). Then subtract 1, multiply 2, square root. Finally multiply by 2 n times'.

Note that this is a potentially unsatisfactory method because at the 'subtract 1' stage much accuracy is lost. See what happens with your calculator or computer if 1.001 is changed to 1.000 01.

Exercise 2A

1 (a) $11 + 10j$ (b) $15 - 8j$ (c) $-46 + 9j$ (d) $\dfrac{5 + 14j}{17}$ (e) $\dfrac{5 - 14j}{13}$

The moduli are $\sqrt{221} = \sqrt{13} \times \sqrt{17}$, $17 = (\sqrt{17})^2$, $\sqrt{2197} = (\sqrt{13})^3$, $\sqrt{13} \div \sqrt{17}$ and $\sqrt{17} \div \sqrt{13}$. The arguments are 0.738, -0.490, 2.948, 1.228 and -1.228; the arguments of z_1 and z_2 are 0.983 and -0.245.

2 (a) $\pm(2 + j)$ (b) $\pm(1.47 + 2.04j)$ (c) $\pm(2.04 - 1.47j)$

3 (a) -2, $1 \pm \sqrt{3}j$ (b) $z^3 + 8 = (z + 2)(z^2 - 2z + 4)$, etc.
(c) $2.01 + 0.421j$, $-1.37 + 1.53j$, $-0.638 - 1.95j$

4 $\cos 3\theta$ is the real part of $(\cos \theta + j \sin \theta)^3$, that is $\cos^3 \theta - 3 \cos \theta \sin^2 \theta$ or $4 \cos^3 \theta - 3 \cos \theta$.

5 $0.284 - 0.736j$, $-7.28 - 1.26j$

Exercise 2B

1 (a) 1, $-\frac{1}{2} \pm \frac{1}{2}\sqrt{3}j$ (b) $\pm\frac{1}{2}\sqrt{3} + \frac{1}{2}j$, $-j$
(c) $1.08 + 0.29j$, $-0.79 + 0.79j$, $-0.29 - 1.08j$ (d) -1, $\frac{1}{2} \pm \frac{1}{2}\sqrt{3}j$
(e) $2j$, $\pm\frac{1}{2}\sqrt{3} - \frac{1}{2}j$ (f) $\pm j$, $\frac{1}{2}\sqrt{3} \pm \frac{1}{2}j$, $-\frac{1}{2}\sqrt{3} \pm \frac{1}{2}j$

2 (a) $z^2 = 3$ or $-\frac{1}{4} \Rightarrow z = \pm\sqrt{3}$ or $\pm\frac{1}{2}j$
(b) $(z^2 - 1)(z^3 + 1) = 0 \Rightarrow z = \pm 1$ or $\frac{1}{2} \pm \frac{1}{2}\sqrt{3}j$
(c) $z^2 = -\frac{1}{2} \pm \frac{1}{2}\sqrt{3}j \Rightarrow z = \pm(\frac{1}{2} + \frac{1}{2}\sqrt{3}j)$ or $\pm(\frac{1}{2} - \frac{1}{2}\sqrt{3}j)$

3 $(z + 1)^4 = 16z^4 \iff 15z^4 - 4z^3 - 6z^2 - 4z - 1 = 0$
$$\iff (z - 1)(3z + 1)(5z^2 + 2z + 1) = 0$$
$$\iff z = 1 \text{ or } -\tfrac{1}{3} \text{ or } -\tfrac{1}{5} \pm \tfrac{2}{5}j$$

4 (a) $4z^3 - 8jz^2 - z + 2j = 0$ (b) $z^3 - z^2 + (-1 + 2j)z + (1 + 2j) = 0$

5 $z = \cos \tfrac{2}{7}k\pi + j \sin \tfrac{2}{7}k\pi, \quad k = 0, 1, 2, \ldots, 6.$
The result follows since
$$\cos \tfrac{12}{7}\pi = \cos \tfrac{2}{7}\pi, \quad \cos \tfrac{10}{7}\pi = \cos \tfrac{4}{7}\pi, \quad \cos \tfrac{8}{7}\pi = \cos \tfrac{6}{7}\pi.$$

6 These represent the fourth roots of $[1, \tfrac{3}{4}\pi] = -\tfrac{1}{2}\sqrt{2} + \tfrac{1}{2}\sqrt{2}j.$

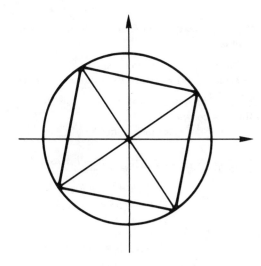

7 $z = \cos(\tfrac{1}{12}\pi + \tfrac{1}{3}k\pi) + j \sin(\tfrac{1}{12}\pi + \tfrac{1}{3}k\pi), \quad k = 0, 1, 2, 3, 4, 5.$
The values of z^5 are the same six numbers.

8 $(z + 1) = z^4 \Rightarrow z + 1 = z$ or $z + 1 = -z$ or $z + 1 = jz$ or $z + 1 = -jz$.
It follows that $z = -\tfrac{1}{2}, \quad -\tfrac{1}{2} \pm \tfrac{1}{2}j$. Alternatively, the equation is equivalent to $4z^3 + 6z^2 + 4z + 1 = 0$, and the solutions follow from the form $(2z + 1)(2z^2 + 2z + 1) = 0$.

9 $z = \dfrac{(1 + 4j) \pm \sqrt{(-3 + 4j)}}{2(1 + j)} = 2 + j \text{ or } \tfrac{1}{2} + \tfrac{1}{2}j$

10 $2.37 - 0.42j, \quad -0.82 + 2.26j, \quad -1.55 - 1.84j$

11 $\cos \tfrac{2}{5}\pi + \cos \tfrac{4}{5}\pi = -\tfrac{1}{2} \Rightarrow c + (2c^2 - 1) = -\tfrac{1}{2},$ where $c = \cos \tfrac{2}{5}\pi$
$$\Rightarrow c = \frac{-1 \pm \sqrt{5}}{4}.$$

Now $\sin 18° = \cos \tfrac{2}{5}\pi$, and this must be the positive value above, i.e. $\tfrac{1}{4}(\sqrt{5} - 1)$.

12 $z + \dfrac{1}{z} = 2 \cos \theta, \quad z^2 + \dfrac{1}{z^2} = 2 \cos 2\theta, \quad z^n + \dfrac{1}{z^n} = 2 \cos n\theta,$

$$z^n - \dfrac{1}{z^n} = 2j \sin n\theta$$

Exercise 2C

1 $\cos 3\theta + j \sin 3\theta = (\cos \theta + j \sin \theta)^3$
$$= \cos^3 \theta + 3j \cos^2 \theta \sin \theta - 3 \cos \theta \sin^2 \theta - j \sin^3 \theta;$$
$\cos 3\theta = \cos^3 \theta - 3 \cos \theta \sin^2 \theta = \cos^3 \theta - 3 \cos \theta (1 - \cos^2 \theta)$
$$= 4 \cos^3 \theta - 3 \cos \theta;$$
$\sin 3\theta = 3 \cos^2 \theta \sin \theta - \sin^3 \theta = 3 \sin \theta - 4 \sin^3 \theta;$
$$\tan 3\theta = \frac{3 \cos^2 \theta \sin \theta - \sin^3 \theta}{\cos^3 \theta - 3 \cos \theta \sin^2 \theta} = \frac{3 \tan \theta - \tan^3 \theta}{1 - 3 \tan^2 \theta}$$

2 $(\cos n\theta + j \sin n\theta)(\cos n\theta - j \sin n\theta) = 1;$
$(\cos \theta + j \sin \theta)^{-m} = (\cos m\theta + j \sin m\theta)^{-1} = \cos m\theta - j \sin m\theta$
$$= \cos(-m\theta) + j \sin(-m\theta)$$

3 $[\cos(\theta/n) + j \sin(\theta/n)]^n = \cos \theta + j \sin \theta$, so $\cos(\theta/n) + j \sin(\theta/n)$ is indeed an nth root of $\cos \theta + j \sin \theta$.

4 (a) $\cos 2\pi + j \sin 2\pi = 1$ (b) $\cos 5\theta - j \sin 5\theta$
(c) $\cos(\pi - 4\theta) + j \sin(\pi - 4\theta) = -\cos 4\theta + j \sin 4\theta$ (d) $\cos 3\theta + j \sin 3\theta$

5 (a) $\cos(4\phi - 4\theta) + j \sin(4\phi - 4\theta)$ (b) $\cos 9\theta + j \sin 9\theta$
(c) $j^4(\cos \theta - j \sin \theta)^4 = \cos 4\theta - j \sin 4\theta$
(d) $(-j)^6(\cos \theta + j \sin \theta)^6 = -\cos 6\theta - j \sin 6\theta$

(e) $\dfrac{1}{(2 \cos^2 \theta + 2j \sin \theta \cos \theta)^2} = \dfrac{1}{4 \cos^2 \theta} \times (\cos \theta + j \sin \theta)^{-2}$

$$= \left(\frac{\cos 2\theta}{4 \cos^2 \theta}\right) - j \left(\frac{\sin 2\theta}{4 \cos^2 \theta}\right)$$

6 $1 + j = [\sqrt{2}, \frac{1}{4}\pi] \implies (1 + j)^n = [2^{n/2}, \frac{1}{4}n\pi]$
$$= 2^{n/2}(\cos \frac{1}{4}n\pi + j \sin \frac{1}{4}n\pi);$$

$(1 + \sqrt{3}j)^n + (1 - \sqrt{3}j)^n = [2, \frac{1}{3}\pi]^n + [2, -\frac{1}{3}\pi]^n$
$$= 2^n(\cos \frac{1}{3}n\pi + j \sin \frac{1}{3}n\pi + \cos \frac{1}{3}n\pi - j \sin \frac{1}{3}n\pi)$$
$$= 2^{n+1} \cos \frac{1}{3}n\pi$$

7 (a) $\frac{1}{2}\sqrt{3} + \frac{1}{2}j$ (b) $\frac{1}{2}\sqrt{2} + \frac{1}{2}\sqrt{2}j$
(c) $\cos \theta + j \sin \theta$ (d) $\cos 5\theta - j \sin 5\theta$

8 $\cos 4\theta = c^4 - 6c^2s^2 + s^4$, $\sin 4\theta = 4c^3s - 4cs^3$, and $\tan 4\theta = \dfrac{4c^3s - 4cs^3}{c^4 - 6c^2s^2 + s^4}$,
writing c for $\cos \theta$ and s for $\sin \theta$.

Hence $\cos 4\theta = c^4 - 6c^2(1 - c^2) + (1 - c^2)^2 = 8c^4 - 8c^2 + 1$

and $\tan 4\theta = \dfrac{4t - 4t^3}{1 - 6t^2 + t^4}$, where $t = \tan \theta$.

9 If $z = \cos \theta + j \sin \theta$,

$$2 \cos \theta = z + \frac{1}{z} \quad \text{and} \quad 2 \cos n\theta = z^n + \frac{1}{z^n}.$$

So $\cos^6 \theta = \dfrac{1}{2^6}\left(z^6 + 6z^4 + 15z^2 + 20 + \dfrac{15}{z^2} + \dfrac{6}{z^4} + \dfrac{1}{z^6}\right)$

$$= \frac{1}{2^5}(10 + 15 \cos 2\theta + 6 \cos 4\theta + \cos 6\theta).$$

$$\int_0^{\pi/3} \cos^6 \theta \, d\theta = \frac{1}{2^5} \left(\tfrac{10}{3}\pi + 3\sqrt{3}\right).$$

10 (a) $\sin^4 \theta = \dfrac{1}{2^4}\left(z^4 - 4z^2 + 6 - \dfrac{4}{z^2} + \dfrac{1}{z^4}\right) = \dfrac{1}{2^3}(3 - 4\cos 2\theta + \cos 4\theta);$

$$\int \sin^4 \theta \, d\theta = \tfrac{1}{8}(3\theta - 2\sin 2\theta + \tfrac{1}{4}\sin 4\theta) + k$$

(b) $\displaystyle\int \cos^5 \theta \, d\theta = \int \frac{1}{2^4}(10\cos\theta + 5\cos 3\theta + \cos 5\theta)\, d\theta$

$$= \frac{1}{2^4}\left(10\sin\theta + \frac{5}{3}\sin 3\theta + \frac{1}{5}\sin 5\theta\right) + k$$

11 $\sin^4 \theta = \left(\dfrac{1 - \cos 2\theta}{2}\right)^2 = \dfrac{1 - 2\cos 2\theta + \cos^2 2\theta}{4}$

$\qquad = \tfrac{1}{4} - \tfrac{1}{2}\cos 2\theta + \tfrac{1}{8}(1 + \cos 4\theta)$, giving the same answer as before.

$\cos^5 \theta = \left(\dfrac{1 + \cos 2\theta}{2}\right)\left(\dfrac{\cos 3\theta + 3\cos\theta}{4}\right)$ using the result from question 1

$\qquad = \tfrac{1}{8}(\cos 3\theta + 3\cos\theta + \cos 2\theta\cos 3\theta + 3\cos 2\theta\cos\theta)$

$\qquad = \tfrac{1}{8}[\cos 3\theta + 3\cos\theta + \tfrac{1}{2}(\cos\theta + \cos 5\theta) + \tfrac{3}{2}(\cos\theta + \cos 3\theta)]$

$\qquad = \tfrac{1}{16}(10\cos\theta + 5\cos 3\theta + \cos 5\theta)$,   again.

Miscellaneous exercise 2

1

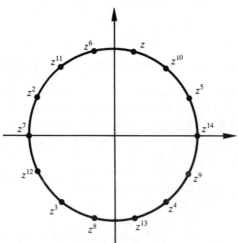

The last pattern arises from $(2z^2 - 1)(z^4 + 1) = 0$, i.e. $2z^6 - z^4 + 2z^2 - 1 = 0$.

2

3 (a) $(z - \sqrt{2} - \sqrt{2}j)(z + \sqrt{2} + \sqrt{2}j)$ (b) $(z - 1 - 4j)(z - 1 + 4j)$
(c) $(2z + 1 - 3j)(2z + 1 + 3j)$ (d) $(z - 2.20 + 0.91j)(z + 2.20 - 0.91j)$
(e) $(z + 2j)^2$

4 (a) $(z + j)(z - \frac{1}{2}\sqrt{3} - \frac{1}{2}j)(z + \frac{1}{2}\sqrt{3} - \frac{1}{2}j)$ (b) $(z + j)(z - \sqrt{3})(z + \sqrt{3})$
(c) $(z + j)(z - j)(z + 2j)(z - 2j)$
(d) $(z + j)(z^3 + z^2 + z - 3) = (z + j)(z - 1)(z^2 + 2z + 3)$
$$= (z + j)(z - 1)(z + 1 - \sqrt{2}j)(z + 1 + \sqrt{2}j)$$

5 $z^5 = -1 \Rightarrow z = [1, \frac{1}{5}\pi]$ or $[1, -\frac{1}{5}\pi]$ or $[1, \frac{3}{5}\pi]$ or $[1, -\frac{3}{5}\pi]$ or $[1, \pi]$.

$[z - \cos\frac{1}{5}\pi - j\sin\frac{1}{5}\pi][z - \cos\frac{1}{5}\pi + j\sin\frac{1}{5}\pi] = z^2 - 2\cos\frac{1}{5}\pi z + 1$,

so $z^5 + 1 = (z + 1)[z^2 - 2\cos\frac{1}{5}\pi z + 1][z^2 - 2\cos\frac{3}{5}\pi z + 1]$.

Now, $\cos\frac{3}{5}\pi = \cos 108° = -\cos 72° = -\sin 18° = -(\sqrt{5} - 1)/4$,

and $\cos\frac{1}{5}\pi = \cos 36° = -\cos 144° = -(2\cos^2 72° - 1) = (\sqrt{5} + 1)/4$.

6 $z^3 + 3jz^2 - 3z - j = z^3 - 3jz^2 - 3z + j \Rightarrow 6jz^2 = 2j \Rightarrow z = \pm\frac{1}{3}\sqrt{3}$.
For $z = \frac{1}{3}\sqrt{3}$,

$$(z + j) = [\tfrac{2}{3}\sqrt{3}, \tfrac{1}{3}\pi], \quad (z - j) = [\tfrac{2}{3}\sqrt{3}, -\tfrac{1}{3}\pi] \quad \text{and} \quad (z + j)^3 = (z - j)^3.$$

Similarly for $z = -\frac{1}{3}\sqrt{3}$.
$(z + j)^4 = (z - j)^4 \Rightarrow z^3 = z \Rightarrow z = 0$ or 1 or -1. These check.

7 $P(z) = (z^2 - 2z + 2)(z^2 - 2z + 5) = 0$ when $z = 1 + j, 1 - j, 1 + 2j, 1 - 2j$.

8 $z^n - 1 = 0 \Rightarrow$ product of the roots is $(-1)^{n-1}$, based on the coefficients in the equation. Alternatively,

$$[1, 0] \times [1, 2\pi/n] \times [1, 4\pi/n] \times \ldots \times [1, 2(n - 1)\pi/n] = [1, (n - 1)\pi] = (-1)^{n-1}.$$

9 $\omega^3 = \cos 2\pi + j\sin 2\pi = 1$;
$\omega^3 - 1 = 0 \Rightarrow (\omega - 1)(\omega^2 + \omega + 1) = 0 \Rightarrow \omega^2 + \omega + 1 = 0$, since $\omega \neq 1$.

(a) $\dfrac{1}{1 + \omega} + \dfrac{1}{1 + \omega^2} = \dfrac{1}{-\omega^2} + \dfrac{1}{-\omega} = -\omega - \omega^2 = 1$

(b) $\dfrac{1}{z - \omega} + \dfrac{1}{z - \omega^2} = \dfrac{2z - \omega^2 - \omega}{z^2 - (\omega^2 + \omega)z + 1} = \dfrac{2z + 1}{z^2 + z + 1}$

(c) $\dfrac{\omega^2}{z - \omega} + \dfrac{\omega}{z - \omega^2} = \dfrac{(\omega^2 + \omega)z - (\omega^4 + \omega^2)}{z^2 + z + 1} = \dfrac{-z + 1}{z^2 + z + 1}$

10 $(z - a - b)(z - a\omega - b\omega^2)(z - a\omega^2 - b\omega) = (z - a - b)(z^2 + (a + b)z + a^2 - ab + b^2)$
$$= z^3 - 3abz - (a^3 + b^3).$$
This equals $z^3 + 3z - 2$ if $ab = -1$ and $a^3 + b^3 = 2$. Eliminating b gives $a^6 - 2a^3 - 1 = 0$, $a^3 = 1 \pm \sqrt{2}$. From this, a and b are 1.342 and -0.745, giving the roots as 0.60, $-0.30 + 1.81j$ and $-0.30 - 1.81j$, rounding to 2 DP.

11 (a) a and b are -3 and 1, giving roots $-2, 1 + 2\sqrt{3}j, 1 - 2\sqrt{3}j$.
(b) $ab = 2, a^3 + b^3 = 4 \Rightarrow a^6 - 4a^3 + 8 = 0$
$$\Rightarrow a^3 = 2 \pm 2j = [2\sqrt{2}, \tfrac{1}{4}\pi] \text{ or } [2\sqrt{2}, -\tfrac{1}{4}\pi].$$
Hence a and b are $[\sqrt{2}, \frac{1}{12}\pi]$ and $[\sqrt{2}, -\frac{1}{12}\pi]$.
Since $\omega = [1, \frac{2}{3}\pi]$,

$$\omega^2 = [1, -\tfrac{2}{3}\pi],$$
$$a\omega + b\omega^2 = [\sqrt{2}, \tfrac{3}{4}\pi] + [\sqrt{2}, -\tfrac{3}{4}\pi] = -2$$

and $\qquad aw^2 + bw = [\sqrt{2}, -\tfrac{7}{12}\pi] + [\sqrt{2}, \tfrac{7}{12}\pi] = 1 - \sqrt{3}.$

Also $\qquad a + b = [\sqrt{2}, \tfrac{1}{12}\pi] + [\sqrt{2}, -\tfrac{1}{12}\pi] = 1 + \sqrt{3}.$

This method is one that can cope with any coefficients. The equations in this question are solved much more easily, of course, by finding that $z = -2$ is one solution and then factorising!

12 Since w and w^2 are complex conjugates, aw is the conjugate of bw^2 if a and b are conjugates, as are also aw^2 and bw. Hence $aw + bw^2$ and $aw^2 + bw$ are real. Moreover, $a + b$ is real.

13 With first approximation 0.5, the second approximation is 0.6 and the third 0.596.

$$z^3 + 3z - 2 = (z - 0.596)(z^2 + 0.596z + 3.356)$$

and the complex roots are $-0.298 \pm 1.808j$.

Exercise 3A

1 (a) Tends to infinity (b) Tends to 0 (c) Tends to 1 (d) Tends to 1

2 (a) Has a limit approximately 0.368 (e^{-1}) (b) Tends to infinity
(c) Tends to 1 (d) Has a limit approximately 2.718 (e).

3 The u-sequence starts 1, 2, 0.5, 8, 0.03125; the v-sequence starts 1, 1.414, 1.189, 1.297, 1.242; the Newton–Raphson sequence starts 1, 1.333, 1.264, 1.260, 1.260.

4 (a) The first five terms are 1, 1.414, 1.554, 1.598, 1.612.
(b) The first five terms are 1, 2, 1.5, 1.667, 1.6.
Both sequences converge on the 'golden ratio', $(1 + \sqrt{5})/2 \approx 1.618$.

5 (i) For large x, $y \approx x + 3$ (ii) y tends to 0 (iii) $1/(2\sqrt{3})$

Exercise 3B

1 (a) Tends to 1 (b) Oscillates infinitely (c) Tends to infinity
(d) Tends to 0 (e) Tends to 0 (f) Tends to 1 (g) Tends to infinity
For (c), we could choose n_0 as 100 (or any larger number) if $k = 100$ and choose n_0 as 1000 if $k = 1000$; for (g), minimum values for n_0 are 10^4 and 10^6. For (a) we could choose n_0 as 20 if $k = 0.01$, and choose n_0 as 30 if $k = 0.001$; for (d), suitable values are 100 and 1000; for (e), suitable values are 200 and 2000; for (f), suitable values are 70 and 700.

2 (a) $\dfrac{n+1}{2n-5} = \dfrac{1 + \dfrac{1}{n}}{2 - \dfrac{5}{n}} \to \dfrac{1}{2}$ (b) $\dfrac{(n+1)^2}{2n(3n-1)} = \dfrac{1 + \dfrac{2}{n} + \dfrac{1}{n^2}}{6 - \dfrac{2}{n}} \to \dfrac{1}{6}$

(c) $\dfrac{\sqrt{n}+1}{n} = \dfrac{1}{\sqrt{n}} + \dfrac{1}{n} \to 0$

(d) $\dfrac{\sqrt{(2n^2 + n)} - n}{n - 1} = \dfrac{\sqrt{\left(2 + \dfrac{1}{n}\right)} - 1}{1 - \dfrac{1}{n}} \to \sqrt{2} - 1$

3 Since $-\dfrac{1}{\sqrt{n}} \le \dfrac{\cos n}{\sqrt{n}} \le \dfrac{1}{\sqrt{n}}$ and $\dfrac{1}{\sqrt{n}} \to 0$ as $n \to \infty$, $\dfrac{\cos n}{\sqrt{n}} \to 0$ as $n \to \infty$.

4 $1 - f(n) = \dfrac{n}{n^2 + n + 1} < \dfrac{n}{n^2} = \dfrac{1}{n}$ for $n > 0$. Also $1 - f(n) > 0$.

Hence $\qquad 0 \le \lim\limits_{n \to \infty} (1 - f(n)) \le 0$, i.e. $f(n) \to 1$ as $n \to \infty$.

5 (a) $\dfrac{u_{n+1}}{u_n} = \dfrac{(n+1)x}{n}$ and $\dfrac{n+1}{n} = 1 + \dfrac{1}{n}$ decreases as n increases.

$\dfrac{u_{20}}{u_{19}} = \dfrac{20 \times 0.9}{19} < 0.95$, so $\dfrac{u_{n+1}}{u_n} < 0.95$ for all $n > 18$.

It follows that $u_{20} < 0.95 \times u_{19}$, $u_{21} < 0.95^2 \times u_{19}$, etc.

Thus $\qquad u_n < 0.95^{n-19} \times u_{19}$ and $u_n \to 0$ as $n \to \infty$.

(b) We can find n_0 such that $v_{n+1}/v_n < 0.98$ for all $n > n_0$ ($n_0 = 50$ will do). The proof then follows the pattern of (a).

(c) $w_{n+1}/w_n < 0.95$ for all $n > 40$. Hence $w_n \to 0$ as $n \to \infty$.

6 If $u_n = x^n/n!$, $u_{n+1}/u_n = x/(n+1) < 0.5$ for all $n > 2x$. By the method of question 5(a), we see that $u_n \to 0$ as $n \to \infty$.

7 $|f(n) + g(n) - l - m| \le |f(n) - l| + |g(n) - m| < \frac{1}{2}k + \frac{1}{2}k$ for all n for which both $n > n_1$ and $n > n_2$. Now $n_1 + n_2$ is certainly greater than both n_1 and n_2, so this will do as n_0. We then have 'for any positive k, however small, $|f(n) + g(n) - l - m| < k$ for all $n > n_0$, proving $f(n) + g(n) \to l + m$ as $n \to \infty$.

The other parts of theorem 2 can be proved in similar (though slightly more complicated) ways.

8 $[\sqrt{(n^2 + 1)} - n][\sqrt{(n^2 + 1)} + n] = [\sqrt{(n^2 + 1)}]^2 - n^2 = n^2 + 1 - n^2 = 1$;

$$\lim_{n \to \infty} [\sqrt{(n^2 + 1)} - n] = \lim_{n \to \infty} \left[\frac{1}{\sqrt{(n^2 + 1)} + n} \right] = 0$$

9 $\dfrac{1}{n+1} < \displaystyle\int_n^{n+1} \dfrac{1}{x}\, dx < \dfrac{1}{n} \ \Rightarrow\ \dfrac{1}{n+1} < \ln(n+1) - \ln n < \dfrac{1}{n}$

$\Rightarrow \dfrac{n}{n+1} < n \ln\left(1 + \dfrac{1}{n}\right) < 1$

$\Rightarrow \qquad 1 \le \lim\limits_{n \to \infty} \ln\left(1 + \dfrac{1}{n}\right)^n \le 1$

$\Rightarrow \qquad \lim\limits_{n \to \infty} \ln\left(1 + \dfrac{1}{n}\right)^n = 1$

$\Rightarrow \qquad \lim\limits_{n \to \infty} \left(1 + \dfrac{1}{n}\right)^n = e$

10 $\dfrac{3}{n+3} < \displaystyle\int_n^{n+3} \dfrac{1}{x}\, dx < \dfrac{3}{n}$ as in question 9

$\Rightarrow \qquad 3 \le \lim\limits_{n \to \infty} \ln\left(1 + \dfrac{3}{n}\right)^n \le 3$

$\Rightarrow$ $\qquad$ $\displaystyle\lim_{n\to\infty}\left(1+\frac{3}{n}\right)^n = e^3 \approx 20.09,$ as suggested in §1.

11 $\left(1+\dfrac{1}{n}\right)^n = 1 + n\left(\dfrac{1}{n}\right) + \dfrac{n(n-1)}{2!}\left(\dfrac{1}{n}\right)^2 + \dfrac{n(n-1)(n-2)}{3!}\left(\dfrac{1}{n}\right)^3 + \ldots$

$\qquad\qquad < 1 + 1 + \frac{1}{2} + \frac{1}{6} + 1 + 1 + \ldots$ if $n \geqslant 3$

$\qquad\qquad < n.$

Also

$\qquad \left(1+\dfrac{2}{\sqrt{n}}\right)^n > 1 + n\left(\dfrac{2}{\sqrt{n}}\right) + \dfrac{n(n-1)}{2!}\left(\dfrac{2}{\sqrt{n}}\right)^2,$ taking three terms only.

$\qquad\qquad = 1 + 2\sqrt{n} + 2n - 2$

$\qquad\qquad > n.$

Both inequalities are crude but quite sufficient for the task ahead.

$$\left(1+\frac{1}{n}\right)^n < \quad n \quad < \left(1+\frac{2}{\sqrt{n}}\right)^n$$

$\Rightarrow \quad \displaystyle\lim_{n\to\infty}\left(1+\frac{1}{n}\right) \leqslant \lim_{n\to\infty} n^{1/n} \leqslant \lim_{n\to\infty}\left(1+\frac{2}{\sqrt{n}}\right)$

$\Rightarrow \qquad\qquad\qquad \displaystyle\lim_{n\to\infty} n^{1/n} = 1.$

Exercise 3C

1 (a) e $\quad$ (b) e^{-1} $\quad$ (c) e^2 $\quad$ (d) e^2

2 The scale factor for 12 months at $1\frac{1}{2}\%$ is $1.015^{12} = 1.1956$, corresponding to a 19.56% annual rate; $1.0075^{24} = 1.1964$, equivalent to a 19.64% annual rate; $(1+18/100n)^n \to e^{0.18} = 1.1972$, so 19.72% is the maximum effective annual rate.

3 $\left(1+\dfrac{x}{n}\right)^n \approx e^x \Rightarrow \left(1+\dfrac{\ln u}{n}\right)^n \approx e^{\ln u} = u$

$\qquad\Rightarrow \quad 1 + \dfrac{\ln u}{n} \quad \approx u^{1/n}$

$\qquad\Rightarrow \qquad \ln u \approx n(u^{1/n} - 1).$

This is a poor algorithm. Its accuracy is much reduced when 1 is subtracted from a number only slightly greater than 1. Large values of m will give extremely inaccurate answers.

4 The rectangle method gives

$$\frac{u^{1/n} - 1}{u^{1/n}} < \int_1^{u^{1/n}} \frac{1}{x}\,dx < u^{1/n} - 1.$$

Hence $\qquad \dfrac{1}{u^{1/n}} < \dfrac{\ln u^{1/n}}{u^{1/n} - 1} < 1$ $\quad$ or $\quad u^{1/n} > \dfrac{n(u^{1/n} - 1)}{\ln u} > 1.$

(a) Since for $u > 1$, $\lim\limits_{n \to \infty} u^{1/n} = 1$,

then $\qquad \lim\limits_{n \to \infty} \left(\dfrac{n(u^{1/n} - 1)}{\ln u} \right) = 1$ or $\lim\limits_{n \to \infty} n(u^{1/n} - 1) = \ln u$.

(b) The above inequality shows that the percentage error is less than $100(u^{1/n} - 1)$.

(c) $100(2^{1/n} - 1) < 1 \quad \Rightarrow \quad 2^{1/n} < 1.01 \quad \Rightarrow \quad n > \dfrac{\ln 2}{\ln 1.01} = 69.7$.

For $n = 70$, $n(u^{1/n} - 1)$ gives $\ln 2 \approx 0.696\,59$.
For $n = 100$, $n(u^{1/n} - 1)$ gives $\ln 2 \approx 0.695\,56$.

5   $0 < x < \tfrac{1}{2}\pi \Rightarrow 0 < \sin x < 1 \qquad$ and $\qquad \sin x < x \Rightarrow \sin x < \sqrt{\sin x} \qquad$ and
$\sqrt{\sin x} < \sqrt{x}$.

Hence $\qquad \displaystyle\int_0^{\pi/2} \sin x \, dx < \int_0^{\pi/2} \sqrt{\sin x} \, dx < \int_0^{\pi/2} \sqrt{x} \, dx$,

$\Rightarrow \qquad 1 < \displaystyle\int_0^{\pi/2} \sqrt{\sin x} \, dx < \left[\tfrac{2}{3} x^{3/2} \right]_0^{\pi/2} \approx 1.312\,47$.

Exercise 3D

1   (a) $y \approx 3/x$ for large x, and $y \to 0$ as $x \to \infty$ $\qquad$ (b) $y \to 3$ as $x \to \infty$

2   (a) $y = x + 2$ $\qquad$ (b) $y = x + 4$ $\qquad$ (c) $y = 4x + 8$
When $x = 100$:   (a) $y = 101.96$ $\qquad$ (b) $y = 103.93$ $\qquad$ (c) $y = 408.05$

3   (a) $\dfrac{\ln x}{x} \to 0$ $\qquad$ (b) $\dfrac{\ln x}{\sqrt{x}} \to 0$ $\qquad$ (c) $x\,e^{-x} \to 0$ $\qquad$ (d) $x^3 e^{-x} \to 0$

(e) $\dfrac{e^x}{x^2 + 10} \to \infty$

4   (a) $\dfrac{\sin 2x}{x} \to 2$ $\qquad$ (b) $x \ln x \to 0$ $\qquad$ (c) $x^2 \ln x \to 0$ $\qquad$ (d) $x^3 e^{-x} \to 0$

(e) $\dfrac{e^x + 10}{x^2} \to \infty$

Exercise 3E

1

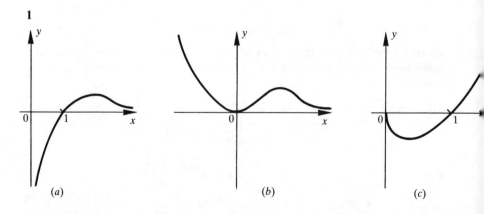

(a)   (b)   (c)

2 $\dfrac{\ln x}{x} \to 0$ as $x \to \infty$ $\Rightarrow$ $x^{1/x} \to e^0 = 1$ as $x \to \infty$;

$\dfrac{\ln x}{x} \to -\infty$ as $x \to 0$ $\Rightarrow$ $x^{1/x} \to 0$ as $x \to 0$.

$y = x^{1/x}$ $\Rightarrow$ $\ln y = \dfrac{1}{x} \ln x$ $\Rightarrow$ $\dfrac{1}{y}\dfrac{dy}{dx} = \dfrac{1}{x^2} - \dfrac{1}{x^2} \ln x$

$\qquad\qquad\qquad\qquad\qquad = 0$, when $x = e$ and $y = e^{1/e} \approx 1.44$.

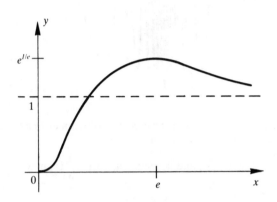

3 $x e^{-\alpha x} = x t^x$ where $t = e^{-\alpha}$; $\alpha > 0$ $\Rightarrow$ $0 < t < 1$;
$x t^x \to 0$ as $x \to \infty$ $\Leftrightarrow$ $n x^n \to 0$ as $n \to \infty$.

4 (a) $\dfrac{\sin x}{3x^2 + 2x} = \left(\dfrac{\sin x}{x}\right)\left(\dfrac{1}{3x + 2}\right) \to \tfrac{1}{2}$ as $x \to 0$ (b) $\dfrac{\sin x - x}{4x - 6} \to 0$ as $x \to 0$

(c) $\dfrac{\sin x - 3x}{5 \sin x - x} = \dfrac{\dfrac{\sin x}{x} - 3}{5\left(\dfrac{\sin x}{x}\right) - 1} \to -\tfrac{1}{2}$ as $x \to 0$

5 (a) $y = \dfrac{\sin x}{x}$ is an even function.

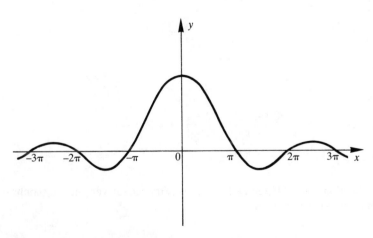

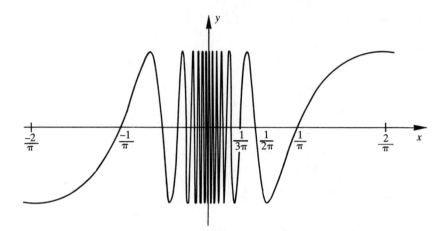

(b) As x approaches 0, the period of the oscillations becomes smaller; the amplitude remains 1; $\sin(1/x)$ is an odd function.

6 $x \sin \dfrac{1}{x} = \dfrac{\sin u}{u} \to 1$ as $x \to \infty$, and hence $u \to 0$; $x \sin \dfrac{1}{x}$ is an even function.

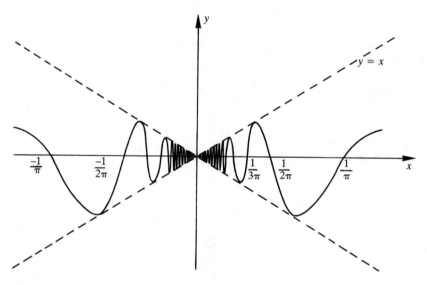

Exercise 3F

1   For $1 < x < 2$, $\dfrac{f(x) - f(1)}{x - 1} = \dfrac{2 - 1}{x - 1} \to \infty$ as $x \to 1$.

For $0 < x < 1$, $\dfrac{f(x) - f(1)}{x - 1} = 0$.

So the function is not differentiable. Of course, the formal working only confirms the evidence provided by a graph.

2 $x \mapsto |x^2 - 1|$ is an example:

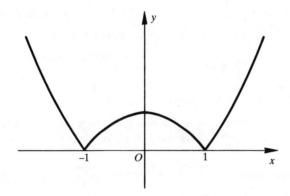

3 (i) $\Rightarrow b = 0$ and $2 = 9p + 3q + 2$, (ii) $\Rightarrow a \neq 1$, (iii) $\Rightarrow 1 = 6p + q$.
All conditions are satisfied if $b = 0, p = \frac{1}{3}, q = -1$ and $a \neq 1$. f' is not differentiable at $x = 3$, so $f''(3)$ does not exist.

4 $f(x) = x^2$ if $x \geq 0$ and $f(x) = -x^2$ if $x < 0$.

For positive x, $\qquad \dfrac{f(x) - f(0)}{x - 0} = x \to 0$ as $x \to 0^+$.

For negative x, $\qquad \dfrac{f(x) - f(0)}{x - 0} = -x \to 0$ as $x \to 0^-$.

Hence $f'(0) = 0$.
(i) f is an odd function since $f(-x) = -f(x)$.
(ii) f is continuous at $x = 0$, as shown by the graph.
(iii) f is differentiable at $x = 0$ (proved above).
$f'(x) = 2x$ for $x \geq 0$ and $f'(x) = -2x$ for $x < 0$. Hence $f'(x) = 2|x|$; f' is not differentiable at $x = 0$ (see Example 5).

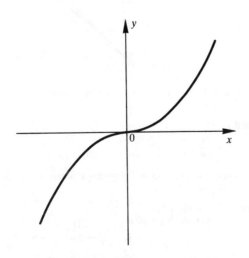

Miscellaneous exercise 3

1 (a) $f(n + 1) = f(n) \times \dfrac{2n + 1}{2n + 2}$; as $n \to \infty$, $f(n) \to 0$. In fact, $f(n)$ is the probability of
getting exactly n heads and n tails in $2n$ tosses of a fair coin.

   (b) $f(n + 1) = f(n) \times \dfrac{(2n + 2)^2 - 1}{(2n + 2)^2}$; as $n \to \infty$, $f(n) \to 2/\pi$, approximately 0.637.

2

n	3	4	5	6
r_n	10	7.071	5.721	4.954

   Further investigation, preferably with a computer, shows that r_n tends to a limit
   approximately equal to 2.300. This is hard to justify theoretically although insight
   can be gained using

   $$\cos x \approx 1 - \tfrac{1}{2}x^2 \text{ for small } x \quad \text{and} \quad \sin \pi y \approx \pi y(1 - y^2)\left(1 - \frac{y^2}{4}\right)\left(1 - \frac{y^2}{9}\right)\dots$$

3 $f(1) = 1.333$, $f(2) = 1.422$, $f(3) = 1.463$
   (a) Each new bracket is greater than 1, so $f(n)$ is an increasing function.
   (b) $f(n)$ can be written

   $$\frac{2}{1}\left(\frac{2 \times 4}{3 \times 3}\right)\left(\frac{4 \times 6}{5 \times 5}\right) \dots \left(\frac{(2n - 2) \times (2n)}{(2n - 1) \times (2n - 1)}\right)\left(\frac{2n}{2n + 1}\right),$$

   and each multiplier of the original fraction $\tfrac{2}{1}$ is less than 1. Hence $f(n) < 2$ for all n.
   (a) and (b) together show that $f(n)$ tends to a limit. This limit is in fact $\pi/2 \approx 1.571$.
   Compare with question 1(b).

4 The binomial expansion shows that $(1 + t)^n > 1 + nt$ if $t > 0$ and $n > 1$. Since
   $1 + nt \to \infty$ as $n \to \infty$, it follows that $(1 + t)^n \to \infty$ as $n \to \infty$. Writing x for $1 + t$ gives
   $x^n \to \infty$ as $n \to \infty$ if $x > 1$.

5 The chord OA and the tangent at O
   give $a = 0.5/(\tfrac{1}{6}\pi)$; $b = 1$. The integral

   lies between $\left[\tfrac{1}{2}ax^2\right]_0^{\pi/6}$ and $\left[\tfrac{1}{2}bx^2\right]_0^{\pi/6}$,

   i.e. between $\pi/24 \approx 0.131$ and
   $\pi^2/72 \approx 0.137$.

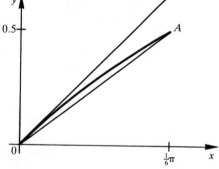

6 $1 < \sec^2 t \Rightarrow \displaystyle\int_0^u 1 \, dt < \int_0^u \sec^2 t \, dt \Rightarrow u < \tan u$. This requires $0 < u < \tfrac{1}{2}\pi$.

7 $\displaystyle\int_0^x u \, du < \int_0^x \tan u \, du \Rightarrow \tfrac{1}{2}x^2 < \ln \sec x$
   $\Rightarrow -\tfrac{1}{2}x^2 > \ln \cos x$
   $\Rightarrow e^{-x^2/2} > \cos x \quad \text{for } 0 < x < \tfrac{1}{2}\pi.$

   The inequality holds for $x = \tfrac{1}{2}\pi$, and $e^{-x^2/2} = \cos x$ when $x = 0$. So $e^{-x^2/2} \geqslant \cos x$
   for $0 \leqslant x \leqslant \tfrac{1}{2}\pi$.

8 (a) The limit is seen to be about 1.5.
   (b) $[\sqrt{(x^2 + 3x)} - \sqrt{(x^2 - 5)}][\sqrt{(x^2 + 3x)} + \sqrt{(x^2 - 5)}]$
   $\qquad\qquad = x^2 + 3x - x^2 + 5 = 3x + 5;$

$$\lim_{x \to \infty} [\sqrt{(x^2 + 3x)} - \sqrt{(x^2 - 5)}] = \lim_{x \to \infty} \left[\frac{3x + 5}{\sqrt{(x^2 + 3x)} + \sqrt{(x^2 - 5)}} \right] = \frac{3}{2}$$

9   $u(x) = x - \sin x \Rightarrow u'(x) = 1 - \cos x \geq 0$. Hence u is an increasing function and

$$\int_1^2 \frac{\sin x}{x^3} dx < \int_1^2 \frac{x}{x^3} dx = \tfrac{1}{2}.$$

Also,

$$\int_1^2 \frac{\sin x}{x^3} dx < \int_1^2 \frac{1}{x^3} dx = \tfrac{3}{8}.$$

Note, moreover, that

$$\sin x > x - \tfrac{1}{6}x^3 \Rightarrow \int_1^2 \frac{\sin x}{x^3} dx > \tfrac{1}{3}.$$

10   $(x - 1)^2 \geq 0 \Rightarrow x^2 + 1 \geq 2x \Rightarrow \dfrac{1}{x} \geq \dfrac{2}{1 + x^2}$ for positive x, with equality only when $x = 1$.

Hence

$$\int_1^{\sqrt{3}} \frac{1}{x} dx > \int_1^{\sqrt{3}} \frac{2}{1 + x^2} dx$$

$$\tfrac{1}{2} \ln 3 > \left[2 \tan^{-1} x \right]_1^{\sqrt{3}} = 2(\tfrac{1}{3}\pi - \tfrac{1}{4}\pi)$$

$$\ln 3 > \tfrac{1}{3}\pi.$$

11   See §4, and Exercise 3E, question 1(a).

$$f(t) = \frac{\ln t}{t} \Rightarrow f'(t) = \frac{1}{t^2} - \frac{\ln t}{t^2} = 0 \quad \text{when } t = e.$$

The maximum point is $(e, 1/e)$.

12   $(1 + \sqrt{x})(1 - \sqrt{x})(1 + x) = (1 - x)(1 + x) = 1 - x^2$, the result follows.
For $0 < x < \tfrac{1}{4}$, $\tfrac{15}{16} < 1 - x^2 < 1$.

Hence

$$\tfrac{15}{16} \int_0^{1/4} (1 - \sqrt{x})(1 + x)\, dx > \int_0^{1/4} \frac{1}{1 + \sqrt{x}} dx > \int_0^{1/4} (1 - \sqrt{x})(1 + x)\, dx$$

$$\Rightarrow \qquad 0.198 \approx \tfrac{89}{450} > \int_0^{1/4} \frac{1}{1 + \sqrt{x}} dx > \tfrac{89}{480} \approx 0.185.$$

The substitution $u = 1 + \sqrt{x}$ gives the integral as $1 - 2 \ln 1.5 \approx 0.189$.

13   (a) The result comes from repeated use of $\sin \theta \cos \theta = \tfrac{1}{2} \sin 2\theta$.

(b) $\displaystyle \lim_{n \to \infty} S(n) = \lim_{n \to \infty} \left(\frac{1/2^{n-1}}{\sin(\pi/2^n)} \right) = \frac{2}{\pi} \lim_{\phi \to 0} \left(\frac{\phi}{\sin \phi} \right) = \frac{2}{\pi}$

14   $\cos \tfrac{1}{4}\pi = \dfrac{1}{\sqrt{2}} \Rightarrow 2 \cos^2 \tfrac{1}{8}\pi = 1 + \dfrac{1}{\sqrt{2}} = \dfrac{\sqrt{2} + 1}{\sqrt{2}} = \dfrac{2 + \sqrt{2}}{2}$

$$\Rightarrow \qquad \cos \tfrac{1}{8}\pi = \frac{\sqrt{(2 + \sqrt{2})}}{2}.$$

Then $2 \cos^2 \tfrac{1}{16}\pi = 1 + \dfrac{\sqrt{(2 + \sqrt{2})}}{2} = \dfrac{2 + \sqrt{(2 + \sqrt{2})}}{2}$

$$\Rightarrow \quad \cos \tfrac{1}{16}\pi = \frac{\sqrt{(2 + \sqrt{(2 + \sqrt{2}))}}}{2}.$$

The process can be continued easily, and we have a simple iterative method of calculating π.

Exercise 4A

1 (a) 21, 28, 36; $S_n = \tfrac{1}{2}n(n + 1)$

(b) 0, 1, 0; $S_n = 0$ when n is even, $S_n = 1$ when n is odd.

(c) $-3, 4, -4$; $S_n = -\tfrac{1}{2}n$ when n is even, $S_n = \tfrac{1}{2}(n + 1)$ when n is odd.

2 (a) Converges with sum to infinity 2   (b) Converges with sum to infinity $\tfrac{2}{3}$

(c) Diverges   (d) Oscillates infinitely

3 $P(A) = \tfrac{1}{6} + (\tfrac{5}{6} \times \tfrac{4}{6}) \times \tfrac{1}{6} + (\tfrac{5}{6} \times \tfrac{4}{6})^2 \times \tfrac{1}{6} + \ldots = \tfrac{6}{16};$

$P(B) = (\tfrac{5}{6} \times \tfrac{2}{6}) + (\tfrac{5}{6} \times \tfrac{4}{6}) \times (\tfrac{5}{6} \times \tfrac{2}{6}) + (\tfrac{5}{6} \times \tfrac{4}{6})^2 \times (\tfrac{5}{6} \times \tfrac{2}{6}) + \ldots = \tfrac{10}{16}$

4 $0.37(1 + 0.01 + 0.01^2 + \ldots) = \tfrac{37}{99}$

5 $T = \sqrt{(2h/g)} + 2[\tfrac{1}{2}\sqrt{(2h/g)} + \tfrac{1}{4}\sqrt{(2h/g)} + \tfrac{1}{8}\sqrt{(2h/g)} + \ldots] = 3\sqrt{(2h/g)}$

6 $P(A) = \tfrac{9}{36} + (\tfrac{27}{36} \times \tfrac{24}{36}) \times \tfrac{9}{36} + (\tfrac{27}{36} \times \tfrac{24}{36})^2 \times \tfrac{9}{36} + \ldots = \tfrac{1}{2};$ $P(B) = \tfrac{1}{2}$

7 We require $-1 < \dfrac{x}{x - 1} < 1$, i.e. $x < \tfrac{1}{2}$. This is perhaps most easily seen from a sketch graph of $y = \dfrac{x}{1 - x}$.

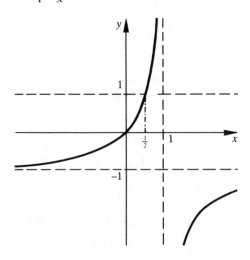

8 $S_n = \left(1 - \dfrac{1}{2}\right) + \left(\dfrac{1}{2} - \dfrac{1}{3}\right) + \left(\dfrac{1}{3} - \dfrac{1}{4}\right) + \ldots + \left(\dfrac{1}{n} - \dfrac{1}{n + 1}\right) = 1 - \dfrac{1}{n + 1};$

sum to infinity = 1.

9 $S_k = \left(1 - \dfrac{1}{3}\right) + \left(\dfrac{1}{3} - \dfrac{1}{5}\right) + \left(\dfrac{1}{5} - \dfrac{1}{7}\right) + \ldots + \left(\dfrac{1}{2k - 1} - \dfrac{1}{2k + 1}\right)$

$= 1 - \dfrac{1}{2k + 1};$

$$\frac{1}{2k+1} < 10^{-6} \quad \Rightarrow \quad k \geqslant 500\,000$$

10 $S_2 = \frac{5}{6}, \quad S_3 = \frac{23}{24}, \quad S_4 = \frac{119}{120};$

$$S_n = \left(\frac{1}{1!} - \frac{1}{2!}\right) + \left(\frac{1}{2!} - \frac{1}{3!}\right) + \left(\frac{1}{3!} - \frac{1}{4!}\right) + \ldots + \left(\frac{1}{n!} - \frac{1}{(n+1)!}\right)$$

$$= 1 - \frac{1}{(n+1)!} \to 1 \quad \text{as } n \to \infty$$

11 $S_n(1 - x) = (1 + x + x^2 + \ldots + x^{n-1}) - nx^n = \dfrac{1 - x^n}{1 - x} - nx^n;$

$S_n \to (1 - x)^{-2} \quad \text{as } n \to \infty$

12 $S_n = \dfrac{d}{dx}(1 + x + x^2 + \ldots + x^{n-1}) = \dfrac{d}{dx}\left(\dfrac{1 - x^n}{1 - x}\right) = \dfrac{(1 - x^n)}{(1 - x)^2} - \dfrac{nx^{n-1}}{1 - x}$

13 (a) 2.929, 3.318, 3.598   (b) 1.550, 1.580, 1.596
    (c) 5.021, 6.414, 7.595

14 (a) 5.187, 5.591, 5.878   (b) 1.635, 1.638, 1.640
    (c) 18.590, 23.075, 26.859
    The series of (b) converges on $\pi^2/6 = 1.645$ (see §3.2); the others diverge.

Exercise 4B

1 If $x > 1$, $x + \frac{1}{2}x^2 + \frac{1}{3}x^3 + \ldots > 1 + \frac{1}{2} + \frac{1}{3} + \ldots$, which is divergent.

2 $1 + \frac{1}{3} + \frac{1}{5} + \ldots > \frac{1}{2} + \frac{1}{4} + \frac{1}{6} + \ldots = \frac{1}{2}(1 + \frac{1}{2} + \frac{1}{3} + \ldots)$, which is divergent.

3 $\displaystyle\sum_2^\infty \frac{1}{\ln r} > \sum_2^\infty \frac{1}{r - 1} = \sum_1^\infty \frac{1}{r}$, which is divergent.

4 (a) $S < 1 + x + \dfrac{x^2}{2!} + \dfrac{x^3}{3!} + \dfrac{x^4}{4!}\left[1 + \dfrac{x}{5} + \left(\dfrac{x}{5}\right)^2 + \left(\dfrac{x}{5}\right)^3 + \ldots\right]$,

   which converges if $0 < x < 4$. Also, S_n is an increasing function of n, so the
   original (exponential) series converges.

   (b) If $k - 1 < x < k$, where k is a positive integer, we can adapt the method of (a) by
   copying the first k terms and showing that the rest are less than the terms of a GP
   with ratio $x/(k + 1)$.

5 (a) This is a generalisation of the idea in question 4: S_n is an increasing function of n
   and $S < u_1 + ku_1 + k^2u_1 + \ldots$, which is convergent.

   (b) Here we write $S < u_1 + u_2 + \ldots + u_m + u_{m+1}(1 + k + k^2 + \ldots)$, and then the
   same argument applies.

6 (a) $\dfrac{u_{r+1}}{u_r} = \left(\dfrac{r}{r+1}\right)x < x < 1$, so the series converges if $0 < x < 1$.

   (b) $\dfrac{u_{r+1}}{u_r} = \left(\dfrac{r+1}{r}\right)^2 x < k$ when $(r + 1)\sqrt{x} < r\sqrt{k}$, i.e. $r > \dfrac{\sqrt{x}}{\sqrt{k} - \sqrt{x}}$.

   We can now invoke question 5(a), taking any k between x and 1.

7 In the term containing x^r, we have the product of $2r$ negative numbers, and the result
   is therefore positive.

$$\frac{u_{r+1}}{u_r} = \frac{(m - r + 1)x}{r}.$$

It is now helpful to write $m = -n$ and $x = -y$, so that n and y are positive. Then

$$\frac{u_{r+1}}{u_r} = \frac{(n+r-1)}{r} < k \quad \text{when} \quad r > \frac{(n-1)y}{k-y},$$

and we can invoke question 5(b), taking any k between y and 1.

8 The limit is $\frac{2}{3}$.

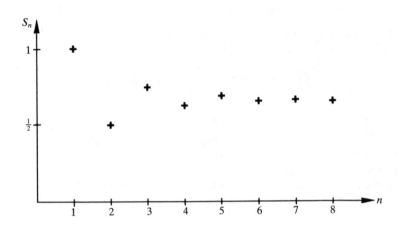

9

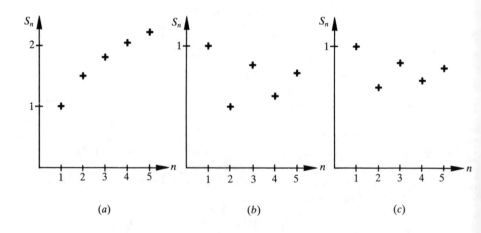

(a) (b) (c)

10 We need to formalise the ideas behind questions 8 and 9. The partial sums S_1, S_3, S_5, ... form a decreasing sequence, while S_2, S_4, S_6, ... form an increasing sequence. This is because

$$S_{2n+1} = S_{2n-1} + u_{2n} \quad + u_{2n+1} < S_{2n-1}$$

and
$$S_{2n+2} = S_{2n} \quad + u_{2n+1} + u_{2n+2} > S_{2n}.$$

This first sequence is bounded below (since $S_{2n+1} > S_{2n} > S_2$) and hence tends to a limit l, and the second sequence is bounded above and tends to a limit m. Since $S_{2n+1} > S_{2p}$ for all n and p, it follows that $l \geqslant m$.

Since $u_n \to 0$, l must equal m. For $S_{2n+1} - S_{2n} = u_{2n+1}$ and letting $n \to \infty$, we have $l - m = 0$. Hence $l = m$, and the alternating series is convergent.

11 These results are immediate. Notice that the corresponding series with all positive terms are divergent (see questions 3 and 1).

12 (a) If $p - 1 < x < p$, the conditions of question 10 apply for all terms beyond the x^p term. This is sufficient.

(b) This is a finite series if m is a positive integer, of course. Otherwise the series alternates eventually, and then

$$\frac{u_{r+1}}{u_r} = \frac{(m - r + 1)x}{r} \quad \text{(see question 7)}$$

implies

$$\left| \frac{u_{r+1}}{u_r} \right| = \left(\frac{m - r + 1}{-r} \right) x,$$

which is less than k if $r > \dfrac{-(m+1)x}{k - x}$. Hence, choosing any k between x and 1

we see that the conditions of question 10 apply and that the series converges.

13 Both are alternating series that satisfy the conditions of question 10 after a few terms.

14 All except (b) and (f) are correct; the harmonic series provides a counter-example for each of the false statements.

15
$$\sum_{11}^{\infty} \left(\frac{1}{r} - \frac{1}{r+1} \right) = \frac{1}{11} = \frac{22}{220} \quad \text{and} \quad \sum_{21}^{\infty} \left(\frac{1}{r} - \frac{1}{r+1} \right) = \frac{1}{21} = \frac{40}{840}.$$

Also
$$\sum_{11}^{\infty} \frac{1}{2} \left(\frac{1}{r-1} - \frac{1}{r+1} \right) = \frac{1}{2} \left(\frac{1}{10} + \frac{1}{11} \right) = \frac{21}{220}$$

and
$$\sum_{21}^{\infty} \frac{1}{2} \left(\frac{1}{r-1} - \frac{1}{r+1} \right) = \frac{1}{2} \left(\frac{1}{20} + \frac{1}{21} \right) = \frac{41}{840}.$$

$$\sum_{1}^{\infty} \frac{1}{r^2} = \sum_{1}^{20} \frac{1}{r^2} + \sum_{21}^{\infty} \frac{1}{r^2} \approx 1.596\,16 + \frac{40.5}{840} = 1.644\,38.$$

The predicted error is less than $\dfrac{0.5}{840} \approx 0.0006$. In fact, the sum to infinity is $1.644\,93$ to 6 SF.

Exercise 4C

1 For both $\sin x$ and $\cos x$,

$$|R_n| = \left| \frac{x^n}{n!} \sin \theta x \right| \quad \text{or} \quad \left| \frac{x^n}{n!} \cos \theta x \right|,$$

depending on whether n is odd or even. In either case,

$$|R_n| \leqslant \left| \frac{x^n}{n!} \right|, \quad \text{so} \quad |R_n| \to 0 \text{ as } n \to \infty.$$

2 $\sin 0.3 \approx 0.3 - \dfrac{0.3^3}{3!} + \dfrac{0.3^5}{5!} = 0.295\,520\,25$; error is less than

$\dfrac{0.3^6}{6!} \sin 0.3 < 3 \times 10^{-7}$.

3 $R_n < \dfrac{1^{10}}{10!} \times e^1 = 7.5 \times 10^{-7}$

4 (a) $\ln 1.3 \approx 0.3 - \dfrac{0.3^2}{2} + \dfrac{0.3^3}{3} - \dfrac{0.3^4}{4} + \dfrac{0.3^5}{5} = 0.262\,461$;

$\ln 0.7 \approx -0.3 - \dfrac{0.3^2}{2} - \dfrac{0.3^3}{3} - \dfrac{0.3^4}{4} - \dfrac{0.3^5}{5} = -0.356\,511$

(b) $f^{(6)}(x) = (-1)^5\, 5!\,(1+x)^{-6}$ so $\dfrac{x^6}{6!} f^{(6)}(\theta x) = -\dfrac{1}{6}\left(\dfrac{-x}{1+\theta x}\right)^6$

(c) Error lies between $\frac{1}{6} \times (0.3/1.3)^6$ and $\frac{1}{6} \times 0.3^6$, i.e. between $0.000\,025$ and $0.000\,122$. (In fact, the error is approximately $0.000\,097$.)

(d) Upper limit is $\frac{1}{6}(0.3/0.7)^6 \approx 0.00103$. On this occasion, Taylor's theorem is not illuminating and an *ad hoc* method is better:

$$\dfrac{x^6}{6} + \dfrac{x^7}{7} + \dfrac{x^8}{8} + \ldots < \dfrac{x^6}{6} + \dfrac{x^7}{6} + \dfrac{x^8}{6} + \ldots = \dfrac{0.3^6}{6} \times \dfrac{1}{0.7} \quad \text{when } x = 0.3$$

$$= 0.000\,173\,6.$$

The error is actually about $0.000\,16$.

5 (a)

$f(x)$	$= \tan x$		$f(0)$	$= 0$
$\Rightarrow f'(x)$	$= \sec^2 x$		$f'(0)$	$= 1$
$\Rightarrow f''(x)$	$= 2 \sec^2 x \tan x$		$f''(0)$	$= 0$
$\Rightarrow f'''(x)$	$= 2 \sec^4 x + 4 \sec^2 x \tan^2 x$		$f'''(0)$	$= 2$
$\Rightarrow f^{(4)}(x)$	$= 16 \sec^4 x \tan x + 8 \sec^2 x \tan^3 x$		$f^{(4)}(0)$	$= 0$
$\Rightarrow f^{(5)}(x)$	$= 16 \sec^6 x + 88 \sec^4 x \tan^2 x + 16 \sec^2 x \tan^4 x$		$f^{(5)}(0)$	$= 16$

$$f(x) \approx x + \dfrac{2}{3!}x^3 + \dfrac{16}{5!}x^5$$

$$= x + \tfrac{1}{3}x^3 + \tfrac{2}{15}x^5.$$

An alternative is to carry out a long division of the leading terms for $\sin x$ by the leading terms for $\cos x$, neglecting terms above x^5:

$$
\begin{array}{r}
x + \frac{1}{3}x^3 + \frac{2}{15}x^5 \\
1 - \frac{1}{2}x^2 + \frac{1}{24}x^4\,\overline{)\,x - \frac{1}{6}x^3 + \frac{1}{120}x^5} \\
\underline{x - \frac{1}{2}x^3 + \frac{1}{24}x^5} \\
\frac{1}{3}x^3 - \frac{1}{30}x^5 \\
\underline{\frac{1}{3}x^3 - \frac{1}{6}x^5} \\
\frac{2}{15}x^5
\end{array}
$$

(b) Since $\dfrac{\mathrm{d}}{\mathrm{d}x}(\sinh x) = \cosh x$ and $\dfrac{\mathrm{d}}{\mathrm{d}x}(\cosh x) = \sinh x$,

we soon get $f(0) = f''(0) = f^{(4)}(0) = 0$, $f'(0) = f'''(0) = f^{(5)}(0) = 1$,

and hence $\sinh x \approx x + \dfrac{x^3}{3!} + \dfrac{x^5}{5!}$.

(c) $f(x) = \tan^{-1} x \implies f'(x) = \dfrac{1}{1 + x^2} \approx 1 - x^2 + x^4.$

This leads immediately, by integration, to $\tan^{-1} x = x - \frac{1}{3}x^3 + \frac{1}{5}x^5$. Other methods are available, of course. This series is taken further in Exercises 4D and 4E.

6 $\left[1 + \left(-\dfrac{x^2}{2} + \dfrac{x^4}{24}\right)\right]^{1/2} \approx 1 + \dfrac{1}{2}\left(-\dfrac{x^2}{2} + \dfrac{x^4}{24}\right) - \dfrac{1}{8}\left(-\dfrac{x^2}{2} + \dfrac{x^4}{4}\right)^2$

$$\approx 1 - \dfrac{x^2}{4} + \dfrac{x^4}{48} - \dfrac{1}{8} \times \dfrac{x^4}{4}$$

$$= 1 - \dfrac{x^2}{4} - \dfrac{x^4}{96}$$

7 (a) $e^h \approx 1 + h + \frac{1}{2}h^2 \implies e^{-x^2/2} \approx 1 - \frac{1}{2}x^2 + \frac{1}{8}x^4$

(b) $\ln(1 + \sin x) \approx \ln(1 + x - \frac{1}{6}x^3)$
$$\approx (x - \tfrac{1}{6}x^3) - \tfrac{1}{2}(x - \tfrac{1}{6}x^3)^2 + \tfrac{1}{3}(x - \tfrac{1}{6}x^3)^3$$
$$\approx x - \tfrac{1}{6}x^3 - \tfrac{1}{2}(x^2) + \tfrac{1}{3}(x^3)$$
$$= x - \tfrac{1}{2}x^2 + \tfrac{1}{6}x^3$$

(c) $(1 + x)^{1/2}(1 - x)^{-1/2} \approx (1 + \tfrac{1}{2}x - \tfrac{1}{8}x^2 + \tfrac{1}{16}x^3)(1 + \tfrac{1}{2}x + \tfrac{3}{8}x^2 + \tfrac{5}{16}x^3)$
$$= 1 + x + \tfrac{1}{2}x^2 + \tfrac{1}{2}x^3$$

(d) $e^x \cos x \approx (1 + x + \tfrac{1}{2}x^2 + \tfrac{1}{6}x^3 + \tfrac{1}{24}x^4)(1 - \tfrac{1}{2}x^2 + \tfrac{1}{24}x^4)$
$$= 1 + x - \tfrac{1}{3}x^3 - \tfrac{1}{6}x^4$$

Exercise 4D

1 $\displaystyle\int_0^1 \dfrac{t^n}{2}\,dt < \int_0^1 \dfrac{t^n}{1 + t}\,dt < \int_0^1 \dfrac{t^n}{1}\,dt \implies \dfrac{1}{2(n + 1)} < |\ln 2 - S_n| < \dfrac{1}{n + 1}.$

The error in using S_{1000} as an approximation to $\ln 2$ lies between about 0.005 and 0.001, which is unsatisfactory!

2 $0 < e^x - 1 < e^c - 1 \implies 0 < e^x - x - 1 < (e^c - 1)x$
$$\implies 0 < e^x - \tfrac{1}{2}x^2 - x - 1 < (e^c - 1)\dfrac{x^2}{2}$$
$$\vdots$$
$$\implies 0 < e^x - E_n(x) < (e^c - 1)\dfrac{x^n}{n!}.$$

But $x^n/n! \to 0$ as $n \to \infty$, so $E_n(x) \to e^x$ as $n \to \infty$.

If $d < x < 0$, $\qquad\qquad e^d - 1 < e^x - 1 < 0$,

and integrating twice from x to 0 gives

$$-x(e^d - 1) < \quad 1 + x - e^x \quad < 0,$$

then $\qquad\dfrac{(-x)^2}{2}(e^d - 1) < e^x - 1 - x - \dfrac{x^2}{2} < 0.$

Continuing the process, we obtain

$$\dfrac{(-x)^n}{n!}(e^d - 1) < (-1)^n[e^x - E_n(x)] < 0,$$

and the required result follows.

3
$$1 - t^2 + t^4 - \ldots + (-1)^{n-1} t^{2n-2} = \frac{1 - (-t^2)^n}{1 - (-t^2)}.$$

Hence
$$\frac{1}{1 + t^2} = 1 - t^2 + t^4 - \ldots + (-1)^{n-1} t^{2n-2} + (-1)^n \frac{t^{2n}}{1 + t^2},$$

and

$$\int_0^x \frac{1}{1 + t^2} \, dt = \int_0^x (1 - t^2 + t^4 - \ldots (-1)^{n-1} t^{2n-2}) \, dt + (-1)^n \int_0^x \frac{t^{2n}}{1 + t^2} \, dt.$$

Now
$$\int_0^x \frac{t^{2n}}{1 + x^2} \, dt < \int_0^x \frac{t^{2n}}{1 + t^2} \, dt < \int_0^x t^{2n} \, dt,$$

i.e.
$$\frac{x^{2n+1}}{(2n + 1)(1 + x^2)} < \int_0^x \frac{t^{2n}}{1 + t^2} \, dt < \frac{x^{2n+1}}{2n + 1}.$$

From this we see that $\int_0^x \frac{t^{2n}}{1 + t^2} \, dt \to 0$ as $n \to \infty$, so the infinite series

$x - \dfrac{x^3}{3} + \dfrac{x^5}{5} + \ldots$ converges, with sum to infinity $\tan^{-1} x$.

4 From question 3, setting $x = 1$ and $n = 1000$, we get

$$\frac{1}{4002} < \int_0^1 \frac{t^{2n}}{1 + t^2} \, dt < \frac{1}{2001},$$

giving an 'error' greater than 2×10^{-4}.

Exercise 4E

1, 2 It is sufficient to take the terms up to and including that in x^{12}. In Basic a simple program could be
```
INPUT X
T = 1
S = 1
FOR I = 1 to 12
T = T*X/I
S = S + T
NEXT T
PRINT X, S
```

3 Subtracting large numbers of comparable size leads to serious loss of accuracy.

4 (a) It gives 1.221 402 instead of 1.221 403.

(b) The error is now about 3×10^{-8} (see question 7). With $((e^{0.5})^2)^2$, the 'method error' is insignificant compared with rounding errors.

5 $x = 1$ gives 2.714.

6 This is easy to program.

7
$$\frac{(x + 3)^2 + 3}{(x - 3)^2 + 3} = \frac{x^2 + 6x + 12}{x^2 - 6x + 12}$$

$$= 1 + \frac{12x}{x^2 - 6x + 12}$$

$$= 1 + x(1 - \tfrac{1}{2}x + \tfrac{1}{12}x^2)^{-1}$$

$$\approx 1 + x[1 - (-\tfrac{1}{2}x + \tfrac{1}{12}x^2) + (-\tfrac{1}{2}x + \tfrac{1}{12}x^2)^2 - (-\tfrac{1}{2}x + \tfrac{1}{12}x^2)^3$$
$$+ (-\tfrac{1}{2}x + \tfrac{1}{12}x^2)^4]$$

$$\approx 1 + x + \tfrac{1}{2}x^2 - \tfrac{1}{12}x^3 + \tfrac{1}{4}x^3 - \tfrac{1}{12}x^4 + \tfrac{1}{144}x^5 + \tfrac{1}{8}x^4 - \tfrac{1}{16}x^5 + \tfrac{1}{16}x^5$$

(omitting terms in x^6 and higher powers)

$$= 1 + x + \tfrac{1}{2}x^2 + \tfrac{1}{6}x^3 + \tfrac{1}{24}x^4 + \tfrac{1}{144}x^5.$$

$\tfrac{1}{144}x^5$ differs from $x^5/5!$ by $(\tfrac{1}{120} - \tfrac{1}{144})x^5 = \tfrac{1}{720}x^5$.

8 (a) $\tan\theta = \tfrac{1}{5}$ $\Rightarrow$ $\tan 2\theta = \dfrac{\tfrac{2}{5}}{1 - \tfrac{1}{25}} = \tfrac{5}{12}$ $\Rightarrow$ $\tan 4\theta = \dfrac{\tfrac{10}{12}}{1 - \tfrac{25}{144}} = \tfrac{120}{119}.$

Hence $\qquad\qquad \tan(4\theta - \tfrac{1}{4}\pi) = \dfrac{\tfrac{120}{119} - 1}{1 + \tfrac{120}{119}} = \tfrac{1}{239}.$

(b) $\tan\alpha = \tfrac{1}{4}$ $\Rightarrow$ $\tan 2\alpha = \tfrac{8}{15}$ and $\tan 3\alpha = \tfrac{47}{52}.$ Then

$$\tan(3\alpha + \beta) = \dfrac{\tfrac{47}{52} + \tfrac{1}{20}}{1 - \tfrac{47}{52} \times \tfrac{1}{20}} = \tfrac{992}{993} \quad\text{and}\quad \tan(3\alpha + \beta - \tfrac{1}{4}\pi) = -\tfrac{1}{1985}.$$

(c) $\theta = \tan^{-1}\tfrac{1}{5}$ $\Rightarrow$ $4\theta - \tfrac{1}{4}\pi = \tan^{-1}\tfrac{1}{239},$ so $\tfrac{1}{4}\pi = 4\tan^{-1}\tfrac{1}{5} - \tan^{-1}\tfrac{1}{239}.$

Similarly, $\qquad \tfrac{1}{4}\pi = 3\tan^{-1}\tfrac{1}{4} + \tan^{-1}\tfrac{1}{20} + \tan^{-1}\tfrac{1}{1985}.$

(d) For each inverse tan, at most six terms of Gregory's series will be required.

9 (a) It will be found that about 30 terms are required to give 6 DP accuracy.

(b) $\ln(1 + x) = \quad x - \tfrac{1}{2}x^2 + \tfrac{1}{3}x^3 - \tfrac{1}{4}x^4 + \tfrac{1}{5}x^5 - \dots$
$\ln(1 - x) = -x - \tfrac{1}{2}x^2 - \tfrac{1}{3}x^3 - \tfrac{1}{4}x^4 - \tfrac{1}{5}x^5 - \dots$

$$\ln\left(\frac{1 + x}{1 - x}\right) = \ln(1 + x) - \ln(1 - x) = 2(x + \tfrac{1}{3}x^3 + \tfrac{1}{5}x^5 + \dots)$$

Only nine non-zero terms are now required for 6 DP accuracy.

(c) When $x < 0.001$, the first two terms of the Taylor series will give an accurate value of $\ln(1 + x)$. So we calculate $\ln 3$ as $2^n \times \ln 3^{2^{-n}}$; this gives 6 DP accuracy.

It is interesting to replace 1.001 by values like 1.002 and 1.0005. Can you explain the way method errors and rounding errors affect the answers? These will depend upon the calculator or computer used.

Miscellaneous exercise 4

1 $P(A) = a + ka + k^2a + \dots = a(1 + k + k^2 + \dots)$ where $k = (1 - a)(1 - b);$
$P(B) = (1 - a)b(1 + k + k^2 + \dots);$
$P(A) = P(B)$ $\Rightarrow$ $a = (1 - a)b$

2 $[a + b = 1 \text{ and } a = (1 - a)b]$ $\Rightarrow$ $a^2 - 3a + 1 = 0$ $\Rightarrow$ $a = \dfrac{3 - \sqrt{5}}{2}.$

Then $\quad b = \dfrac{-1 + \sqrt{5}}{2}$ and $\dfrac{b}{a} = \dfrac{(-1 + \sqrt{5})(3 + \sqrt{5})}{(3 - \sqrt{5})(3 + \sqrt{5})} = \dfrac{1 + \sqrt{5}}{2}.$

The irrationality of $\sqrt{5}$ makes such a game hard to realise!

3 $S_2 = \dfrac{x(1 + x^2) + x^2}{1 - x^4} = \dfrac{x + x^2 + x^3}{1 - x^4};$

$S_3 = \dfrac{(x + x^2 + x^3)(1 + x^4) + x^4}{1 - x^8}$

$= \dfrac{x + x^2 + x^3 + x^4 + x^5 + x^6 + x^7}{1 - x^8} = \dfrac{x(1 - x^7)}{(1 - x)(1 - x^8)}$

A pattern is established, which can be proved by induction if required:

$$S_n = \frac{x - x^{2^n}}{(1 - x)(1 - x^{2^n})}.$$

(a) If $|x| < 1$, $x^{2^n} \to 0$ as $n \to \infty$, so $S_n \to \dfrac{x}{1 - x}$

(b) If $|x| > 1$, $\dfrac{x - x^{2^n}}{1 - x^{2^n}} \to 1$ as $n \to \infty$, so $S_n \to \dfrac{1}{1 - x}$

4 $(r - \tfrac{1}{2})(r + \tfrac{1}{2}) = r^2 - \tfrac{1}{4} < r^2$

$(r - \tfrac{39}{80})(r + \tfrac{41}{80}) = r^2 + \tfrac{2}{80}r - \tfrac{1599}{6400} = r^2 + \dfrac{160r - 1559}{6400} > r^2$ for $r \geqslant 10$

$$\frac{1}{(r - \tfrac{39}{80})(r + \tfrac{41}{80})} < \frac{1}{r^2} < \frac{1}{(r - \tfrac{1}{2})(r + \tfrac{1}{2})}$$

$\Rightarrow$
$$\frac{1}{r - \tfrac{39}{80}} - \frac{1}{r + \tfrac{41}{80}} < \frac{1}{r^2} < \frac{1}{r - \tfrac{1}{2}} - \frac{1}{r + \tfrac{1}{2}}$$

$\Rightarrow$
$$\frac{1}{10 - \tfrac{39}{80}} < \sum_{10}^{\infty} \frac{1}{r^2} < \frac{1}{10 - \tfrac{1}{2}}$$

$\Rightarrow$
$$\frac{80}{761} < \sum_{10}^{\infty} \frac{1}{r^2} < \frac{2}{19}$$

$\Rightarrow$
$$\frac{80}{761} + \sum_{1}^{9} \frac{1}{r^2} < \sum_{1}^{\infty} \frac{1}{r^2} < \frac{2}{19} + \sum_{1}^{9} \frac{1}{r^2}.$$

This gives $\displaystyle\sum_{1}^{\infty} \frac{1}{r^2}$ with an accuracy of $\tfrac{1}{2}(\tfrac{2}{19} - \tfrac{80}{761}) \approx 0.000\,14$.

5
$$\int_n^{n+1} \frac{1}{\sqrt{x}}\,dx < \frac{1}{\sqrt{n}} < \int_{n-1}^{n} \frac{1}{\sqrt{x}}\,dx \quad \text{(from Figure 4)}$$

$\Rightarrow 2(\sqrt{(n+1)} - \sqrt{n}) < \dfrac{1}{\sqrt{n}} < 2(\sqrt{n} - \sqrt{(n-1)})$.

Alternatively,

$$\sqrt{n}(\sqrt{(n+1)} - \sqrt{n}) = \sqrt{(n^2 + n)} - n < \sqrt{(n^2 + n + \tfrac{1}{4})} - n = \tfrac{1}{2}, \quad \text{etc.}$$

Then $\displaystyle\sum_{1}^{100} \frac{1}{\sqrt{r}} > 2(\sqrt{101} - \sqrt{1}) > 18$ and $\displaystyle\sum_{2}^{100} \frac{1}{\sqrt{r}} < 2(\sqrt{100} - 1) = 18$,

implying
$$\sum_{1}^{100} \frac{1}{\sqrt{r}} < 19.$$

6 The expression gives the sum of the areas of n rectangles, each with width $1/n$, under the graph of $y = 1/x$ between $x = 1$ and $x = 2$. This tends to $\displaystyle\int_1^2 \frac{1}{x}\,dx$ as $n \to \infty$.

Hence
$$\lim_{n \to \infty} \left(\frac{1}{n + 1} + \frac{1}{n + 2} + \ldots + \frac{1}{2n} \right) = \ln 2.$$

7 $S_{2n} = 1 - \tfrac{1}{2} + \tfrac{1}{3} - \tfrac{1}{4} + \ldots - 1/2n$
$= (1 + \tfrac{1}{2} + \tfrac{1}{3} + \tfrac{1}{4} + \ldots + 1/2n) - 2(\tfrac{1}{2} + \tfrac{1}{4} + \tfrac{1}{6} + \ldots + 1/2n)$
$= (1 + \tfrac{1}{2} + \tfrac{1}{3} + \tfrac{1}{4} + \ldots + 1/2n) - (1 + \tfrac{1}{2} + \tfrac{1}{3} + \ldots + 1/n)$
$= \dfrac{1}{n + 1} + \dfrac{1}{n + 2} + \ldots + \dfrac{1}{2n};$

$S_{2n} \to \ln 2$ as $n \to \infty$ $\Rightarrow$ $S_n \to \ln 2$ as $n \to \infty$.

8 $\dfrac{d}{dx}(x \ln x - x) = \ln x + 1 - 1 = \ln x$

(b) This follows from a diagram similar to Figures 4 and 5.

(c) $\displaystyle\int_1^{100} \ln x \, dx < \sum_2^{100} \ln r < \int_2^{101} \ln x \, dx$

$\Rightarrow \left[x \ln x - x \right]_1^{100} < \ln 100! < \left[x \ln x - x \right]_2^{101}$

$\Rightarrow \qquad\qquad 361.5 < \ln 100! < 365.8$

(d) This gives $362.6 < \ln 100! < 364.9$.

9 (a) $(1 - h)^{-1/2} \approx 1 + \frac{1}{2}h + \frac{3}{8}h^2 + \frac{5}{16}h^3$; $(1 - x^2)^{-1/2} \approx 1 + \frac{1}{2}x^2 + \frac{3}{8}x^4 + \frac{5}{16}x^6$
  (b) $\sin^{-1} x \approx x + \frac{1}{6}x^3 + \frac{3}{40}x^5 + \frac{5}{112}x^7$
  (c) $(1 + x^2)^{-1/2} \approx 1 - \frac{1}{2}x^2 + \frac{3}{8}x^4 - \frac{5}{16}x^6$; $\sinh^{-1} x \approx x - \frac{1}{6}x^3 + \frac{3}{40}x^5 - \frac{5}{112}x^7$
  (d) The polynomial gives 0.390 028, whereas $\sinh^{-1} 0.4 = 0.390 035$.

10 $(1 + 2x)^{1/2} (1 - 3x)^{-1/2} \approx (1 + x - \frac{1}{2}x^2)(1 + \frac{3}{2}x + \frac{27}{8}x^2) \approx 1 + \frac{5}{2}x + \frac{35}{8}x^2$

11 When $x = 0$, $y = c$; when $x = 20$, $y = c \cos(20/c)$.
  Sag $= 1 \Rightarrow c + 1 = c \cosh(20/c) \approx c[1 + \frac{1}{2}(20/c)^2] \Rightarrow c \approx 200$.

12 (a) The total area of the rectangles is $(1 + \frac{1}{2} + \frac{1}{3} + \frac{1}{4} + \frac{1}{5})$, while the area under the curve from $x = 1$ to $x = 6$ is $\ln 6$.

  (b) Increasing n increases the number of shaded regions and hence the total area. The area of the rth shaded area is less than the area of a rectangle of width 1 and height $\left(\dfrac{1}{r} - \dfrac{1}{r+1} \right)$, and hence u_n is less than $1 - \dfrac{1}{n+1}$. Since u_n is a bounded increasing sequence, it has a limit.

  (c) $v_n - u_n = \ln(n + 1) - \ln n = \ln \left(\dfrac{n+1}{n} \right) \to 0$ as $n \to \infty$. Hence $v_n \to \gamma$ as $n \to \infty$.

  (d) $1 + \frac{1}{2} + \frac{1}{3} + \ldots + \frac{1}{25000} > \ln 25\,000 > 10$

13

n	2	10	100	10 000
u_n	0.401 39	0.531 07	0.572 26	0.576 72
v_n	0.806 85	0.626 38	0.582 21	0.577 72

14 (a) $\cos(2m + 1)\theta + j \sin(2m + 1)\theta = (\cos \theta + j \sin \theta)^{2m+1}$.
  Expanding the right-hand side and picking out the terms containing j gives

$$\sin(2m + 1)\theta = \binom{2m + 1}{1} c^{2m} s - \binom{2m + 1}{3} c^{2m-2} s^3 + \ldots$$

(writing c, s for $\cos \theta$ and $\sin \theta$),

$$= s^{2m+1} \left[\binom{2m + 1}{1} \left(\frac{c}{s} \right)^{2m} + \binom{2m + 1}{3} \left(\frac{c}{s} \right)^{2m-2} + \ldots \right],$$

which is the desired result since $\cot \theta = c/s$.

(b) $\theta = \dfrac{k\pi}{2m + 1}$ $\Rightarrow$ $\sin(2m + 1)\theta = 0$, so for $k = 1, \quad 2, \quad 3, \quad \ldots, \quad m,$

$\cot^2\left(\dfrac{k\pi}{2m + 1}\right)$ is a solution of

$$\binom{2m + 1}{1} x^m - \binom{2m + 1}{3} x^{m-1} + \ldots + (-1)^m = 0$$

But these m values are all different, so they constitute all the roots of the equation.

(c) The sum of the roots is

$$\binom{2m + 1}{3} \div \binom{2m + 1}{1} = \dfrac{(2m + 1)(2m)(2m - 1)}{3!} \div (2m + 1)$$

$$= \dfrac{m(2m - 1)}{3}.$$

(d) $0 < x < \tfrac{1}{2}\pi$

$\Rightarrow$ $\sin x < x < \tan x$

$\Rightarrow$ $\dfrac{1}{\tan x} < \dfrac{1}{x} < \dfrac{1}{\sin x}$

$\Rightarrow$ $\cot^2 x < \dfrac{1}{x^2} < \text{cosec}^2 x$

$\Rightarrow$ $\cot^2 x < \dfrac{1}{x^2} < 1 + \cot^2 x$

(e) From (d),

$$\sum_{1}^{m} \cot^2\left(\dfrac{k\pi}{2m + 1}\right) < \sum_{1}^{m} \left(\dfrac{2m + 1}{k\pi}\right)^2 < m + \sum_{1}^{m} \cot^2\left(\dfrac{k\pi}{2m + 1}\right),$$

giving

$$\dfrac{m(2m - 1)}{3} < \left(\dfrac{2m + 1}{\pi}\right)^2 \sum_{1}^{m} \dfrac{1}{k^2} < m + \dfrac{m(2m - 1)}{3} = \dfrac{2m(m + 1)}{3}.$$

(f) $\dfrac{\pi^2}{6} \times \dfrac{2m(2m - 1)}{(2m + 1)^2} < \sum_{1}^{m} \dfrac{1}{k^2} < \dfrac{\pi^2}{6} \times \dfrac{4m(m + 1)}{(2m + 1)^2}.$

Let $m \to \infty$: $\dfrac{\pi^2}{6} \leq \lim_{m \to \infty} \sum_{1}^{m} \dfrac{1}{k^2} \leq \dfrac{\pi^2}{6}$, giving $\sum_{1}^{\infty} \dfrac{1}{k^2} = \dfrac{\pi^2}{6}.$

15 $((t^2 - 6)^2 - 12)/24 = 1 - \tfrac{1}{2}t^2 + \tfrac{1}{24}t^4$, the first three terms of the series for cos t. This gives an accurate value if $t < 0.005$.

The algorithm finds cos x by finding a suitable n such that $|x|/2^n$ is small enough, working out its cosine, then using the double angle formula, $\cos 2\theta = 2\cos^2\theta - 1$, n times.

16 $e^x = 1 + x + \dfrac{x^2}{2!} + \ldots + \dfrac{x^{n+1}}{(n + 1)!} + \ldots$ $\Rightarrow$ $e^x > \dfrac{x^{n+1}}{(n + 1)!}$

$\Rightarrow$ $\dfrac{x^n}{e^x} < \dfrac{(n + 1)!}{x}.$

Since $(n + 1)!/x \to 0$ as $x \to \infty$, and $x^n/e^x > 0$ given $x > 0$, it follows that $x^n/e^x \to 0$ as $x \to \infty$.

17 $0 < t - \sin t$

⇒ $0 < \frac{1}{2}x^2 + \cos x - 1$ (integrating between limits of 0 and x)

⇒ $0 < \int_0^x (\frac{1}{2}t^2 + \cos t - 1)\, dt$

⇒ $0 < \dfrac{x^3}{3!} + \sin x - x.$

This means that $\sin x > x - x^3/3!$. Two more similar integrations give $\sin x < x - x^3/3! + x^5/5!$, and the process can be continued indefinitely.

Thus $S_{2m} < \sin x < S_{2m+1}.$

Now $S_{2m+1} - S_{2m} \to 0$ as $m \to \infty$, so S_{2m} and S_{2m+1} tend to the same limit l as $m \to \infty$.

Moreover, $l \leqslant \sin x \leqslant l,$ so $l = \sin x.$

For negative values, $t - \sin t < 0$

⇒ $\int_x^0 (t - \sin t)\, dt < 0$

⇒ $1 - \frac{1}{2}x^2 - \cos x < 0$

⇒ $\left[t - \frac{1}{6}t^3 - \sin t \right]_x^0 < 0$

⇒ $\sin x - x + \dfrac{x^3}{3!} < 0,$ etc.

Exercise 5A

1   (a)   (b)

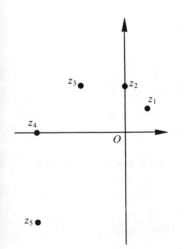

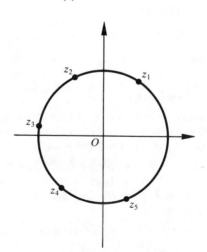

All points lie on the unit circle.

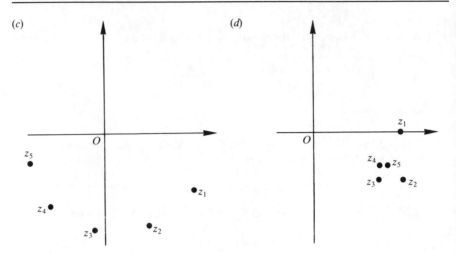

(c)

(d)

$\arg z_1 = -32°$; $|z_5| = 0.75 |z_1|$

(e)

$z_4 = 1\tfrac{1}{5} + \tfrac{3}{5}j$; $z_5 = 1\tfrac{1}{3} + \tfrac{2}{3}j$

2 The sequence in (c) converges to 0; that in (d) to $0.8–0.4j$ (the solution of $z = 1 - \tfrac{1}{2}jz$). In (e), the limit is a solution of $z = j/z + 1$, i.e. of $z^2 - z - j = 0$. The methods of Chapter 3 give this as $1.300 + 0.625j$ to 3 DP.

3 $R = r^n$ and $\phi = n\theta$, giving $R = r^{\phi/\theta}$. This may be written as $R = e^{m\phi}$, where $e^m = r^{1/\theta}$, i.e. $m = (1/\theta) \ln r$. If ϕ is allowed to take any real value, $R = e^{m\phi}$ gives an equiangular spiral; integer values of n give only isolated points on this curve, of course.

4 $|z^n/n!| = |z|^n/n!$. We can choose an integer m greater than $|z|$, and then

$$\frac{|z|^n}{n!} < \frac{|z|^m}{m!} \times \left(\frac{|z|}{m}\right)^{n-m} \quad \text{for all } n > m.$$

It follows that as $n \to \infty$, $|z^n/n!| \to 0$, and hence the points on the Argand diagram representing $z^n/n!$ spiral in towards the origin.

5 For any chosen $k > 0$, there exists n_0 such that $|x_n + y_n j - a - bj| < k$ for all $n > n_0$. But $|x_n + y_n j - a - bj| = \sqrt{((x_n - a)^2 + (y_n - b)^2)}$, which is greater than $|x_2 - a|$ and also greater than $|y_n - b|$. So for any chosen $k > 0$, there exists n_0 such that $|x_n - a| < k$ for all $n > n_0$; i.e. x_n tends to a as n tends to infinity. Similarly, y_n tends to b.

6 (a)   (b)

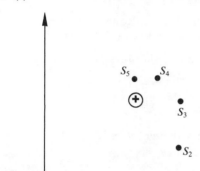

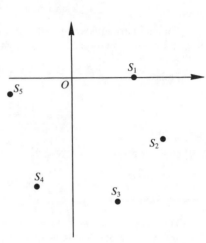

(c)   (d)

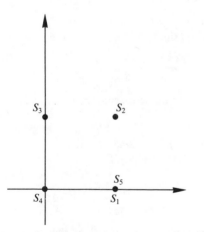

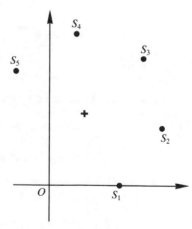

The points lie on a circle centre $\frac{1}{2} + j$.

Only (a) converges.

7 The usual methods of summing geometric series work just as well with complex series.

Then $$S_n = \frac{1 - z^n}{1 - z} \to \frac{1}{1 - z} \quad \text{as } n \to \infty \quad \text{if } |z| < 1.$$

When $z = \frac{1}{2} + \frac{1}{2}j$, $\dfrac{1}{1-z} = \dfrac{1}{\frac{1}{2} - \frac{1}{2}j} = 1 + j$

8   When $z = \cos\theta + j\sin\theta$, $z^n = \cos n\theta + j\sin n\theta$

and $\dfrac{1-z^n}{1-z} = \dfrac{1 - \cos n\theta - j\sin n\theta}{1 - \cos\theta - j\sin\theta} = \dfrac{1 - \cos n\theta - j\sin n\theta}{2\sin^2\frac{1}{2}\theta - 2j\sin\frac{1}{2}\theta\cos\frac{1}{2}\theta}$

$$= \dfrac{[(1 - \cos n\theta) - j\sin n\theta]\,(\sin\frac{1}{2}\theta + j\cos\frac{1}{2}\theta)}{2\sin\frac{1}{2}\theta(\sin\frac{1}{2}\theta - j\cos\frac{1}{2}\theta)\,(\sin\frac{1}{2}\theta + j\cos\frac{1}{2}\theta)}.$$

The real part equals $C = 1 + \cos\theta + \cos 2\theta + \ldots + \cos(n-1)\theta$
and the imaginary part equals $S = \sin\theta + \sin 2\theta + \ldots + \sin(n-1)\theta$.

Thus $C = \dfrac{(1 - \cos n\theta)\sin\frac{1}{2}\theta + \sin n\theta\cos\frac{1}{2}\theta}{2\sin\frac{1}{2}\theta}$

$$= \dfrac{\sin\frac{1}{2}\theta + \sin(n - \frac{1}{2})\theta}{2\sin\frac{1}{2}\theta}$$

and $S = \dfrac{(1 - \cos n\theta)\cos\frac{1}{2}\theta - \sin n\theta\sin\frac{1}{2}\theta}{2\sin\frac{1}{2}\theta}$

$$= \dfrac{\cos\frac{1}{2}\theta - \cos(n - \frac{1}{2})\theta}{2\sin\frac{1}{2}\theta}.$$

These results only hold if $z \neq 1$, i.e. $\theta \neq 2k\pi$. If $\theta = 2k\pi$, $C = 1 + 1 + 1 + \ldots + 1 = n$
and $S = 0$. Note that as $\theta \to 0$, $C \to n$ and $S \to 0$.

9 $1 + \frac{1}{2}\cos\theta + \frac{1}{4}\cos 2\theta + \frac{1}{8}\cos 3\theta + \ldots$ is the real part of

$$\dfrac{1}{1 - \frac{1}{2}(\cos\theta + j\sin\theta)} = \dfrac{2}{[(2 - \cos\theta) - j\sin\theta]} \cdot \dfrac{[(2 - \cos\theta) + j\sin\theta]}{[(2 - \cos\theta) + j\sin\theta]}.$$

This is $\dfrac{4 - 2\cos\theta}{(2 - \cos\theta)^2 + \sin^2\theta} = \dfrac{4 - 2\cos\theta}{5 - 4\cos\theta}.$

This is valid since $|\cos\theta + j\sin\theta| = 1 < 2$ and the series converges if $|z| < 2$.

10
$$S_n = 1 + 2z + 3z^2 + \ldots + nz^{n-1}$$
$$-2z\,S_n = \quad -2z - 4z^2 + \ldots - 2(n-1)z^{n-1} - 2nz^n$$
$$z^2 S_n = \qquad\qquad z^2 + \ldots + (n-2)z^{n-1} + (n-1)z^n + nz^{n+1}.$$

When we add up, most of the terms cancel, leaving

$$(1 - z)^2 S_n = 1 - (n+1)z^n + nz^{n+1}.$$

If $|z| < 1$, the right-hand side tends to 1 as n tends to ∞, for reasons similar to those
discussed in Chapter 4, §4 and Exercise 4E. The sum to infinity of the given series is
$(1 - z)^{-2}$.

11 (*a*)   (*b*)

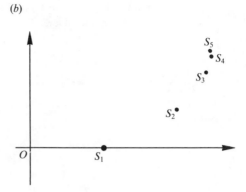

The series converges very rapidly.   The series converges less rapidly but S_5 and S_4 are very close.

Exercise 5B

1 (*a*) $\cos 2 + j \sin 2 \approx -0.42 + 0.91j$ (*b*) $-\frac{1}{2}\sqrt{2} + \frac{1}{2}\sqrt{2}\,j \approx -0.71 + 0.71j$
    (*c*) $e^3(\cos 1 - j \sin 1) \approx 10.85 - 16.90j$ (*d*) $\cos \theta - j \sin \theta$

2 (*a*) $4\,e^{\pi j/2}$ (*b*) $7\,e^{\pi j}$ (*c*) $2\,e^{\pi j/3}$ (*d*) $2\,e^{4\pi j/3}$ or $2\,e^{-2\pi j/3}$

3 (*a*) Modulus 7, argument $\frac{3}{2}\pi$ (*b*) $[1, 1]$ (*c*) $[e^2, 1]$
    (*d*) A rhombus on an Argand diagram shows the modulus to be $2\cos(\theta - \phi)$ and the argument to be $(\theta + \phi)$. Alternatively, we may use trigonometric formulae to obtain the same answers:

$$e^{2j\theta} + e^{2j\phi} = \cos 2\theta + j \sin 2\theta + \cos 2\phi + j \sin 2\phi$$
$$= 2\cos(\theta + \phi)\cos(\theta - \phi) + 2j \sin(\theta + \phi)\cos(\theta - \phi)$$
$$= 2\cos(\theta - \phi)[\cos(\theta + \phi) + j \sin(\theta + \phi)]$$

4 (*a*) $1 + e^{\theta j} = (1 + \cos \theta) + j \sin \theta$
        $= 2\cos^2 \frac{1}{2}\theta + 2j \sin \frac{1}{2}\theta \cos \frac{1}{2}\theta$
        $= 2\cos \frac{1}{2}\theta (\cos \frac{1}{2}\theta + j \sin \frac{1}{2}\theta)$
    $\Rightarrow$ modulus $= 2\cos^2 \frac{1}{2}\theta$, argument $= \frac{1}{2}\theta$.
    This question may also be treated as a special case of question 3(*d*).
    (*b*) $1/(\sin \theta + j \cos \theta) = \sin \theta - j \cos \theta$
            $= -j(\cos \theta + j \sin \theta)$
            $= \cos(\theta - \frac{1}{2}\pi) + j \sin(\theta - \frac{1}{2}\pi)$
    $\Rightarrow$ modulus $= 1$, argument $= \theta - \frac{1}{2}\pi$.
    There are many different ways of looking at this question.
    (*c*) $1 - e^{\theta j}$ can be shown to have modulus $2\sin \frac{1}{2}\theta$ and argument $(\frac{1}{2}\theta - \frac{1}{2}\pi)$ and hence, using (*a*), $(1 - e^{\theta j})/(1 + e^{\theta j})$ has modulus $\tan \frac{1}{2}\theta$ and argument $-\frac{1}{2}\pi$. The diagram gives these answers directly.

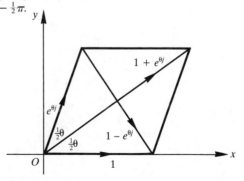

5 $e^{z+2\pi j} = e^z \times e^{2\pi j} = e^z \times (\cos 2\pi + j \sin 2\pi) = e^z$.

Similarly, $e^{z+2k\pi j} = e^z$ for all $k \in \mathbb{Z}$. Hence e^z can be said to have period $2\pi j$.

6 (a)

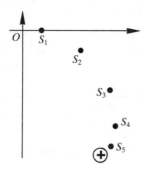

The limit is $3.99 - 6.22j$.

(b)

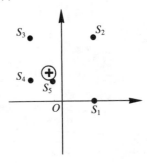

The limit is $-0.42 + 0.91j$.

(c)

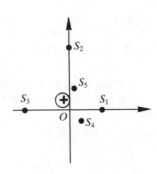

The limit is $-0.15 + 0.33j$.

7 (a)

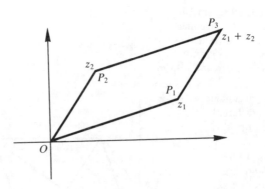

$$OP_3 \leqslant OP_1 + OP_2$$
$$\Rightarrow |z_1 + z_2| \leqslant |z_1| + |z_2|$$

(b) $\left| 1 + \dfrac{z}{3} + \dfrac{z^2}{3 \times 4} + \dots \right| \leqslant 1 + \dfrac{|z|}{3} + \dfrac{|z|^2}{3 \times 4} + \dots$

$$< 1 + \dfrac{|z|}{3} + \dfrac{|z|^2}{3^2} + \dots$$

$$= \left(1 - \dfrac{|z|}{3} \right)^{-1} \quad \text{if } |z| < 3$$

(c) $\qquad R_n(z) = \dfrac{z^n}{n!} \left(1 + \dfrac{z}{n+1} + \dfrac{z^2}{(n+1)(n+2)} + \dots \right)$

$$\Rightarrow \ |R_n(z)| < \dfrac{|z|^n}{n!} \left(1 - \dfrac{|z|}{n+1} \right)^{-1} \quad \text{if } |z| < n+1$$

(d) However large $|z|$ may be, the result in (c) will hold for all sufficiently large n. Moreover, $|z|^n/n! \to 0$ as $n \to 0$, so $|R_n(z)| \to 0$ and the exponential series converges for all z.

Applying the result in (c) to question 6(c), we see that we have proved that the point S_5 is within a distance 0.74 of the limiting point.

8 With $z = -1 + 2j$, $\ |R_8(z)| < \dfrac{(\sqrt{5})^8}{8!} \left(1 - \dfrac{\sqrt{5}}{9} \right)^{-1} < 0.021$

9 The methods of Chapter 4 show that the series converges if $|z| < 1$, as in (a), and diverges if $|z| > 1$, as in (b). Argand diagrams can be drawn to illustrate these examples. When $|z| = 1$, the situation is more complicated.

When $z = j$, $\ S = (-\tfrac{1}{2} + \tfrac{1}{4} - \tfrac{1}{6} + \dots) + j(1 - \tfrac{1}{3} + \tfrac{1}{5} - \dots)$

and our experience of alternating series shows that the series converges. The real part equals $-\tfrac{1}{2}(1 - \tfrac{1}{2} + \tfrac{1}{3} - \dots)$, with sum to infinity $-\tfrac{1}{2} \ln 2$. The imaginary part equals $j \tan^{-1} 1 = \tfrac{1}{4}\pi j$.

Now $\qquad\qquad -\ln(1 - j) = -\ln(\sqrt{2}\, e^{-\pi j/4})$
$$\qquad\qquad\qquad = -\tfrac{1}{2}\ln 2 + \tfrac{1}{4}\pi j.$$
For (a), $\qquad\quad -\ln(1 - z) = -\ln(\tfrac{1}{2} - \tfrac{1}{2}j)$
$$\qquad\qquad\qquad = -\ln(1 - j) + \ln 2$$
$$\qquad\qquad\qquad = \tfrac{1}{2}\ln 2 + \tfrac{1}{4}\pi j.$$

10 (a) $\ln 2 + 3j$ (b) $\ln 5 + \tan^{-1} \tfrac{4}{3} j$ (c) θj
Any multiple of $2\pi j$ could be added to each of these answers.

11 (a) $\cos 5$ (b) $\cosh 2 \cos 5 + j \sinh 2 \sin 5$ (c) 1

Miscellaneous exercise 5

1 $x^2 - 2\cos\theta x + 1$;
$x^8 = 1 \ \Rightarrow \ x = [1, \theta]$ where $\theta = 2k\pi/8$ and $k = -3, -2, -1, 0, 1, 2, 3, 4$;
$x^8 - 1 = (x - e^{-3\pi j/4})(x - e^{-2\pi j/4}) \dots (x - e^{-4\pi j/4})$
$\qquad = (x + 1)(x - 1)(x + j)(x - j)(x^2 - 2\cos\tfrac{1}{4}\pi x + 1)(x^2 - 2\cos\tfrac{3}{4}\pi x + 1)$
$\qquad = (x + 1)(x - 1)(x^2 + 1)(x^2 - \sqrt{2}x + 1)(x^2 + \sqrt{2}x + 1)$

2 (a) $(z - e^{\theta j})(z - e^{-\theta j}) = (z - \cos \theta - j \sin \theta)(z - \cos \theta + j \sin \theta)$

(b) (i) $(z^2 - e^{\theta j})(z^2 - e^{-\theta j}) = (z - e^{\theta j/2})(z + e^{\theta j/2})(z - e^{-\theta j/2})(z + e^{-\theta j/2})$

(ii) $\qquad\qquad = (z^2 - 2 \cos \tfrac{1}{2}\theta z + 1)(z^2 + 2 \cos \tfrac{1}{2}\theta z + 1)$.

If the answer is checked by multiplying these final factors, the coefficient of z^2

is $1 + 1 - 4 \cos^2 \tfrac{1}{2}\theta = 2(1 - 2 \cos^2 \tfrac{1}{2}\theta) = -2 \cos \theta$.

3 $\qquad S_1 = \sinh a + \sinh 2a + \sinh 3a + \ldots + \sinh na$

$\qquad = \tfrac{1}{2}(e^a + e^{2a} + e^{3a} + \ldots + e^{na}) - \tfrac{1}{2}(e^{-a} + e^{-2a} + e^{-3a} + \ldots + e^{-na})$

$\qquad = \tfrac{1}{2}e^a \left(\dfrac{1 - e^{na}}{1 - e^a} \right) - \tfrac{1}{2}e^{-a}\left(\dfrac{1 - e^{-na}}{1 - e^{-a}} \right),$

and this can be expressed in hyperbolic functions using $e^a = \cosh a + \sinh a$, etc. Similarly,

$$S_2 = \sin a + \sin 2a + \ldots + \sin na$$

$$= \frac{1}{2j}(e^{ja} + e^{2ja} + \ldots) - \frac{1}{2j}(e^{-ja} + e^{-2ja} + \ldots)$$

$$= \frac{1}{2j}e^{ja}\left(\frac{1 - e^{jna}}{1 - e^{ja}}\right) - \frac{1}{2j}e^{-ja}\left(\frac{1 - e^{-jna}}{1 - e^{-ja}}\right)$$

$$= \frac{1}{j} \times \text{imaginary part of } e^{ja}\left(\frac{1 - e^{jna}}{1 - e^{ja}}\right).$$

This can yield the result of Exercise 5A, question 8 with n replaced by $n + 1$. Alternatively, we can proceed as follows:

$\qquad 2 \sin \tfrac{1}{2}a \times S_2 = 2 \sin \tfrac{1}{2}a \sin a + 2 \sin \tfrac{1}{2}a \sin 2a + \ldots + 2 \sin \tfrac{1}{2}a \sin na$

$\qquad\qquad = (\cos \tfrac{1}{2}a - \cos \tfrac{3}{2}a) + (\cos \tfrac{3}{2}a - \cos \tfrac{5}{2}a)$

$\qquad\qquad \quad + \ldots + (\cos(n - \tfrac{1}{2})a - \cos(n + \tfrac{1}{2})a)$

$\qquad\qquad = \cos \tfrac{1}{2}a - \cos(n + \tfrac{1}{2})a.$

Hence $\qquad\qquad S_2 = \dfrac{\cos \tfrac{1}{2}a - \cos(n + \tfrac{1}{2})a}{2 \sin \tfrac{1}{2}a}.$

This method applied to the first series gives

$$S_1 = \frac{\cosh(n + \tfrac{1}{2})a - \cosh \tfrac{1}{2}a}{2 \sinh \tfrac{1}{2}a}.$$

As a check, notice that for small a

$$S_2 \approx \frac{(1 - (\tfrac{1}{2}a)^2) - (1 - ((n + \tfrac{1}{2})a)^2)}{2 \times \tfrac{1}{2}a}, \quad \text{using } \sin \theta \approx \theta \text{ and } \cos \theta \approx 1 - \tfrac{1}{2}\theta^2$$

$$= \tfrac{1}{2}[(n + \tfrac{1}{2})^2 - (\tfrac{1}{2})^2]a$$

$$= \tfrac{1}{2}n(n + 1)a$$

Also $\qquad \sin a + \sin 2a + \sin 3a + \ldots + \sin na \approx \sum_{1}^{n} ia = \tfrac{1}{2}n(n + 1)a.$

The Taylor approximation for $\cosh u$ is $1 + \tfrac{1}{2}u^2$, and this accounts for the change of sign in the result for S_1 compared with that for S_2.

4 This 'proof' is plausible but we have yet to discuss differentiation and integration of functions of a complex variable.

5 (a) The proof is exactly as in Chapter 1, §1.

(b) These follow immediately from the definitions.

(c) $\cos(z_1 + z_2) = \cosh(jz_1 + jz_2)$
$\qquad = \cosh jz_1 \cosh jz_2 + \sinh jz_1 \sinh jz_2$
$\qquad = \cos z_1 \cos z_2 + (j \sin z_1)(j \cos z_2)$
$\qquad = \cos z_1 \cos z_2 - \sin z_1 \sin z_2$

Alternatively, just use the definitions.

(d) $\cos(z + 2n\pi) = \cos z \cos 2n\pi - \sin z \sin 2n\pi$
$\qquad = \cos z.$

Similarly, $\cosh(z + 2n\pi j) = \cosh z.$

(e) $\cos(a + bj) = \cos a \cos bj - \sin a \sin bj$
$\qquad = \cos a \cosh b + j \sin a \sinh(bj^2)$
$\qquad = \cos a \cosh b - j \sin a \sinh b$

(f) If $\cos z = 2$ and $z = a + bj$, where a and b are real, then

$$\cos a \cosh b = 2 \quad \text{and} \quad \sin a \sinh b = 0.$$

$\sinh b$ cannot be 0, since this would require $\cos a = 2$; so $\sin a = 0$. Now $\cos a > 0$, since $\cosh b > 0$; consequently $a = 2k\pi$ and $\cosh b = 2$. All solutions are given by $z = 2k\pi + j \cosh^{-1} 2$.

Exercise 6A

1 (a) $\frac{1}{3} \tan^3 x - \tan x + x + k$ $\qquad$ (b) $\frac{1}{4} - \frac{1}{2} + \left[\ln \sec x \right]_0^{\pi/4} = -\frac{1}{4} + \frac{1}{2} \ln 2 \approx 0.0966$

(c) $\dfrac{5}{6} \times \dfrac{3}{4} \times \dfrac{1}{2} \times \dfrac{\pi}{2} = \dfrac{5\pi}{32} \approx 0.491$

(d) $\dfrac{10}{11} \times \dfrac{8}{9} \times \dfrac{6}{7} \times \dfrac{4}{5} \times \dfrac{2}{3} \times 2 \approx 0.739$

2 $\displaystyle\int_0^{\pi/2} \cos^7 x \, dx = \int_0^{\pi/2} \sin^7 y \, dy = \frac{6}{7} \times \frac{4}{5} \times \frac{2}{3} \times 1 = \frac{16}{35} \approx 0.457$

3 $\qquad u_n = \displaystyle\int \cos^n x \, dx = \int \cos^{n-1} x \cos x \, dx$

$\qquad\quad = \cos^{n-1} x \sin x - \displaystyle\int \sin x \times (n-1) \cos^{n-2} x \times (-\sin x) \, dx$

$\qquad\quad = \cos^{n-1} x \sin x + (n-1) \displaystyle\int \cos^{n-2} x \, (1 - \cos^2 x) \, dx;$

$\qquad n u_n = \cos^{n-1} x \sin x + (n-1) u_{n-2};$

$\displaystyle\int \cos^6 x \, dx = \frac{1}{6} \cos^5 x \sin x + \frac{5}{6} \times \frac{1}{4} \cos^3 x \sin x$
$\qquad\qquad\qquad + \frac{5}{6} \times \frac{3}{4} \times \frac{1}{2} \cos x \sin x + \frac{5}{6} \times \frac{3}{4} \times \frac{1}{2} x + k$

4 $\left[-\frac{1}{4} \sin^3 x \cos x - \frac{3}{4} \times \frac{1}{2} \sin x \cos x + \frac{3}{4} \times \frac{1}{2} x \right]_0^{\pi/4} = (3\pi - 8)/32 \approx 0.0445$

5 $\displaystyle\int_0^a (a^2 - x^2)^{3/2} \, dx = a^4 \int_0^{\pi/2} \cos^4 u \, du = \frac{3}{16} \pi a^4$

6 $u_n = \displaystyle\int \sec^{n-2} x \sec^2 x \, dx = \sec^{n-2} x \tan x - \int \tan x \times (n-2) \sec^{n-2} x \tan x \, dx$
$\qquad = \sec^{n-2} x \tan x - (n-2) \displaystyle\int \sec^{n-2} x \, (\sec^2 x - 1) \, dx;$

$(n-1)u_n = \sec^{n-2} x \tan x + (n-2)u_{n-2};$

$u_4 = \frac{1}{3} \sec^2 x \tan x + \frac{2}{3} \tan x + k;$

$u_5 = \frac{1}{4} \sec^3 x \tan x + \frac{3}{4} \times \frac{1}{2} \sec x \tan x + \frac{3}{4} \times \frac{1}{2} \ln(\sec x + \tan x) + k$

7   $u_n = \int x^n e^x \, dx = x^n e^x - nu_{n-1};$

$u_5 = x^5 e^x - 5x^4 e^x + 20x^3 e^x - 60x^2 e^x + 120x e^x - 120 e^x + k$

8   $u_n = \int_1^e 1 \times (\ln x)^n \, dx = \left[x(\ln x)^n \right]_1^e - \int x \times n(\ln x)^{n-1} \times \frac{1}{x} \, dx = e - nu_{n-1};$

$u_4 = e - 4e + 12e - 24e + 24e - 24 = 9e - 24 \approx 0.465.$

The substitution $y = \ln x$ reveals the connection with question 7.

9   $u_n = \int \cosh^n x \, dx = \cosh^{n-1} x \sinh x - \int \sinh x \times (n-1) \cosh^{n-2} x \sinh x \, dx$

$$= \cosh^{n-1} x \sinh x - (n-1) \int \cosh^{n-2} x (\cosh^2 x - 1) \, dx;$$

$$nu_n = \cosh^{n-1} x \sinh x + (n-1)u_{n-2};$$

$$v_n = \int \sinh^n x \, dx \;\; \Rightarrow \;\; nv_n = \sinh^{n-1} x \cosh x - (n-1)v_{n-2}$$

10   $x = a \tan \theta$ gives $\int_0^a \frac{1}{(a^2 + x^2)^3} \, dx = \frac{1}{a^5} \int_0^{\pi/4} \cos^4 \theta \, d\theta = \frac{1}{a^5} \left(\frac{8 + 3\pi}{32} \right)$

11   $u_n = \int x^n \cos x \, dx = x^n \sin x - n \int x^{n-1} \sin x \, dx$

$$= x^n \sin x + nx^{n-1} \cos x - n(n-1)u_{n-2}$$

Exercise 6B

1   (a) $\left[\frac{1}{7} \sin^7 x \right]_0^{\pi/2} = \frac{1}{7}$ (b) $\frac{6}{13} \times \frac{4}{11} \times \frac{2}{9} \times \frac{1}{7} = 0.005\,33$

2   $\qquad\qquad u_{m,n} = \int_0^\pi \sin^{m-1} x \times \sin x \cos^n x \, dx$

$$= \left[-\frac{1}{n+1} \sin^{m-1} x \cos^{n+1} x \right]_0^\pi$$

$$+ \int_0^\pi \frac{1}{n+1} \cos^{n+1} x \times (m-1) \sin^{m-2} x \cos x \, dx$$

$$= 0 + \frac{m-1}{n+1} \int_0^\pi \cos^n x(1 - \sin^2 x) \sin^{m-2} x \, dx \quad \text{if } m > 1$$

$$= \frac{m-1}{n+1} (u_{m-2,n} - u_{m,n}).$$

Hence $\qquad u_{m,n} = \frac{m-1}{m+n} u_{m-2,n}.$

3   $\int_0^a (a^2 - x^2)^{5/2} \, dx = \int_0^\pi a^6 \cos^6 \theta \, d\theta = a^6 \times \frac{5}{6} \times \frac{3}{4} \times \frac{1}{2} \times \frac{1}{2}\pi = \frac{5}{32}\pi a^6;$

$\int_0^a x^2(a^2 - x^2)^{5/2} \, dx = \int_0^\pi a^8 \sin^2 \theta \cos^6 \theta = a^8 \times \frac{1}{8} \times \frac{5}{32}\pi = \frac{5}{256}\pi a^8$

4 (a) $v_{m,n} = \int_0^1 x^m (1-x)^n \, dx$

$$= \left[\frac{1}{m+1} x^{m+1} (1-x)^n \right]_0^1 - \int_0^1 \frac{1}{m+1} x^{m+1} \times - n(1-x)^{n-1} \, dx$$

$$= \frac{n}{m+1} v_{m+1,n-1}$$

(b) $v_{3,4} = \frac{4}{4} \times \frac{3}{5} \times \frac{1}{6} \times \frac{1}{7} \int_0^1 x^7 \, dx = \frac{1}{280} = 0.003\,57;$

$$v_{0.5,4} = \frac{4}{1.5} \times \frac{3}{2.5} \times \frac{2}{3.5} \times \frac{1}{4.5} \int_0^1 x^{4.5} \, dx = 0.0739$$

5 $v_{m,n} = \frac{n}{m+1} \times \frac{n-1}{m+2} \times \dots \times \frac{1}{m+n} v_{m+n,0}$

$$= \frac{m!\,n!}{(m+n)!} \times \frac{1}{m+n+1}$$

$$= \frac{m!\,n!}{(m+n+1)!}$$

6 This follows from integration by parts or the substitution $x = 1 - y$.

7 $v_{m,n} = 2 \int_0^{\pi/2} \sin^{2m+1} \theta \cos^{2n+1} \theta \, d\theta$

The first reduction formula of §2 then gives the result as the reduction formula of question 4(a).

8

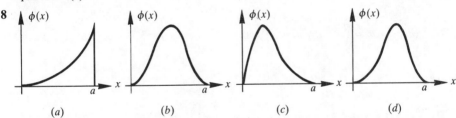

(a)   (b)   (c)   (d)

$\int_0^a \phi(x) \, dx = 1 \implies k = \dfrac{(m+n+1)!}{m!\,n!\,a^{m+n+1}},$ using the result of question 5.

$$\mu = k \times \frac{(m+1)!\,n!\,a^{m+n+2}}{(m+n+2)!} = \frac{(m+1)a}{m+n+2}$$

9 $\sigma^2 = \dfrac{(m+2)(m+1)a^2}{(m+n+3)(m+n+2)} - \left[\dfrac{(m+1)a}{m+n+2} \right]^2 = \dfrac{(m+1)(n+1)a^2}{(m+n+3)(m+n+2)^2}.$

Note that we should expect σ to be symmetrical in m and n.

Miscellaneous exercise 6

1 $I_2 - I_1 = \int_0^{\pi/4} (\cos^4 x - \sin^4 x) \, dx$

$$= \int_0^{\pi/4} (\cos^2 x - \sin^2 x)(\cos^2 x + \sin^2 x) \, dx$$

$$= \int_0^{\pi/4} \cos 2x \, dx = \tfrac{1}{2};$$

$$I_1 + I_2 = \int_0^{\pi/4} \sin^4 x \, dx + \int_0^{\pi/4} \cos^4 x \, dx$$

$$= \int_0^{\pi/4} \sin^4 x \, dx + \int_{\pi/4}^{\pi/2} \sin^4 y \, dy, \quad \text{putting } y = \tfrac{1}{2}\pi - x \text{ in } I_2,$$

$$= \int_0^{\pi/2} \sin^4 x \, dx = \tfrac{3}{16}\pi \quad \text{(see Exercise 6A, question 5)}.$$

2 $u_n = \int_0^t x^n e^{-x} \, dx = -t^n e^{-t} + n u_{n-1}$

$$= -e^{-t}(t^n + nt^{n-1} + n(n-1)t^{n-2} + \ldots + n!t) + n!u_0$$
$$\text{and} \qquad u_0 = -e^{-t} + 1.$$

Hence $\qquad e^t \int_0^t \dfrac{x^n}{n!} e^{-x} \, dx = e^t - \left(1 + t + \dfrac{t^2}{2!} + \ldots + \dfrac{t^n}{n!} \right),$

and the integral tends to 0 as $n \to \infty$.

So $\qquad 1 + t + \dfrac{t^2}{2!} + \ldots + \dfrac{t^2}{n!} + \ldots \quad$ converges to e^t for all t.

3 $u_n = \dfrac{1}{\sqrt{(2\pi)}} \int_{-\infty}^{\infty} x^{n-1} \times x \, e^{-x^2/2} \, dx = \dfrac{1}{\sqrt{(2\pi)}} \left[-x^{n-1} e^{-x^2/2} \right]_{-\infty}^{\infty} + (n-1)u_{n-2}$

$$= (n-1)u_{n-2}$$

(a) $u_2 = u_0 = 1$ (b) $u_3 = 2u_1 = 0$ (c) $u_4 = 3u_2 = 3$

4 (a) $V = 2\pi a^3 \displaystyle\int_0^{\pi/2} \sin t \cos^2 t \, dt = \tfrac{2}{3}\pi a^3;$

$$MI = 2\pi\rho a^5 \int_0^{\pi/2} \sin^3 t \cos^2 t \, dt = \tfrac{4}{15}\pi\rho a^5$$

(b) $V = 6\pi a^3 \displaystyle\int_0^{\pi/2} \sin^5 t \cos^4 t \, dt = \tfrac{16}{105}\pi a^3;$

$$MI = 6\pi\rho a^5 \int_0^{\pi/2} \sin^{11} t \cos^4 t \, dt = \tfrac{10}{15} \times \tfrac{8}{13} \times \tfrac{6}{11} \times \tfrac{16}{105}\pi\rho a^5$$

5 $A = \displaystyle\int y \, dx = 3a^2 \int_0^{\pi/2} \sin^2 t \cos^4 t \, dt = \tfrac{3}{32}\pi a^2;$

$$A\bar{x} = 3a^3 \int_0^{\pi/2} \sin^5 t \cos^4 t \, dt = \tfrac{8}{105}a^3$$

Hence $\qquad\qquad\qquad \bar{x} = 256a/315\pi \approx 0.259a.$

The mid-point of the arc is $(a \sin^3 \tfrac{1}{4}\pi, \, a \cos^3 \tfrac{1}{4}\pi)$ or $(0.354a, 0.354a)$, so the centre of mass lies within the lamina.

6 (*a*)

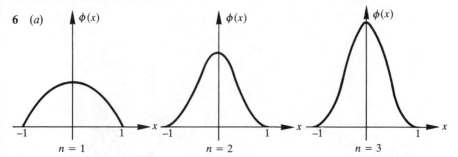

$$n = 1 \qquad\qquad\qquad n = 2 \qquad\qquad\qquad n = 3$$

(*b*) $x = \sin u$ gives

$$\int_{-1}^{1} (1 - x^2)^n \, dx = \int_{-\pi/2}^{\pi/2} \cos^{2n+1} u \, du$$

$$= \frac{2n}{2n+1} \times \frac{2n-2}{2n-1} \times \ldots \times \frac{4}{5} \times \frac{2}{3} \times 2.$$

Hence $\qquad \dfrac{1}{k} = 2 \times \dfrac{2}{3} \times \dfrac{4}{5} \times \ldots \times \dfrac{2n}{2n+1}.$

(*c*) $\sigma^2 = k \displaystyle\int_{-\pi/2}^{\pi/2} \sin^2 u \cos^{2n+1} u \, du = \dfrac{1}{2n+3} \times k \int_{-\pi/2}^{\pi/2} \cos^{2n+1} u \, du$

$$= \frac{1}{2n+3}$$

(*d*) $y = k(1 - x^2)^n \quad\Rightarrow\quad \dfrac{dy}{dx} = -2nkx(1 - x^2)^{n-1}$

$$\Rightarrow \qquad \frac{1}{y}\frac{dy}{dx} = \frac{-2nx}{1-x^2}$$

$$\Rightarrow \qquad \frac{\sigma}{y'} \times \frac{1}{\sigma^2}\frac{dy'}{dx'} = \frac{-2n\sigma x'}{1-\sigma^2 x'^2}$$

$$\Rightarrow \qquad \frac{1}{y'}\frac{dy'}{dx'} = \frac{-2n\sigma^2 x'}{1-\sigma^2 x'^2} = \frac{-2nx'}{1/\sigma^2 - x'^2} = \frac{-2nx'}{2n+3-x'^2}.$$

For large n, $\dfrac{1}{y'}\dfrac{dy'}{dx'} \approx -x'$, the differential equation for the standardised normal probability function.

(*e*) When $x = 0$, $\phi(x) = k$ in the original model. For the standardised model, $y = k\sigma$ when $x = 0$. Hence $k\sigma \approx 1/\sqrt{(2\pi)}$ for large n.

(*f*) $2\pi \approx \dfrac{1}{k^2\sigma^2} \quad\Rightarrow\quad \pi \approx \left(\dfrac{2n+3}{2}\right) \times \dfrac{1}{k^2}$

$$= (n + 1.5)\left[2 \times \frac{2}{3} \times \frac{4}{5} \times \ldots \times \frac{2n}{2n+1}\right]^2.$$

$n = 100$ gives 3.165, $n = 1000$ gives 3.144, $n = 5000$ gives 3.142.

Exercise 7A

1 (*a*) $K = 2$, $L = 5$ (*b*) $K = -2$ (*c*) $K = \frac{6}{5}$, $L = -\frac{3}{5}$

2 (*a*) $A\,e^{-3t}$, $2t + 5 + A\,e^{-3t}$ (*b*) $-2\,e^t + A\,e^{4t}$
(*c*) $\frac{6}{5} \sin t - \frac{3}{5} \cos t + A\,e^{-2t}$

3 (a) 3, $A\,e^{-6t}$ (b) $3t-1$, $A\,e^{-6t}$ (c) $\frac{1}{3}e^{-t}$, $A\,e^{-10t}$
(d) $2\sin t + 3\cos t$, $A\,e^{-10t}$

4 (a) $x = 3 - e^{-6t}$ (b) $x = 3t - 1 + 3\,e^{-6t}$

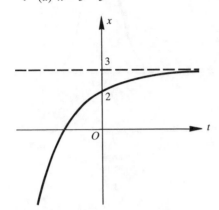

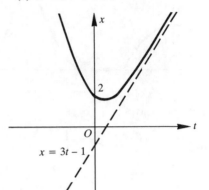

(c) $x = \frac{1}{3}e^{-t} + \frac{5}{3}e^{-10t}$ (d) $x = 2\sin t + 3\cos t - e^{-10t}$

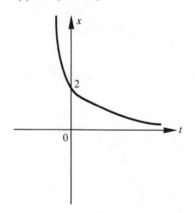

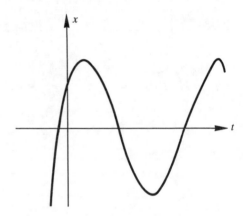

Exercise 7B

1 (a) $n = 3 \pm \sqrt{21}$ (b) $-2, -5$ (c) $4 \pm \sqrt{5}$ (d) $-3 \pm j$

2 (a) $x = A\,e^{-2t} + B\,e^{-7t}$ (b) $x = A\,e^{(-7+\sqrt{40})t} + B\,e^{(-7-\sqrt{40})t}$

3 $x = A\,e^{-t} + B\,e^{-2t}$, where $A + B = 4$ and $-A - 2B = 5$. So $A = 13$, $B = -9$.
$x = 0$ when $e^{t} = \frac{9}{13}$, i.e. $t \approx -0.37$.

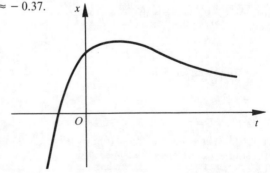

4 (a) $n = \pm 5j$ (b) $n = -3 \pm 5j$
Because $e^{5jt} = \cos 5t + j \sin 5t$ and $e^{-5jt} = \cos 5t - j \sin 5t$, we expect solutions of the form given.

5 We require $p^2 - q^2 + ap + b = 0$ and $2pq + aq = 0$. These equations are satisfied if $p = -\frac{1}{2}a$, $q = \pm\frac{1}{2}\sqrt{(4b - a^2)}$, and these values are real (and non-zero) if $a \neq 0$, and $4b - a^2 > 0$.

6 (a) $x = \frac{1}{2}\sqrt{5}(e^{(-3+\sqrt{5})t} - e^{(-3-\sqrt{5})t})$ (b) $x = \frac{3}{4}\sin 4t + 2\cos 4t$
(c) $x = e^{-2t}(\frac{2}{3}\sin 3t + \cos 3t)$

7

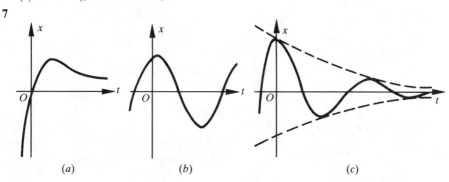

(a)   (b)   (c)

8 $A + B = 1$ and $(-2 + 3j)A + (-2 - 3j)B = 0$ $\Rightarrow$ $A = \frac{1}{2} - \frac{1}{3}j$ and $B = \frac{1}{2} + \frac{1}{3}j$.
Then $e^{-2t}[A(\cos 3t + j \sin 3t) + B(\cos 3t - j \sin 3t)]$ simplifies   to
$e^{-2t}(\frac{2}{3}\sin 3t + \cos 3t)$.

Exercise 7C

1 (a) $x = A e^{-t} + B e^{-7t}$ (b) $x = e^{-2t}(A \sin \sqrt{3}t + B \cos \sqrt{3}t)$
(c) $A e^t + B e^{7t}$ (d) $x = A e^{(-3+\sqrt{2})t} + B e^{(-3-\sqrt{2})t}$
(e) $x = A e^{-t/2} + B e^{-2t}$ (f) $x = e^{-t}(A \sin 4t + B \cos 4t)$

2 (a) $x = \frac{50}{48} e^{-2t} - \frac{2}{48} e^{-50t}$, $|x| < 0.001$ for all $t > 3.5$
(b) $x = \frac{25}{21} e^{-4t} - \frac{4}{21} e^{-25t}$, $|x| < 0.001$ for all $t > 1.8$
(c) $x = e^{-8t}(\frac{4}{3}\sin 6t + \cos 6t)$; the bracket has amplitude $\frac{5}{3}$, so we can take T as $\ln 0.0006/(-8) \approx 0.93$. The minimum T is in fact nearer 0.85.
(d) $x = e^{-6t}(\frac{3}{4}\sin 8t + \cos 8t)$; the bounding exponential curves have $|x| = 0.001$ when $t \approx \ln 0.0008/(-6) = 1.2$.
The first two graphs are like Figure 8, the other two like Figure 9. The point of the question is to illustrate the fact that with heavy damping the motion dies away more rapidly with the *smaller* damping constant (part (b) rather than (a)), while with light damping the oscillations die away more rapidly with the *larger* damping constant (part (c) rather than (d)).

3 Initial velocity = $1.5/3 = 0.5$ m s^{-1}; spring constant = $3 g/0.12 \approx 245$ N m^{-1}. If x is the displacement in metres from the equilibrium position, then

$$3\ddot{x} = -245x, \quad \text{or} \quad \ddot{x} + \omega^2 x = 0 \quad \text{with } \omega \approx 9.04.$$
$$x = a \sin \omega t, \quad \text{where } a\omega = 0.5 \text{ and } a \approx 0.055 \text{ m}$$

The period = $2\pi/\omega \approx 0.70$ s, and amplitude = 5.5 cm.

4 $x = (1.0/\omega) \sin \omega t + 0.02 \cos \omega t$, giving an oscillation of amplitude 11.2 cm. The spring remains stretched throughout the motion.

5   $\dot{x} = 0 \Rightarrow -k \sin \omega t + \omega \cos \omega t = 0 \Rightarrow \tan \omega t = \omega/k$.
At maximum points,

$$\sin \omega t = + \omega/\sqrt{(\omega^2 + k^2)}, \quad \text{and} \quad x = \frac{\omega}{\sqrt{(\omega^2 + k^2)}} e^{-kt}.$$

6   $e^{-15k} = 0.5 \Rightarrow k = 0.046$. Also $\omega = \sqrt{(n^2 - k^2)} \Rightarrow n = 12.57$.

7   Percentage error in g = percentage error in ω^2. But $\omega^2/n^2 = 1 - (k^2/n^2)$, so the percentage error in g is $100k^2/n^2 = 0.0014\%$. This is not very serious!

Exercise 7D

1   (a) $-2\frac{1}{2}$ (b) $\frac{1}{10} e^{-2t}$ (c) $\frac{1}{2}t + 1$ (d) $7t + 21$ (e) $-\frac{1}{4} \sin 3t$
(f) $\frac{1}{10} \sin t + \frac{1}{5} \cos t$

2   (a) $x = -5 + A e^{-t} + B e^{3t}$ (b) $x = -\frac{1}{2} e^t + A e^{3t} + B e^{-3t}$
(c) $x = \frac{1}{18} e^{3t} + A \sin 3t + B \cos 3t$ (d) $x = -\frac{1}{3} e^{-2t} + 2 + A e^{-t} + B e^{-5t}$
(e) $x = -\frac{1}{7} \cos 2t + A e^{\sqrt{3}t} + B e^{-\sqrt{3}t}$
(f) $x = -\frac{1}{5} \sin 3t - \cos 3t + A \sin 2t + B \cos 2t$
(g) $x = -\frac{1}{5} \cos t + A e^{-t/2} + B e^{-2t}$

3   The particular integrals are $\left(\dfrac{2-j}{10}\right) e^{jt}$ and $\left(\dfrac{2+j}{10}\right) e^{-jt}$. Now

$$\frac{1}{2}\left[\left(\frac{2-j}{10}\right)(\cos t + j \sin t) + \left(\frac{2+j}{10}\right)(\cos t - j \sin t)\right] = \tfrac{1}{10} \sin t + \tfrac{1}{5} \cos t,$$

as expected.

4   (a) $-\frac{5}{222} \sin 3t - \frac{7}{222} \cos 3t$ (b) $\frac{41}{202} \sin 2t - \frac{3}{101} \cos 2t$

5   (a) $x = 3 + A \sin t + B \cos t$, where $2 = 3 + B$ and $10 = A$; the solution is
$x = 3 + 10 \sin t - \cos t$.
(b) $x = 7 - 6 \sin \frac{1}{2}t - 3 \cos \frac{1}{2}t$
(c) $x = \frac{1}{5} \sin t - \frac{1}{10} \cos t + e^{-t} (\frac{9}{20} \sin 2t + \frac{11}{10} \cos 2t)$

Exercise 7E

1   $F = ma \Rightarrow mg - mkv = m\dfrac{d^2y}{dt^2} \Rightarrow \dfrac{d^2y}{dt^2} + k\dfrac{dy}{dt} = g \Rightarrow y = \dfrac{gt}{k} + A + B e^{-kt}$.

The initial conditions give $A = -B = -g/k^2$.

2   The weight balances the Archimedean upthrust, so the equation of motion is

$$M\ddot{z} = -n^2(z - z_0) - \lambda Mn(\dot{z} - a \sin pt),$$
i.e. $$M\ddot{z} + \lambda Mn\dot{z} + n^2 z = n^2 z_0 + \lambda Mna \sin pt.$$

The CF provides transient terms only; the long-term solution is given by the PI, which is

$$z = z_0 + K \sin pt + L \cos pt,$$

where $-MKp^2 - \lambda MnLp + n^2K = \lambda Mna$ and $-MLp^2 + \lambda MnKp + n^2L = 0$.

$p = n/\sqrt{M}$ reduces these equations, and we get $K = 0$ and $L = -a/p$.

3   $\dfrac{d^2\theta}{dx^2} = \mu^2\theta \Rightarrow \theta = A e^{\mu x} + B e^{-\mu x}$; $\theta \to 0$ as $x \to \infty \Rightarrow A = 0$, and the required solution is $\theta = \theta_0 e^{-\mu x}$.

4 $\dot{\theta} = k(T_1 - \theta) - \frac{1}{6}k(\theta - T)$ leads to $\dot{\theta} + \frac{7}{6}k\theta = k(T_1 - \frac{1}{3}T_0) + \frac{1}{6}kT_0\,e^{-kT/6}$. The CF is $C\,e^{-7kt/6}$ and the PI has the form $A + B\,e^{-kt/6}$, so the complete solution has the given form;

$$A = \frac{6}{7}(T_1 - \frac{1}{3}T_0) = \frac{6}{7}T_1 - \frac{2}{7}T_0.$$

5 $\dot{T} = -a(T - T_0) + b(\theta - \theta_0)$ and $\dot{\theta} = -k(\theta - \theta_0) + c(T - \theta)$. The first equation gives

$$c\dot{T} + acT = acT_0 + bc(\theta - \theta_0) = acT_0 + bc\phi, \quad \text{where } \phi = \theta - \theta_0.$$

The second equation gives

$$cT = \dot{\phi} + k\phi + c\phi + c\theta_0 \quad \text{and} \quad c\dot{T} = \ddot{\phi} + (k + c)\dot{\phi}.$$

Hence $[\ddot{\phi} + (k + c)\dot{\phi}] + a[\dot{\phi} + (k + c)\phi + c\theta_0] = acT_0 + bc\phi,$

i.e. $\ddot{\phi} + (a + c + k)\dot{\phi} + (ac + ak - bc)\phi = ac(T_0 - \theta_0).$

If $ac + ak > bc$, there is a steady-state temperature given by the PI

$$\phi = ac(T_0 - \theta_0)/(ac + ak - bc).$$

Then $\theta = \theta_0 + ac(T_0 - \theta_0)/(ac + ak - bc).$

6 Upthrust $= U = V\rho g = (A - x/36) \times 10^3 \times 10 = 10^4(A - x/36)$. This equals 800 when $A = A_0$ and $x = 3.6 \times 10^{-2}$;   hence $A_0 = 8.1 \times 10^{-2}$.

$$U - 800 - 20\ddot{x} - 200\dot{x} = 80\ddot{x}$$
$$\Rightarrow \qquad\qquad \ddot{x} + 2\dot{x} = -8 + U/100$$
$$\Rightarrow \qquad\qquad \ddot{x} + 2\dot{x} + \tfrac{100}{36}x = -8 + 100(A_0 + a\sin\omega t).$$

The CF is $e^{-t}(A\cos nt + B\sin nt)$, where $n = \frac{4}{3}$. The PI is $x = 3.6 \times 10^{-2} + K\sin\omega t + L\cos\omega t$, where K and L may be found in terms of a and ω by those with perseverance.

7 (a) $2\ddot{x} = -8x \Rightarrow x = A\cos 2t + B\sin 2t$. The initial conditions give $A = 0.05, B = 0$. Hence $a = 0.05, \omega = 2$.

  (b) $\ddot{x} = -8(x - y) \Rightarrow \ddot{x} + 4x = 12\sin t \Rightarrow x = A'\cos 2t + B'\sin 2t + 4\sin t$. The initial condition, $x = \dot{x} = 0$ when $t = 0$, gives $A' = 0$, $B' = -2$, and hence $x = 4\sin t(1 - \cos t)$. This has period 2π.

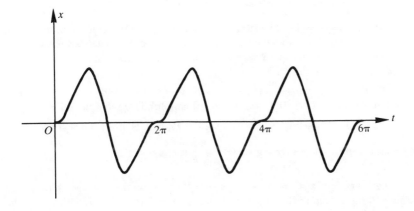

Miscellaneous exercise 7

1 $y = A\sqrt{(\cos x)}$
  $\Rightarrow\ y^2 = A^2 \cos x$

  $\Rightarrow\ 2y\dfrac{dy}{dx} = -A^2 \sin x$

  $\Rightarrow\ 2y\dfrac{d^2y}{dx^2} + 2\left(\dfrac{dy}{dx}\right)^2 = -A^2 \cos x = -y^2.$

  $y = B\sqrt{(\sin x)}$ is a solution similarly, but the differential equation is not linear, and $y = A\sqrt{(\cos x)} + B\sqrt{(\sin x)}$ is not a solution unless $A = 0$ or $B = 0$.

2 $\dot{x} = kx(1 - x)$, where $x = \frac{1}{2}$ when $t = 0$ and $\frac{1}{2} \div 24 = k \times \frac{1}{2} \times \frac{1}{2}$. Then

  $kt = \displaystyle\int \frac{1}{x(1 - x)}\,dx = \int \left(\frac{1}{x} + \frac{1}{1 - x}\right)dx = \ln\left(\frac{x}{1 - x}\right) + A,\quad$ where $A = 0$.

  When $t = 12$, $\dfrac{x}{1 - x} = e$, i.e. $x \approx 0.73$.

3 $n(n - 1) - 7n + 12 = 0 \Rightarrow n = 2$ or 6.
  $t^2\ddot{x} - 7t\dot{x} + 12x = 10t + 36$ has CF $At^2 + Bt^6$ and PI $x = Kt + L$, where

  $$-7Kt + 12Kt + 12L \equiv 10t + 36,\quad K = 2 \quad\text{and}\quad L = 3.$$

  $$t^2\ddot{x} - 6t\dot{x} + 12x = \ln t \ \Rightarrow\ x = At^3 + Bt^4 + K\ln t + L$$

  where $K = \frac{1}{12}$ and $L = \frac{7}{144}$.

4 $\dfrac{dy}{dx} - y\tan x = -4\sin x$ has CF $A\sec x$ and PI $y = 2\cos x$. The complete solution is $y = A\sec x + 2\cos x$ and the boundary condition gives $A = 0$. The second term of the differential equation is not defined when $x = (n + \frac{1}{2})\pi$, so the solution $y = 2\cos x$ is only appropriate for $-\frac{1}{2}\pi < x < \frac{1}{2}\pi$.

5 (a) $\dfrac{dy}{dx} - \left(\dfrac{x + 1}{x}\right)y = 0 \Rightarrow \dfrac{1}{y}\dfrac{dy}{dx} = 1 + \dfrac{1}{x} \Rightarrow \ \ln y = x + \ln x + A$
  $\Rightarrow y = Bx\,e^x.$

  A PI is $y = -2x$, so the complete solution is $y = Bx\,e^x - 2x$.
  (b) $\dfrac{d^2y}{dx^2} + 4y = \cos x \ \Rightarrow\ y = A\cos 2x + B\sin 2x + \frac{1}{3}\cos x$

6 $\ddot{x} + x = \sin 2t \Rightarrow x = A\cos t + B\sin t - \frac{1}{3}\sin 2t$. The initial condition, $x = \dot{x} = 0$ when $t = 0$, gives $A = 0$ and $B = \frac{2}{3}$, so $x = \frac{2}{3}\sin t(1 - \cos t)$. The solution curve is similar to the curve on page 269, and the maximum and minimum points occur where $\cos t = -\frac{1}{2}$, $x = \pm\frac{1}{2}\sqrt{3}$.

7 $x = e^{-3t}(A\cos t + B\sin t) + \sin 2t - 2\cos 2t$, where $A = 2$ and $B = -2\,e^{3\pi/2}$. For large t, $x \approx \sin 2t - 2\cos 2t$, a sine wave with amplitude $\sqrt{5}$ and period π.

8 $r = A\,e^{\omega t} + B\,e^{-\omega t}$, where $A + B = a$ and $A\omega - B\omega = 0$. Hence $r = a\cosh \omega t$.

9 $mg - mk\dot{r} = m\ddot{r} \ \Rightarrow\ \ddot{r} + k\dot{r} = g \ \Rightarrow\ r = \dfrac{t}{k}g + A + e^{-kt}\mathbf{B}$

10 $m\ddot{\mathbf{r}} = m\mathbf{g} - k\mathbf{r} \ \Rightarrow\ \mathbf{r} = m\mathbf{g}/k + \mathbf{A}\cos \omega t + \mathbf{B}\sin \omega t$, where $\omega^2 = k/m$. If the string remains taut, the path is an ellipse in a plane defined by $\mathbf{A}$ and $\mathbf{B}$ with centre the position of equilibrium.

11 The amplitude of the PI is $7/(100 - \omega^2)$. The phenomenon of resonance (see Chapter 10) is suggested by the asymptote $\omega = 10$ in the graph.

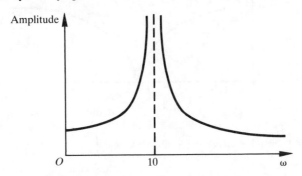

12 $\dfrac{\mathrm{d}}{\mathrm{d}x}\left(\dfrac{f''}{f}\right) = \dfrac{f'''}{f} - \dfrac{f''f'}{f^2} = 0$ since $ff''' = f'f''$. Hence $\dfrac{f''}{f} = A$, i.e. $f'' = Af$.

$f(x) = B\,e^{\alpha x} + C\,e^{-\alpha x}$ is a solution for any B, C, α; also $f(x) = D\sin(\beta x + \gamma)$ for any D, β, γ.

Exercise 8A

1 A is $(1, 4)$. Arc length $OA = \displaystyle\int_0^{\pi/4} (2\cos 2t + 4)\,\mathrm{d}t = 1 + \pi = 4.14$; direct distance $OA = \sqrt{17} = 4.12$. Similarly, arc $AB = \pi - 1 = 2.14$; $AB = 1.94$.

2 (a) Speed $= \sqrt{(20^2 + (12 - 10t)^2)}$;

$$\text{distance} = \int_0^{2.4} \sqrt{(20^2 + (12 - 10t)^2)}\,\mathrm{d}t = 40\int_{-0.6}^{0.6} \sqrt{(1 + u^2)}\,\mathrm{d}u,$$

where $u = \dfrac{12 - 10t}{20}$.

(b) $d = 40\left[\tfrac{1}{2}v + \tfrac{1}{4}\sinh 2v\right]_{-\sinh^{-1}0.6}^{\sinh^{-1}0.6} = 50.7\text{ m}$

3 8.27, 8.25

4 $2\left[\tfrac{1}{4}u + \tfrac{1}{8}\sinh 2u\right]_0^{\sinh^{-1}2} = 2.96$

5 $s = \displaystyle\int_0^2 \sqrt{(1 + \sinh^2 x)}\,\mathrm{d}x = \int_0^2 \cosh x\,\mathrm{d}x = \sinh 2 = 3.63$

6 $s = \displaystyle\int_0^1 \sqrt{(1 + e^{2x})}\,\mathrm{d}x \approx 2.00$, using Simpson's rule with two strips.

7 (a) $s = \displaystyle\int_1^5 \sqrt{(1 + 1/x^4)}\,\mathrm{d}x \approx 4.29$

(b) $s = \displaystyle\int_1^e \sqrt{(1 + 1/x^2)}\,\mathrm{d}x \approx 2.01$; this should be the same as question 6.

8

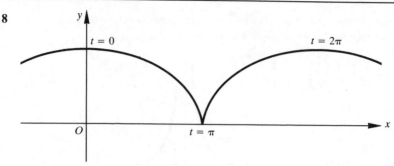

$$s = a \int_0^{2\pi} \sqrt{((1 + \cos t)^2 + (-\sin t)^2)}\ dt = a \int_0^{2\pi} \sqrt{(2 + 2\cos t)}\ dt$$

$$= 2a \int_0^{\pi} 2\cos \tfrac{1}{2}t\ dt = 8a$$

Care must be taken to use the positive square root (see §5).
    Alternatively, the arc length could be written

$$s = a \int_0^{\pi} 2\cos \tfrac{1}{2}t\ dt + a \int_{\pi}^{2\pi} -2\cos \tfrac{1}{2}t\ dt.$$

9 (a) The formula gives $\displaystyle\int_0^{\pi/2} a\ dt = \tfrac{1}{2}\pi a$, the length of the quarter-circle.

(b) The formula gives $\displaystyle\int_0^{\pi/2} \sqrt{2}a \sin 2t\ dt = \sqrt{2}a$, the length of the line segment.

(c) $s = \displaystyle\int_0^{\pi/2} \tfrac{3}{2}a \sin 2t\ dt = \tfrac{3}{2}a$; the curve is an astroid.

10

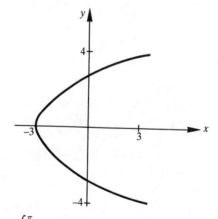

$$s = \int_0^{\pi} \sqrt{((-6 \sin 2t)^2 + (-4 \sin t)^2)}\ dt$$

$$= \int_0^{\pi} 4 \sin t\ \sqrt{(9 \cos^2 t + 1)}\ dt$$

$$= \int_{\sinh^{-1}(-3)}^{\sinh^{-1}3} \tfrac{4}{3} \cosh^2 u\ du, \quad \text{putting } 3 \cos t = \sinh u$$

$$= 15.1$$

Exercise 8B

1 $\dot{y} = \dot{r}\sin\theta + r\dot{\theta}\cos\theta$ and $\dot{x}^2 + \dot{y}^2 = \dot{r}^2 + r^2\dot{\theta}^2$. In this way, the result of §2 is deduced from the result of §1.

2 $\dfrac{ds}{d\theta} = a\surd(\sin^2\theta + (1 - \cos\theta)^2) = a\surd(4\sin^2\tfrac{1}{2}\theta)$;

$$\int_0^{\pi/2} 2a\sin\tfrac{1}{2}\theta\,d\theta : \int_{\pi/2}^{\pi} 2a\sin\tfrac{1}{2}\theta\,d\theta = \surd2 - 1 : 1$$

3 $s = \displaystyle\int_0^{\pi} \tfrac{5}{4}e^{3\theta/4}\,d\theta = \left[\tfrac{5}{3}e^{3\theta/4}\right]_0^{\pi} = 15.9$

4 $s = \displaystyle\int_0^{3\pi} \cos^2\tfrac{1}{3}\theta\,d\theta = \tfrac{3}{2}\pi = 4.71$.

The inner loop has length $\displaystyle\int_{\pi}^{2\pi} \cos^2\tfrac{1}{3}\theta\,d\theta = \tfrac{1}{2}\pi - \tfrac{3}{4}\surd3 = 0.27$.

5 (a) The formula gives $s = \displaystyle\int_0^{\pi/3} \surd3\,\sec^2\theta\,d\theta = 3$. This checks with the graph, a segment of the straight line $x = \surd3$.

   (b) The formula gives $s = 4\alpha$. It is an arc of the circle $x^2 + y^2 = 4y$, subtending an angle 2α at the centre.

6

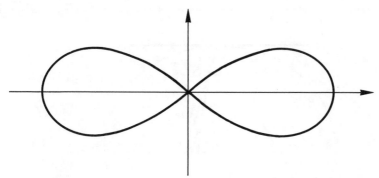

Each loop has length $2\displaystyle\int_0^{\pi/4} \surd(\cos^2 2\theta + 4\sin^2 2\theta)\,d\theta$. Simpson's rule with two strips gives a value of 2.42.

Exercise 8C

1 (a) $\psi = \tan^{-1}x$ (b) $\psi = x$ (c) $\tan\psi = \dfrac{-\sin t}{1 + \cos t} = -\tan\tfrac{1}{2}t,\quad \psi = -\tfrac{1}{2}t$

   (d) For $n = 1$, $\tan\psi = -\tan t$ and $\psi = -t$; this is a circle property.

   For $n = 2$, $\tan\psi = -1$, which is correct for a line segment with gradient -1.

   For $n = 3$, $\tan\psi = -\cot t$ and $\psi = -\tfrac{1}{2}\pi + t$ when $0 < t < \tfrac{1}{2}\pi$.

2 (a) $\tan\psi = -\dfrac{1}{x^2} \;\Rightarrow\; \tan\beta = \dfrac{1}{x^2}$. Also $\tan\alpha = \dfrac{1}{x} \div x$.

   (b) $\tan\delta = \dfrac{\sec^2 t}{\sec t \tan t} = \dfrac{1}{\sin t}$, while $\tan\gamma = \dfrac{\tan t}{\sec t} = \sin t$. Hence $\delta = \tfrac{1}{2}\pi - \gamma$.

3 $\tan \delta = \dfrac{\cosh u}{\sinh u}$; $\tan \gamma = \dfrac{\sinh u}{\cosh u}$

4 (a) $\cot \phi = \frac{3}{4}$ at all points   (b) Area $= \displaystyle\int_0^1 \frac{1}{2} e^{3\theta/2}\, d\theta = 1.16$

5 Area $= \frac{3}{2}\pi a^2$. $\cot \phi = \dfrac{\sin \theta}{1 - \cos \theta} = \cot \frac{1}{2}\theta$; scrutiny of the graph shows that it is correct to deduce that $\phi = \frac{1}{2}\theta$ when $0 < \theta < 2\pi$.

6 (a) $\cot \phi = -\tan \frac{1}{3}\theta$. When $\theta = \frac{1}{2}\pi$, $\phi = \frac{2}{3}\pi$; when $\theta = \pi$, $\phi = \frac{5}{6}\pi$. Generally, $\phi = \frac{1}{3}\theta + \frac{1}{2}\pi$.

(b) (i) $A_1 = \displaystyle\int_0^{3\pi/2} \frac{1}{2} \cos^6 \frac{1}{3}\theta\, d\theta = \frac{3}{2} \int_0^{\pi/2} \cos^6 u\, du = \frac{3}{2} \times \frac{5}{6} \times \frac{3}{4} \times \frac{1}{2} \times \frac{1}{2}\pi$

(ii) $A_2 = \dfrac{3}{2} \displaystyle\int_0^{\pi/3} \cos^6 u\, du = \dfrac{3}{2}\left(\dfrac{3\sqrt{3}}{32} + \dfrac{5\pi}{48}\right)$, using the reduction formula or the methods of Chapter 2.

Hence the area of the inner loop $= 2(A_1 - A_2) = 0.0037$.

7 $A = 2 \times \frac{1}{2} \displaystyle\int_0^{\pi/4} \cos^2 2\theta\, d\theta = \frac{1}{8}\pi$; $\cot \phi = -2\tan 2\theta = -2\sqrt{3}$ when $\theta = \frac{1}{6}\pi$. From a diagram, we see that ϕ is obtuse. Hence $\phi = \pi - \tan^{-1}(1/2\sqrt{3})$.

8

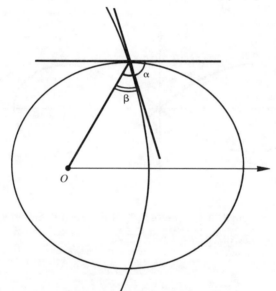

$\cot \alpha = -1/\sqrt{3}$ and $\cot \beta = \sqrt{3}/2$; hence $\alpha - \beta = 1.24$ radians.

9 (a) (i) $A = \displaystyle\int_0^\alpha \frac{3}{2} \sec^2 \theta\, d\theta = \frac{3}{2} \tan \alpha$

(ii) $\cot \phi = \tan \alpha$ when $\theta = \alpha$,
   as $\phi = \frac{1}{2}\pi - \alpha$.
   Area $OPN = \frac{1}{2} \times \sqrt{3} \times \sqrt{3} \tan \alpha$
   $= \frac{3}{2} \tan \alpha$.

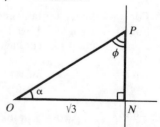

(i) $A = \displaystyle\int_0^\alpha 8 \sin^2 \theta \, d\theta$

$= 4\alpha - 2 \sin 2\alpha$

$=$ area of minor segment

(ii) $\cot \phi = \cot \alpha \Rightarrow \phi = \alpha$

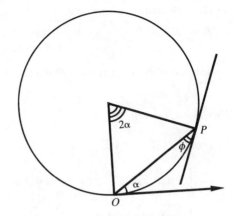

Exercise 8D

1 (a) $\rho = (1 + x^2)^{3/2}$ (b) $\rho = \sec x$ (c) $\rho = -4a \cos \tfrac{1}{2}t$

2 $\sqrt{2}$ and 1. The first curve is the image of the second under a rotation through $45°$ and enlargement with scale factor $\sqrt{2}$.

3 K equals 1 and 0.071 for $y = \cosh x, 0,$ and 0.061 for $y = \sinh x$. These answers make sense in terms of the graphs.

4 (a) 1.29   (b) 1.01   (c) 0.505
The effect of a one-way stretch on ρ is unpredictable, but the last two answers are correct because (b) is an enlargement of (c).

5 $\tfrac{9}{5}$, $\tfrac{25}{3}$, $17^{3/2}/15 = 4.67$

6 $\psi = \theta + \cot^{-1} \tfrac{3}{4} \Rightarrow \dfrac{d\psi}{d\theta} = 1$. Also $\dfrac{ds}{d\theta} = \tfrac{5}{4} e^{3\theta/4}$, so $\dfrac{ds}{d\psi} = \dfrac{ds}{d\theta} \div \dfrac{d\psi}{d\theta} = \tfrac{5}{4}r.$

7 $\psi = \theta + \tan^{-1} \theta \Rightarrow \dfrac{d\psi}{d\theta} = 1 + \dfrac{1}{1 + \theta^2} = \dfrac{2 + \theta^2}{1 + \theta^2};$

$\dfrac{ds}{d\theta} = a\sqrt{(1 + \theta^2)}$ and $\dfrac{ds}{d\psi} = \dfrac{a(1 + \theta^2)^{3/2}}{2 + \theta^2}$

8 $\dfrac{d\psi}{d\theta} = 1 - \left(\dfrac{r^{-1}r'' - r^{-2}r'^2}{1 + r^{-2}r'^2} \right) = 1 - \dfrac{rr'' - r'^2}{r^2 + r'^2} = \dfrac{r^2 + 2r'^2 - rr''}{r^2 + r'^2};$

$\dfrac{ds}{d\theta} = \sqrt{(r^2 + r'^2)}, \quad \rho = \dfrac{(r^2 + r'^2)^{3/2}}{r^2 + 2r'^2 - rr''}$

9 $r' = 3\sqrt{3}/2, r'' = 6,$ giving $\rho = \tfrac{3}{4} \times 7^{3/2}.$

10 The assertion in the question is easily justified if standard results for conic sections are known. Using the usual notation, $l = 6, e = 2$ from the polar equation and $l = a(e^2 - 1) = b^2/a$ gives $a = 2, b = 2\sqrt{3}$. The question as set is straightforward.

11 $\rho = \tfrac{4}{3}a \sin \tfrac{1}{2}\theta$ except at the cusp where $\theta = 0$. Note, though, that $\rho \to 0$ as $\theta \to 0$.

12 $\rho = 4a \sin \tfrac{1}{2}t$ except when $t = 0,$ but $\rho \to 0$ as $t \to 0$. $\rho = 2\sqrt{2}a$ when $t = \tfrac{1}{2}\pi$ and $\rho = 4a$ when $t = \pi$.

13 $(2, -16)$ and $(-2, 16)$.

$$K = y''(1 + y'^2)^{-3/2} \quad \Rightarrow \quad K' = y'''(1 + y'^2)^{-3/2} - 3y'y''^2(1 + y'^2)^{-5/2}$$
$$= y''' \quad \text{when } y' = 0.$$

The curvature is not greatest at the turning points.

Miscellaneous exercise 8

1 $\displaystyle s = 2\int_0^1 \sqrt{(1 + 4x^2)}\,dx$

$\displaystyle = \int_0^a \cosh^2 u\,du, \quad$ putting $x = \tfrac{1}{2}\sinh u$, and where $a = \sinh^{-1} 2$

$\displaystyle = \int_0^a (\tfrac{1}{2} + \tfrac{1}{2}\cosh 2u)\,du$

$= \tfrac{1}{2}a + \tfrac{1}{4}\sinh 2a$

$= \tfrac{1}{2}a + \tfrac{1}{2}\sinh a \cosh a = \tfrac{1}{2}\sinh^{-1} 2 + \tfrac{1}{2} \times 2 \times \sqrt{5}$

2

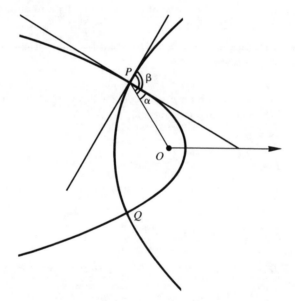

The curves intersect at $[2, \tfrac{2}{3}\pi]$ and $[2, -\tfrac{2}{3}\pi]$. For the first curve,

$$-\frac{1}{r^2}\frac{dr}{d\theta} = -\sin\theta, \quad \text{and hence } \cot\alpha = \sqrt{3} \text{ and } \alpha = \tfrac{1}{6}\pi.$$

Similarly, $\cot\beta = -\tfrac{1}{3}\sqrt{3}$ and $\beta = \tfrac{2}{3}\pi$.

It follows that $\beta - \alpha = \tfrac{1}{2}\pi$, and by symmetry the curves intersect at right angles at Q also.

3

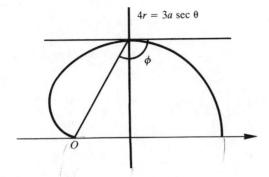

$4r = 3a \sec \theta$

$4r = 3a \sec \theta$ is the line $x = \frac{3}{4}a$. It meets the cardioid at $[\frac{3}{2}a, \frac{1}{3}\pi]$. $\cot \phi = -\dfrac{1}{\sqrt{3}} \Rightarrow \phi = \frac{2}{3}\pi$, hence the line and curve intersect at right angles.

4 $\cot \phi = \dfrac{1}{r} \dfrac{dr}{d\theta} = \dfrac{1}{\theta} \Rightarrow \phi = \tan^{-1}\theta$ for $0 < \theta < \frac{1}{2}\pi$.

$$\psi = \theta + \phi = \theta + \tan^{-1}\theta \quad \text{and} \quad \dfrac{d\psi}{d\theta} = 1 + \dfrac{1}{1+\theta^2} = \dfrac{2a^2 + r^2}{a^2 + r^2}.$$

$$\dfrac{ds}{d\theta} = \sqrt{(a^2 + a^2\theta^2)} = \sqrt{(a^2 + r^2)}, \quad \text{hence} \quad \rho = \dfrac{(a^2 + r^2)^{3/2}}{2a^2 + r^2}.$$

5

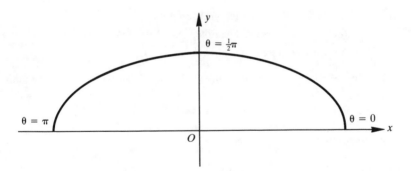

$K = \dfrac{\dot{x}\ddot{y} - \ddot{x}\dot{y}}{(\dot{x}^2 + \dot{y}^2)^{3/2}} = \dfrac{1}{2a}$ when $\theta = \frac{1}{2}\pi$. So the centre of curvature is $(0, -\frac{3}{2}a)$.

6 $x = r\cos\theta = a\sin^3\frac{1}{3}\theta\cos\theta$

$\Rightarrow \quad \dfrac{dx}{d\theta} = a\sin^2\frac{1}{3}\theta(\cos\frac{1}{3}\theta\cos\theta - \sin\frac{1}{3}\theta\sin\theta)$

$\qquad = a\sin^2\frac{1}{3}\theta\cos\frac{4}{3}\theta;$

$\dfrac{dy}{d\theta} = a\sin^2\frac{1}{3}\theta\sin\frac{4}{3}\theta.$

Hence $\tan\psi = \tan\frac{4}{3}\theta.$

$$\dfrac{ds}{d\theta} = a\sin^2\frac{1}{3}\theta, \quad \dfrac{d\psi}{d\theta} = \frac{4}{3} \Rightarrow \pi = \frac{3}{4}a\sin^2\frac{1}{3}\theta.$$

7 $s = a \int_0^{2\pi} \sqrt{(1.25 - \cos t)}\, dt \approx 6.7\pi a$, using Simpson's rule.

8 $s = 4 \int_0^{\pi/2} \sqrt{(25 \sin^2 t + 9 \cos^2 t)}\, dt \approx 25.6$, a little more than the circumference of a circle of radius 4.

9 $A = \frac{1}{2} \int_{-\pi/6}^{\pi/6} \cos^6 3\theta\, d\theta = \frac{1}{6} \int_{-\pi/2}^{\pi/2} \cos^6 u\, du = \frac{5}{6} \times \frac{5}{6} \times \frac{3}{4} \times \frac{1}{2} \times \pi \approx 0.164$

10 $A = \frac{1}{8} \times \frac{3}{4} \times \frac{1}{2} \times \pi \approx 0.147$

11 (a) $\dfrac{dy}{du} = \dfrac{e^u}{e^u - 1} - \dfrac{e^u}{e^u + 1} = \dfrac{2e^u}{e^{2u} - 1} = \dfrac{2}{e^u - e^{-u}} = \dfrac{1}{\sinh u}$

(b) $s = \displaystyle\int_0^1 \sqrt{(1 + e^{2x})}\, dx$

$= \displaystyle\int_{\sinh^{-1} 1}^{\sinh^{-1} e} \dfrac{1 + \sinh^2 u}{\sinh u}\, du, \quad$ putting $x = \ln \sinh u$

$= \left[\ln(e^u - 1) - \ln(e^u + 1) + \cosh u \right]_{\sinh^{-1} 1}^{\sinh^{-1} e}$

$= 2.0035 \quad$ (to 5 SF)

Exercise 9A

1 (b) 4 (e) $\frac{1}{2}\pi$ The other integrals do not exist.

2 (a) $\frac{1}{4}$ (c) $\frac{1}{3}$ (e) $\frac{1}{16}\pi$ The other integrals do not exist.

3 (a) Does not exist because of problems near $x = 1.5$.

(b) $\left[x \ln x - x \right]_u^1 = -1 - u \ln u + u \to -1$ as $u \to 0$. Hence the integral equals -1.

(c) $-\frac{1}{4}$, since $\left[\frac{1}{2}x^2 \ln x - \frac{1}{4}x^2 \right]_u^1 \to -\frac{1}{4}$ as $u \to 0$.   (d) $\frac{1}{2}$

(e) Substituting $y = x - 1$, we get $\displaystyle\lim_{u \to 0} \left[\frac{2}{3}y^{3/2} + 2y^{1/2} \right]_u^4 = 9\frac{1}{3}$.

(f) $\displaystyle\lim_{u \to \infty} \left[\cos(1/x) \right]_1^u = 1 - \cos 1 \approx 0.46$

4 (a) $\displaystyle\int_1^5 \dfrac{\sqrt{x}}{x - 1}\, dx > \int_1^5 \dfrac{1}{x - 1}\, dx$.   The integral is not convergent, since

$\displaystyle\int_u^5 \dfrac{1}{x - 1}\, dx \to \infty$ as $u \to 1$.

(b) $y = \dfrac{\sin x}{x^2}$ behaves like $y = \dfrac{1}{x}$ for small x, suggesting that the given integral does not converge. To formalise this, we can start by noting that

$$\int_0^\pi \dfrac{\sin x}{x^2}\, dx > \int_0^\pi \dfrac{x - \frac{1}{6}x^3}{x^2}\, dx.$$

(c) $\displaystyle\int_0^\infty \dfrac{1}{1 + x^3}\, dx < \int_0^1 1\, dx + \int_1^\infty \dfrac{1}{x^3}\, dx = 1.5$, so the integral converges.

(d) $\displaystyle\int_0^\pi \frac{1}{\sqrt{(\sin x)}}\,dx = 2\int_0^{\pi/2} \frac{1}{\sqrt{(\sin x)}}\,dx < 2\int_0^{\pi/2} \frac{\sqrt 2}{\sqrt x}\,dx$, which is convergent.

(e) $\sin x \approx x$ for small x, so question 3(b) suggests that the integral converges. For a proof, it is sufficient to note that

$$0 > \int_0^{\pi/2} \ln \sin x\, dx > \int_0^{\pi/2} \ln(\tfrac12 x)\, dx.$$

(f) $\displaystyle\int_0^1 \frac{1}{\sinh x}\,dx > \int_0^1 \frac{1}{2x}\,dx$ shows the integral does not exist.

(g) $\displaystyle\int_1^\infty \frac{1}{\sinh x}\,dx < \int_1^\infty 4\,e^{-x}\,dx$ shows that the integral converges.

Alternatively, we can argue that

$$\sinh x = x + \frac{x^3}{3!} + \frac{x^5}{5!} + \dots$$
$$> \tfrac16 x^3 \quad \text{for } x>0.$$

Hence $$\int_1^\infty \frac{1}{\sinh x}\,dx < \int_1^\infty \frac{6}{x^3}\,dx.$$

5 (a) $k = \tfrac{1}{20}$ (b) $\mu = 20$

6 (a) $\sec\theta = \cosh u \;\Rightarrow\; \tan\theta = \sinh u$

(b) $\sec\theta\tan\theta\,\dfrac{d\theta}{du} = \sinh u \;\Rightarrow\; \dfrac{d\theta}{du} = \dfrac{1}{\cosh u}$

$$\Rightarrow\quad \int_0^a \frac{1}{\cosh u}\,du = \int_0^{\sec^{-1}\cosh a} 1\,d\theta = \sec^{-1}\cosh a.$$

This tends to $\tfrac12\pi$ as a tends to infinity.
  Alternatively, we may write

$$\int_0^a \frac{1}{\cosh u}\,du = \int_0^a \frac{2\,e^u}{e^{2u}+1}\,du$$
$$= \Big[\,2\tan^{-1} e^u\,\Big]_0^a$$
$$\rightarrow 2(\tfrac12\pi) - 2(\tfrac14\pi) \quad \text{as } a\rightarrow\infty.$$

Exercise 9B

1

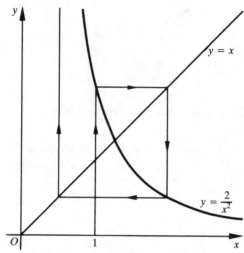

2 (*a*) $l = \frac{1}{2}(\sqrt{5} + 1) \approx 1.62$, the 'golden ratio'.

(*b*)

i	x_i	e_i	e_{i+1}/e_i
1	2	0.3820	– 0.3090
2	1.5	– 0.1180	– 0.4120
3	1.6667	0.0486	– 0.3708
4	1.6	– 0.0180	– 0.3863
5	1.625	– 0.0070	– 0.3803
6	1.6154	– 0.0026	—

For this question and the next, a computer program is most helpful; the program will need only slight modification for other questions in this chapter.

(*c*)

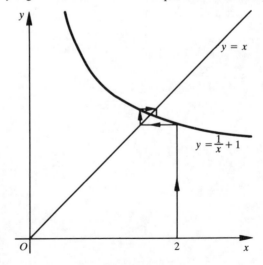

(d) $f'(l) = -0.3820$, which is consistent with the last column of the table.

3 (a) $l = \frac{1}{2}(\sqrt{5} + 1)$, as in question 2.

i	x_i	e_i	e_{i+1}/e_i
1	1	-0.6180	0.3298
2	1.4142	-0.2038	0.3153
3	1.5538	-0.0643	0.3109
4	1.5981	-0.0200	0.3096
5	1.6118	-0.0062	0.3091
6	1.6161	-0.0019	—

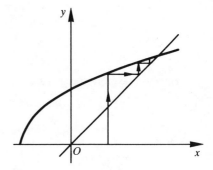

$f'(l) = 0.3090$

(b) $l = \frac{1}{2}(5 - \sqrt{13})$

i	x_i	e_i	e_{i+1}/e_i
1	1	0.3028	0.3394
2	0.8	0.1028	0.2994
3	0.728	0.0308	0.2850
4	0.7060	0.0088	0.2806
5	0.6997	0.0025	0.2794
6	0.6979	0.0007	—

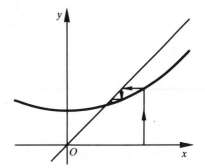

$f'(l) = 0.2789$

(c) $l = 2 - \sqrt{7}$

i	x_i	e_i	e_{i+1}/e_i
1	1	1.6458	-0.2153
2	-1	-0.3542	-0.1292
3	-0.6	0.0458	-0.1404
4	-0.6522	0.0009	$-0,1390$
5	-0.6449	-0.0064	-0.1388
6	-0.6459	-0.0001	—

$f'(l) = -0.1390$

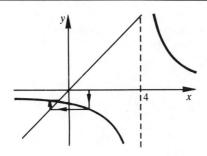

4 In question 2, sequences with other positive values of x_1 will tend to the same limit. Negative values of x_1 have the same result unless $x_i = 0$ for some i, e.g.

$$x_1 = -\tfrac{3}{5} \;\Rightarrow\; x_2 = -\tfrac{2}{3} \;\Rightarrow\; x_3 = -\tfrac{1}{2} \;\Rightarrow\; x_4 = -1 \;\Rightarrow\; x_5 = 0$$
$$\Rightarrow\; x_6 \text{ not defined,}$$

whereas

$$x_1 = -\tfrac{2}{5} \;\Rightarrow\; x_2 = -\tfrac{3}{2} \;\Rightarrow\; x_3 = \tfrac{1}{3} \;\Rightarrow\; x_4 = 4 \;\Rightarrow\; x_5 = \tfrac{5}{4} \;\Rightarrow\; x_6 = \tfrac{9}{5}, \text{ etc.}$$

There is one more special case:

$$x_1 = \tfrac{1}{2}(1 - \sqrt{5}) \;\Rightarrow\; x_2 = \tfrac{1}{2}(1 - \sqrt{5}), \quad \text{etc.}$$

In question 3(a), all values of x_1 greater than or equal to -1 give sequences with the same limit.

In question 3(b), $-\tfrac{1}{2}(5 + \sqrt{13}) < x_1 < \tfrac{1}{2}(5 + \sqrt{13})$ gives convergence on $\tfrac{1}{2}(5 - \sqrt{13})$, $x_1 = \pm\tfrac{1}{2}(5 + \sqrt{13})$ gives $l = \tfrac{1}{2}(5 + \sqrt{13})$, and other values of x_1 give divergent sequences.

In question 3(c), all values of x_1 less than 4 give convergence on $2 - \sqrt{7}$, as well as 'most' values greater than 4 (the exceptions are similar to those in question 2).

5 $x_{i+1} = \dfrac{1}{x_i} + 1$ and $l = \dfrac{1}{l} + 1$

$$\Rightarrow\; x_{i+1} - l = \dfrac{1}{x_i} - \dfrac{1}{l} = -\dfrac{x_i - l}{lx_i}$$

$$\Rightarrow\qquad \dfrac{e_{i+1}}{e_i} = -\dfrac{1}{lx_i}.$$

This is consistent with the last column of the table in the answer to question 2.

6 (a) $\dfrac{1}{x_{i+1} + l}$ (b) $\dfrac{x_i + l}{5}$ (c) $\dfrac{-l}{x_i - 4}$

7 (a) Converges slowly on $\sqrt{10}$; $e_{20} \approx 6 \times 10^{-6}$
   (b) Converges rapidly on $\sqrt{10}$; $e_5 < 10^{-8}$

8 (a) Converges very slowly with limit 2, $x_{250} \approx 1.984$. The graph of $y = \tfrac{1}{4}(x^2 + 4)$ touches $y = x$ at $x = 2$.   (b) Diverges

9 (a) $x_2 = 2$, $x_3 = -1$, $x_4 = \tfrac{1}{2}$, $x_5 = 2$, etc.
   (b) $x_2 = 4$, $x_3 = -2$, $x_4 = 1$, $x_5 = 4$, etc.
   (c) $x_2 = \tfrac{8}{5}$, $x_3 = \tfrac{3}{4}$, $x_4 = -\tfrac{2}{3}$, $x_5 = 5$, etc.

The cobweb diagram for (a) is a closed loop and so the sequence cycles. For (b), the diagram is merely an enlargement with the centre the origin and scale factor 2, and that is why all the values in the sequence are doubled. Similar sequences are generated by other starting values, apart from 0 and 1.

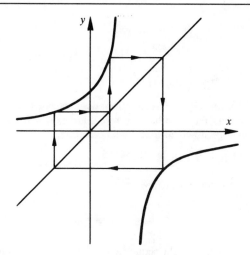

Exercise 9C

1 All x terms are positive, so $e_{i+1}/e_i = -1/lx_i$, so the error sequence alternates.

$$\left.\begin{array}{l} x_1 > l \ \Rightarrow \ l > x_2 > 1 \\ x_1 < l \ \Rightarrow \ x_2 > l \ \Rightarrow \ l > x_3 > 1 \end{array}\right\}$$

so there exists an early term in the sequence for which $l > x_j > 1$.
Then $|e_{j+1}/e_j| < 1/l$ and $x_{j+1} > l$, and it follows that $|e_{j+2}/e_{j+1}| < 1/l^2$.
Hence $|e_{j+2}/e_j| < 1/l^3$ and $l > x_{j+2} > 1$.
We deduce that $|e_{j+2r}| < (1/l^3)^r |e_j|$ and $e_{j+2r} \to 0$ as $r \to \infty$.
$|e_{j+2r+1}| < |e_{j+2r}|$ now implies $e_{j+2r+1} \to 0$ as $r \to \infty$.

2 $x_1 = 2,$ $x_{i+1} = (x_i + 10)/(x_i + 1),$ and $l = \sqrt{10}$

$$\Rightarrow \quad x_{i+1} - \sqrt{10} = \frac{x_i + 10}{x_i + 1} - \sqrt{10} = \frac{x_i + 10 - \sqrt{10}x_i - \sqrt{10}}{x_i + 1}$$

$$= \frac{-(\sqrt{10} - 1)}{x_i + 1}(x_i - \sqrt{10})$$

$$\Rightarrow \qquad\qquad \frac{e_{i+1}}{e_i} = -\left(\frac{\sqrt{10} - 1}{x_i + 1}\right).$$

As in question 1, we need to show that $x_i \geq 2$ for all i. Then it follows that $|e_{i+1}/e_i| < 0.8$ for all n, and hence $e_n \to 0$ as $n \to \infty$. The sequence converges, and the relation between e_i and e_{i+1} represents first-order convergence.

3 $x_{i+1} - 1 = -(x_i - 1)^2$, i.e. $e_{i+1} = -e_i^2$, where $l = 1$. If $|e_1| > 1$, the sequence diverges; if $0 < x_1 < 2$, then $|e_1| < 1$, and we have second-order convergence.

4 This is a Newton–Raphson iteration for $\sqrt[3]{6}$.

$$x_{i+1} - l = x_i - l - \left(\frac{x_i^3 - l^3}{3x_i^2}\right), \quad \text{where } l = \sqrt[3]{6}$$

$$= (x_i - l)\left[1 - \frac{x_i^2 + x_i l + l^2}{3x_i^2}\right]$$

$$= \frac{(x_i - l)^2(2x_i + l)}{3x_i^2}$$

$$\Rightarrow \quad e_{i+1} = \left(\frac{2x_i + l}{3x_i^2}\right)e_i^2.$$

$e_1 \approx 0.2$ and $x_i > 1.5$ for all i. The relation demonstrates rapid second-order convergence. Notice that if x_1 (and hence e_1) were large, $e_2 \approx \frac{2}{3}e_1$, $e_3 \approx \frac{2}{3}e_2$, etc. The sequence would converge slowly at first, then accelerate.

5   The sequence continues 2, 3, 5, 8, 13, 21, 34, 55.

$$u_{i+1} = u_i + u_{i-1} \quad \Rightarrow \quad \frac{u_{i+1}}{u_i} = 1 + \frac{u_{i-1}}{u_i}$$

$$\Rightarrow \quad v_{i+1} = 1 + \frac{1}{v_i}.$$

$v_2 = 1$, $v_3 = 2$, and we then have the sequence of Exercise 9B, question 2.

$$v_{i+1} - l = \frac{v_i + 1 - lv_i}{v_i}$$

$$= \frac{v_i + l^2 - l - lv_i}{v_i}, \quad \text{since } l^2 = l + 1$$

$$= -\left(\frac{l-1}{v_i}\right)(v_i - l).$$

So
$$\frac{e_{i+1}}{e_i} = -\left(\frac{l-1}{v_i}\right).$$

$(l-1)/v_2 < 0.7$ and $(l-1)/v_3 < 0.4$. Hence $v_4 > v_2$ and the sequence continues to converge.

6   $z_2 = 0.5 + 1.5j$, $z_3 = 1.1 + 0.7j$.

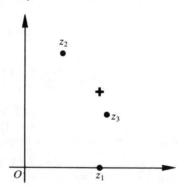

If $l = 1 + j$, $l^2 = 2j$ and $z_{i+1} - l = \frac{i+j}{2} + \frac{j}{z_i} - l$

$$= \frac{l}{2} + \frac{l^2}{2z_i} - l$$

$$= -\frac{l}{2z_i}(z_i - l)$$

$$\Rightarrow \qquad e_{i+1} = -\frac{le_i}{2z_i}.$$

$|e_3| < 0.4 \Rightarrow |z_3| > 1$ and $|e_4/e_3| < |l/2| < 0.8 \Rightarrow |e_4| < 0.4 \times 0.8$
$\phantom{|e_3| < 0.4} \Rightarrow |z_4| > 1$ and $|e_5/e_4| < 0.8 \Rightarrow |e_5| < 0.4 \times 0.8^2$,   etc.

The sequence does converge.

7 $z_2 = 0.5 + j$, $z_3 = 1.05 + 0.9j$.

$$z_{i+1} = \tfrac{1}{2}z_i + \frac{j}{z_i} \Rightarrow z_{i+1} - l = \frac{z_i^2 + l^2 - 2lz_i}{2z_i}, \quad \text{where } l = 1 + j, \quad l^2 = 2j$$

$$\Rightarrow \qquad e_{i+1} = \frac{1}{2z_i} \times e_i^2.$$

$|e_2| = 0.5, |e_3| < 0.2$. It is clear that $|z_i| > 1$ for all $i > 1$, and we have second-order convergence.

8   This question demonstrates another way of proving that the sequence converges with limit $\sqrt{2}$: $x_i > 1$ for all $i > 1$, and then $|x_{i+1}^2 - 2| < \tfrac{1}{4}|x_i^2 - 2|$.
    We can deduce that $x_n{}^2 - 2 \to 0$ as $n \to \infty$.

9   We get $e_{n+1} = -\left(\dfrac{\sqrt{5}-1}{x_{n+1}}\right)e_n$, and hence the i-sequence alternates.

$$\begin{aligned} e_1 > 0 \Rightarrow \left.\begin{array}{l} e_{2n+1} > 0 \\ e_{2n} < 0 \end{array}\right\} &\Rightarrow \left.\begin{array}{l} x_{2n+1} > \sqrt{5} \\ x_{2n} < \sqrt{5} \end{array}\right\} \end{aligned}$$

$$e_{n+2} = \frac{(\sqrt{5}-1)^2}{(x_n + 1)(x_{n+1} + 1)}e_n.$$

Now $x_i < \sqrt{5} \Rightarrow x_{i+1} > \sqrt{5}$, and $x_i > \sqrt{5} \Rightarrow x_{i+1} > 1$. Either way, $x_{i+1} > 1$ and $e_{n+2} < \left(\dfrac{\sqrt{5}-1}{2}\right)^2 e_n$. Results (a), (b) and (c) follow immediately from this last relation.

10   The sequence starts $1, 3, \tfrac{5}{3}, \tfrac{11}{5}, \tfrac{21}{11}, \tfrac{43}{21}$, suggesting a limit of 2.

$$u_{n+2} - 2 = -\frac{1}{u_{n+1}}(u_{n+1} - 2) = \frac{1}{u_n u_{n+1}}(u_n - 2).$$

But from the original inductive definition, $u_n u_{n+1} = u_n + 2$.

Hence $$u_{n+2} - 2 = \frac{1}{u_n + 2}(u_n - 2).$$

The proof is immediate when we note that $\dfrac{1}{u_n + 2} < \tfrac{1}{2}$ for all n.

11 (a) If a limit l exists, it satisfies $l = 1 - \tfrac{1}{2}jl$, i.e. $l = 0.8 - 0.4j$.
      Then $z_{i+1} - l = -\tfrac{1}{2}j(z_i - l)$, and since $|-\tfrac{1}{2}j| = \tfrac{1}{2}$, the sequence converges.
      This question is equivalent to summing the infinite GP

$$1 + (-\tfrac{1}{2}j) + (-\tfrac{1}{2}j)^2 + (-\tfrac{1}{2}j)^3 + \ldots$$

(b) $z_i = a + bj \implies z_{i+1} = \left(1 + \dfrac{b}{a^2 + b^2}\right) + \left(\dfrac{a}{a^2 + b^2}\right)j$ forms the basis for a computer program to generate the sequence. It transpires that there is a limit, approximately $1.3002 + 0.6248j$. This is a solution of the equation $l = 1 + j/l$, which can be obtained from $\dfrac{1 + \sqrt{(1 + 4j)}}{2}$. Now $z_{i+1} - l = \left(\dfrac{1 - l}{z_i}\right)(z_i - l)$, and since $\left|\dfrac{1 - l}{z_i}\right| \approx 0.5$, we can see how quickly the sequence converges.

Miscellaneous exercise 9

1 (a) $I = \displaystyle\int_0^\infty \dfrac{1}{1 + x^3}\,dx$

$= \displaystyle\int_0^1 \dfrac{1}{1 + x^3}\,dx + \int_1^\infty \dfrac{1}{1 + x^3}\,dx < \int_0^1 1\,dx + \int_1^\infty \dfrac{1}{x^3}\,dx = 1.5$

(b) Also $I < \displaystyle\int_0^1 1\,dx + \int_1^2 \dfrac{1}{1 + x^2}\,dx + \int_2^\infty \dfrac{1}{x^3}\,dx < 1.45$

(c) The integrand may be written as

$$\dfrac{\frac{1}{3}}{1 + x} + \dfrac{-\frac{1}{3}x + \frac{2}{3}}{1 - x + x^2} = \dfrac{\frac{1}{3}}{1 + x} - \dfrac{\frac{1}{6}(-1 + 2x)}{1 - x + x^2} + \dfrac{\frac{1}{2}}{\frac{3}{4} + (\frac{1}{2} - x)^2},$$

giving

$$I = \lim_{u \to \infty}\left[\frac{1}{3}\ln(1 + x) - \frac{1}{6}\ln(1 - x + x^2) - \frac{1}{\sqrt{3}}\tan^{-1}\left(\frac{1 - 2x}{\sqrt{3}}\right)\right]_0^u$$

$$= \lim_{u \to \infty}\left[\frac{1}{6}\ln\frac{(1 + x)^2}{1 - x + x^2} - \frac{1}{\sqrt{3}}\tan^{-1}\left(\frac{1 - 2x}{\sqrt{3}}\right)\right]_0^u$$

$$= \frac{2\pi}{3\sqrt{3}}.$$

2 (a) $\displaystyle\int_0^{\pi/2} \ln\cos x\,dx = \int_{\pi/2}^0 \ln\sin u\,(-du) = I$

(b) $\displaystyle\int_0^{\pi/2} \ln\sin 2x\,dx = \int_0^\pi \ln\sin v\,(\tfrac{1}{2}dv) = \int_0^{\pi/2} \ln\sin v\,dv = I$

(c) From   (b), $I = \displaystyle\int_0^{\pi/2} (\ln 2 + \ln\sin x + \ln\cos x)\,dx = \tfrac{1}{2}\pi\ln 2 + 2I$;   hence $I = -\tfrac{1}{2}\pi\ln 2.$

3 $\displaystyle\int_u^1 x^{-1/2}\,dx \to 2$ as $u \to 0$. Hence we say that $\displaystyle\int_0^1 x^{-1/2}\,dx$ converges. Similarly,

$\displaystyle\int_1^\infty x^{-\alpha}\,dx$ means the limit as $u \to \infty$ of $\displaystyle\int_1^u x^{-\alpha}\,dx$, provided that this limit exists, which it does if $\alpha > 1$.

The diagram shows the arc of the curve $y = \sin\theta$, the chord OA which has equation $y = (2/\pi)\theta$ and the tangent at O which has equation $y = \theta$.

It is clear that $\dfrac{2}{\pi}\theta \leqslant \sin\theta \leqslant \theta$ for $0 \leqslant \theta \leqslant \tfrac{1}{2}\pi.$

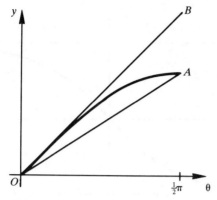

It follows that $\sqrt{\dfrac{2}{\pi}}\,\theta^{1/2} \;\leqslant\; \sqrt{(\sin\theta)} \;\leqslant\; \theta^{1/2}$ in this interval,

and hence $\sqrt{\dfrac{\pi}{2}}\,\theta^{-1/2} \;\geqslant\; \dfrac{1}{\sqrt{(\sin\theta)}} \;\geqslant\; \theta^{-1/2}.$

Integrating between u and $\tfrac{1}{2}\pi$, then letting u tend to 0, we get the required result.

The substitution $x = -\ln\sin\theta$ transforms the given integral to $\sqrt{2}\displaystyle\int_0^{\pi/2}\dfrac{d\theta}{\sqrt{(\sin\theta)}}$, which has been shown to converge. Its value lies between $2\sqrt{\pi}$ and $\pi\sqrt{2}$.

4 $\displaystyle\int_0^u\dfrac{e^{-t}}{(1+e^{-2t})^{1/2}}\,dt = \Big[-\sinh^{-1}(e^{-t})\Big]_0^u \to \sinh^{-1}1$ as $u\to\infty$

5 $y = \sinh^{-1}x \;\Rightarrow\; x = \sinh y \;\Rightarrow\; \sqrt{(1+x^2)} = \cosh y.$
Then

$x + \sqrt{(1+x^2)} = \sinh y + \cosh y = e^y,$ and $y = \sinh^{-1}x = \ln\{x + \sqrt{(1+x^2)}\}.$

It follows that $\sinh^{-1}x - \ln x = \ln\left\{1 + \sqrt{\left(\dfrac{1}{x^2}+1\right)}\right\}$

$\to \ln 2$ as $x\to\infty.$

Then $\displaystyle\int_1^u\left\{\dfrac{1}{(1+x^2)^{1/2}} - \dfrac{1}{x}\right\}dx \to \ln 2 - \ln(1+\sqrt{2})$ as $u\to\infty.$

6 Gradient $= 1$ when $x = 0$. $x = \sinh u$ transforms

$$I_1 = \int_1^\infty\dfrac{dx}{(1+x^2)^{3/2}} \quad\text{to}\quad \int_0^\infty\operatorname{sech}^2 u\,du.$$

Now $\displaystyle\int_0^a\operatorname{sech}^2 u\,du = \tanh a \to 1$ as $a\to\infty$, and hence $I_1 = 1.$

$$I_n = \int_0^\infty\operatorname{sech}^{2n}u\,du$$

$$= \Big[\tanh u\,\operatorname{sech}^{2n-2}u\Big]_0^\infty + \int_0^\infty(2n-2)\tanh^2 u\,\operatorname{sech}^{2n-2}u\,du,$$

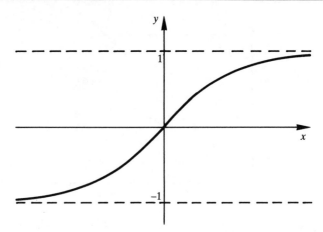

leading directly to $I_n = \dfrac{2n-2}{2n-1} I_{n-1}$ (using $\tanh^2 u = 1 - \operatorname{sech}^2 u$),

or
$$I_n = \left[\frac{x}{(1+x^2)^{n+1/2}} \right]_0^\infty + \int_0^\infty \frac{(2n+1)x^2}{(1+x^2)^{n+3/2}}\, dx$$

$$= (2n+1) \int_0^\infty \frac{(1+x^2)-1}{(1+x^2)^{n+3/2}}\, dx$$

$$= (2n+1)(I_n - I_{n+1}).$$

This leads to
$$I_{n+1} = \frac{2n}{2n+1} I_n \quad \text{or} \quad I_n = \frac{2n-2}{2n-1} I_{n-1}.$$

$I_3 = \tfrac{4}{5} I_2 = \tfrac{4}{5} \times \tfrac{2}{3} I_1 = \tfrac{8}{15}.$

7   $(1+x)^{-1} \approx 1 - x + x^2 - x^3$ for small x.

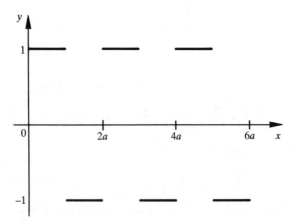

$$I = \int_0^{2na} e^{-kx} f(x)\, dx = \int_0^a e^{-kx}\, dx + \int_a^{2a} -e^{-kx}\, dx + \ldots + \int_{(2n-1)a}^{2na} -e^{-kx}\, dx$$

$$= \frac{1}{k} (1 - 2 e^{-ak} + 2 e^{-2ak} - \ldots + e^{-2nak})$$

$$= \frac{1}{k}(1 - 2t + 2t^2 - \ldots + t^{2n})$$

$$= \frac{1}{k}\left(\frac{2 + 2t^{2n+1}}{1 + t} - 1 - t^{2n}\right).$$

As n tends to ∞, I tends to

$$\frac{1}{k}\left(\frac{2}{1 + t} - 1\right) = \frac{1}{k}\left(\frac{1 - t}{1 + t}\right)$$

$$= \frac{1}{k}\left(\frac{1 - e^{-ak}}{1 + e^{-ak}}\right) = \frac{1}{k}\left(\frac{e^{ak/2} - e^{-ak/2}}{e^{ak/2} + e^{-ak/2}}\right)$$

$$= \frac{1}{k}\tanh\left(\frac{ak}{2}\right).$$

8 $x_n - x_{n-1} = -\frac{1}{2}(x_{n-1} - x_{n-2})$
$\Rightarrow \quad x_n - x_{n-1} = (-\frac{1}{2})^{n-2}(x_2 - x_1) = (-\frac{1}{2})^{n-2}.$
Then $x_n - x_1 = (-\frac{1}{2})^{n-2} + (-\frac{1}{2})^{n-3} + \ldots + 1 = \dfrac{1 - (-\frac{1}{2})^{n-1}}{1 + \frac{1}{2}},$

and $x_n \to 1 + \frac{2}{3}$ as $n \to \infty$.

9   The proof is similar to that for question 8, starting with

$$\frac{x_n}{x_{n-1}} = \left(\frac{x_{n-1}}{x_{n-2}}\right)^{-1/2}, \qquad \frac{x_n}{x_{n-1}} = \left(\frac{x_2}{x_1}\right)^{(-1/2)^{n-2}}.$$

We find that $\dfrac{x_n}{x_1} \to \left(\dfrac{x_2}{x_1}\right)^{2/3}$ as $n \to \infty$, so $x_n \to x_1^{1/3} x_2^{2/3}$.

10   Since $0 < \sin \theta < \theta$ for $0 < \theta < \frac{1}{2}\pi$, $u_{r+1} < u_r$, and all the terms of the sequence are positive. Hence the sequence tends to a limit. The limit is a solution of $l = \sin l$, and this is 0.

Also $u_{r+1} = \sin(u_r) > \dfrac{2}{\pi} u_r$ (see the diagram on page 287),

and hence $u_n > \left(\dfrac{2}{\pi}\right)^{n-1} u_1 > \left(\dfrac{2}{\pi}\right)^n x.$

11   (a) We find $x_4 = x_1$ (provided $x_1 \neq 0, 1$), and hence $x_{n+3} = x_n$.
     (b) $x_{n+4} = x_n$ (c) $x_{n+6} = x_n$ (d) $x_n \to 2$ as $n \to \infty$.

12   (a) Converges slowly on 0   (b) Second-order convergence on $\frac{1}{2}$ (c) Diverges
     (d) The sequence oscillates apparently in an unpredictable way. In fact, if $x_1 = \sin^2 \theta$, then $x_2 = \sin^2 2\theta$, $x_3 = \sin^2 4\theta$, etc.

13 $Z = \dfrac{Z + a}{Z + 1} \Rightarrow Z^2 = a.$ When $a = j, z_1 = 1 \Rightarrow z_2 = \frac{1}{2} + \frac{1}{2}j \Rightarrow z_3 = \frac{3}{5} + \frac{4}{5}j.$

The limit is $\frac{1}{2}\sqrt{2} + \frac{1}{2}\sqrt{2}j.$

14   (a) $z_1 = 1 + j$, $z_2 = \frac{3}{4} + j$, $z_3 = \frac{18}{27} + \frac{26}{27}j$, $z_4 = \frac{161}{256} + \frac{240}{256}j$,

     $z_5 = \frac{1900}{3125} + \frac{2876}{3125}j = 0.608 + 0.92032j.$

The sequence is converging slowly.

(b) $z_n = 1 + j + \dfrac{n(n-1)}{2!} \dfrac{j^2}{n^2} + \dfrac{n(n-1)(n-2)}{3!} \dfrac{j^3}{n^3} + \ldots$

$\approx 1 + j + \dfrac{j^2}{2!} + \dfrac{j^3}{3!} + \ldots$ when n is large

$= e^j = \cos 1 + j \sin 1$

$\approx 0.54 - 0.84j.$

The result $\lim\limits_{n \to \infty} (1 + x/n)^n = e^x$ applies for complex numbers as well as real numbers (see Chapter 3).

15   (a) When $z = j$, $S_n = (\frac{1}{2} - \frac{1}{4} + \frac{1}{6} - \ldots) + j(1 - \frac{1}{3} + \frac{1}{5} - \ldots)$
$= \frac{1}{2}(1 - \frac{1}{2} + \frac{1}{3} - \ldots) + j(1 - \frac{1}{3} + \frac{1}{5} - \ldots)$
$= \frac{1}{2} \ln 2 + (\tan^{-1} 1)j$
$= \frac{1}{2} \ln 2 + \frac{1}{4}\pi j.$

Now $\ln(1 + j) = \ln(\sqrt{2}\, e^{(\pi/4)j}) = \frac{1}{2} \ln 2 + \frac{1}{4}\pi j.$

(b) When $z = \frac{1}{2}j$,

$S_n = \frac{1}{2}\{\frac{1}{4} - \frac{1}{2}(\frac{1}{4})^2 + \frac{1}{3}(\frac{1}{4})^3 - \ldots\} + j\{\frac{1}{2} - \frac{1}{3}(\frac{1}{2})^3 + \frac{1}{5}(\frac{1}{2})^5 - \ldots\}$
$= \frac{1}{2} \ln(1 + \frac{1}{4}) + (\tan^{-1} \frac{1}{2})j$
$S_n = \ln(1 + \frac{1}{2}j)$ since $|1 + \frac{1}{2}j| = \sqrt{\frac{5}{4}}$ and $\arg(1 + \frac{1}{2}j) = \tan^{-1} \frac{1}{2}.$

Exercise 10A

1   (a) $\dot{u} = 10\, e^{5t}$, giving $u = 2\, e^{5t} + A$ and $x = 2\, e^t + A\, e^{-4t}.$
    (b) $\dot{u} = 3$, giving $u = 3t + A$ and $x = 3t\, e^{-4t} + A\, e^{-4t}.$
The right-hand side of the second differential equation belongs to the complementary function; the particular integral is shown to have an extra factor of t.

2   (a) $x = u\, e^{-2t} \Rightarrow \dot{x} = (\dot{u} - 2u)\, e^{-2t} \Rightarrow \ddot{x} = (\ddot{u} - 4\dot{u} + 4u)\, e^{-2t}.$
    Hence $\ddot{x} + 5\dot{x} + 6x = 0 \Rightarrow \ddot{u} + \dot{u} = 0 \Rightarrow \dot{u} + u = A$
                              $\Rightarrow u = A + B\, e^{-t} \Rightarrow x = A\, e^{-2t} + B\, e^{-3t}.$
Thus the method of Chapter 7 does give all possible solutions.

    (b) $x = v\, e^{-3t} \Rightarrow \ddot{x} = (\ddot{v} - 6\dot{v} + 9v)\, e^{-3t}.$ We then get $\ddot{v} - \dot{v} = 0$, giving
    $v = B + A\, e^t$ and $x = B\, e^{-3t} + A\, e^{-2t}.$

3   The substitution gives the SHM equation, $\ddot{u} + u = 0$, with solution $u = A \sin t + B \cos t$. Hence $x = e^{-3t}(A \sin t + B \cos t)$. This method avoids the use of complex numbers.

4   Now we get $\ddot{u} = 0$, and so $\dot{u} = A$ and $u = At + B$. The general solution is $x = (At + B)\, e^{-3t}.$

5   (a) $\ddot{x} + 5\dot{x} + 6x = e^{-2t} \Rightarrow \ddot{u} + \dot{u} = 1.$ A PI is given by $u = t$, for then $\dot{u} = 1$, $\ddot{u} = 0$. For the original differential equation, therefore, $t\, e^{-2t}$ is a PI.
    (b) $\ddot{x} + 100x = \cos 10t \Rightarrow \ddot{u} \sin 10t + 20\dot{u} \cos 10t = \cos 10t.$ PIs are $u = \frac{1}{20}t$ and $x = \frac{1}{20}t \sin 10t.$
    (c) $\ddot{u} = 4$ leads to $x = 2t^2\, e^{-3t}$ as a PI.
    (d) $\ddot{u} = 4t + 5$ leads to $x = (\frac{2}{3}t^3 + \frac{5}{2}t^2)\, e^{-3t}$ as a PI.

6   We get $\ddot{u} \cos 10t - 20\dot{u} \sin 10t = \cos 10t.$ No simple solution is apparent.

Exercise 10B

1 (a) $x = \frac{10}{3} + A e^{-t} + B e^{-3t}$ (b) $x = 2 + e^{-2t} (A \sin t + B \cos t)$
   (c) $x = \frac{5}{2} + (A + Bt) e^{-2t}$ (d) $x = \frac{5}{2}t + \frac{1}{2} + (A + Bt) e^{-2t}$

2 $\dot{x} = K(1 - 2t) e^{-2t}$; $\ddot{x} = K(-4 + 4t) e^{-2t}$
   (a) We require $K e^{-2t} = 12 e^{-2t}$. The PI is $12t e^{-2t}$.   (b) $4t e^{-2t}$ (c) $-4t e^{-2t}$
   The complete solutions are:
   (a) $x = 12t e^{-2t} + A e^{-2t}$ (b) $x = 4t e^{-2t} + A e^{-2t} + B e^{-5t}$
   (c) $x = -4t e^{-2t} + A e^{-2t} + B e^{t}$

3 $K = \frac{5}{2}$

4 The PIs are $x = -\frac{3}{2}jt\, e^{jt}$ and $x = \frac{3}{2}jt\, e^{-jt}$. Hence for $\ddot{x} + x = 6 \cos t$, a PI is

$$-\tfrac{3}{2}jt\, e^{jt} + \tfrac{3}{2}jt\, e^{-jt} = -3jt \times \tfrac{1}{2}(e^{jt} - e^{-jt})$$
$$= 3t \sin t.$$

5 (a) $-\frac{1}{3} e^{-2t} + A e^{-t} + B e^{-5t}$ (b) $\frac{1}{2}t\, e^{-t} + A e^{-t} + B e^{-5t}$
   (c) $\frac{1}{8}e^{-t} + (A + Bt) e^{-5t}$ (d) $\frac{1}{2}t^2\, e^{-5t} + (A + Bt) e^{-5t}$
   (e) $\frac{6}{26} \sin t - \frac{9}{26} \cos t + A\, e^{-t} + B e^{-5t}$ (f) $-\frac{3}{2}t \cos t + A \sin t + B \cos t$

6

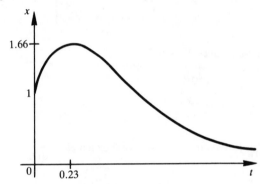

   (a) $x = 10t\, e^{-3t} + e^{-3t}$ (b) The maximum value is ≈ 1.66.

7 (a) $x = -3 e^{-t} + 4 e^{-t/4}$; the maximum point is $(\frac{4}{3} \ln 3,\, 3^{2/3}) \approx (1.46, 2.08)$.
   (b) $x = (1 + \frac{5}{2}t) e^{-t/2}$; the maximum point is $(\frac{8}{5},\, 5 e^{-0.8}) \approx (1.6, 2.25)$. The motion
   with critical damping has a larger maximum value but dies away more rapidly.

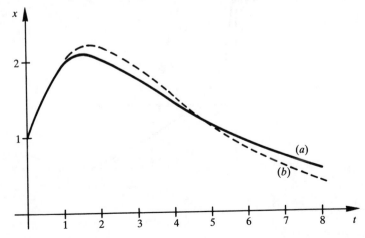

Exercise 10C

1 (*a*) Maximising the amplitude implies minimising
$$[(13 - \omega^2)^2 + 16\omega^2] = \omega^4 - 10\omega^2 + 169.$$

(*b*) This is effected when $\omega^2 = 5$, the period is $2\pi/\omega$ and the frequency is $\omega/2\pi$.

2 (*a*) $\ddot{x} + a\dot{x} + bx = 0$ gives damped oscillations of frequency $n/2\pi$, where $n^2 = b - \frac{1}{4}a^2$, provided that $b > \frac{1}{4}a^2$.

(*b*) The amplitude of the PI is $\dfrac{c}{\sqrt{[(b - \omega^2)^2 + a^2\omega^2]}}$, and the resonant frequency is $\omega/2\pi$, where $\omega^2 = b - \frac{1}{2}a^2$. $\omega^2 \approx n^2$ if a is small compared with b.

3 The steady-state current is the PI $H \sin \omega t + K \cos \omega t$, where H and K are given by
$$\left.\begin{array}{r}\left(\dfrac{1}{C} - L\omega^2\right) H - R\omega K = 0 \\[4mm] R\omega H + \left(\dfrac{1}{C} - L\omega^2\right) K = E_0\omega\end{array}\right\}$$

Squaring and adding gives the amplitude
$$A = \frac{E_0\omega}{\sqrt{\left[\left(\dfrac{1}{C} - L\omega^2\right)^2 + R^2\omega^2\right]}} = \frac{E_0}{\sqrt{\left[\left(\dfrac{1}{\omega C} - L\omega\right)^2 + R^2\right]}}.$$

(*a*) $\left(\dfrac{1}{\omega C} - \omega L\right)^2$ has a minimum value of 0, when $\omega = \dfrac{1}{\sqrt{(LC)}}$.

(*b*) Then $A = E_0/R$.

(*c*) $f'(\omega) = -\dfrac{1}{\omega^2 C} - L = - 2L$ when $\omega = \dfrac{1}{\sqrt{(LC)}}$.

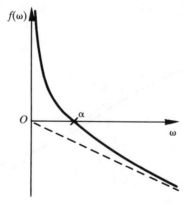

(*d*) $\dfrac{10^3}{2\pi\sqrt{15}} = 41$ Hz

(e)

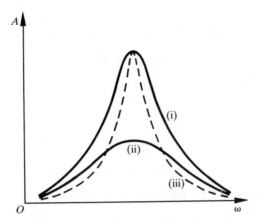

All have the same resonant frequency. The peak value in (ii) is smaller, since R is greater. The graph in (iii) is steeper and narrower, because L is larger and hence $f(\omega)$ changes more rapidly near the maximum point (see (c)).

4 One would like R to be as small as possible. Highly selective circuits would have large L and correspondingly small C. The product LC is determined by the frequency chosen. Components with large inductance will inevitably have some resistance.

5 We want $f(\omega) = 1/\omega C - \omega L = \pm \sqrt{3}R$ so that $A = E_0/2R$. Now $f'(\Omega) = -2L$ (see question $3(c)$), so $\omega_1 \approx \Omega + \sqrt{3}R/2L$ and $\omega_2 \approx \Omega - \sqrt{3}R/2L$. Hence $\omega_1 - \omega_2 \approx \sqrt{3}R/L$. As a percentage of Ω this is $100R\sqrt{(3C/L)}$, which for the data of question $3(e)$ gives (i) 0.45%, (ii) 1.1%, (iii) 0.22%.

6 $m_0\ddot{z} + \dfrac{F_0 z}{Z_0} = cV^2 \cos(kVt)$ gives resonance when the natural frequency equals the

forcing frequency. Then $\dfrac{F_0}{m_0 Z_0} = (kV)^2 = \omega^2$, say.

The wind speed $= \dfrac{1}{k}\sqrt{\left(\dfrac{F_0}{m_0 Z_0}\right)}$.

Writing the differential equation as $\ddot{z} + \omega^2 z = a \cos \omega t$, where $a = cV^2/m_0$, we have CF $A \cos \omega t + B \sin \omega t$ and PI $Kt \sin \omega t$, where K is given by $2K\omega \cos \omega t = a \cos \omega t$, i.e. $K = a/2\omega$.

The general solution is $z = A \cos \omega t + B \sin \omega t + \left(\dfrac{a}{2\omega}\right) t \sin \omega t$, and the initial conditions $z = \dot{z} = 0$ when $t = 0$ give $A = 0$ and $B = 0$.

7 (a) $\alpha = 1$ gives resonance; $\alpha \approx 1$ gives large-amplitude oscillations.
   (b) Small α means high frequency oscillations, modelling rapid alternations between braking and accelerating.

Miscellaneous exercise 10

1 $y = \dfrac{1}{z} \Rightarrow \dfrac{dy}{dx} = -\dfrac{1}{z^2}\dfrac{dz}{dx}$.

The differential equation then becomes $x^2 \dfrac{dz}{dx} + 3xz = 2$.

$z = \dfrac{K}{x}$ is a PI if $-K + 3K = 2$, i.e. if $K = 1$.

$$x^2 \frac{dz}{dx} + 3xz = 0 \quad \Rightarrow \quad \frac{1}{z} \frac{dz}{dx} = -\frac{3}{x}$$

$$\Rightarrow \quad \ln z = -3 \ln x + c \quad \Rightarrow \quad z = \frac{A}{x^3} \text{ is the CF.}$$

Hence $\dfrac{1}{y} = \dfrac{A}{x^3} + \dfrac{1}{x}$, and the initial condition gives $A = 0$. The required solution is merely $y = x$. A check is easy.

2 $y = z^{-1/2} \quad \Rightarrow \quad \dfrac{dy}{dx} = -\tfrac{1}{2} z^{-3/2} \dfrac{dz}{dx}$. This leads to $x^3 \dfrac{dz}{dx} + 4x^2 z = -2$, and the standard methods provide a general solution $\dfrac{1}{y^2} = z = -\dfrac{1}{x^2} + \dfrac{A}{x^4}$. The initial conditions give $A = 5$ and hence $y = \dfrac{x^2}{\sqrt{(5 - x^2)}}$, but this can only be accepted for values of x less than $\sqrt{5}$.

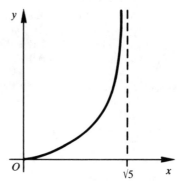

3 $y = \ln u \quad \Rightarrow \quad \dfrac{dy}{dx} = \dfrac{1}{u} \dfrac{du}{dx}$. We then obtain $\dfrac{1}{u} \dfrac{du}{dx} = \dfrac{1}{u} + \dfrac{1}{x}$, i.e $x \dfrac{du}{dx} - u = x$.

This has CF Ax, but a PI may prove elusive.

A second substitution, $u = xv$, gives $x \dfrac{dv}{dx} = 1$, and hence we get a solution $v = \ln x$;

so $u = Ax + x \ln x$ and $e^y = Ax + x \ln x$. Since $y = 1$ when $x = 1$, $A = e$. Finally, we have $y = \ln(ex + x \ln x)$, with the condition that $ex + x \ln x > 0$, i.e. $x > e^{-e}$.

4 $\dfrac{dy}{dx} = \dfrac{dy}{dt} \times \dfrac{dt}{dx} = e^{-t} \dfrac{dy}{dt}; \quad \dfrac{d^2y}{dx^2} = -e^{-t} \dfrac{dt}{dx} \dfrac{dy}{dt} + e^{-t} \dfrac{d^2y}{dt^2} \dfrac{dt}{dx}$

$\qquad = -e^{-2t} \dfrac{dy}{dt} + e^{-2t} \dfrac{d^2y}{dt^2}$.

The differential equation becomes $\dfrac{d^2y}{dt^2} + 2 \dfrac{dy}{dt} - 3y = 0$, giving

$$y = A e^t + B e^{-3t} = Ax + B/x^3.$$

Alternatively, we may try $y = x^n$ in the original equation. This is a solution if $n(n-1) + 3n - 3 = 0$, i.e. if $n = 1$ or -3.

5 $\dfrac{q}{C} + Ri + L\dfrac{di}{dt} = E \Rightarrow L\dfrac{d^2i}{dt^2} + R\dfrac{di}{dt} + \dfrac{1}{C}i = 0$. The current is non-oscillatory if the auxiliary equation has real roots, i.e. if $R^2 \geqslant 4L/C$.

6 The extra acceleration is proportional to $(\dot{y} - V)$. We may take the constant of proportion as β/V, leading to the required equation. The equation is satisfied if $y = x = L$, $\dot{y} = V$ and $\ddot{x} = 0$.

(a) In the test,
$$\ddot{x} + \frac{\alpha}{L}x = \alpha\left(\frac{y_0}{L} - 2\right).$$

Measuring time from the start of the test, $x = y_0 - L$ and $\dot{x} = V$ when $t = 0$. The solution is
$$x = (y_0 - 2L) + A\cos\Omega t + B\sin\Omega t, \quad \text{where } \Omega^2 = \alpha L,$$

and we find that
$$A = L \quad \text{and} \quad B = V/\Omega.$$

A crash is avoided if the amplitude of the oscillatory terms, $\sqrt{(A^2 + B^2)}$, is less than $2L$. This requires
$$L^2 + \frac{V^2}{\Omega^2} < 4L^2, \quad \text{giving } \alpha > \frac{V^2}{3L}.$$

(b) $f(t) = (\alpha Vt/L) + (b\alpha/L)\cos\omega t - (b\beta\omega/V)\sin\omega t$; resonance occurs if $\Omega = v$, and this would cause problems!

7 (a) $\omega = A/x^3$

(b) $\dfrac{dx}{dy} = \dfrac{1}{1-y^2}$ leads to $x = \frac{1}{2}\ln\left(\dfrac{1+y}{1-y}\right) + 1$, i.e. $y = \dfrac{e^{2x-2} - 1}{e^{2x-2} + 1}$. $y = c/x$ is a solution of (B) if $-c + c^2 = \frac{3}{4}$, i.e. $c = -\frac{1}{2}$ or $\frac{3}{2}$.

The given substitution reduces (B) to
$$\frac{d^2z}{dx^2} + \frac{3}{x}\frac{dz}{dx} = 0, \quad \text{giving } z = \frac{A}{x^2} + B, \quad y = \frac{-2A}{x(A + B\,x^2)} + \frac{3}{2x}.$$

We note that the two special solutions found earlier correspond to $B = 0$ and $A = 0$ respectively.
$$y = \frac{-6}{x(3 + x^2)} + \frac{3}{2x}$$

is a solution, with $y = 0$ when $x = 1$.

8 (a) $\ddot{x} = \dot{y} - 4\dot{x} = -4\dot{x} - 4x$. The boundary conditions imply that $\dot{x} = 1$ when $t = 0$, and we obtain the solution $x = t\,e^{-2t}$. From $y = \dot{x} + 4x$, we find $y = (1 + 2t)\,e^{-2t}$.

(b) $\dot{w} = \dot{u} + \dot{v} = -(u + v)^2 = -w^2$ and $w = 1$ when $t = 0$. So $t = 1/w - 1$, i.e. $w = (1 + t)^{-1}$ or $u = (1 + t)^{-1} - v$. The second differential equation then becomes $\dot{v} + (1 + t)^{-1}v = \frac{1}{2}v^2$. $v = 1/z$ leads to the equation $\dot{z} - (1 + t)^{-1}z = -\frac{1}{2}$, which is similar to the equation for u in question 3. The solution here is $1/v = z = A(1 + t) - \frac{1}{2}(1 + t)\ln(1 + t)$, and the boundary conditions give $A = 1$. No problems arise when taking the reciprocal of the right-hand side provided that $t < e^2 - 1$, as stated; then u is given by $(1 + t)^{-1} - v$.

Exercise 11A

1

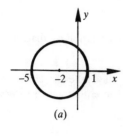

(a)

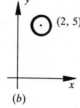

(b)

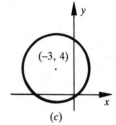

(c)

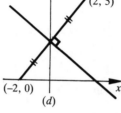

(d)

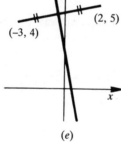

(e)

(f)

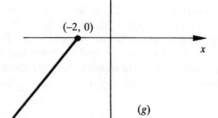

(g)

2

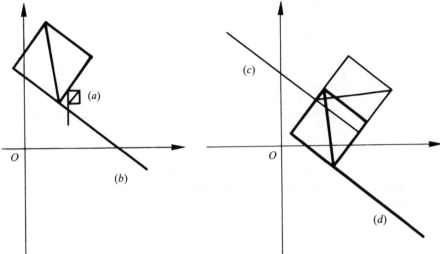

(a)

(b)

(c)

(d)

3 $\mathbf{OB'} = \begin{bmatrix} 10 \\ 5 \end{bmatrix} = 5\begin{bmatrix} 2 \\ 1 \end{bmatrix} = 5\mathbf{OB}$

4 The invariant point is seen to be C. It is given by

$$z = (3 + 4j)z + (2 - 6j), \quad \text{i.e. } z = \frac{-2 + 6j}{2 + 4j} = 1 + j.$$

The transformation is a rotation (through $\tan^{-1} \frac{4}{3}$) and enlargement about C, the scale factor being 5.

5 (a) $|z - 4 - j| = |z - 4 - j - 2 + 3j|$, i.e. $|z - 4 - j| = |z - 6 + 2j|$; there are, of course, many other descriptions of this line.
(b) $|z*| = |z* - 2 + 3j|$ or $|z| = |z - 2 - 3j|$
(c) $|jz| = |jz - 2 + 3j|$ or $|z| = |z + 2j + 3|$
We may either use previous experience of transformations of graphs, replacing z wherever it occurs by (a) $z - 4 - j$, (b) $z*$ and (c) jz, or proceed from diagrams of the image lines.

Exercise 11B

1 Body: $z = 20 + 10j + 10e^{\theta j}$, $0 \leqslant \theta < 2\pi$
   Head: $z = 20 + 25j + 5e^{\theta j}$, $0 \leqslant \theta < 2\pi$
   Whiskers: $z = t + 25j$, $12 \leqslant t \leqslant 15$ and $25 \leqslant t \leqslant 28$
   $z = (20 + 25j) + t(4 + j)$, $5/\sqrt{17} \leqslant t \leqslant 2$
   $z = (20 + 25j) + t(-4 + j)$, $5/\sqrt{17} \leqslant t \leqslant 2$

2 (a) $x^2 + y^2 = 25$ (b) $(x - 2)^2 + (y - 1)^2 = 9$ (c) $4x + 2y = 5$
   (d) $2x^2 + 2y^2 + 4x + 2y = 5$

3 (a) Centre $(4, 0)$, radius 2   (b) Centre $(-4\frac{1}{2}, -1)$, radius $\frac{1}{2}\sqrt{45}$
   (c) Centre $(3\frac{1}{3}, 0)$, radius $1\frac{2}{3}$
   In (b), the equation can be written as $3|z + 4| = |z - 8j|$, while in (c) we may write
   $|2z - 5| = |z|$ or $2|z - 2\frac{1}{2}| = |z|$.

4 (a) The line $x = 3$ (b) $y = 2$ (c) $y = -2$
   (d) The circle of radius 2 with centre the origin

5　　$\sqrt{((x + 3)^2 + y^2)} = 4 + \sqrt{((x - 3)^2 + y^2)}$
$\Rightarrow$　$x^2 + 6x + 9 + y^2 = 16 + 8\sqrt{((x - 3)^2 + y^2)} + x^2 - 6x + 9 + y^2$
$\Rightarrow$　　　　　　$3x - 4 = 2\sqrt{((x - 3)^2 + y^2)}$
$\Rightarrow$　$9x^2 - 24x + 16 = 4(x^2 - 6x + 9 + y^2)$
$\Rightarrow$　　　　　$5x^2 - 4y^2 = 20.$

All points on the locus are points of the hyperbola $5x^2 - 4y^2 = 20$, but some of the steps of the working above are not reversible. The locus consists of the branch of the hyperbola further from $(-3, 0)$ than from $(3, 0)$, i.e. the right-hand branch.

Exercise 11C

1　*A* and *B* are invariant; *C* $(2 + 4j)$ maps onto *G* $(\frac{2}{5} + \frac{4}{5}j)$, and *G* maps onto *C*; *D* maps onto *j*, *E* onto $-\frac{2}{5} + \frac{4}{5}j$ and *F* onto $1 + j$. The circle maps onto itself and the line *CDE* maps onto the smaller circle in the diagram.

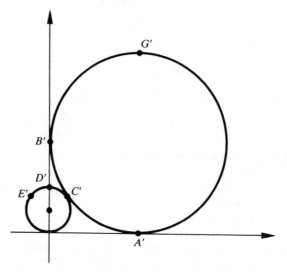

2　$\left| \dfrac{1}{w} - 4j \right| = 4 \left| \dfrac{1}{w} + 1 \right|$　$\Rightarrow$　　　　$|1 - 4jw| = 4 |1 + w|$

　　　　　　　　　　　　$\Rightarrow$　　　　$|\tfrac{1}{4} - jw| = |1 + w|$
　　　　　　　　　　　　$\Rightarrow$　$|\tfrac{1}{4}j + w| \times |-j| = |1 + w|$
　　　　　　　　　　　　$\Rightarrow$　　　　$|w + \tfrac{1}{4}j| = |w + 1|.$

This gives the perpendicular bisector of the line joining $(-1, 0)$ and $(0, -\frac{1}{4})$.

3　$\left| \dfrac{1}{w} - 3 + 4j \right| = 5$　$\Rightarrow$　　　　$|1 + (-3 + 4j)w| = 5 |w|$

　　　　　　　　　　$\Rightarrow$　$\left| \dfrac{1}{-3 + 4j} + w \right| \times |-3 + 4j| = 5 |w|$

　　　　　　　　　　$\Rightarrow$　　$\left| \dfrac{-3 - 4j}{25} + w \right| = |w|.$

As in question 2, a circle through the origin has mapped onto a straight line.

4   Two parallel lines not through the origin map onto two circles which touch at the origin.

5   (a)   This has been illustrated in question 1. In the diagram below, if $OP = p$, $OQ = q$ and $OR = r$, then $q = \frac{1}{2}(p + r)$. But $OP' = 1/p$, etc. and $1/q \neq \frac{1}{2}(1/p + 1/r)$, so Q' is not the mid-point of $P'R'$.

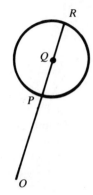

   (b) C' is the reflection of O in the line.

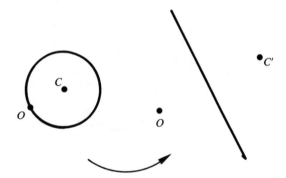

6   The points inside the larger circle map onto points outside its image but points inside the second circle map onto points inside its image.

7 $A'C'$ is a diameter of the circle $OA'B'C'$, so angle $A'B'C'$ is a right angle. This means $A'B'$ and $B'C'$ are the images of two circles OAB and OBC which intersect at right angles.

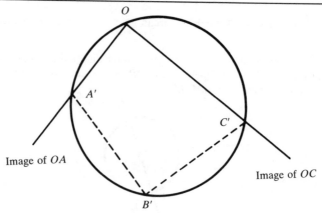

8 In the image diagram, $A'B'$ is parallel to $C'D'$. It follows that the circles OAB and OCD in Figure 22 touch at O. Note that the unmarked point of intersection of the circles in the image diagram is the image of the point where the common tangents AB and CD meet (when produced) in Figure 22.

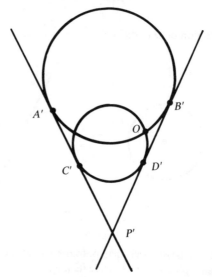

9 All the possible chords $P'Q'$ have the same length since they all subtend an angle α at O. Hence they touch a circle C' concentric with l'. All the possible circles OPQ in the original figure must touch C, the circle whose image is C'.

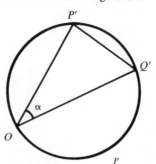

Exercise 11D

1 $7 - 3j$ and $2 - 4j$, or $5 + 7j$ and $6j$.

2

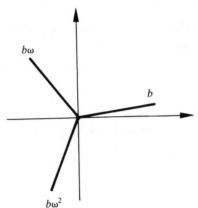

b, $b\omega$, $b\omega^2$ give an equilateral triangle, and adding a to each complex number merely effects a translation. Alternatively, it is sufficient to show that

$$(a + b\omega) - (a + b) = -\omega[(a + b\omega^2) - (a + b)], \quad \text{which is true since } \omega^3 = 1.$$

3

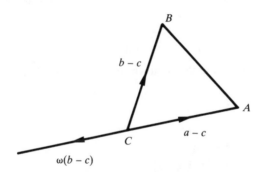

In the diagram, $a - c = -\omega(b - c)$.

Hence $a + b\omega - c(1 + \omega) = 0$,   i.e. $a + b\omega + c\omega^2 = 0$,

since $\omega^3 = 1 \implies (\omega - 1)(\omega^2 + \omega + 1) = 0$
                    $\implies \omega^2 + \omega + 1 = 0$ since $\omega \neq 1$.

If the triangle is labelled clockwise, then $a + b\omega^2 + c\omega = 0$ is achieved by interchanging b and c throughout.

4 $l = \frac{1}{2}(p + s) = \frac{1}{2}(1 + j)a + \frac{1}{2}(1 - j)p$; $m = \frac{1}{2}(p + v) = \frac{1}{2}(-1 + j)a + \frac{1}{2}(1 + j)p$.
By inspection, $m = jl$, so OL is equal and perpendicular to OM.

5 As in question 4,

$p = \frac{1}{2}(1 + j)b + \frac{1}{2}(1 - j)c$, $q = \frac{1}{2}(1 + j)c + \frac{1}{2}(1 - j)a$, $r = \frac{1}{2}(1 + j)a + \frac{1}{2}(1 - j)b$.

PQ is represented by $q - p = \frac{1}{2}(1 - j)a - \frac{1}{2}(1 + j)b + jc$,

and **CR** is represented by $r - c = \frac{1}{2}(1 + j)a + \frac{1}{2}(1 - j)b - c$.

The result follows when we notice that $r - c = j(q - p)$.

6 $1 + b\omega^2 + c\omega = 0$ (see question 3), and hence $a - l = a + b\omega^2 + c\omega$.

Similarly, $b - m = b + c\omega^2 + a\omega$ and $c - n = c + a\omega^2 + b\omega$.
Hence $b - m = \omega(a - l)$ and $c - n = \omega(b - m)$.

Consequently $AL = BM = CN$, and the lines meet at angles of $120°$.

7 Call the centres P, Q and R,

then $p = \tfrac{1}{3}(b + c + l)$, $q = \tfrac{1}{3}(c + a + m)$, $r = \tfrac{1}{3}(a + b + n)$.

Hence

$$q - p = \tfrac{1}{3}(a + m - b - l) = \tfrac{1}{3}[(a - l) - (b - m)]$$

and $r - q = \tfrac{1}{3}[(b - m) - (c - n)] = \omega(q - p)$ (see question 6).

This means $QR = PQ$ and angle $PQR = 60°$, implying that triangle PQR is equilateral.

Miscellaneous exercise 11

1 $|(5 + 5j) - (2 + j)| = 5 = |(6 + 4j) - (2 + j)|$. The fourth vertex is given by $9 + 8j$.

2 We should require $c - a = (\tfrac{1}{2} + \tfrac{1}{2}\sqrt{3}j)(b - a)$. If A and B have integer coordinates, the coordinates of C will contain $\sqrt{3}$.

3 In the diagram opposite, **OP'** represents $1 + j(z - 1)$. A $90°$ rotation about $(0, 2)$ is given by $z \mapsto 2j + j(z - 2j)$.
The combined transformation is

$$z \mapsto 2j + j\{1 + j(z - 1) - 2j\} = -z + 3 + 3j.$$

This is a $180°$ rotation about the point where $z = -z + 3 + 3j$, i.e. $(\tfrac{3}{2}, \tfrac{3}{2})$.

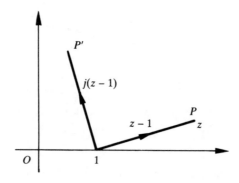

4 $z \mapsto 4j - \{1 + j(z - 1)\} \Leftrightarrow z \mapsto -jz - 1 + 5j$. The invariant point is given by $z = -jz - 1 + 5j$, i.e. $z = \dfrac{-1 + 5j}{1 + j} = 2 + 3j$. The point is $(2, 3)$.

5 $z \mapsto b + \omega(z - b)$ followed   by $z \mapsto a + \omega(z - a)$ is   equivalent   to
$z \mapsto a + \omega\{b + \omega(z - b) - a\}$.   The   invariant   point   being C means
$c = a + \omega\{b + \omega(c - b) - a\}$,

i.e. $a(1 - \omega) + b(\omega - \omega^2) + c(\omega^2 - 1) = 0$
$\Rightarrow \quad a \qquad\qquad + b\omega \qquad\quad - c(1 + \omega) \;= 0$
$\Rightarrow \quad a \qquad\qquad + b\omega \qquad\quad + c\omega^2 \qquad = 0$

6

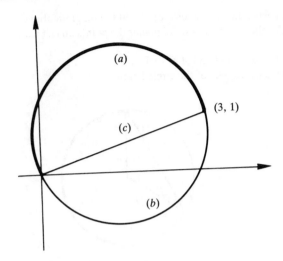

7 (*a*) $OP + PA = 10 = OA \Rightarrow P$ lies in the line segment OA.

(*b*) The locus is the continuation of the line OA beyond A.

(*c*) The line OA, omitting the segment from O to A.

(*d*) The line segment OA.

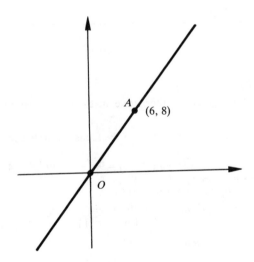

8 (*a*) The perpendicular bisector of OA in the diagram above.

(*b*) An Apollonius circle with diameter the points on OA with x-coordinates 4.8 and 8.

(*c*) An ellipse with O and A as foci.

(*d*) The major arc OA of the circle below.

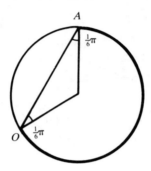

(*e*) The two arcs of the hyperbola $xy - 4x - 3y = 0$ shown below.

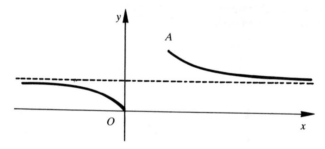

9 $zz^* = (a + bj)(a - bj) = a^2 + b^2 = |z|^2.$

The subsequent working gives an alternative method for treating simple loci algebraically.

10 $(z + 8)(z^* + 8) = 4(z + 2)(z^* + 2) \Rightarrow zz^* = 16 \Rightarrow$ locus is a circle, centre the origin, radius 4.

$$(z - j)(z^* - j) = 9(z - 4 - 9j)(z^* - 4 + 9j)$$
$$\Rightarrow \quad 8zz^* - 36z + 80jz - 36z^* - 80jz^* + 872 = 0$$
$$\Rightarrow \quad zz^* - \tfrac{9}{2}z + 10jz - \tfrac{9}{2}z^* - 10jz + 109 = 0$$
$$\Rightarrow \quad (z - \tfrac{9}{2} - 10j)(z^* - \tfrac{9}{2} + 10j) = 11\tfrac{1}{4}$$
$$\Rightarrow \quad |z - \tfrac{9}{2} - 10j| = \sqrt{11\tfrac{1}{4}}$$

This confirms the result of Example 2, page 141.

11

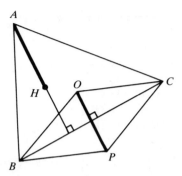

(a) $OB = OC \Rightarrow p = b + c$ where $OBPC$ is a rhombus

(b) $\Rightarrow h = a + b + c$ represents the point on the altitude through A a distance equal to OP from A.

(c) Writing $h = b + (c + a) = c + (a + b)$ shows that H lies on each of the other two altitudes of triangle ABC.

12

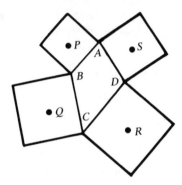

$p = \frac{1}{2}(1 + j)a + \frac{1}{2}(1 - j)b, \quad q = \frac{1}{2}(1 + j)b + \frac{1}{2}(1 - j)c,$ etc.
We soon see that $s - q = j(r = p)$, and the required properties are immediate deductions.

Exercise 12A

1 (a) $z = 20x - 8y - 4$ (b) $z = \frac{1}{4}x + \frac{1}{2}y + \frac{3}{2}$
   (c) $z = 5x + 6y - 4$ (d) $z = \frac{1}{2}x - \frac{3}{2}y + 3$

2 (a) $\cos(x + 5y)$, $5\cos(x + 5y)$ (b) $px^{p-1}y^q$, $qx^p y^{q-1}$
   (c) $-2xy/(x^2 + y^2)^2$, $(x^2 - y^2)/(x^2 + y^2)^2$ (d) $-y/(x^2 + y^2)$, $x/(x^2 + y^2)$

3 $\dfrac{\partial z}{\partial t}$ is the vertical velocity of a particular point of the surface of the pond; $\dfrac{\partial z}{\partial r}$ is the gradient of a section of the surface in a radial direction.

4 $\dfrac{\partial L}{\partial v}$ is the rate of change of lift with speed; $\dfrac{\partial L}{\partial \rho}$ is the rate of change of lift with density.

5 (a) $10, -2$ (b) $-\frac{1}{32}, -\frac{1}{4}$ (c) $2, -6$ (d) $0, \frac{3}{2}$

6 (*a*)

x	y	z	$\dfrac{\partial z}{\partial x}$	$\dfrac{\partial z}{\partial y}$
3	1	34	29	15
3.2	1	40.17	32.72	15.8
3	1.1	35.59	29.42	16.83
3.2	1.1	41.84	33.14	17.71

$40.17 - 34 \approx 41.84 - 35.59 \approx 0.2 \times 29$; $35.59 - 34 \approx 41.84 - 40.17 \approx 0.1 \times 15$

(*b*) $\dfrac{\partial^2 z}{\partial x^2} = 18,\quad \dfrac{\partial^2 z}{\partial y^2} = 18,\quad \dfrac{\partial^2 z}{\partial x\,\partial y} = \dfrac{\partial^2 z}{\partial y\,\partial x} = 4$

$32.72 - 29 \approx 33.14 - 29.42 \approx 0.2 \times 18$; $16.83 - 15 \approx 17.71 - 15.8 \approx 0.1 \times 18$

$29.42 - 29 \approx 33.14 - 32.72 \approx 0.1 \times 4$; $15.8 - 15 \approx 17.71 - 16.83 \approx 0.2 \times 4$

8 (*a*) $\dfrac{\partial^2 z}{\partial x\,\partial y}$ is the rate of change with respect to x of the gradient of sections through the surface in planes perpendicular to the x-axis.

(*b*) The increase in z is the sum of the increases when x is increased by δx keeping y constant, then y is increased by δy keeping x constant (or vice versa). These increases are approximately $\dfrac{\partial z}{\mathrm{d}x}\,\partial x$ and $\dfrac{\partial z}{\mathrm{d}y}\,\delta y$. The smaller the values of δx and δy, the better the approximation will be.

Exercise 12B

1 (*a*) 10.2%   (*b*) 1.8%   (*c*) 10.2%

2 If r is increased by a small amount δr while h remains constant, $\delta V \approx \delta r \times$ curved surface area; if h is increased by a small amount δh while r remains constant, $\delta V = \delta h \times$ area of one end.

3 $S = 2\pi r^2 + 2\pi r h \Rightarrow \dfrac{\partial S}{\partial r} = 4\pi r + 2\pi h$ and $\dfrac{\partial S}{\partial h} = 2\pi r$; $\delta r = 0.05$ and $\delta h = 0.05$, give $\delta S \approx 2.83$.

and
$$f(2.05, 3.05) - f(2, 3) = 65.69 - 62.83 = 2.86,$$
$$f(2, 3) - f(1.95, 2.95) = 62.83 - 60.04 = 2.79.$$

4 2% error in distance and 4.2% error in time would give an error in average speed of up to 6.2%. The time error has the greater effect.

5 $(pu + qv)\%$

6 Between 2% and 3%, depending on the relative sizes of x and y: nearer 2% if x: y is large, nearer 3% if x: y is small.

7

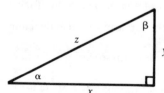

$$\delta z \approx \frac{x}{\sqrt{(x^2 + y^2)}}\,\delta x + \frac{y}{\sqrt{(x^2 + y^2)}}\,\delta y = \cos\alpha\,\delta x + \cos\beta\,\delta y.$$

This is as expected, since a small change δx in x alters z by an amount approximately equal to $\cos\alpha\,\delta x$.

Exercise 12C

1 (a) Saddle point   (b) Maximum   (c) Minimum   (d) Saddle point
For (a), $(0, 1, -1)$ is below and $(1, 0, 5)$ is above the saddle point;
for (d), $(1, 1, 3)$ is below and $(1, 0, 5)$ above.

2 $\frac{1}{6}, \frac{1}{3}, -\frac{1}{108}, -\frac{1}{54}, -\frac{1}{54}, -\frac{1}{27}$

3 (a) $\frac{5}{3}, -\frac{8}{3}, -\frac{16}{27}, \frac{40}{27}, -\frac{100}{27}$ (b) $\frac{1}{2}, \frac{5}{2}, -\frac{1}{16}, \frac{3}{16}, -\frac{5}{16}$

4 9, 12, 0, 6, 4.
$f(2 + h, 3 + k) \approx 18 + 9h + 12k + 6hk + 2k^2.$
But $(2 + h)(3 + k)^2 = 18 + 9h + 12k + 6hk + 2k^2 + hk^2.$

5 (a) $f(2 + h, 3 + k) \approx 3 - h + 2k + \frac{1}{3}h^2 - \frac{2}{3}hk + \frac{1}{3}k^2$
$= 3.53$ when $h = -0.1, k = 0.2.$
In fact, $f(1.9, 3.2) = 3.531$ (to 4 SF).
(b) $f(2 + h, 3 + k) \approx 5 + 6h - 4k + 6h^2 - 10hk + 4k^2$
$= 4.02$ when $h = -0.1, k = 0.2.$
In this case, $f(1.9, 3.2) = 3.923$ (to 4 SF).
(c) It pays to write $f(x, y) = \dfrac{1}{2(x - y)} + \dfrac{1}{2(x + y)}$ before differentiating.
$f(2 + h, 3 + k) \approx -0.4 - 0.52h + 0.48k - 0.496h^2 + 1.008hk - 0.496k^2$
$= -0.296\,96$ when $h = -0.1, k = 0.2.$
$f(1.9, 3.2) = -0.2866$ (to 4 SF).

6 (a) $\dfrac{\partial z}{\partial x} = \dfrac{\partial z}{\partial y} = 0$ when $x = 15, \ y = 6. \ f(15 + h, 6 + k) = -45 + h^2 - 4hk + 5k^2,$
giving $(15, 6, -45)$ as a minimum point.

(b) $\dfrac{\partial z}{\partial x} = \dfrac{\partial z}{\partial y} = 0$ when $x = 4, \ y = -1. \ f(4 + h, -1 + k) = 16 - h^2 - 2hk - 3k^2,$
giving $(4, -1, 16)$ as a maximum point.

7 (a) $f(0 + h, 0 + k) \approx 4hk + k^2$ gives $(0, 0, 0)$ as a saddle point.

(b) $\dfrac{\partial z}{\partial x} = \dfrac{\partial z}{\partial y} = 0 \ \Rightarrow \ \left.\begin{array}{r} 8x^3 + 4y = 0 \\ 4x + 2y = 0 \end{array}\right\}$

$\Rightarrow \ 8x^3 - 8x = 0$
$\Rightarrow \ x = 0 \text{ or } 1 \text{ or } -1.$

$f(1 + h, -2 + k) \approx -2 + 12h^2 + 4hk + k^2$ gives $(1, -2, -2)$ as a minimum point.
(c) Similarly, $(-1, 2, -2)$ is a minimum point. Note that the surface has $180°$ rotational symmetry about the z-axis, since replacing x by $-x$ and y by $-y$ leaves z unchanged.

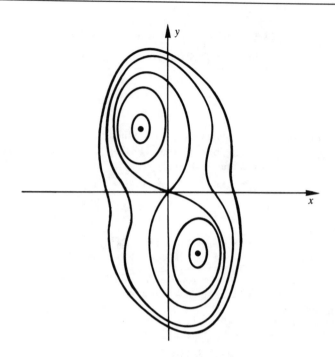

8 $\dfrac{\partial z}{\partial x} = \left(\dfrac{y+8}{y}\right)\left(1 - \dfrac{9y}{x^2}\right)$ and $\dfrac{\partial^2 z}{\partial x^2} = \left(\dfrac{y+8}{y}\right)\left(\dfrac{18y}{x^3}\right)$. When $x = \sqrt{(9y)}$, $\dfrac{\partial z}{\partial x} = 0$

and $\dfrac{\partial^2 z}{\partial x^2} > 0$, so the section through the surface has a minimum point. Similarly,

when $y = \sqrt{(8x/3)}$, the section perpendicular to the x-axis has a minimum point. The minimum point of the surface occurs where $x^2 = 9y$ and $3y^2 = 8x$. It is (6, 4, 81). Second derivatives must be calculated to prove this is indeed a minimum point.

9 (a) $z = 6x^2 + 4x + 72$ gives a parabola with minimum point where $x = -\tfrac{1}{3}$.

(b) $\dfrac{\partial z}{\partial x} = 2xy + 4 = 0$ when $xy = -2$. $\dfrac{\partial^2 z}{\partial x^2} = 2y$, so the section has a maximum point when $y < 0$ and a minimum when $y > 0$.

(c) $\dfrac{\partial z}{\partial y} = x^2 + 4y$ and $\dfrac{\partial^2 z}{\partial y^2} = 4$, so the sections have minimum points when $y = -\tfrac{1}{4}x^2$.

(d) (2, −1, 6) satisfies $xy = -2$ and $y = -\tfrac{1}{4}x^2$; (b) and (c) show that it is a saddle point.

AB is a gulley, dropping as one goes from *A* towards *B*. *CDE* is a ridge, dropping from *C* to *D* then rising as one proceeds towards *E*. *FDG* is a gulley, rising from *F* to *D* then dropping from *D* to *G*.

Miscellaneous exercise 12

1 $-2z\dfrac{\partial z}{\partial x} = 5 \Rightarrow \dfrac{\partial z}{\partial x} = -\tfrac{1}{2}$ at *P*. Similarly, $\dfrac{\partial z}{\partial y} = -\tfrac{1}{2}$ and the tangent to S_1 is $z = -\tfrac{1}{2}x - \tfrac{1}{2}y + 6\tfrac{1}{2}$. The tangent plane to S_2 at *P* is $z = 4x + 2y - 5$. The direction of the intersection curve *C* at *P* is perpendicular to both normal vectors.

$\begin{bmatrix} \frac{1}{2} \\ \frac{1}{2} \\ 1 \end{bmatrix}$ and $\begin{bmatrix} 4 \\ 2 \\ -1 \end{bmatrix}$. It is given by $\begin{bmatrix} 5 \\ -9 \\ 2 \end{bmatrix}$.

2 $f(x, y) = x^2 y + 2$

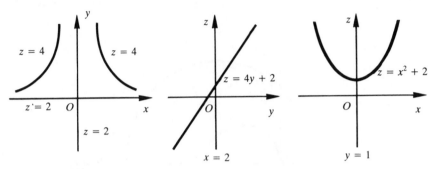

3 $\left.\begin{array}{l} 1010 = 1005 + \alpha + \beta \\ 995 = 1005 - \alpha + 2\beta \end{array}\right\} \Rightarrow \alpha = 6\frac{2}{3}$ and $\beta = -1\frac{2}{3}$, and hence $\dfrac{\partial p}{\partial x} = 6\frac{2}{3}$ and

$\dfrac{\partial p}{\partial y} = -1\frac{2}{3}$ at O. Isobars are parallel to $4x - y = 0$ and the pressure is greatest

(on $x^2 + y^2 = 4$) at $\left(\dfrac{8}{\sqrt{17}}, -\dfrac{2}{\sqrt{17}} \right)$.

4 From the diagram, it is clearly impossible to choose a value for $f(0, 0)$ to make the function continuous.

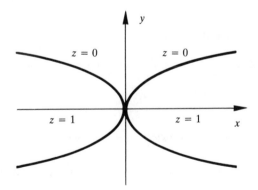

5 $x^2 + y^2 - x = 0 \implies r^2 = r\cos\theta \implies r = 0$ or $r = \cos\theta$. But $r = \cos\theta$ already includes the origin, so all points are given by $r = \cos\theta$.

$$f(x, y) = 1 \implies r = \cos\theta + 1.$$

$f(x, y) \to 1$ as one approaches the origin along the cardioid, but 0 as one approaches along the circle.

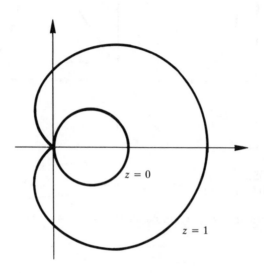

$z = 0$

$z = 1$

6 $-\sin A \dfrac{\partial A}{\partial a} = -\dfrac{2a}{2bc}$; $-\sin A \dfrac{\partial A}{\partial b} = \dfrac{1}{2c} - \dfrac{c^2 - a^2}{2b^2 c}$; $\delta A \approx \dfrac{\partial A}{\partial a}\,\delta a + \dfrac{\partial A}{\partial b}\,\delta b$.

For the triangle specified, $\dfrac{\partial A}{\partial a} = \tfrac{5}{12}$, $\dfrac{\partial A}{\partial b} = -\tfrac{1}{4}$.

If $\delta a = \pm\tfrac{1}{16}$ and $\delta b = \mp\tfrac{1}{16}$, $\delta A \approx \tfrac{8}{12} \times \tfrac{1}{16}$ radians $= \pm\tfrac{1}{24}$ radians $\approx \pm 2.4°$.

7 $d = \dfrac{l\sin\beta}{\sin(\beta - \alpha)}$ is the sine rule.

$\dfrac{\partial d}{\partial\alpha} = l\sin\beta\cot(\beta - \alpha)\operatorname{cosec}(\beta - \alpha) = 3l$ when $\alpha = \tfrac{1}{6}\pi$, $\beta = \tfrac{1}{3}\pi$,

and $\dfrac{\partial d}{\partial\beta} = l\cos\beta\operatorname{cosec}(\beta - \alpha) - l\sin\beta\cot(\beta - \alpha)\operatorname{cosec}(\beta - \alpha) = -2l$.

When $\delta\alpha = 0.01\alpha$ and $\delta\beta = -0.01\beta$, $\delta d \approx 7l\pi/600$, representing 2.1% of the value $d = l\sqrt{3}$.

8 At $(2, 1)$, $\dfrac{\partial f}{\partial x} = 3$ and $\dfrac{\partial f}{\partial y} = -3$. $f(x, y) \approx -2 + 3x - 3y$. If $f(x, y) = (\alpha x + \beta y)^\gamma$, the first equation gives $\gamma = 3$, the second equation gives $\alpha + \beta = 0$, and $f(2, 1) = 1$ gives $2\alpha + \beta = 1$. Hence $\alpha = 1$, $\beta = -1$, $\gamma = 3$.

Exercise 13A

1 (a) 20.5   (b) 105   (c) 336

2 (i) (a) $11\frac{5}{6}$. The values of z at the corners are 10, 13, 11, and 16, and at $(\frac{1}{2}, \frac{1}{2})$, $z = 11.5$. The answer is reasonable whichever method of checking is employed.

    (b) 120. In this example, the checks give 141 and 109.5, neither of them particularly reassuring!

    (c) $245\frac{1}{3}$. The simple checks are unsatisfactory here, since the surface has a minimum point where $x = 0$ and $y = 0$.

  (ii) (a) $\frac{7}{36}$ (b) $\frac{4}{9}$ (c) $2\frac{2}{15}$

4 $I = \displaystyle\int_0^2 (4x^2 - \tfrac{5}{2}x^2 + 21x)\,dx = 46.$

  (*Check*: average height × area of base = $\frac{1}{3}(21 + 29 + 19) \times 2 = 46$.)

5 The limits are y and 2.

$$I = \int_0^2 [(8 - 2y^2) - 5y(2 - y) + 21(2 - y)]\,dy$$

$$= \int_0^2 (50 - 31y + 3y^2)\,dy$$

$$= 46$$

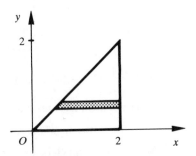

6 $I = \displaystyle\int_1^2 [(3 - y)^3 - 1 + 2y\{(3 - y)^2 - 1\} + 6y^2(3 - y - 1)]\,dy$

$$= \int_1^2 [(3 - y)^3 - 1 + 16y - 4y^3]\,dy$$

$$= \left[-\tfrac{1}{4}(3 - y)^4 - y + 8y^2 - y^4 \right]_1^2$$

$$= 11\tfrac{3}{4}.$$

(*Check*: $\frac{1}{3}(13 + 26 + 35) \times \frac{1}{2} \approx 12$; the check is only approximate because the surface is curved.)

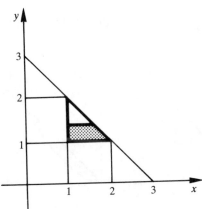

7

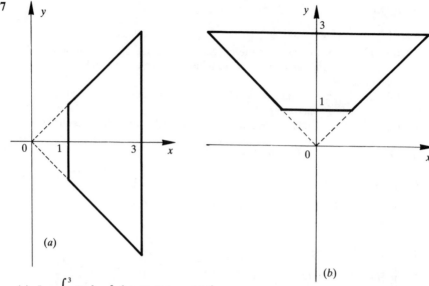

(a)

(b)

(a) $I_1 = \int_1^3 (2x^3 - \frac{2}{3}x^3 + 20x)\, dx = 106\frac{2}{3}$.

The domain has area 8 and at each vertex $z = 10$. But elsewhere in the domain, $z > 10$, so the answer is reasonable.

(b) $I_2 = 53\frac{1}{3}$, as much below 8×10 as the previous answer is above 80.

8 (a) $I = \int_0^1 \int_y^1 (x + y)\, dx\, dy = \frac{1}{2}$

(b) $\qquad I_2 = \int_0^4 \int_0^{\sqrt{y}} (x + y)\, dx\, dy = \int_0^4 (\frac{1}{2}y + y^{3/2})\, dy = 16.8$.

Also, $I_2 = \int_0^2 \int_{x^2}^4 (x + y)\, dy\, dx = \int_0^2 (4x - x^3 + 8 - \frac{1}{2}x^4)\, dx = 16.8$.

(c) $I_3 = \int_0^2 \int_0^{\sqrt{(4 - y^2)}} (x + y)\, dx\, dy = \int_0^2 \left[\frac{1}{2}(4 - y^2) + y(4 - y^2)^{1/2}\right] dy = 5\frac{1}{3}$

9

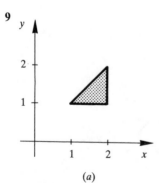

(a)

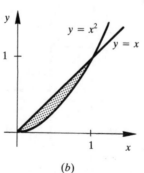

(b)

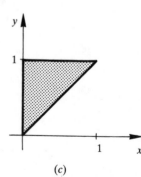

(c)

(a) $\displaystyle\int_1^2\int_y^2 z\,dx\,dy$

(b) $\displaystyle\int_0^1\int_{x^2}^x (x^2+y^2)\,dy\,dx = \int_0^1 (x^3 - x^4 + \tfrac{1}{3}x^3 - \tfrac{1}{3}x^6)\,dx = \tfrac{3}{35}$

(c) $\displaystyle\int_0^1\int_x^1 e^{-y^2}\,dy\,dx$. This cannot be evaluated, but the original form gives

$$\int_0^1 y\,e^{-y^2}\,dy = \left[-\tfrac{1}{2}e^{-y^2}\right]_0^1 = \tfrac{1}{2}(1 - e^{-1}).$$

Exercise 13B

1 $\displaystyle\int_0^{\pi/2}\int_0^1 (r\cos\theta)(r\sin\theta)r\,dr\,d\theta = \left[\tfrac{1}{4}r^4\right]_0^1 \times \left[\tfrac{1}{2}\sin^2\theta\right]_0^{\pi/2} = \tfrac{1}{8}$

2 The domain is triangle OAB; $OP = OC\sec(\theta - \tfrac{1}{4}\pi) = 1/\sqrt{2}\sec(\theta - \tfrac{1}{4}\pi)$.

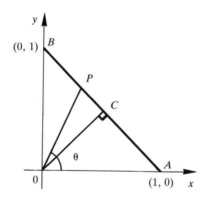

The integral equals

$$\int_0^{\pi/2}\int_0^{1/\sqrt{2}\sec(\theta - \pi/4)} \frac{1}{r} \times r\,dr\,d\theta = \int_0^{\pi/2} \frac{1}{\sqrt{2}}\sec(\theta - \tfrac{1}{4}\pi)\,d\theta$$

$$= \frac{1}{\sqrt{2}}\left[\ln((\sec(\theta - \tfrac{1}{4}\pi) + \tan(\theta - \tfrac{1}{4}\pi))\right]_0^{\pi/2}$$

$$= \frac{1}{\sqrt{2}}(\ln(\sqrt{2}+1) - \ln(\sqrt{2}-1))$$

3   Using polar coordinates as shown,

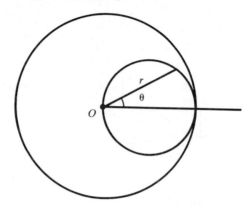

$$V = \int_{-\pi/2}^{\pi/2} \int_0^{a\cos\theta} \sqrt{(a^2 - r^2)}\, r\, dr\, d\theta$$

$$= 2 \int_0^{\pi/2} \left[-\tfrac{1}{3}(a^2 - r^2)^{3/2} \right]_0^{a\cos\theta} d\theta$$

$$= 2 \int_0^{\pi/2} (\tfrac{1}{3}a^3 - \tfrac{1}{3}a^3 \sin^3\theta)\, d\theta$$

$$= \tfrac{1}{3}a^3\pi - \tfrac{4}{9}a^3 \int_0^{\pi/2} \sin\theta\, d\theta \quad \text{(using the reduction formula)}$$

$$= \tfrac{1}{3}a^3\pi - \tfrac{4}{9}a^3.$$

The original limits are kept; one must be careful to note that

$$(a^2 \sin^2\theta)^{3/2} = a^3 \sin^3\theta \text{ when } \theta > 0 \quad \text{and} \quad -a^3 \sin^3\theta \text{ when } \theta < 0.$$

4 (a)
$$\int_0^1 \int_0^{\sqrt{(1-y^2)}} (x + 2y)\, dx\, dy = \int_0^1 (\tfrac{1}{2}(1 - y^2) + 2y\sqrt{(1 - y^2)})\, dy$$

$$= \left[\tfrac{1}{2}y - \tfrac{1}{6}y^3 - \tfrac{2}{3}(1 - y^2)^{3/2} \right]_0^1 = 1$$

or
$$\int_0^{\pi/2} \int_0^1 (r\cos\theta + 2r\sin\theta)r\, dr\, d\theta = \left[\tfrac{1}{3}r^3 \right]_0^1 \times \left[\sin\theta - 2\cos\theta \right]_0^{\pi/2}$$

$$= \tfrac{1}{3} \times 3 = 1$$

(b)
$$\int_0^1 \int_0^{\sqrt{(1-y^2)}} x\sqrt{y}\, dx\, dy = \int_0^1 \tfrac{1}{2}(y^{1/2} - y^{5/2})\, dy = \tfrac{1}{3} - \tfrac{1}{7} = \tfrac{4}{21}$$

or
$$\int_0^{\pi/2} \int_0^1 r^{3/2} \cos\theta \sqrt{(\sin\theta)} \times r\, dr\, d\theta = \left[\tfrac{2}{7}r^{7/2} \right]_0^1 \times \left[\tfrac{2}{3}(\sin\theta)^{3/2} \right]_0^{\pi/2} = \tfrac{4}{21}$$

(c) The Cartesian form is unsuitable, but

$$\int_0^{\pi/2} \int_0^1 \frac{1}{\sqrt{(r^2 + 1)}}\, r\, dr\, d\theta = \left[\sqrt{(r^2 + 1)} \right]_0^1 \times \left[\theta \right]_0^{\pi/2} = \tfrac{1}{2}\pi(\sqrt{2} - 1).$$

(d) $\int_0^{\pi/2} \int_0^1 (1 - r)r\, dr\, d\theta = \tfrac{1}{12}\pi$

5   The Cartesian equation of the sphere, $x^2 + y^2 + z^2 = a^2$, gives $z = \sqrt{(a^2 - r^2)}$ for the top half when $r^2 = x^2 + y^2$. The integral follows.

$$V = 2\pi \left[-\tfrac{1}{3}(a^2 - r^2)^{3/2} - \tfrac{1}{2}br^2 \right]_0^{\sqrt{(a^2 - b^2)}} = 2\pi \left(-\tfrac{1}{3}b^3 + \tfrac{1}{3}a^3 - \tfrac{1}{2}a^2b + \tfrac{1}{2}b^3 \right)$$

$$= \tfrac{2}{3}\pi \, (2a^3 - 3a^2b + b^3)$$
$$= \tfrac{1}{3}\pi \, (a - b)(2a^2 - 2ab - b^2)$$
$$= \tfrac{1}{3}\pi \, (a - b)^2 \, (2a + b).$$

Simple checks arise from replacing b by 0 and a by $-a$. Taking thin discs perpendicular to the z–axis gives

$$V = \int_b^a \pi \, (a^2 - z^2) \, \mathrm{d}z = \tfrac{1}{3}\pi \, (2a^3 - 3a^2b + b^3).$$

Exercise 13C

1 (a) $\displaystyle\int_0^{100}\int_0^{100} (x + 2y) \, \mathrm{d}x \, \mathrm{d}y = \int_0^{100} (\tfrac{1}{2} \times 10^4 + 2 \times 10^2 y) \, \mathrm{d}y = \tfrac{3}{2} \times 10^6$

(b) $\displaystyle k \int_0^{100}\int_0^{100 - y} (x + 2y) \, \mathrm{d}x \, \mathrm{d}y = k \int_0^{100} (\tfrac{1}{2}(100 - y)^2 + 200y - 2y^2) \, \mathrm{d}y$

$$= k \left[-\tfrac{1}{6}(100 - y)^3 + 100y^2 - \tfrac{2}{3}y^3 \right]_0^{100} = \tfrac{1}{3}$$

(c) We get $k \times 10^8 [\tfrac{1}{3} + \tfrac{3}{4} + \tfrac{2}{3}] = \tfrac{700}{6}$

For parts (a) and (b), and also for the first three parts of question 2, the answers may be obtained easily from (base area) × (average height).

2 (a) 0.147   (b) 0.107   (c) 0.171   (d) 0.197   (e) 55.6   (f) 61.1   (g) 5.5

Note that $E(X + Y) = E(X) + E(Y)$ and $E(Y - X) = E(Y) - E(X)$.

3 $k = 7.2 \times 10^{-13}$, $P(X < 20) = 0.104$, $P(50 < Y < 60) = 0.163$

4 $\displaystyle E(X + Y) = \iint (x + y) \, \phi(x, y) \, \mathrm{d}x \, \mathrm{d}y$

$$= \iint x \, \phi(x, y) \, \mathrm{d}x \, \mathrm{d}y + \iint y \, \phi(x, y) \, \mathrm{d}x \, \mathrm{d}y = E(X) + E(Y)$$

5   This follows from the fact that

$$P(x < X < x + \delta x \text{ and } y < Y < y + \delta y) = P(x < X < x + \delta x) \times P(y < Y < y + \delta y).$$

$$E(XY) = \iint xy \, f(x) \, g(y) \, \mathrm{d}x \, \mathrm{d}y$$

$$= \int x \, f(x) \, \mathrm{d}x \times \int y \, g(y) \, \mathrm{d}y = mn.$$

6   The probability is

$$\frac{1}{2\pi} \iint e^{-x^2/2} \times e^{-y^2/2} \, \mathrm{d}x \, \mathrm{d}y \quad \text{over the domain}$$

$$= \frac{1}{2\pi} \int_0^{2\pi}\int_0^a e^{-r^2/2} \times r \, \mathrm{d}r \, \mathrm{d}\theta = 1 - e^{-a^2/2}$$

$$\to 1 \quad \text{as } a \to \infty$$

Miscellaneous exercise 13

1 $\displaystyle\int_0^1 \int_{-y}^{3y} (x + y)^{1/2}\, dx\, dy = \int_0^1 \tfrac{2}{3}(4y)^{3/2}\, dy = \tfrac{16}{3}\int_0^1 y^{3/2}\, dy = \tfrac{32}{15}$

2 $\displaystyle\int_0^a \int_{-y/\sqrt3}^{y/\sqrt3} x^2 y^3\, dx\, dy = \int_0^a \frac{2}{9\sqrt3} y^6\, dy = \frac{2a^7}{63\sqrt3};\quad \iint x^3 y^2\, dx\, dy = 0$

3 $\displaystyle I = \int_0^4 \int_x^{2\sqrt x} \frac{y}{\{(4 - x)(4x - y^2)\}^{1/2}}\, dy\, dx$

$\displaystyle = \int_0^4 \frac{1}{(4 - x)^{1/2}}\left[-(4x - y^2)^{1/2}\right]_x^{2\sqrt x}\, dx$

$\displaystyle = \int_0^4 x^{1/2}\, dx = \tfrac{16}{3}$

4 $g(x) = -1 + \sqrt{(x^2 + 1)};$

$\displaystyle I = \int_0^1 \frac{1}{x}\left[-\left(\frac{1}{y + 1}\right)\right]_0^{g(x)}\, dx$

$\displaystyle = \int_0^1 \left(\frac{1}{x} - \frac{1}{x\sqrt{(x^2 + 1)}}\right)\, dx$

$\displaystyle = \lim_{a \to 0}\left[\ln x - \ln\{x/(1 + \sqrt{(1 + x^2)})\}\right]_a^1$

$\displaystyle = \lim_{a \to 0}\left[\ln(1 + \sqrt{(1 + x^2)})\right]_a^1$

$= \ln(1 + \sqrt2) - \ln 2$

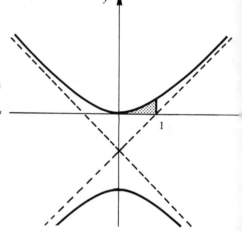

5 $\displaystyle\iint dx\, dy = \tfrac{8}{3}a^2;\quad \iint y\, dx\, dy = \tfrac{32}{15}a^3;$

$\displaystyle\iint y^2\, dy\, dx = \int_{-a}^a \left[\tfrac{1}{3}y^3\right]_0^{2(a^2 - x^2)/a}\, dx$

$\displaystyle = 2 \times \frac{1}{3} \times \frac{8}{a^3}\int_0^a (a^6 - 3a^4 x^2 + 3a^2 x^4 - x^6)\, dx$

$\displaystyle = \tfrac{256}{105}a^4;$

$\displaystyle F = \iint \rho g(L - y)\, dx\, dy = \rho g L \times \tfrac{8}{3}a^2 - \rho g \times \tfrac{32}{15}a^3 = \tfrac{8}{15}\rho g a^2(5L - 4a);$

$\displaystyle M = \rho g L \times \tfrac{32}{15}a^3 - \rho g \times \tfrac{256}{105}a^4 = \tfrac{32}{105}\rho g a^3(7L - 8a)$

6 (a) $\displaystyle F = \int_0^b \int_0^{ay/b} \rho y\, dx\, dy = \tfrac{1}{3}\rho a b^2$

(b) $F = 2 \displaystyle\int_0^{\pi/2} \int_0^{a(1+\cos\theta)} \rho r \cos\theta \times r \, dr \, d\theta$

$= \tfrac{2}{3}\rho a^3 \displaystyle\int_0^{\pi/2} \cos\theta(1+\cos\theta)^3 \, d\theta$

$= \tfrac{2}{3}\rho a^3 \displaystyle\int_0^{\pi/2} \cos\theta + 3\cos^2\theta + 3\cos^3\theta + \cos^4\theta \, d\theta$

$= \tfrac{2}{3}\rho a^3 \left(1 + \dfrac{3}{2} \times \dfrac{\pi}{2} + 3 \times \dfrac{2}{3} + \dfrac{3}{4} \times \dfrac{1}{2} \times \dfrac{\pi}{2}\right) = \rho a^3(2 + \tfrac{5}{8}\pi)$

Exercise 14A

1 (a) $\left.\begin{array}{l} u = 4 - y^2 \\ v = 4y \end{array}\right\}$ $\Rightarrow$ $u = 4 - \tfrac{1}{16}v^2$ (b) $\left.\begin{array}{l} u = x^2 - 16 \\ v = 8x \end{array}\right\}$ $\Rightarrow$ $u = \tfrac{1}{64}v^2 - 16$

   (c) $\left.\begin{array}{l} u = x^2 - 9 \\ v = 6x \end{array}\right\}$ $\Rightarrow$ $u = \tfrac{1}{36}v^2 - 9$

2 (a) For the first parabola, $\dfrac{du}{dv} = -\tfrac{1}{2}v = -3$ when $v = 6$; for the second,

   $\dfrac{du}{dv} = \tfrac{1}{18}v = \tfrac{1}{3}$ when $v = 6$. The gradients of $A'B'C'$ and $B'E'$ are $-\tfrac{1}{3}$ and 3 at B',
   so the curves cross at right angles.

   (b) The gradients of $B'C'$ and $C'D'$ at C' are $-\tfrac{1}{4}$ and 4; the gradients of $D'E'$ and
   $B'E'$ at E' are $-\tfrac{2}{3}$ and $\tfrac{3}{2}$. In both cases, the image curves cross at right angles.

3 $u = x^2 - y^2 = x^2 - (x+2)^2 = -4x - 4$; $v = 2xy = 2x(x+2) = 2x^2 + 4x$.

   $\dfrac{du}{dx} = -4$ and $\dfrac{dv}{dx} = 8$ when $x = 1$, so $\begin{bmatrix} -4 \\ 8 \end{bmatrix}$ is a tangent vector. $\begin{bmatrix} -1 \\ 2 \end{bmatrix}$ is a simpler
   tangent vector.

   $\begin{bmatrix} -1 \\ 2 \end{bmatrix} \cdot \begin{bmatrix} 1 \\ 3 \end{bmatrix} = \sqrt5 \times \sqrt{10} \times \cos\theta = -1 + 6 = 5$ $\Rightarrow$ $\cos\theta = \dfrac{1}{\sqrt2}$

   $\Rightarrow$ $\theta = 45°$.

   The angle DBE has been preserved by the transformation.

4 Tangent vectors are $\begin{bmatrix} -2 \\ 1 \end{bmatrix}$, $\begin{bmatrix} -1 \\ 3 \end{bmatrix}$ and $\begin{bmatrix} 1 \\ 2 \end{bmatrix}$ at D'. The angle between $\begin{bmatrix} -2 \\ 1 \end{bmatrix}$ and

   $\begin{bmatrix} -1 \\ 3 \end{bmatrix}$, and that between $\begin{bmatrix} -1 \\ 3 \end{bmatrix}$ and $\begin{bmatrix} 1 \\ 2 \end{bmatrix}$, are both 45°

5 A: $1 + j \mapsto 6 - 6j$
   B: $1 + 3j \mapsto 1.2 - 3.6j$
   C: $1 + 4j \mapsto 0.71 - 2.82j$
   D: $2 + 4j \mapsto 1.2 - 2.4j$
   E: $2 + 3j \mapsto 1.85 - 2.77j$

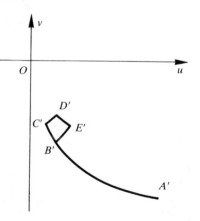

For $A'B'C'$, $u = \dfrac{12}{1 + y^2}$, $v = \dfrac{-12y}{1 + y^2}$, and a tangent vector is $\begin{bmatrix} -8 \\ 15 \end{bmatrix}$ when $y = 4$.

For $C'D'$, $u = \dfrac{12x}{x^2 + 16}$, $v = \dfrac{-48}{x^2 + 16}$, and a tangent vector is $\begin{bmatrix} 15 \\ 8 \end{bmatrix}$ when $x = 1$.

These are perpendicular vectors.

6

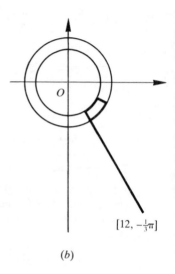

$[12, -\tfrac{1}{3}\pi]$

(b)

7 (a)

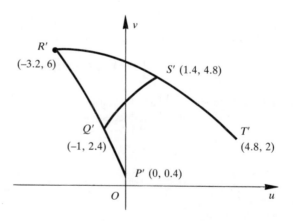

(b) $u = \tfrac{1}{5}(x^2 - y^2) = \tfrac{1}{5}(x^2 - (2x - 1)^2) = \tfrac{1}{5}(-3x^2 + 4x - 1)$;
$v = \tfrac{1}{5}(2xy) \quad = \tfrac{1}{5}(4x^2 - 2x)$

(c) $\begin{bmatrix} \dfrac{du}{dx} \\ \dfrac{dv}{dx} \end{bmatrix} = \begin{bmatrix} \tfrac{1}{5}(-6x + 4) \\ \tfrac{1}{5}(8x - 2) \end{bmatrix} = \begin{bmatrix} -\tfrac{8}{5} \\ \tfrac{14}{5} \end{bmatrix} = +\tfrac{2}{5}\begin{bmatrix} -4 \\ 7 \end{bmatrix}$ when $x = 2$.

For the image of QS, $u = \frac{1}{3}(x^2 - 9)$, $v = \frac{1}{3}(6x)$, and the tangent vector

$$\begin{bmatrix} \dfrac{du}{dx} \\[2mm] \dfrac{dv}{dx} \end{bmatrix} = \begin{bmatrix} \frac{2}{3}x \\[1mm] \frac{6}{3} \end{bmatrix} = \frac{2}{3}\begin{bmatrix} 2 \\ 3 \end{bmatrix} \quad \text{when } x = 2.$$

(d) $\alpha = \tan^{-1} 2 = \cos^{-1}(1/\sqrt{5})$, while the angle between $\begin{bmatrix} -4 \\ 7 \end{bmatrix}$ and $\begin{bmatrix} 2 \\ 3 \end{bmatrix}$ is given by

$\sqrt{(4^2 + 7^2)} \times \sqrt{(2^2 + 3^2)} \cos\theta = -8 + 21 \Rightarrow \cos\theta = 1/\sqrt{5}$. Hence $\alpha = \theta$.

8   P'' is $(0.4, 0.8)$, Q'' is $(-0.2, 3.6)$, R'' is $(-2, 8)$, S'' is $(3, 6)$ and T'' is $(6.8, 2.4)$. Again we find that angles are preserved by the transformation.

Exercise 14B

1   $f'(z) = -12/z^2$ so $f'(1 + j) = 6j = [6, \frac{1}{2}\pi]$. In the neighbourhood of the base of the flagpole there has been an enlargement $\times 6$ and a rotation through a right angle.

$f'(1 + 3j) = \frac{24}{25} + \frac{18}{25}j = [1.2, \tan^{-1}\frac{3}{4}]; \quad f'(2 + 4j) = \frac{9}{25} + \frac{12}{25}j = [0.6, \tan^{-1}\frac{4}{3}].$

These are consistent with Figure 7.

2   (a) $f'(z) = 2z - 6$, and $f'(6 + 4j) = 6 + 8j$. The local enlargement factor is $|6 + 8j| = 10$, so the image of the lantern has area approximately $2 \times 10^2 = 200$ units.

(b) $f'(6 + 4j) = \dfrac{-5 + 38j}{26}$, which has modulus 1.47.

The area of $A'B'C'D' \approx 4.34$ units.

3   $f'(1 + j) = \dfrac{1-j}{2}; \quad f'(1 + j) = \frac{1}{2}j.$ If $ABCD$ is small, each length is approximately halved and the whole region is approximately rotated through a right angle.

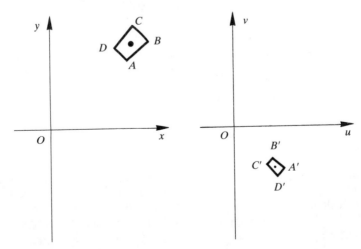

4   (a) $(x + yj) \mapsto 2(x + yj) + (x - yj) = 3x + yj$; this is a $\times 3$ stretch in the x-direction.

(b) $(x + yj) \mapsto 3(x + yj) + (x - yj) = 4x + 2yj$; this is a $\times 4$ stretch in the x-direction together with a $\times 2$ stretch in the y-direction.

Neither stretch preserves angles, so neither function is differentiable.

5 $f(z) = e^z \Rightarrow f(x + yj) = e^{x+yj} = e^x \times e^{yj} = e^x (\cos y + j \sin y)$.
Hence $u = e^x \cos y$, $v = e^x \sin y$.

$x = 1 \Rightarrow u^2 + v^2 = e^2$, a circle of radius e.
$y = 1 \Rightarrow v/u = \tan 1$, a line through the origin; but $e^x > 0$ for all x, so the image is only the part of this line in the first quadrant.

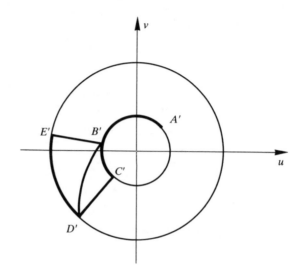

6

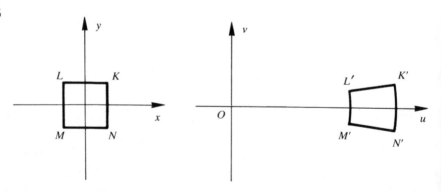

The images of KN and LM are arcs of radius e^b and e^{-b}. The difference between these radii is approximately $2b$ if b is small. The images of KL and MN are segments of lines through the origin at angles of $\pm b$ radians to the x-axis. Hence the areas $L'M'$ and $K'N'$ both have length approximately $2b$. $f'(0) = 1$ since the small square has been neither enlarged nor rotated.

$$\frac{f(a + h) - f(a)}{h} = e^a \left(\frac{e^h - 1}{h} \right).$$

Now for any complex number h, e^h is defined as the sum to infinity of the series

$1 + h + \dfrac{h^2}{2!} + \dfrac{h^3}{3!} + \ldots$, and it follows that $\dfrac{e^h - 1}{h}$ is the sum to infinity of

$S = 1 + \dfrac{h}{2!} + \dfrac{h^2}{3!} + \ldots$, this series certainly being convergent. As h tends to 0,

S tends to 1, and hence $f(z) = e^z \Rightarrow f'(a) = e^a$.

7   Working from first principles,

$$f(b) - f(a) = \frac{b - 2j}{jb + 1} - \frac{a - 2j}{ja + 1}$$

$$= \frac{(b - 2j)(ja + 1) - (a - 2j)(jb + 1)}{(jb + 1)(ja + 1)} = \frac{-(b - a)}{(jb + 1)(ja + 1)}.$$

$$\lim_{b \to a} \left(\frac{f(b) - f(a)}{b - a} \right) = \lim_{b \to a} \left(\frac{-1}{(jb + 1)(ja + 1)} \right) = \frac{-1}{(ja + 1)^2}.$$

The product and quotient rules may be used, but first one should make quite sure they are appropriate for functions of a complex variable. The proofs are identical to those for real functions.

8   Each complex number has two distinct square roots. To make $z \mapsto z^{1/2}$ a one-to-one transformation, the codomain must be restricted. The suggestion here gives one possible way to do this.

$$(x + yj)^{1/2} = u + vj \implies x + yj = (u + vj)^2$$
$$\implies \left. \begin{array}{l} x = u^2 - v^2 \\ y = 2uv \end{array} \right\}$$

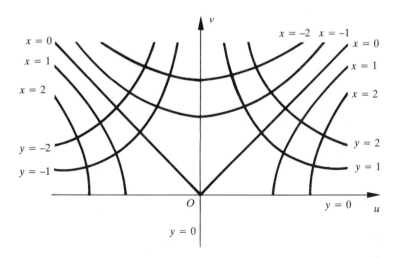

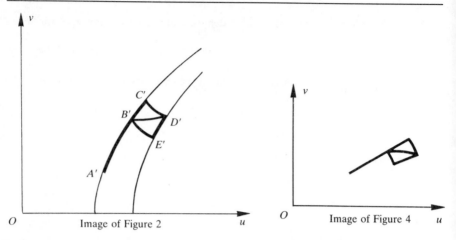

Image of Figure 2 · Image of Figure 4

9 Some are; some are not. Look first to see whether the meridians and lines of latitude cross at right angles. This is not sufficient evidence. Mercator's projection, for example, is a conformal transformation, but to achieve this the lines of latitude must be drawn further and further apart as one goes away from the equator, since two meridians on a globe get closer as one approaches a pole. This map, and any other conformal representation of a spherical surface on a plane, has a variable scale.

Exercise 14C

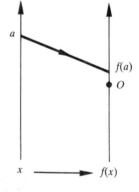

1 We wish to find a point on the left-hand number line (the domain) mapping onto O. Given a number a such that $f(a) \approx 0$, we can obtain a better answer by using $f'(a)$, the local scale factor of the variable stretch which transforms one number line onto the other. For a small displacement $-f(a)$ in the codomain is approximately effected by a displacement $-f(a)/f'(a)$ in the domain. Our next approximation is consequently

$$a - \frac{f(a)}{f'(a)}.$$

2 The Newton–Raphson process for real numbers breaks down if $f'(a) = 0$. It is less effective if the second derivative is large near the solution point. If the graph of the function is as shown below, a bad choice of starting value (e.g. b) can lead to an infinite oscillation.

One should be on the look out for similar difficulties when using the process with complex numbers.

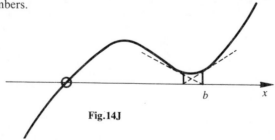

Fig. 14J

3 $f(3 + 5j) = -4; f'(3 + 5j) = -50 + 90j$; the second approximation is

$$(3 + 5j) - \left(\frac{-4}{-50 + 90j}\right) = 2.981 + 4.966j.$$

4 $f(2 - j) = 2 + 4j; f'(2 - j) = 19 + 8j$; the second approximation is $1.84 - 1.14j$.

5 With the equation of question 4,

$$f(a + bj) = (a^3 - 3ab^2 - 10ab - 20) + (3a^2b - b^3 + 5a^2 - 5b^2)j;$$

$$f'(a + bj) = (3a^2 - 3b^2 - 10b) + (6ab + 10a)j.$$

The important computer instructions are
```
C = A ↑ 3 − 3*A*B*B − 10*A*B − 20
D = 3*A*A*B − B ↑ 3 + 5*A*A − 5*B*B
E = 3*A*A − 3*B*B − 10*B
F = 6*A*B + 10*A
A = A − (C*E + D*F)/(E*E + F*F)
B = B − (D*E − C*F)/(E*E + F*F)
```

Repeated application of the process starting with $(2 - j)$ gives a solution $1.832\,85 - 1.156\,55j$. With different starting values we soon obtain the other solutions $-1.130\,76 + 1.349\,91j$ and $-0.702\,09 - 5.193\,36j$.

6 $|f(z)| > |z^3| - |3 + j| \times |z| - |8 + 4j|$
$\qquad = 27 - 3\sqrt{10} - \sqrt{80}$ when $|z| = 3$
$\qquad > 27 - 10 - 9$
$\qquad = 8.$

Similar arguments show that $|f(z)| > 0$ if $|z| > 3$. All the solutions of $f(z) = 0$ must therefore lie within the circle $|z| = 3$.

The values of $f(z)$ are shown below.

✖	✖	✖	✖	✖
$32 + 16j$	$24 - 3j$	$10 - 10j$	$-4 - 5j$	$-12 + 12j$
✖	✖	✖	✖	✖
$13 + 14j$	$14 + 4j$	$9 + 0j$	$4 + 2j$	$5 + 10j$
✖	✖	✖	✖	✖
$6 + 6j$	$10 + 5j$	$8 + 4j$	$6 + 3j$	$10 + 2j$
✖	✖	✖	✖	✖
$11 - 2j$	$12 + 6j$	$7 + 8j$	$2 + 4j$	$3 - 6j$
✖	✖	✖	✖	✖
$28 - 4j$	$20 + 13j$	$6 + 18j$	$-8 + 11j$	$-16 - 8j$

Suitable starting values for the Newton–Raphson process are $1 + j$, $1 - j$ and -2. The solutions (to 5 DP) are

$$1.070\,69 + 1.532\,97j, \quad 1.473\,42 - 1.130\,39j \quad \text{and} \quad -2.544\,11 - 0.402\,58j.$$

Note that the sum of the roots is zero, as the coefficient of z^2 in the equation is zero.

Miscellaneous exercise 14

1   $z^4 + jz = z \quad \Rightarrow \quad z = 0$ or $z^3 = 1 - j = [\sqrt{2}, -\frac{1}{4}\pi]$

$\Rightarrow \quad z = 0$ or $z = [2^{1/6}, -\frac{1}{12}\pi]$ or $z = [2^{1/6}, \frac{7}{12}\pi]$ or $z = [2^{1/6}, -\frac{9}{12}\pi]$

$\Rightarrow \quad z = 0$ or $z = 1.08 - 0.29j$ or $z = -0.29 + 1.08j$ or

$$z = -0.79 - 0.79j$$

2   $az + cz^* = (\alpha + j\beta)(x + jy) + (\gamma + j\delta)(x - jy)$

$$\Rightarrow \quad \mathbf{A} = \begin{bmatrix} \alpha + \gamma & -\beta + \delta \\ \beta + \delta & \alpha - \gamma \end{bmatrix}.$$

T has an inverse if and only if det $\mathbf{A} \neq 0$, i.e. $\alpha^2 - \gamma^2 + \beta^2 - \delta^2 \neq 0$.

But $|a| \neq |c| \quad \Leftrightarrow \quad (\alpha^2 + \beta^2) \neq (\gamma^2 + \delta^2) \quad \Leftrightarrow \quad \alpha^2 - \gamma^2 + \beta^2 - \delta^2 \neq 0.$

3   $\arg\left(\dfrac{z_3 - z_1}{z_3 - z_2}\right) = \arg(z_3 - z_1) - \arg(z_3 - z_2)$

$= $ angle of rotation from P_2P_3 to P_1P_3.

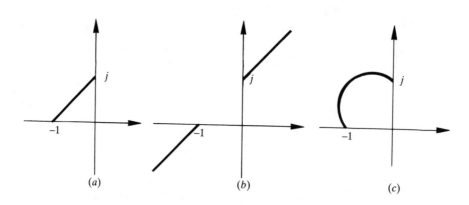

(a) $\qquad\qquad\qquad\qquad$ (b) $\qquad\qquad\qquad\qquad$ (c)

4 (a) $|w| = 1 \iff |z + j| = |z - 1|$
   (b) $|w| = 2$ is an Apollonius circle.
   (c) The locus is a semi-circle.

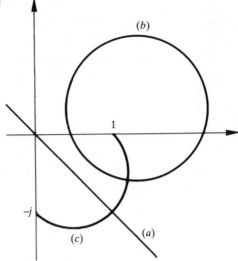

(b)

1

$-j$

(c)   (a)

5 $z = e^{u + vj} = e^u (\cos v + j \sin v) \implies |z| = e^u;$ $\arg z = v - 2n\pi.$
   $z = 1 + jt \implies u = \frac{1}{2} \ln(1 + t^2),$ $v = \tan^{-1} t.$
   When $t = 0$, $u = 0$ and $v = 0$; when $t = 1$, $u = 0.35$ and $v = 0.79$; when t is large and
   positive, $v \approx \frac{1}{2}\pi$; when t is small, $u \approx \frac{1}{2}t^2$ and $v \approx t.$

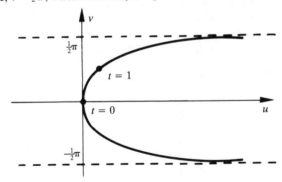

v

$\frac{1}{2}\pi$

$t = 1$

$t = 0$ u

$-\frac{1}{2}\pi$

6

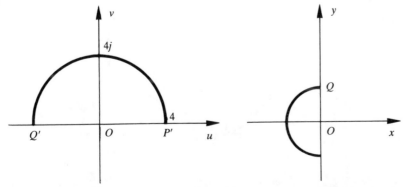

v

$4j$

Q' O P' u

y

Q

O x

7 $|z - 1 - j| = 1$ is a circle centre $(1, 1)$, radius 1.

$$z \mapsto jz^* \Leftrightarrow x + yj \mapsto j(x - yj) = y + xj \Leftrightarrow \text{reflection in } y = x.$$

Hence $z \mapsto jz^* - 1$ maps W onto the circle centre $(0, 1)$, radius 1. Since $(f(z))^* = -jz - 1$, then $g(z) = 1/(f(z))^*$, and we require an inversion with centre the origin, giving as image the line $y = \frac{1}{2}$.

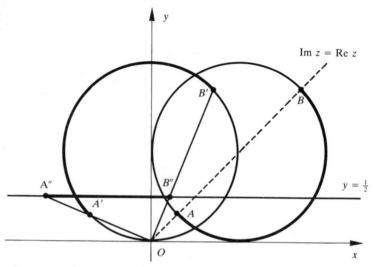

A'' is the point of $y = \frac{1}{2}$ on OA' produced, while B'' is the point on OB'. The final image of the required half of W is the line segment $A''B''$. As a check, we can show that $g(1) = -\frac{1}{2} + \frac{1}{2}j$ and $g(2 + j) = \frac{1}{2}j$.

8 $\arg\left(\dfrac{z_1 - z}{z_2 - z}\right)$ is the angle of rotation from PP_2 to PP_1. If P_2 represents 1 and P_1 $3 + j\sqrt{3}$, then the locus of P is an arc of a circle through P_1 and P_2. This includes 0 since $z = 0$ satisfies the equation.

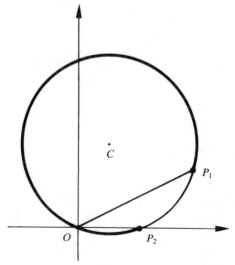

The centre C lies on the perpendicular bisectors of OP_1 and OP_2. Now $j(3 + j\sqrt{3})$ corresponds to a vector at right angles to OP_1, so the parametric equation given is indeed the perpendicular bisector of OP_2. Re $z = \frac{1}{2}$ when $t = \frac{1}{3}\sqrt{3}$, $z = \frac{1}{2} + \frac{3}{2}\sqrt{3}j$. Hence C is $(\frac{1}{2}, \frac{3}{2}\sqrt{3})$ and the radius $= OC = \sqrt{7}$.

9 $\text{Im}(e^z) = e^x \sin y$; $\text{Re}(e^{-z}) = e^{-x} \cos y$; $\text{Im}(e^{-z}) = -e^{-x} \sin y$
All of these repeat every time y increases by 2π, so $\sinh z$ has period $2\pi j$.

$\text{Re}(\sinh z) = \frac{1}{2}(e^x \cos y - e^{-x} \cos y) = \sinh x \cos y$,
and similarly $\text{Im}(\sinh z) = \cosh x \sin y$.

$\text{Im}(z) = \frac{1}{4}\pi$ $\Rightarrow$ $\cos y = \sin y = \frac{1}{2}\sqrt{2}$ $\Rightarrow$ $v^2 - u^2 = \frac{1}{2}(\cosh^2 x - \sinh^2 x) = \frac{1}{2}$
$\text{Re}(z) = 1$ $\Rightarrow$ $(u/\sinh 1)^2 + (v/\cosh 1)^2 = 1$.

The ellipse and hyperbola intersect at right angles because the transformation is conformal.

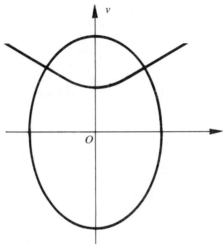

10 $u = e^x \cos y$; $v = e^x \sin y$;
$\dot{u}^2 + \dot{v}^2 = (e^x \dot{x} \cos y - e^x \dot{y} \sin y)^2 + (e^x \dot{x} \sin y + e^x \dot{y} \cos y)^2$
$= e^{2x} (\dot{x}^2 + \dot{y}^2)$.

Hence length of $C' = \displaystyle\int e^x (\dot{x}^2 + \dot{y}^2)^{1/2}\, dt$ between appropriate limits

$= \displaystyle\int_0^1 e^t \sqrt{(1 + \frac{1}{4}\pi^2)}\, dt$ in the example given

$= (e - 1)(1 + \frac{1}{4}\pi^2)$.

11

$$|z - j| = 2$$
$$\Rightarrow \quad (z - j)(z^* + j) = 2$$
$$\Rightarrow \quad zz^* + jz - jz^* - 1 = 0$$
$$\Rightarrow \quad 1 + \frac{j}{z^*} - \frac{j}{z} - \frac{1}{zz^*} = 0$$
$$\Rightarrow \quad \frac{1}{zz^*} + \frac{j}{z} - \frac{j}{z^*} - 1 = 0.$$

Hence if z lies on S, so does $1/z$.

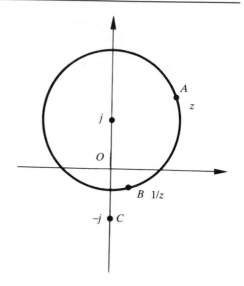

$$\frac{(1/z) + j}{z + j} = \frac{(z^* - j)(1/z + j)}{|z + j|^2} = \frac{(z^* - j)(1 + jz)}{z\,|z + j|^2}$$

$$= \frac{jzz^* + z + z^* - j}{z\,|z + j|^2} = \frac{(z - z^* + j) + z + z^* - j}{z\,|z + j|^2} = \frac{2}{|z + j|^2}$$

Hence A, B and C are collinear.

Exercise 15A

1

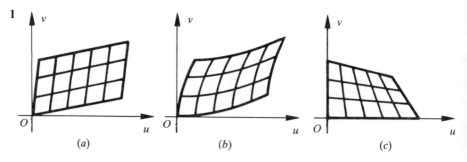

(a)   (b)   (c)

(a) At $(3, 2)$ – and elsewhere – the lines are in the directions $\begin{bmatrix} 1 \\ \frac{1}{5} \end{bmatrix}$ and $\begin{bmatrix} \frac{1}{10} \\ 1 \end{bmatrix}$.

(b) At $(3, 2)$, the tangent vectors are $\begin{bmatrix} 1 \\ \frac{3}{10} \end{bmatrix}$ and $\begin{bmatrix} \frac{4}{10} \\ 1 \end{bmatrix}$.

(c) At $(3, 2)$, the tangent vectors are $\begin{bmatrix} \frac{8}{10} \\ -\frac{1}{10} \end{bmatrix}$ and $\begin{bmatrix} -\frac{3}{10} \\ \frac{17}{20} \end{bmatrix}$.

2 $x = 5 \implies y = v - 1.25 \implies u = 5 + 0.1(v - 1.25)^2$, which represents the parabola $u = 0.1v^2$ translated by $\begin{bmatrix} 5 \\ 1.25 \end{bmatrix}$.

$y = 3 \implies x = u - 0.9 \implies v = 3 + 0.05(u - 0.9)^2$, another parabola.

3 $\begin{bmatrix} \delta x \\ \delta y \end{bmatrix} \to \begin{bmatrix} 0.9\ \delta x & -0.15\ \delta y \\ 0.2\ \delta x & +1.3\ \delta y \end{bmatrix} = \begin{bmatrix} 0.9 & -0.15 \\ 0.2 & 1.3 \end{bmatrix} \begin{bmatrix} \delta x \\ \delta y \end{bmatrix}$

For question 1, the corresponding matrices are

$\begin{bmatrix} 1 & 0.1 \\ 0.2 & 1 \end{bmatrix}, \begin{bmatrix} 1 & 0.4 \\ 0.3 & 1 \end{bmatrix}$ and $\begin{bmatrix} 0.8 & -0.3 \\ -0.1 & 0.85 \end{bmatrix}$.

4 $u = xy,\ v = y/x \implies x^2 = u/v,\ y^2 = uv \implies x = \sqrt{(u/v)},\ y = \sqrt{(uv)}$ if $x, y > 0$.

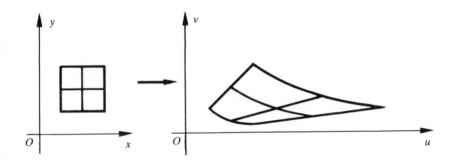

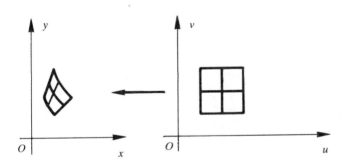

The matrices are $\begin{bmatrix} 3 & 2 \\ -\frac{3}{4} & \frac{1}{2} \end{bmatrix}$ and $\begin{bmatrix} \frac{1}{6} & -\frac{2}{3} \\ \frac{1}{4} & 1 \end{bmatrix}$. These are inverse matrices, anticipating property (2) of §2.2.

Exercise 15B

1 (a) $\begin{bmatrix} 1 & 0.1 \\ 0.2 & 1 \end{bmatrix}$ (b) $\begin{bmatrix} 1 & 0.2y \\ 0.1x & 1 \end{bmatrix}$ (c) $\begin{bmatrix} 1 - 0.1y & -0.1x \\ -0.05y & 1 - 0.05x \end{bmatrix}$

2 (a)

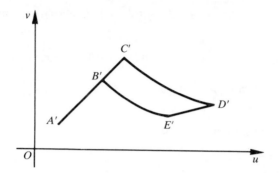

(b) $J = \begin{bmatrix} y & x \\ -y/x^2 & 1/x \end{bmatrix}$. When $x = 1$ and $y = 3$, $J = \begin{bmatrix} 3 & 1 \\ -3 & 1 \end{bmatrix}$, representing a 90°

clockwise rotation and a two-way stretch; when $x = 2$ and $y = 4$, $J = \begin{bmatrix} 4 & 2 \\ -1 & \frac{1}{2} \end{bmatrix}$.

(c) $\det J = 2y/x = 4.67$ when $x = 1.5$ and $y = 3.5$. This is the area scale factor at the centre of the flag.

(d) The image curves $C'D'$ and $B'E'$ have equations $uv = 16$ and $uv = 9$. The trapezium under $B'C'$ has area 3.5 and the trapezium under $D'E'$ has area 3.5 also.

So $\text{area } B'C'D'E' = (3.5 + \int_4^8 \frac{16}{u} \, du) - (\int_3^6 \frac{9}{u} \, du + 3.5)$

$$= 7 \ln 2$$
$$\approx 4.85.$$

This is approximately the area scale factor found in (c).

3 $J' = \begin{bmatrix} \dfrac{1}{2\sqrt{(uv)}} & -\dfrac{u}{2\sqrt{v^3}} \\ \dfrac{\sqrt{v}}{2\sqrt{u}} & \dfrac{\sqrt{u}}{2\sqrt{v}} \end{bmatrix} = \begin{bmatrix} \dfrac{1}{2y} & -\dfrac{x^2}{2y} \\ \dfrac{1}{2x} & \dfrac{x}{2} \end{bmatrix}$,

the inverse of the matrix J in question 2.

4 $J = \begin{bmatrix} 1 & 1 \\ \dfrac{\sqrt{y}}{2\sqrt{x}} & \dfrac{\sqrt{x}}{2\sqrt{y}} \end{bmatrix}$; $J' = \begin{bmatrix} \dfrac{x}{x-y} & -\dfrac{2\sqrt{(xy)}}{x-y} \\ \dfrac{-y}{x-y} & \dfrac{2\sqrt{(xy)}}{x-y} \end{bmatrix}$; $\det J = \dfrac{x-y}{2\sqrt{(xy)}}$.

On this occasion, obtaining J' as the inverse of J is considerably less complicated than obtaining x and y as functions of u and v, then differentiating to find $\dfrac{\partial(x, y)}{\partial(u, v)}$ from its definition.

5

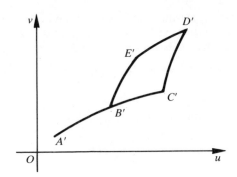

$\dfrac{\partial(u, v)}{\partial(x, y)} = \begin{bmatrix} 2x & 2y \\ 2y & 2x \end{bmatrix}$ and the determinant is $4(x^2 - y^2) = -40$ at $(1\tfrac{1}{2}, 3\tfrac{1}{2})$; the negative sign indicates that a reflection is involved. The area of $B'C'D'E'$ is approximately 40.

6   $\mathbf{J} = \begin{bmatrix} 2x & -2y \\ 2y & 2x \end{bmatrix}$, which is of the form $r\begin{bmatrix} \cos\theta & -\sin\theta \\ \sin\theta & \cos\theta \end{bmatrix}$ as expected, since the transformation is conformal. $r = \det \mathbf{J} = 4(x^2 + y^2) = 58$ when $x = 1\tfrac{1}{2}$ and $y = 3\tfrac{1}{2}$. Consequently, the area of $B'C'D'E' \approx 58$.

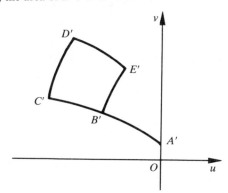

7

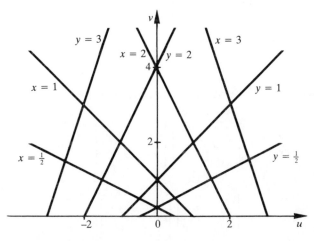

Every number pair (x, y) with $x, y > 0$ gives a point in the uv-plane with $v > 0$. It is clear from the diagram that every point for which $v > 0$ arises from some point (x, y) in the domain, and this can be proved algebraically from the following working:

$$u = x - y, \ v = xy \ \Rightarrow \ u = x - v/x \ \Rightarrow \ x^2 - ux - v = 0$$

$$\Rightarrow \qquad x = \frac{u}{2} + \sqrt{\left(\frac{u^2}{4} + v^2\right)},$$

the positive square root being taken to ensure $x > 0$.

Similarly,
$$y = -\frac{u}{2} + \sqrt{\left(\frac{u^2}{4} + v^2\right)}.$$

Since $\sqrt{\left(\dfrac{u^2}{4} + v^2\right)} > \dfrac{u}{2}$, the function is indeed one-to-one.

$$\mathbf{J} = \frac{\partial(u, v)}{\partial(x, y)} = \begin{bmatrix} 1 & -1 \\ y & x \end{bmatrix} = \begin{bmatrix} 1 & -1 \\ 1 & 1 \end{bmatrix} \quad \text{when } x = 1 \text{ and } y = 1.$$

This gives an enlargement $\times \sqrt{2}$ and rotation of $45°$ followed by a reflection in the vertical axis, which is consistent with the diagram.

When $x = 2$ and $y = 2$,

$$\mathbf{J} = \begin{bmatrix} 1 & -1 \\ 2 & 2 \end{bmatrix} \quad \text{as expected,}$$

and when $x = 1$ and $y = 2$,

$$\mathbf{J} = \begin{bmatrix} 1 & -1 \\ 2 & 1 \end{bmatrix}, \quad \text{again consistent with the diagram.}$$

Since $\det \mathbf{J} = x + y$, $\qquad \mathbf{J}' = \mathbf{J}^{-1} = \begin{bmatrix} \dfrac{x}{x+y} & \dfrac{1}{x+y} \\ -\dfrac{y}{x+y} & \dfrac{1}{x+y} \end{bmatrix},$

so $\quad \dfrac{\partial x}{\partial u} = \dfrac{x}{x+y}, \quad \dfrac{\partial x}{\partial v} = \dfrac{1}{x+y}, \quad \dfrac{\partial y}{\partial u} = -\dfrac{y}{x+y} \quad \text{and} \quad \dfrac{\partial y}{\partial v} = \dfrac{1}{x+y}.$

Now $x = \dfrac{u}{2} + \sqrt{\left(\dfrac{u^2}{4} + v^2\right)} \ \Rightarrow \ \dfrac{\partial x}{\partial u} = \dfrac{1}{2} + \dfrac{u}{4} \div \sqrt{\left(\dfrac{u^2}{4} + v^2\right)}$

$$= \tfrac{1}{2} + \tfrac{1}{4}(x - y)/\tfrac{1}{2}(x + y)$$

$$= \dfrac{x}{x+y}.$$

The other partial derivatives can be obtained similarly.

8 $\dfrac{\partial(s, t)}{\partial(u, v)} \times \dfrac{\partial(u, v)}{\partial(x, y)} = \begin{bmatrix} \dfrac{\sqrt{v}}{2\sqrt{u}} & \dfrac{\sqrt{u}}{2\sqrt{v}} \\ 1 & -1 \end{bmatrix} \begin{bmatrix} y^3 & 3xy^2 \\ 3x^2y & x^3 \end{bmatrix}$

$$= \begin{bmatrix} \dfrac{x}{2y} & \dfrac{y}{2x} \\ 1 & -1 \end{bmatrix} \begin{bmatrix} y^3 & 3xy^2 \\ 3x^2y & x^3 \end{bmatrix}$$

$$= \begin{bmatrix} 2xy^2 & 2x^2y \\ y^3 - 3x^2y & 3xy^2 - x^3 \end{bmatrix}.$$

But $s = x^2y^2$ and $t = xy^3 - x^3y$, so $\dfrac{\partial(s, t)}{\partial(x, y)} = \begin{bmatrix} 2xy^2 & 2x^2y \\ y^3 - 3x^2y & 3xy^2 - x^3 \end{bmatrix}.$

9 $\dfrac{\partial(x, y)}{\partial(r, \theta)} = \begin{bmatrix} \cos\theta & -r\sin\theta \\ \sin\theta & r\cos\theta \end{bmatrix};$ determinant $= r$.

$$\frac{\partial(r, \theta)}{\partial(x, y)} = \begin{bmatrix} \dfrac{x}{\sqrt{(x^2 + y^2)}} & \dfrac{y}{\sqrt{(x^2 + y^2)}} \\ -\dfrac{y}{x^2 + y^2} & \dfrac{x}{x^2 + y^2} \end{bmatrix};$$

determinant $= \dfrac{1}{\sqrt{(x^2 + y^2)}} = \dfrac{1}{r}$, of course.

If $\dfrac{\partial(r, \theta)}{\partial(x, y)}$ is expressed in polars, as $\begin{bmatrix} \cos\theta & \sin\theta \\ -\dfrac{\sin\theta}{r} & \dfrac{\cos\theta}{r} \end{bmatrix}$, it is seen to be the inverse of

$\dfrac{\partial(x, y)}{\partial(r, \theta)}$. The significance of the determinants is brought out in Chapter 16.

10

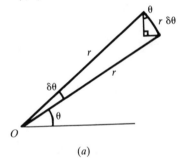

(a)

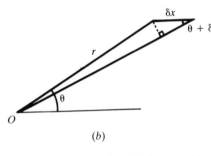

(b)

Diagram (a) shows that $\delta x \approx -r\,\delta\theta\sin\theta$ when r is kept constant but θ is increased by a small amount. In the limit, we get $\dfrac{\partial x}{\partial\theta} = -r\sin\theta$.

In diagram (b), $\delta\theta$ is negative. $\delta r \approx \delta x\cos(\theta + \delta\theta)$ and $-r\,\delta\theta \approx \delta x\sin(\theta + \delta\theta)$.

These lead to $\qquad \dfrac{\partial r}{\partial x} = \cos\theta, \quad \dfrac{\partial\theta}{\partial x} = -\dfrac{\sin\theta}{r}.$

Note that these results occurred in question 9 also.

11 To solve simultaneous equations $u = f(x, y) = 0$, $v = g(x, y) = 0$, we use the relation

$$\begin{bmatrix} \delta x \\ \delta y \end{bmatrix} \approx \frac{\partial(x, y)}{\partial(u, v)} \begin{bmatrix} \delta u \\ \delta v \end{bmatrix}.$$

If (a, b) is an approximate solution of $f(x, y) = 0$, $g(x, y) = 0$, then

$$\begin{bmatrix} a \\ b \end{bmatrix} - \mathbf{J}^{-1} \begin{bmatrix} f(a, b) \\ g(a, b) \end{bmatrix}$$

usually gives a better approximation, where

$$J = \frac{\partial(u, v)}{\partial(x, y)}$$

and J^{-1} is here evaluated for $x = a$, $y = b$.

In the example suggested, $f(3, 5) = -1$, $g(3, 5) = -2$.

$$J = \begin{bmatrix} 2x + 3y & 3x - 2y \\ 4x - y & -x + 10y \end{bmatrix} = \begin{bmatrix} 21 & -1 \\ 7 & 47 \end{bmatrix} \quad \text{when } x = 3, y = 5$$

$$\Rightarrow \quad J^{-1} = \frac{1}{994} \begin{bmatrix} 47 & 1 \\ -7 & 21 \end{bmatrix} \qquad \text{when } x = 3, y = 5,$$

and the next approximation is

$$\begin{bmatrix} 3 \\ 5 \end{bmatrix} - \frac{1}{994} \begin{bmatrix} 47 & 1 \\ -7 & 21 \end{bmatrix} \begin{bmatrix} -1 \\ -2 \end{bmatrix} \approx \begin{bmatrix} 3.049 \\ 5.035 \end{bmatrix}.$$

12 (a) $\begin{bmatrix} 3x^2 - 3y^2 & -6xy \\ 6xy & 3x^2 - 3y^2 \end{bmatrix}$; $f'(z) = 3z^2 = (3x^2 - 3y^2) + 6xyj$

(b) $\left.\begin{array}{l} u = e^x \cos y \\ v = e^x \sin y \end{array}\right\} \Rightarrow \frac{\partial(u, v)}{\partial(x, y)} = \begin{bmatrix} e^x \cos y & -e^x \sin y \\ e^x \sin y & e^x \cos y \end{bmatrix}$;

$f'(z) = e^z = e^x \cos y + j e^x \sin y$

(c) $\left.\begin{array}{l} u = x/(x^2 + y^2) \\ v = -y/(x^2 + y^2) \end{array}\right\} \Rightarrow \frac{\partial(u, v)}{\partial(x, y)} = \begin{bmatrix} \dfrac{x^2 - y^2}{(x^2 + y^2)^2} & \dfrac{-2xy}{(x^2 + y^2)^2} \\ \dfrac{2xy}{(x^2 + y^2)^2} & \dfrac{y^2 - x^2}{(x^2 + y^2)^2} \end{bmatrix}$;

$$f'(z) = \frac{-1}{z^2} = \frac{y^2 - x^2}{(x^2 + y^2)^2} + \frac{2xy}{(x^2 + y^2)^2} j$$

(a), (b) and (c) suggest the Cauchy–Riemann equations which are developed further in questions 13, 14 and 15.

(d) $\left.\begin{array}{l} u = 4x \\ v = 2y \end{array}\right\} \Rightarrow \frac{\partial(u, v)}{\partial(x, y)} = \begin{bmatrix} 4 & 0 \\ 0 & 2 \end{bmatrix}$, representing a two-way stretch.

13 $\left.\begin{array}{l} x = u^2 - v^2 \\ y = 2uv \end{array}\right\} \Rightarrow \frac{\partial(x, y)}{\partial(u, v)} = \begin{bmatrix} 2u & -2v \\ 2v & 2u \end{bmatrix}$

$$\Rightarrow \frac{\partial(u, v)}{\partial(x, y)} = \frac{1}{4(u^2 + v^2)} \begin{bmatrix} 2u & 2v \\ -2v & 2u \end{bmatrix}.$$

Hence $\dfrac{\partial u}{\partial x} = \dfrac{u}{2(u^2 + v^2)}$. Now $f'(z) = \frac{1}{2}\left(\dfrac{1}{u + vj}\right) = \dfrac{u}{2(u^2 + v^2)} - \dfrac{v}{2(u^2 + v^2)} j$,

giving $\dfrac{\partial u}{\partial x} = \dfrac{u}{2(u^2 + v^2)}$.

14 $\begin{bmatrix} \dfrac{\partial u}{\partial x} & \dfrac{\partial u}{\partial y} \\ \dfrac{\partial v}{\partial x} & \dfrac{\partial v}{\partial y} \end{bmatrix} = \begin{bmatrix} r \cos \theta & -r \sin \theta \\ r \sin \theta & r \cos \theta \end{bmatrix} \Rightarrow \dfrac{\partial u}{\partial x} = \dfrac{\partial v}{\partial y}$ and $\dfrac{\partial u}{\partial y} = -\dfrac{\partial v}{\partial x}$

15 The required equations come from the chain rule, or alternatively from $f'(z) = r \cos \theta + r \sin \theta \times j$.

Miscellaneous exercise 15

1 $J = \begin{bmatrix} 2x & -2y \\ 2y & 2x \end{bmatrix} = \begin{bmatrix} 2 & -2 \\ 2 & 2 \end{bmatrix}$ at (1, 1); this represents an enlargement with scale factor $2\sqrt{2}$ and a rotation through $\frac{1}{4}\pi$ radians.

2 $\dfrac{\partial(x, y)}{\partial(\theta, \lambda)} = \begin{bmatrix} 1 & 0 \\ 0 & \sec \lambda \end{bmatrix};$

$\dfrac{\partial(u, v)}{\partial(\theta, \lambda)} = \begin{bmatrix} 2(\sec \lambda + \tan \lambda) \cos \theta & 2(\sec \lambda + \tan \lambda) \sec \lambda \sin \theta \\ -2(\sec \lambda + \tan \lambda) \sin \theta & 2(\sec \lambda + \tan \lambda) \sec \lambda \cos \theta \end{bmatrix}.$

Hence $\dfrac{\partial(\theta, \lambda)}{\partial(x, y)} = \begin{bmatrix} 1 & 0 \\ 0 & \cos \lambda \end{bmatrix}$

and $\dfrac{\partial(u, v)}{\partial(x, y)} = \dfrac{\partial(u, v)}{\partial(\theta, \lambda)} \times \dfrac{\partial(\theta, \lambda)}{\partial(x, y)} = 2(\sec \lambda + \tan \lambda) \begin{bmatrix} \cos \theta & \sin \theta \\ -\sin \theta & \cos \theta \end{bmatrix},$

representing an enlargement with scale factor $2(\sec \lambda + \tan \lambda)$ and rotation through θ. Thus in a Mercator chart the scale varies from place to place, but angles are represented correctly.

3

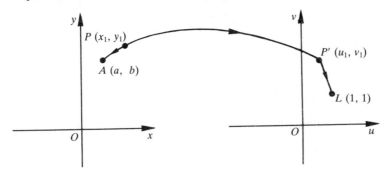

$P'L = \begin{bmatrix} 1 - u_1 \\ 1 - v_1 \end{bmatrix} = \begin{bmatrix} \partial u \\ \partial v \end{bmatrix} \approx J \begin{bmatrix} \partial x \\ \partial y \end{bmatrix} = J \begin{bmatrix} a - x_1 \\ b - y_1 \end{bmatrix}.$

When $u = x + \dfrac{x}{x^2 + y^2}$ and $v = y - \dfrac{y}{x^2 + y^2},$

$$J = \tfrac{4}{25} \begin{bmatrix} 7 & -1 \\ 1 & 7 \end{bmatrix} \quad \text{at (1, 2).}$$

Note that the transformation is equivalent to $z \mapsto z + 1/z$.

The second approximation is given by

$$\begin{bmatrix} a \\ b \end{bmatrix} \approx \begin{bmatrix} x_1 \\ y_1 \end{bmatrix} + J^{-1} \begin{bmatrix} \partial u \\ \partial v \end{bmatrix}.$$

Since $u_1 = 1.2$ and $v_1 = 1.6$, we get

$$\begin{bmatrix} a \\ b \end{bmatrix} \approx \begin{bmatrix} 1 \\ 2 \end{bmatrix} + \tfrac{25}{4} \times \tfrac{1}{50} \begin{bmatrix} 7 & 1 \\ -1 & 7 \end{bmatrix} \begin{bmatrix} -0.2 \\ -0.6 \end{bmatrix} = \begin{bmatrix} 0.75 \\ 1.5 \end{bmatrix}.$$

4 $\dfrac{\partial(x, y, z)}{\partial(r, \theta, \phi)} = \begin{bmatrix} \sin\theta\cos\phi & r\cos\theta\cos\phi & -r\sin\theta\sin\phi \\ \sin\theta\sin\phi & r\cos\theta\sin\phi & r\sin\theta\cos\phi \\ \cos\theta & -r\sin\theta & 0 \end{bmatrix}.$

Its determinant is

$\cos\theta \begin{vmatrix} r\cos\theta\cos\phi & -r\sin\theta\sin\phi \\ r\cos\theta\sin\phi & r\sin\theta\cos\phi \end{vmatrix} + r\sin\theta \begin{vmatrix} \sin\theta\cos\phi & -r\sin\theta\sin\phi \\ \sin\theta\sin\phi & r\sin\theta\cos\phi \end{vmatrix}$

$= \cos\theta \times r^2 \sin\theta\cos\theta + r\sin\theta \times r\sin^2\theta$
$= r^2 \sin\theta(\cos^2\theta + \sin^2\theta)$
$= r^2 \sin\theta.$

5 $\dfrac{\partial u}{\partial x} = \dfrac{\partial v}{\partial y}$ and $\dfrac{\partial u}{\partial y} = -\dfrac{\partial v}{\partial x}$ $\Rightarrow$ $\dfrac{\partial^2 u}{\partial x^2} = \dfrac{\partial^2 v}{\partial x\,\partial y} = \dfrac{\partial^2 v}{\partial y\,\partial x} = -\dfrac{\partial^2 u}{\partial y^2}$

Exercise 16A

1 (a) $A = \displaystyle\int_0^4 (3\sqrt{x} - \tfrac{3}{8}x^2)\,dx = \left[2x^{3/2} - \tfrac{1}{8}x^3\right]_0^4 = 8;$

$\displaystyle\iint x\,dy\,dx = \int_0^4 (3x^{3/2} - \tfrac{3}{8}x^3)\,dx = \left[\tfrac{6}{5}x^{5/2} - \tfrac{3}{32}x^4\right]_0^4 = \tfrac{72}{5};$

$\displaystyle\iint y\,dy\,dx = \tfrac{1}{2}\int_0^4 (9x - \tfrac{9}{4}x^4\,dx = \tfrac{1}{2}\left[\tfrac{9}{2}x^2 - \tfrac{9}{320}x^5\right]_0^4 = \tfrac{108}{5}$

(b) $8\bar{y} = \displaystyle\int_0^6 y\{\sqrt{(\tfrac{8}{3}y)} - \tfrac{1}{9}y^2\}\,dy$

(c) $8\bar{y} = \displaystyle\int_0^4 \tfrac{1}{2}(3\sqrt{x} + \tfrac{3}{8}x^2)(3\sqrt{x} - \tfrac{3}{8}x^2)\,dx,$ since the centre of the strip is

$\tfrac{1}{2}(y_1 + y_2)$ above the *x*-axis.

2 $A = 100,\quad \bar{x} = 3\tfrac{3}{4},\quad \bar{y} = 7$

3 $A = \pi,\quad \bar{x} = (\pi/2) - (2/\pi),\quad \bar{y} = \tfrac{3}{4}$

4 $V\bar{x} = \displaystyle\int_0^1 \int_0^{1-x} (5x - 2x^2 - xy)\,dy\,dx$

$= \displaystyle\int_0^1 \{5x - 5x^2 - 2x^2 + 2x^3 - \tfrac{1}{2}(x - 2x^2 + x^3)\}\,dx$

$= \tfrac{5}{8};$

$V\bar{y} = \displaystyle\int_0^1 \int_0^{1-x} (5y - 2xy - y^2)\,dy\,dx$

$= \displaystyle\int_0^1 \{\tfrac{5}{2}(1 - x)^2 - x + 2x^2 - x^3 - \tfrac{1}{3}(1 - x)^3\}\,dx$

$= \tfrac{2}{3};$

$V\bar{z} = \displaystyle\int_0^1 \int_0^{1-x} \tfrac{1}{2}(5 - 2x - y)^2\,dy\,dx$

$= \displaystyle\int_0^1 \left[-\tfrac{1}{6}(5 - 2x - y)^3\right]_0^{1-x}\,dx$

$$= \int_0^1 \tfrac{1}{6}\{(5 - 2x)^3 - (4 - x)^3\}\, dx$$

$$= 4\tfrac{1}{24}.$$

Hence $\bar{x} = \tfrac{5}{16}$, $\bar{y} = \tfrac{1}{3}$, $\bar{z} = 2\tfrac{1}{48}$.

5 The equations of the top radius and the circle are $x = y \cot \alpha$ and $x = \sqrt{(a^2 - y^2)}$.

$$a^2 \alpha \bar{x} = \int_0^{a\sin\alpha} (a^2 - y^2 - y^2 \cot^2 \alpha)\, dy = \int_0^{a\sin\alpha} (a^2 - y^2 \operatorname{cosec}^2 \alpha)\, dy = \tfrac{2}{3}a^3 \sin \alpha.$$

Since $x = r \cos \theta$, $a^2 \alpha \bar{x} = \int_{-\alpha}^{\alpha} \int_0^a r^2 \cos \theta\, dr\, d\theta = \tfrac{2}{3}a^3 \sin \alpha.$

From either method, it follows that $\bar{x} = \dfrac{2a \sin \alpha}{3\alpha}$.

6 (a) $\displaystyle \int_0^3 \int_0^2 (\tfrac{1}{2} + y + z)\, dy\, dz = \int_0^3 (1 + 2 + 2z)\, dz = 18$

(b) $\displaystyle \int_0^3 \int_0^2 (\tfrac{1}{3} + y^2)\, dy\, dz = \int_0^3 (\tfrac{2}{3} + \tfrac{8}{3})\, dz = 10$

7 (a) $\displaystyle \int_0^2 \int_0^{2-z} \int_0^{2-y-z} (x + y + z)\, dx\, dy\, dz = \tfrac{1}{2} \int_0^2 \int_0^{2-z} \{4 - (y + z)^2\}\, dy\, dz$

$$= \tfrac{1}{2} \int_0^2 \{8 - 4z - \tfrac{1}{3}(8 - z^3)\}\, dz = 2$$

(b) By symmetry, $\displaystyle \iiint y^2\, dx\, dy\, dz = \iiint x^2\, dx\, dy\, dz$ over the tetrahedron.

$$\int_0^2 \int_0^{2-z} \int_0^{2-y-z} x^2\, dx\, dy\, dz = \int_0^2 \int_0^{2-z} \tfrac{1}{3}(2 - y - z)^3\, dy\, dz$$

$$= \int_0^2 \tfrac{1}{12}(2 - z)^4\, dz = \tfrac{8}{15}.$$

Hence $\displaystyle \iiint (x^2 + y^2)\, dx\, dy\, dz = \tfrac{16}{15}.$

8 $V = 60$; $Vx = \displaystyle \int_0^3 \int_0^2 \int_0^{4x-y+5} x\, dz\, dy\, dx = 108$;

$$V\bar{y} = 58; \quad V\bar{z} = \int_0^3 \int_0^2 \tfrac{1}{2}(4x - y + 5)^2\, dy\, dx$$

$$= \int_0^3 \{(4x + 5)^3 - (4x + 3)^3\}\, dx = 337.$$

Hence $\bar{x} = \tfrac{9}{5}$, $\bar{y} = \tfrac{29}{30}$, $\bar{z} = \tfrac{337}{60}$.

9 $V = 58$, $V\bar{x} = 61\tfrac{1}{2}$, so $\bar{x} = \tfrac{123}{116}$

10 (a) $\displaystyle I = \int_{-1/2}^{1/2} \rho x^2\, dx = \tfrac{1}{12}\rho l^3 = \tfrac{1}{12}\,Ml^2$

(b) For a ring of radius r and width δr, $\delta I \approx 2\pi r^2\, \delta r\, \rho$, and hence

$$I = \int_0^a 2\pi r^3 \rho\, dr = \tfrac{1}{2}Ma^2$$

(c) For a disc of thickness δx at right angles to the axis at a distance x from the centre, $\delta I \approx \frac{1}{2}\pi(a^2 - x^2)\,\delta x\,\rho \times (a^2 - x^2)$, and hence

$$I = \int_{-a}^{a} \frac{1}{2}\pi\rho(a^2 - x^2)^2 \, dx = \frac{8}{15}\pi\rho a^5 = \frac{2}{5}Ma^2.$$

11 (a) $\rho \displaystyle\int_0^3 \int_0^2 \int_0^{4x-y+5} (x^2 + y^2) \, dz \, dy \, dx = 310\rho$ (b) 182ρ

12 Perpendicular distance $= \dfrac{ap + bq + c}{\sqrt{(a^2 + b^2)}}$; $I = \rho \displaystyle\int_0^6 \int_0^3 \dfrac{(2x - y)^2}{5} \, dx \, dy$, since the equation of AC is $2x - y = 0$, taking AB and AD along the x- and y-axes respectively; $I = \frac{108}{5}\rho$.

13 The plane through (p, q, r) perpendicular to $\begin{bmatrix} 1 \\ 1 \\ 1 \end{bmatrix}$ has equation $x + y + z = p + q + r$.

This meets the line where $t = \frac{1}{3}(p + q + r)$.

$$I = \rho \int_0^1 \int_0^1 \int_0^1 \left\{ \left(\frac{2x - y - z}{3} \right)^2 + \left(\frac{2y - x - z}{3} \right)^2 + \left(\frac{2z - x - y}{3} \right)^2 \right\} dx \, dy \, dz$$

$$= \frac{1}{9}\rho \int_0^1 \int_0^1 \int_0^1 (6x^2 + 6y^2 + 6z^2 - 6xy - 6yz - 6zx) \, dx \, dy \, dz$$

$$= \frac{1}{6}\rho$$

Exercise 16B

1 (a) $\left| \dfrac{\partial(u, v)}{\partial(x, y)} \right| = \left| \begin{matrix} 1 & 1 \\ -1 & 1 \end{matrix} \right| = 2$, the reciprocal of $\left| \dfrac{\partial(x, y)}{\partial(u, v)} \right|$.

(b) $\left| \dfrac{\partial(x, y)}{\partial(u, v)} \right| = \left| \begin{matrix} \frac{1}{3}u^{-2/3} v^{2/3} & \frac{2}{3}u^{1/3} v^{-1/3} \\ \frac{2}{3}u^{-1/3} v^{1/3} & \frac{1}{3}u^{2/3} v^{-2/3} \end{matrix} \right| = -\frac{1}{3}$, as expected.

2 $\left| \dfrac{\partial(u, v)}{\partial(x, y)} \right| = \left| \begin{matrix} 2x & -2y \\ 2y & 2x \end{matrix} \right| = 4(x^2 + y^2)$; area $= \displaystyle\int_3^4 \int_1^2 4(x^2 + y^2) \, dx \, dy = 58\frac{2}{3}$

3 (a) $\displaystyle\int_0^6 \int_{-3}^0 \frac{1}{27}(2v - u)(v - 2u) \, du \, dv = 35$

(b) $\displaystyle\int_1^3 \int_4^6 xy \times \frac{1}{4x} \, du \, dv = \int_1^3 \int_4^6 \frac{1}{8}(u + v) \, du \, dv = 3\frac{1}{2}$

(c) $\displaystyle\int_0^{\pi/2} \int_2^3 \frac{1}{2}r^3 \sin 2\theta \, dr \, d\theta = 8\frac{1}{8}$

4 $\displaystyle\int_5^8 \int_2^4 \frac{1}{8xy} \, du \, dv = \int_5^8 \int_2^4 \frac{1}{8}u^{-1/2} v^{-1/2} \, du \, dv = \frac{1}{4}\left[u^{1/2} \right]_2^4 \times \left[v^{1/2} \right]_5^8 \approx 0.173$

5 $\left| \dfrac{\partial(u, v)}{\partial(x, y)} \right| = \left| \begin{matrix} 1 - \dfrac{y^2}{x^2} & \dfrac{2y}{x} \\ \dfrac{2x}{y} & -\dfrac{x^2}{y^2} + 1 \end{matrix} \right| = -\left(\dfrac{x^2 + y^2}{xy} \right)^2;$

$I = \displaystyle\int_0^b \int_0^a 1 \, du \, dv = ab$

6 $A = \dfrac{1}{2\sqrt{2}} \displaystyle\int_1^3 \int_4^6 (u - v)^{-1/2}\, du\, dv = 0.843$ (to 3 SF);

$A\bar{x} = \dfrac{1}{4} \displaystyle\int_1^3 \int_4^6 du\, dv = 1$, so $\bar{x} = 1.19$ (to 3 SF)

7   This question can be answered without using multiple integrals. Or, taking rings round the x-axis as elements,

$$V = \iint 2\pi y\, dx\, dy = \int_0^{\pi/2} \int_2^3 2\pi r^2 \sin\theta\, dr\, d\theta = \tfrac{38}{3}\pi;$$

$$V\bar{x} = \iint x \times 2\pi y\, dx\, dy = 2\pi \times 8\tfrac{1}{8} \quad \text{(see question 3}(c));$$

$$\text{Moment of inertia} = \iint y^2 \times 2\pi\rho y\, dx\, dy = 2\pi\rho \int_0^{\pi/2} \int_2^3 r^4 \sin^3\theta\, dr\, d\theta.$$

Hence $\bar{x} = 1.28$ and moment of inertia $= 117\rho$

8 $A = \displaystyle\int_0^{2\pi} \tfrac{1}{2}a^2(1 + \cos\theta)^2\, d\theta = \tfrac{3}{2}\pi a^2;$

$$A\bar{x} = \iint r\cos\theta \times r\, dr\, d\theta$$

$$= \tfrac{1}{3}a^3 \int_0^{2\pi} \cos\theta(1 + \cos\theta)^3\, d\theta$$

$$= \tfrac{1}{3}a^3\{3 \times \tfrac{1}{2} \times 2\pi + \tfrac{3}{4} \times \tfrac{1}{2} \times 2\pi\},$$

using reduction formulae and noting that odd powers of $\cos\theta$ give zero when integrated between these limits. Hence $\bar{x} = \tfrac{5}{6}a$.

9 $k \displaystyle\iint e^{-3(x+y)^2}\, dx\, dy \quad = 1$

$\Rightarrow\ k \displaystyle\int_0^3 \int_{-u}^u e^{-3u^2} \times \tfrac{1}{2}\, dv\, du = 1, \quad$ putting $u = x + y,\ v = y - x$, as in Example 4

$\Rightarrow\ k \displaystyle\int_0^3 u\, e^{-3u^2}\, du \quad = 1$

$\Rightarrow\ k\left[-\tfrac{1}{6}e^{-3u^2} \right]_0^3 \quad = 1 \ \Rightarrow\ k = 6$

10 (a) $\displaystyle\iint x \, dx \, dy = \int_0^b \left[\tfrac{1}{2} x^2 \right]_0^{a\sqrt{(1 - y^2/b^2)}} dy$

$\qquad\qquad = \tfrac{1}{2} a^2 \displaystyle\int_0^b (1 - y^2/b^2) \, dy$

$\qquad\qquad = \tfrac{1}{3} a^2 b.$

Similarly, $\displaystyle\iint y \, dx \, dy = \tfrac{1}{3} ab^2.$

(b) $\left| \dfrac{\partial(x, y)}{\partial(r, \theta)} \right| = abr,$ so

$\displaystyle\iint (x + y) \, dx \, dy = ab \int_0^{\pi/2} \int_0^1 r^2 (a \cos \theta + b \sin \theta) \, dr \, d\theta = \tfrac{1}{3} ab(a + b).$

Exercise 16C

1 Evaluating directly gives

$r^2 \sin \theta (\cos^2 \theta \cos^2 \phi + \sin^2 \theta \sin^2 \phi + \cos^2 \theta \sin^2 \phi + \sin^2 \theta \cos^2 \phi)$
$= r^2 \sin \theta (\cos^2 \theta + \sin^2 \theta)(\cos^2 \phi + \sin^2 \varphi)$
$= r^2 \sin^2 \theta.$

2 The integral equals $\left[\tfrac{1}{4} r^4 \right]_0^a \times \left[\tfrac{1}{2} \sin^2 \theta \right]_0^{\pi/2} \times \left[\phi \right]_0^{2\pi} = \tfrac{1}{4} \pi a^4.$

3 (a) $\displaystyle\int_0^1 \int_0^{\sqrt{(1-z)^2}} \int_0^{\sqrt{(1-y^2-z^2)}} xyz \, dx \, dy \, dz = \tfrac{1}{2} \int_0^1 \int_0^{\sqrt{(1-z^2)}} (yz - y^3 z - yz^3) \, dy \, dz$

$\qquad\qquad = \tfrac{1}{2} \displaystyle\int_0^1 \{ \tfrac{1}{2}(z - z^3) - \tfrac{1}{4}(z - 2z^3 + z^5) - \tfrac{1}{2}(z^3 - z^5) \} \, dz$

$\qquad\qquad = \displaystyle\int_0^1 (\tfrac{1}{4} z - \tfrac{1}{2} z^3 + \tfrac{1}{4} z^5) \, dz = \tfrac{1}{48}$

(b) $\displaystyle\int_0^{\pi/2} \int_0^{\pi/2} \int_0^1 r^3 \sin^2 \theta \cos^2 \theta \sin \phi \cos \phi \times r^2 \sin^2 \theta \, dr \, d\theta \, d\phi$

$\qquad\qquad = \left[\tfrac{1}{6} r^6 \right]_0^1 \times \left[\tfrac{1}{4} \sin^4 \theta \right]_0^{\pi/2} \times \left[\tfrac{1}{2} \sin^2 \phi \right]_0^{\pi/2} = \tfrac{1}{48}$

4 $V = \displaystyle\int_0^b \int_0^{2\pi} \int_0^{\sqrt{(a^2 - r^2)}} r \, dz \, d\theta \, dr = 2\pi \int_0^b r\sqrt{(a^2 - r^2)} \, dr = \tfrac{2}{3}\pi \{ a^3 - (a^2 - b^2)^{3/2} \};$

$V\bar{z} = \displaystyle\int_0^b \int_0^{2\pi} \int_0^{\sqrt{(a^2 - r^2)}} zr \, dz \, d\theta \, dr = \pi \int_0^b (a^2 r - r^3) \, dr = \tfrac{1}{4}\pi(2a^2 b^2 - b^4).$

Hence $\bar{z} = \tfrac{3}{8}(2a^2 b^2 - b^4)/\{ a^3 - (a^2 - b^2)^{3/2} \}.$

$I = \rho \displaystyle\int_0^b \int_0^{2\pi} \int_0^{\sqrt{(a^2 - r^2)}} r^3 \, dz \, d\theta \, dr = 2\pi\rho \int_0^b r^3 \sqrt{(a^2 - r^2)} \, dr$

$\qquad = - \pi\rho \left[\tfrac{2}{3} a^2 u^{3/2} - \tfrac{2}{5} u^{5/2} \right]_{a^2}^{a^2 - b^2}$

$\qquad = \pi\rho \{ \tfrac{4}{15} a^5 - \tfrac{2}{3} a^2 (a^2 - b^2)^{3/2} + \tfrac{2}{5}(a^2 - b^2)^{5/2} \}$

5 $M = \pi\rho \int_{-b}^{b} 2a\sqrt{(b^2 - z^2)}\, dz = \pi^2\rho ab^2;$

$M\bar{x} = \tfrac{2}{3}\rho \int_{-b}^{b} \{6a^2(b^2 - z^2)^{1/2} + 2(b^2 - z^2)^{3/2}\}\, dz = 2\pi\rho a^2 b^2 + \tfrac{1}{2}\pi\rho b^4;$

$\bar{x} = \dfrac{2a}{\pi} + \dfrac{b^2}{2\pi a}$

6 $A = \tfrac{3}{2}\pi a^2;$

$V = \int_0^{2\pi} \int_0^{a(1 - \cos\theta)} 2\pi(6a - r\cos^2\theta)\, r\, dr\, d\theta$

$= 2\pi a^3 \int_0^{2\pi} \{3(1 - 2c + c^2) - \tfrac{1}{3}(c - 3c^2 + 3c^3 - c^4)\}\, d\theta, \quad \text{where } c = \cos\theta.$

The odd powers of $\cos\theta$ contribute nothing; the reduction formula completes the integration to give

$$V = 2\pi a^3(6\pi + 4 \times \tfrac{1}{2} \times 2\pi + \tfrac{1}{3} \times \tfrac{3}{4} \times \tfrac{1}{2} \times 2\pi) = 20.5\pi a^3.$$

7 (a) $\left| \dfrac{\partial(u, v, w)}{\partial(x, y, z)} \right| = 3, \quad \text{so } V = \int_7^{11} \int_5^9 \int_2^4 \tfrac{1}{3}\, du\, dv\, dw = \tfrac{32}{3}$

(b) $\iiint z\, dx\, dy\, dz = \tfrac{1}{9} \int_7^{11} \int_5^9 \int_2^4 (u - 2v + w)\, du\, dv\, dw = -\tfrac{64}{9}$

(c) $\bar{z} = -\tfrac{64}{9} \div \tfrac{32}{3} = -\tfrac{2}{3}.$ But the centre of mass is the geometrical centre of the parallelepiped. $u = 2, v = 5, w = 7$ gives $z = -\tfrac{1}{3}$, while $u = 4, v = 9, w = 11$ gives $z = -1$. Since opposite vertices have $z = -\tfrac{1}{3}$ and $z = -1$, the centre has $z = \tfrac{1}{2}(-\tfrac{1}{3} - 1) = -\tfrac{2}{3}.$

8 $u = 2x + 3y, v = 5x - y$ gives $\left| \dfrac{\partial(u, v)}{\partial(x, y)} \right| = -17;$ area $= \tfrac{1}{17} \times 6 \times 5 = \tfrac{30}{17}.$ Although many elementary methods are available, all lead to much lengthier calculations.

Miscellaneous exercise 16

1 D is a cylinder of radius a and height b.

$$I = \int_0^b \int_0^{2\pi} \int_0^a r^2 \cos^2\theta\, r\, dr\, d\theta\, dz = b \times \int_0^{2\pi} \cos^2\theta \times \int_0^a r^3\, dr = \tfrac{1}{4}\pi a^4 b$$

2

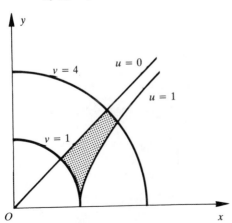

The integral $\displaystyle\iint_D xy^3 \, dx \, dy$ is best evaluated in terms of u and v.

Now $\dfrac{\partial(u, v)}{\partial(x, y)} = \begin{vmatrix} 2x & -2y \\ 2x & 2y \end{vmatrix}$ has determinant $8xy$, hence

$$\iint xy^3 \, dx \, dy = \tfrac{1}{8}\iint y^2 \, du \, dv = \tfrac{1}{16}\iint (v - u) \, du \, dv.$$

The limits are now obvious, and $\tfrac{1}{16}\displaystyle\int_1^4 \int_0^1 (v - u) \, du \, dv$ works out as $\tfrac{3}{8}$.

3

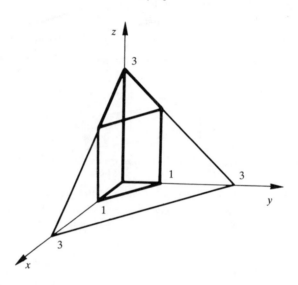

No integration is needed to obtain $V = \tfrac{7}{6}$.

$$\bar{x} = \frac{1}{V} \int_0^1 \int_0^{1-x} \int_0^{3-x-y} x \, dz \, dy \, dx$$

$$= \frac{1}{V} \int_0^1 \int_0^{1-x} (3x - x^2 - xy) \, dy \, dx$$

$$= \frac{1}{V} \int_0^1 (\tfrac{5}{2}x - 3x^2 + \tfrac{1}{2}x^3) \, dx$$

$$= \tfrac{9}{28}$$

4 $\dfrac{\partial(u, v)}{\partial(x, y)} = \begin{vmatrix} y\,e^x & e^x \\ -y\,e^{-x} & e^{-x} \end{vmatrix}$, and the Jacobian has determinant equal to

$2y = 2\sqrt{u}\sqrt{v}$.

$$\text{Area} = \iint_D dx \, dy = \int_{1/2}^2 \int_2^4 \frac{du \, dv}{2\sqrt{u}\sqrt{v}} = \tfrac{1}{2} \times \left[2\sqrt{u}\right]_2^4 \times \left[2\sqrt{v}\right]_{1/2}^2 = 2(\sqrt{2} - 1);$$

$$A\bar{y} = \iint y \, dx \, dy = \int_{1/2}^2 \int_2^4 \tfrac{1}{2} \, du \, dv = \tfrac{3}{2}, \text{ hence } \bar{y} = \tfrac{3}{4}(\sqrt{2} + 1)$$

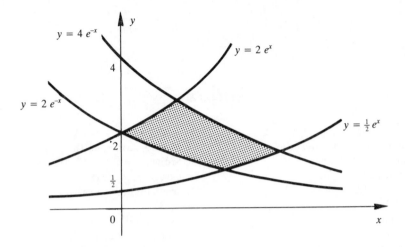

5 $V = \int_b^a \int_0^{2\pi} \int_{-\sqrt{(a^2-r^2)}}^{\sqrt{(a^2-r^2)}} r\, dz\, d\theta\, dr = 2\pi \int_b^a 2r\sqrt{(a^2-r^2)}\, dr = \tfrac{4}{3}\pi(a^2-b^2)^{3/2}$

$I = $ moment of inertia $= \int_b^a \int_0^{2\pi} \int_{-\sqrt{(a^2-r^2)}}^{\sqrt{(a^2-r^2)}} \rho r^3\, dz\, d\theta\, dr$ where $\rho = $ density

$$= 2\pi\rho \int_b^a 2r(r^2 - a^2 + a^2)\sqrt{(a^2-r^2)}\, dr$$

$$= 2\pi\rho \int_b^a \{-2r(a^2-r^2)^{3/2} + 2a^2r(a^2-r^2)^{1/2}\}\, dr$$

$$= 2\pi\rho\{-\tfrac{2}{5}(a^2-b^2)^{5/2} + \tfrac{2}{3}a^2(a^2-b^2)^{3/2}\}$$

$$= \tfrac{1}{5}M(2a^2 + 3b^2).$$

As $b \to a$, $I \to Ma^2$, the formula for a hoop of radius a; as $b \to 0$, $I \to \tfrac{2}{5}Ma^2$, the formula for a uniform sphere.

6 $\dfrac{\partial(x, y)}{\partial(r, \theta)} = \begin{bmatrix} a\cos\theta & -ar\sin\theta \\ \tfrac{2}{3}a\sin\theta & \tfrac{2}{3}ar\cos\theta \end{bmatrix}$, which has determinant $\tfrac{2}{3}a^2r$.

$$M = \iint m\, dx\, dy = \tfrac{2}{3}a^2 \iint mr\, dr\, d\theta = \tfrac{2}{3}m_0a^2 \iint r(1-r^2)\, dr\, d\theta.$$

$r = 1$ gives points on the edge of the disc, with the boundary traversed once as θ goes from 0 to 2π. Hence the limits of integration are as stated, and $M = \tfrac{1}{3}\pi m_0 a^2$.

Moment of inertia about $OY = \tfrac{2}{3}m_0a^4 \int_0^{2\pi} \int_0^1 r(1-r^2) \times r^2\cos^2\theta\, d\theta$

$$= \tfrac{1}{18}\pi m_0 a^4$$

$$= \tfrac{1}{12}Ma^2$$

Index

Addition formulae for hyperbolic
functions, 1, 11, 63
Apollonius circle, 140
Arc length, 91
Area
elements of, 165, 170, 208
of polar curves, 96
under the Normal curve, 215
Astroid, 104
Average scale factor, 183

Binomial series, convergence of, 42
Bivariate probability density, 172

Cardioid, 95, 100, 103, 176, 214
Catenary, 3, 51
Cauchy-Riemann equations, 199
Centre of gravity, 217
Centre of mass, 70, 202, 213
Chain rule for Jacobian matrices,
197
Circle of Apollonius, 140
Circular functions
and hyperbolic functions, 2, 63
of complex numbers, 64
Complementary function, 73, 90, 125
Complex derivative, 182
Complex number geometry, 136
Complex numbers 12
exponential function of, 57
logarithm function of, 61
roots of equations, 13
series, 56
Conformal transformations, 184
Continuity, 31
Convergence, of sequences, 21, 112
of series, 38, 56
Critical damping, 90, 126
Cube roots of unity, 18, 148
Curvature, 103
Cycloid, 93

De Moivre, Abraham, 16
De Moivre's theorem, 12, 16, 60
Descartes' method, 18
Determinant of Jacobian matrix, 208,
213
Differentiability, 32, 185
Differential equations, 71, 124
Differential geometry, 91
Double integrals, 165, 203
change of variables in, 208
with polar coordinates, 170

Electrical circuits, 84, 130
Equiangular spiral, 100
Euler's constant, 52
Euler's relation, 55
Exponential function of z, 58
Exponential series (real), convergence
of, 43
Exponential series (complex),
convergence of, 58

First order approximations, 157
Functions
mapping $\mathbb{C} \mapsto \mathbb{C}$, 136, 177
mapping $\mathbb{R} \mapsto \mathbb{R}$, 26
mapping $\mathbb{R}^2 \mapsto \mathbb{R}^2$, 192
of several variables ($\mathbb{R}^n \mapsto \mathbb{R}$), 151

Geometric inversion, 144, 182
Geometric series of real terms, 39
of complex terms, 56
Geometry, complex plane, 146
differential, 91
Gregory series, 48

Harmonic series, 40
Hyperbola, 6, 11
Hyperbolic functions, 1
and circular functions, 2, 63
application to integration, 7

344